Ownership and Appropriation

ASA Monographs

ISSN 0066–9679

The Relevance of Models for Social Anthropology, ed M. Banton
Political Systems and the Distribution of Power, ed M. Banton
Anthropological Approaches to the Study of Religion, ed M. Banton
The Social Anthropology of Complex Societies, ed M. Banton
The Structural Study of Myth and Totemism, ed E.R. Leach
Themes in Economic Anthropology, ed R. Firth
History and Social Anthropology, ed I.M. Lewis
Socialization: The Approach from Social Anthropology, ed P. Mayer
Witchcraft Confessions and Accusations, ed M. Douglas
Social Anthropology and Language, ed E. Ardener
Rethinking Kinship and Marriage, ed R. Needham
Urban Ethnicity, ed A. Cohen
Social Anthropology and Medicine, ed J.B. Loudon
Social Anthropology and Law, ed I. Hamnett
The Anthropology of the Body, ed J. Blacking
Regional Cults, ed R.P. Werbner
Sex and Age as Principles of Social Differentiation, ed J. La Fontaine
Social and Ecological Systems, ed P C Burnham and R.F. Ellen
Social Anthropology of Work, ed S. Wallman
The Structure of Folk Models, ed L. Holy and L. Stuchlik
Religious Organization and Religious Experience, ed J. Davis
Semantic Anthropology, ed D. Parkin
Social Anthropology and Development Policy, ed R. Grillo and A. Rew
Reason and Morality, ed J. Overing
Anthropology at Home, ed A. Jackson
Migrants, Workers, and the Social Order, ed J.S. Eades
History and Ethnicity, ed E. Tonkin, M. McDonald and M. Chapman
Anthropology and the Riddle of the Sphinx: Paradox and Change in the Life Course, ed
    P. Spencer
Anthropology and Autobiography, ed J. Okely and H. Callaway
Contemporary Futures: Perspectives from Social Anthropology, ed S. Wallman
Socialism: Ideals, Ideologies and Local Practice, ed C.M. Hann
Environmentalism: The View from Anthropology, ed K. Milton
Questions of Consciousness, eds A.P. Cohen and N. Rapport
After Writing Culture: Epistemology and Praxis in Contemporary Anthropology, eds
    A. James, A. Dawson and J. Hockey
Ritual, Performance, Media, ed F. Hughes-Freeland
The Anthropology of Power, ed A. Cheater
An Anthropology of Indirect Communication, ed J. Hendry and C.W. Watson
Elite Cultures, ed C. Shore and S. Nugent
Participating in Development, ed P. Sillitoe, A. Bicker and J. Pottier
Human Rights in Global Perspective, ed R.A. Wilson and J.P. Mitchell
The Qualities of Time, ed W. James and D. Mills
Locating the Field: Space, Place and Context in Anthropology, ed S. Coleman and P. Collins
Anthropology and Science: Epistemologies in Practice, ed J. Edwards, P. Harvey and P. Wade
Creativity and Cultural Improvisation, ed E. Hallam and T. Ingold
Anthropology and the New Cosmopolitanism: Rooted, Feminist and Vernacular Perspectives,
    ed P. Werbner
Thinking Through Tourism, ed J. Scott and T. Selwyn

Ownership and Appropriation

Edited by
Veronica Strang and Mark Busse

Oxford • New York

English edition
First published in 2011 by
Berg
Editorial offices:
First Floor, Angel Court, 81 St Clements Street, Oxford OX4 1AW, UK
175 Fifth Avenue, New York, NY 10010, USA

Berg is the imprint of Oxford International Publishers Ltd.

Library of Congress Cataloging-in-Publication Data

A catalogue record for this book is available from the Library of Congress.

British Library Cataloguing-in-Publication Data

A catalogue record for this book is available from the British Library.

ISBN   978 1 84788 684 2 (Cloth)
         978 1 84788 685 9 (Paper)
e-ISBN 978 1 84788 841 9 (Institutional)
         978 1 84788 840 2 (Individual)

Typeset by JS Typesetting Ltd, Porthcawl, Mid Glamorgan
Printed in the UK by the MPG Books Group

www.bergpublishers.com

Contents

List of Figures   vii

Notes on Contributors   ix

Acknowledgements   xiii

Foreword
Chris Hann   xv

1   Introduction: Ownership and Appropriation
     Mark Busse and Veronica Strang   1

Part One – Subjects, Personhood and Peoplehood

2   Sharing, Stealing and Borrowing Simultaneously
     Marilyn Strathern   23

3   On Having Achieved Appropriation: *Anak Berprestasi* in Kepri,
     Indonesia
     Nicholas Long   43

4   Appropriating an Authentic Bodily Practice from Japan: On 'Being
     There', 'Having Been There' and 'Virtually Being There'
     Tamara Kohn   65

5   Dreaming in Thread: From Ritual to Art and Property(s) Between
     Katie Glaskin   87

6   'Possessing Culture': Political Economies of Community Subjects
     and their Properties
     Rosemary J. Coombe   105

Contents

Part Two – Materiality and Immateriality

7   Cultural Appropriation
The Honourable Sir Edward Taihakurei Durie KNZM   131

8   One Hundred Years of Land Reform on the Gazelle Peninsula: A
Baining Point of View
Colin Filer and Michael Lowe   149

9   Fluid Forms: Owning Water in Australia
Veronica Strang   171

10 Appropriating Fish, Appropriating Fishermen: Tradable Permits,
Natural Resources and Uncertainty
Monica Minnegal and Peter Dwyer   197

11 Can't Find Nothing on the Radio: Radio Spectrum Policy and
Governance in Nepal
Michael Wilmore and Pawan Prakash Upreti   217

Part Three – Ownership as Social Communication

12 The Village That Wasn't There: Appropriation, Domination and
Resistance
Adam Kaul   239

13 'Not Just Pretty Pictures': Relative Autonomy and the Articulations
of Yolngu Art in its Contexts
Howard Morphy   261

Index   287

List of Figures

3.1 A group of *anak berprestasi* carrying trophies and decorated
with sashes bearing the name of 'Kepri Province'.   44

3.2 An *anak berprestasi* from Kepri Province.   49

3.3 Students from Kepri encounter a team dressed in fashionable
blazers at the national debating finals in Jakarta.   54

4.1 Aikido uses the energy of the attack to pin or throw the assailant.   67

4.2 Instructor from Japan demonstrating with the author at a seminar
in Australia.   68

4.3 Visiting foreign students in Iwama dojo, Japan.   70

8.1 Map of census units and alienated land titles in the vicinity of
Lassul Bay.   152

8.2 The cocoa fermentary at Nambung plantation.   163

8.3 The labourers' compound at Nambung plantation.   164

8.4 The Agmark purchasing point on New Kavern plantation.   164

8.5 Noticeboard at the Agmark purchasing point.   165

9.1 Millaa Millaa waterfall, North Queensland.   172

9.2 Water rights poster, Mexico City.   174

9.3 Farm dam in the Brisbane River catchment.   180

9.4 Swimmer, Lake Eacham, North Queensland.   183

9.5 Tree planting on the Brisbane River.   186

11.1 Nepal, Radio Signal Propagation Map 2008.   226

12.1 Zones of development in Doolin.   245

12.2 New developments in Doolin.   246

12.3 Signposting at Fitz's Cross.   246

13.1 Painting of the Wawilak sisters by Wuyulwuy Wanambi.   265

13.2 'The same' painting of the Wawilak sisters by Wuyulwuy Wanambi.   266

13.3 Djungguwan ceremonial ground.   268

13.4 Re-enactment of Gandala's journey.   268

13.5 Male initiate with face painting.   269

13.6 Yirrkala church panels.   271

13.7 The ancestral crocodile, Bäru.   276

13.8 The journey of the Djan'kawu.   277

13.9 Painting by Djambawa Marawili.   279

13.10 Dancers from Blue Mud Bay.   281

Notes on Contributors

Mark Busse is a Senior Lecturer in Social Anthropology at the University of Auckland. He received a PhD in anthropology from the University of California at San Diego, and has carried out long-term ethnographic research among Boazi-speaking peoples in the Lake Murray-Middle Fly region of Papua New Guinea. He also worked at the Papua New Guinea National Museum from 1990 to 1999, first as Curator of Anthropology and then as Assistant Director for Science and Research. His research concerns social organization, inequality, kinship and marriage, exchange and reciprocity, and intellectual and cultural property.

Rosemary J. Coombe is the Senior Canada Research Chair in Law, Communication and Culture at York University where she teaches in the Communication and Culture, Sociolegal Studies, and Social and Political Thought graduate programmes. She is educated in anthropology and law, and publishes in the fields of cultural anthropology, cultural studies, and law and society. She is currently working on a book exploring the proliferation of cultural rights and cultural properties under conditions of informational capital and neoliberal governmentality. A full list of her projects and publications may be found at www.yorku.ca/rcoombe

The Honourable Sir Edward Taihakurei Durie BA, LLB, KNZM has a long record in the legal administration of Maori affairs. He was a judge of the Maori Land Court from 1974, having practised as a lawyer specializing in Maori land matters, and was appointed Chief Judge of that Court in 1980. He also established the Waitangi Tribunal, which hears Maori claims against the State especially in relation to historical losses, and chaired the Tribunal for twenty years. He was appointed to the High Court in 1998 and served also as a New Zealand Law Commissioner engaged in law reform. He has maintained a particular interest in the incorporation of Maori custom. He has honorary doctorates from three New Zealand Universities.

Peter Dwyer was appointed as an honorary research associate of the anthropology programme at the University of Melbourne after a long career in zoology. His primary research interests concern questions of socio-ecology and change among societies of the Strickland-Bosavi region of Papua New Guinea. More recently he became involved in the anthropology of communities of commercial fishermen in south-eastern Australia during a period when their industry has been subject to major changes in management arrangements imposed by State and Federal agencies.

Colin Filer has a PhD in Social Anthropology from the University of Cambridge. He has taught anthropology and sociology at the Universities of Glasgow and Papua New Guinea, and was formerly head of the Social and Environmental Studies Division at the PNG National Research Institute. Since 2001 he has been Convener of the Resource Management in Asia-Pacific Program at The Australian National University. His research interests include the social context, organization and impact of policies, programmes and projects in the mining, petroleum, forestry and conservation sectors, with particular reference to Papua New Guinea and other parts of Melanesia.

Katie Glaskin is an Associate Professor in Anthropology at the University of Western Australia. Her research interests include legal and applied anthropology, with a focus on Indigenous Australia, native title, customary land and marine tenure and property relations; dreams and concepts of personhood; death; creativity and innovation; memory and emotion. Additional research interests include the anthropology of sleep and the relations between humans and humanoid robots in Japan. She is the co-editor of *Customary Land Tenure and Registration in Australia and Papua New Guinea: Anthropological Perspectives* (ANU E-press, 2007) and *Mortality, Mourning and Mortuary Practices in Indigenous Australia* (Ashgate, 2008).

Adam Kaul is Assistant Professor of Anthropology at Augustana College, Illinois, where he co-founded an anthropology program in 2008. He has conducted fieldwork in western Ireland and in the American Midwest. His research interests are in tourism, ethnomusicology, globalization and economic anthropology. Among his publications are 'The Limits of Commodification in Traditional Irish Music Sessions' (*JRAI* 2007) and *Turning the Tune: Traditional Music, Tourism, and Social Change in an Irish Village* (Berghahn 2009). Currently he is conducting ethnographic fieldwork on tourism at former utopian communities in the American Midwest.

Tamara Kohn is a Senior Lecturer in Anthropology at the University of Melbourne. Previously she lectured for fourteen years at Durham University. She studied at Berkeley (BA), University of Pennsylvania (MA) and Oxford (DPhil, and Junior Research Fellow). Field research experiences in Scotland, Nepal, California and Japan are linked by a common interest in migration, identity and transnational communities of embodied practice. Her publications include

The Discipline of Leisure (Berghahn 2007, ed. with S. Coleman), *Extending the Boundaries of 'Care'* (Berg 1999, ed. with R. McKechnie), and 'Becoming an Islander through Action in the Scottish Hebrides' (*JRAI* 2002).

Nicholas Long is a Lecturer in Social Anthropology at the University of Cambridge, where he also completed his undergraduate and doctoral studies. His research interests concern socio-political change in Indonesia's Riau Archipelago, and developing anthropological approaches to 'achievement'. Other recent publications include 'How to Win a Beauty Contest in Tanjung Pinang', in *Review of Indonesian and Malaysian Affairs*, 'Fruits of the Orchard: Land, Space, and State in Kepulauan Riau' in *SOJOURN*, and 'Haunting Malayness: the Multicultural Uncanny in a New Indonesian Province' in the *JRAI*.

Michael Lowe has a PhD in Human Geography from The Australian National University. He has previously lived and worked in both East and West New Britain Provinces of Papua New Guinea. Since 2005 he has been the Rural Livelihoods Coordinator on an AusAID-funded community development programme in Solomon Islands. His primary field of interest is change – both technical and social – in smallholder agrarian communities.

Monica Minnegal is a Senior Lecturer in Anthropology at the University of Melbourne. Her interest is in the reconfiguring of social and ecological relationships that occurs as people grapple with modernization and globalization. She has written about change in societies of the Strickland-Bosavi region of Papua New Guinea as they become more aware of their marginal place in the world; and change among commercial fishermen in south-east Australia as they are increasingly marginalized in the decision-making that affects their lives.

Howard Morphy is Professor of Anthropology and Director of the Research School of Humanities and the Arts at The Australian National University. He has published widely in the anthropology of art, aesthetics, performance, museum anthropology, Aboriginal social organization, the history of anthropology, visual anthropology and religion. His current focus is on the use of digital media in anthropological research and publication. His books include *Ancestral Connections: Art and an Aboriginal System of Knowledge* (University of Chicago Press, 1991), *Aboriginal Art* (Phaidon, 1998), *The Anthropology of Art: A Reader* (with Morgan Perkins, Blackwell, 2006) and *Becoming Art: Exploring Cross-Cultural Categories* (Berg, 2007).

Veronica Strang is a Professor of Social Anthropology at the University of Auckland. Prior to studying anthropology she worked as a writer/researcher on environmental issues, and contributed to The Brundtland Report. She received her DPhil at the University of Oxford in 1994, and has written extensively on water, land and resource issues in Australia and the UK. She is the author of *Uncommon Ground: Cultural Landscapes and Environmental Values* (1997); *The Meaning of Water* (2004); and *Gardening the World: Agency, Identity, and the Ownership of Water* (2009). In 2007 she was named as one of UNESCO's Les Lumières de L'Eau.

Marilyn Strathern is Emeritus Professor of Social Anthropology at the University of Cambridge, and Fellow of Girton College. The appropriateness or otherwise of the concept of property has intrigued her ever since she carried out fieldwork in the Highlands of Papua New Guinea, the concept being one to which she returned more recently in work (with PNG lawyers and anthropologists) on intellectual property rights. She arrived at this topic via a detour that took in English kinship and issues in the (then) new reproductive technologies. At the joint ASA, ASAANZ, AAS Auckland conference in 2008 she was inaugurated as Life President of the ASA.

Pawan Prakash Upreti is a radio professional who pioneered radio mapping and digital audio technology implementation during the rapid growth of the Nepali FM radio sector over the past ten years. Working as a digital media trainer and technical advisor, he designed and conducted training programmes for hundreds of technicians and media managers, on community radio and cable television, digital audio editing, digital storytelling, community multimedia centres and rural video production. In 2007–2009 he completed the first radio mapping and comprehensive technical assessment of FM radio stations in Nepal, Chad and Niger.

Michael Wilmore is a Senior Lecturer in the Discipline of Media at the University of Adelaide. He received his doctorate in anthropology from the University of London, having previously graduated with a Masters degree in social anthropology from University College London. Apart from his on-going research into development communications and media in Nepal, he has conducted ethnographic research into the working practices of UK archaeologists as part of a UCL research project funded by the British Academy.

Acknowledgements

The conference from which the chapters in this volume were drawn was financially supported by the Wenner Gren Foundation; the Royal Anthropological Institute; The Australian Anthropological Society; the University of Auckland and the ASA itself. Other support was given to the event by the Association of Social Anthropologists of Aotearoa/New Zealand and the AAA. The enthusiastic participation in the conference by anthropologists from all around the world ensured that many new ideas flowed into this volume, and the text has benefited at various stages from generous feedback from colleagues. The editors would like to thank in particular Chris Hann, who kindly read and commented on the entire draft manuscript and provided much sage advice. The various stages of production have also been assisted by the helpful input of James Staples (the ASA Publications officer) and Berg's editorial team.

Foreword
Chris Hann

As Veronica Strang and Mark Busse note in their Introduction, the ownership of property has been a prominent theme in the work of anthropologists since the emergence of the academic discipline in the nineteenth century. In the last decades of European imperialism, evolutionist theories gave way to more subtle analyses of the contemporaneous interplay between collective and individualized forms of land tenure. The subject was then temporarily occluded from the anthropological agenda. In the post-war welfare states (characterized by 'embedded liberalism'), ownership rights seemed less important than issues of (re-) distribution and control. After a brief neo-Marxist interlude, studies of consumption became much more popular than studies of productive property. This pattern has persisted, though it has been modified by the impact of neoliberal ideology and massive privatization in both capitalist countries and the countries of the former Soviet bloc. At the beginning of a new century, anthropological interests have shifted again, away from 'real property' towards the intangible, with the familiar principles of market economy being extended into new domains of knowledge and 'culture'.

The essays in this volume reflect and illuminate this conjuncture, which the editors have marked by a conceptual shift of their own by substituting 'appropriation' for the more familiar 'property'. If the anthropologists of the colonial era were still preoccupied with the application of legalistic definitions, as set out systematically in *Notes and Queries*, their successors are much more interested in exploring local semantic fields and subjectivities. Previously taken-for-granted notions of 'persons', 'things' and 'relations' are now thoroughly destabilized. 'Appropriation' used to refer to the assertion of an exclusive claim of ownership to something that was not owned at all. This *herrenlose* thing was, in the classical theories, not even possessed. Gradually, however, the supply of virgin lands and abandoned things diminished, new justificatory theories were needed, and the term 'appropriation' came to be applied in new ways. For example, it was often used in the twentieth century to describe how socialist authorities seized the peasants' land in order to establish collective farms. From the point of view of the peasant, appropriation in this case meant the replacement of a strong exclusive ownership right with a nebulous inclusive right.

Given this background (and the term has a much more complex history in ecclesiastical law), it is interesting to consider why and how anthropologists should come to appropriate 'appropriation' at this moment in history. In fact Daniel Miller has been using the term for some time already, in order to demonstrate how persons are constituted through material culture. By extending the terms appropriation and materiality in this manner, several contributors to this collection show how these processes can also be constitutive for communities or peoples. How the ensuing collectivities then pursue ownership claims over things other than their own collective identities opens up urgent issues of social justice all over the world. Seen from this point of view, the 'cultural turn' in the discipline need not initiate a turning away from issues previously investigated under rubrics such as 'political economy' or 'legal anthropology'. Rather, this new focus on appropriation should enable anthropologists to contribute more effectively to interdisciplinary debates and to give them a distinctive voice in the public sphere.

In any case, conservatives worried that the term 'property' is in danger of becoming a nineteenth-century heirloom in the stock of concepts of the contemporary anthropologist should be reassured by the editors' retention of 'ownership'. Indeed, Strang and Busse convey a sense of cumulative knowledge, unusual in postmodern times. Their innovative thrust is to emphasize symbolic communication and the *processual* character of the phenomena we subsume under the headings 'appropriation' and 'ownership'. Later editions of *Notes and Queries* implicitly reflected the rigidities of the paradigm of structural-functionalism. Legal anthropologists have shown how new specifications of ownership by colonial authorities often distorted the more dynamic processes of the preceding era. By contrast, the editors appeal for more fluid approaches to a social reality that is also taken to be fluid. If productive land was the basis of most earlier theorizing, water, the contested object of multiple ownership claims in Veronica Strang's case study, appears as the exemplary property object of the present era. The message seems to be that we need to correct the discipline's historic bias towards structure and rooted patiency by paying more attention to process and fluid agency.

This line of argumentation stimulates me to invoke an epistemological trope that is prominent in these chapters. Concepts such as process and structure can only exist alongside each other, or in each other's shadow. Thus, in the valuable contribution by the Honourable Taihakurei Durie we read that contemporary Maori understandings of land ownership continue to differ radically from those of the dominant settler society. The principles he identifies as valid today seem remarkably similar to those codified in celebrated monographs by Max Gluckman and Bronislaw Malinowski, or in C.R. Meek's compendium covering the British empire in its entirety (*Land Law in the Colonies*, 1948). The reality of New Zealand society has seen an on-going large-scale exodus of Maori from their native regions. Yet Durie informs us that this process has not been accompanied by radical changes in Maori land tenure: now, as in the past, they refuse to entertain the possibility that material benefits should accrue to an absentee owner. This rigidity, to which Durie is clearly sympathetic, may be variously understood as a consequence of colonial legislation, a defensive response to white domination, or a deliberate commitment to hold on to a valued *local* fluidity. My point is simply that all assertions of ownership and appropriation are in some sense concerned with regulating social life, with the imposition of order on disorder, even those whose aim is to create a space for fluidity.

Introduction

Ownership and Appropriation

Mark Busse and Veronica Strang

In a world of finite resources, expanding populations, and widening structural inequalities, the ownership of things is increasingly contested. Not only are the commons – such as water and airwaves – being rapidly enclosed and privatized, but there are also growing conflicts over the ownership of ideas, culture, 'heritage', people and even parts of people. Understanding how human groups understand and decide ownership is therefore both central to anthropological debates and of enormous practical consequence. In 2008 a joint international conference in Auckland brought together the anthropology associations of the UK and the Commonwealth, New Zealand and Australia to consider the theme of 'Ownership and Appropriation'. The goal of the conference was to extend the area of anthropological theorizing which had been dominated by the term *property* by shifting the focus from property and property relations to notions and acts of owning and appropriating which precede, underwrite and inform property relations. This volume presents some of the ideas that emerged from that event.

Anthropology and Property: A Brief Historical Overview

Chris Hann (1998, 2005, 2007) and Caroline Humphrey and Katherine Verdery (2004) have recently traced anthropology's long interest in property, which stretches back at least to Lewis Henry Morgan and Marcel Mauss. Morgan associated the development of ideas of property with social evolution, suggesting that 'dominance [of property] as a passion over all other passions marks the commencement of civilization' (Morgan 1974:6). Hann (2005:112; 2007:291) cogently observes that Mauss's study of *The Gift* (1990 [1925]), in its examination of changes in how people relate to one another via things, can be read as a history of changing ideas of property. In the 1930s Bronislaw Malinowski (1935) and Raymond Firth (1939) provided early treatments of individual and communal ownership, while three decades later Max Gluckman (1965) demonstrated the close relationship between Barotse land ownership and social structure.

The sixth edition of *Notes and Queries on Anthropology*, originally published in 1951, includes elements which have gained new relevance in contemporary anthropological discussions of property and ownership, including the essays in this volume. It begins with the observation that: 'The concepts of property and ownership are closely linked. Ownership is best defined as the sum total of rights which various persons or groups of persons have over things; the things thus owned are property' (1967:148–9). Definitions of ownership in terms of rights continue (e.g. Hann 2005:111–12; 2007:291) despite critiques of the sometimes ethnocentric assumptions that the language of rights makes about what constitutes a person (Humphrey and Verdery 2004:6). Most contemporary anthropologists and legal scholars, however, define property as a social relationship between persons with respect to things, which includes, for example, rights to exclude others (Macpherson 1978:3–5; Hann 1998:4–5, 2005:111; Humphrey and Verdery 2004:5).

Notes and Queries goes on to state that ideas about property vary both cross-culturally and within single societies 'according to the nature of the property and the type of ownership right involved'.[1] Anthropology has played, and continues to play, a critical role in relativizing property, in documenting cross-cultural variations both in persons and things, and in relationships between persons and between persons and things. It has also demonstrated the ways in which the materiality (or immateriality) of objects of ownership affects the character of relations between people with respect to them, a point taken up in detail in this volume by Veronica Strang, Monica Minnegal and Peter Dwyer, and Michael Wilmore and Pawan Upreti.

The last twenty years has seen renewed anthropological interest in property, coinciding with the rise of neoliberal ideology and its emphasis on free markets and private property, and the collapse of socialism in Eastern Europe and the former Soviet Union. The latter event led to a scramble for previously state-owned resources, a process that has been extensively documented by anthropologists (Cartwright 2001; Eidson 2006; Hann 2006, 2007; Humphrey 2002; Verdery 2003).

Over the last decade, theoretical writing by Hann (1998), Strathern (1999), and Humphrey and Verdery (2004), among others, has demonstrated the relevance of anthropology to articulating the complexity of property relations. Anthropology has also made significant contributions to global debates about intellectual, biological and cultural property (Brown 1998, 2003; Coombe 1998; Geismar 2005, 2008; Hirsch and Strathern 2004; Kalinoe and Leach 2004; Posey 2004; Ziff and Rao 1997). These include examinations of the role of creativity in the construction of intellectual property (Leach 2004; Moutu 2009), and the movement of intellectual property out of national and international legal realms and into local and everyday discourses (Geismar 2005; Strathern and Hirsch

2004; Van Meijl 2009). They have also exposed the reification of intellectual and cultural property: for example, the reification of culture in cases of claims over 'expressions of culture', and the reifications of peoples, as new 'interest groups' emerge through processes of claiming (Strathern and Hirsch 2004:8; cf. Busse 2009; Coombe, this volume; Recht 2009).

The Dynamics of Owning

In her essay 'Possession as the Origin of Property', Carol Rose (1994:11–23) asks how ownership comes about. Some things are owned as a result of exchange or inheritance, but how do never-before-owned things come to be owned? How do new ideas, newly discovered resources, or previously unowned resources such as minerals, water, or radio frequencies, come to belong to particular persons, groups, or corporations? John Locke classically proposed that the owner of a thing is the person who uses her or his labour to modify a previously unowned thing and, in so doing, establishes ownership of it. In the case of land, Locke argued, the labour that justifies ownership is cultivation or development (Garnsey 2007:144; cf. Ryan 1984:14–48). But as Rose notes (1994:12), Locke's theory of ownership raises questions: how much of something can be owned by virtue of labour – for example, why should the cultivation of a piece of land give rights to that land, rather than just to the crops produced?

In contrast, eighteenth-century theorists such as David Hume, Jean-Jacques Rousseau and Immanuel Kant argued that possession or occupation, rather than labour, is the basis of property. As Kant observed, the development of land can only happen if there is prior possession. Hence he objected to the dispossession of indigenous peoples from their land because this ignored their prior possession of it (Garnsey 2007:148; cf. Ryan 1984:81–2). Pierre-Joseph Proudhon echoed Kant's position and wrote, 'To labour it is necessary to occupy' (Proudhon 1970 [1840]:84; Garnsey 2007:146–8, 155–73). Occupation and possession here are examples of social action, an idea further developed by Rose and a significant theme of the papers in this volume.

The ideas of Hume, Rousseau and Kant – and not those of Locke – provide the basis for Anglo-American common law about property which locates the basis of property in possession or occupancy. But, Rose asks, 'what counts as possession?' and 'why does possession count as a claim to title?' (1994:12). At the centre of these two questions lies what Rose terms the 'clear-act principle': to possess something requires both a declaration of an intention to appropriate and an on-going assertion of ownership (1994:13). From this point of view possession is a statement or an act of communication, and it is the labour of communicating claims and maintaining this communication that constitutes the 'labour' justifying ownership. Rose's position assumes both an audience and a symbolic system in which understandable statements of appropriation and on-going ownership can be expressed, and she writes, 'It is not enough … for the property claimant to say simply "It's mine", through some act or gesture; in order for the statement to have any force, some relevant community must understand the claim that it makes and take that claim seriously' (1994:18).

The chapters in this volume extend the central observation contained in Rose's analysis: that ownership is a culturally and historically specific system of symbolic communication through which people act and through which they negotiate social and political relations. This perspective highlights ownership as a set of processes through which people assert and contest rights rather than a static bundle or structure of rights.[2] The acts which constitute possession – which announce it and continue to assert it – need not be verbal, but their intelligibility is critical to their success, as is the power and social positions of the actors making such statements. Anthropology, with its long history of documenting the cross-cultural diversity of ideas of personhood and agency, of power relations, and of symbolic systems and social processes, is particularly well placed to examine ownership and appropriation as on-going processes of symbolic communication and negotiation.

Appropriation – the act of making something one's own – is fundamental to a claim of original ownership. But such acts are not confined to laying claims to things that are previously 'un-owned'. Appropriation is also part of the process of owning objects obtained through exchange or inheritance, as actors make fully their own objects that previously belonged to others. In this expanded sense, *appropriation* covers a range of actions, from those that can be framed positively in terms of agency and creativity (Hirsch and Strathern 2004; Kalinoe and Leach 2004; Strang 2005), to others (such as theft) that are more negative, and still others (such as enslavement and appropriation through violence) that are nefarious (Bales 1999).

What emerges is a sense that acts of appropriation, and acts of communicating and upholding ownership, are processual rather than static in their form. This presents property relations not only as 'social relations between people' (Hann 1998:4) but also situates them more within wider processes of interaction between people, and between people and the physical environments that they inhabit. The purpose of this volume, therefore, is to highlight the fluidity of ownership and appropriation, exploring these as social actions rather than as legal categories. This brings to the fore a reality that there are multiple ways of owning and appropriating, some of which run counter to and thus challenge dominant frameworks. Clearly a willingness to encompass subaltern and alternate forms presents a risk that recognizable concepts of ownership will simply dissolve. At the same time, it helps to illuminate the complex realities of ownership as fluid and ephemeral processes of 'holding things' that – though temporarily crystallized through legal artefacts – can also be undermined and appropriated in a range of ways. The chapters therefore focus on the fluidities inherent in owning and appropriating, including their conceptual undercurrents.

Thus Marilyn Strathern considers the conceptual flows in notions of ownership, exploring how concepts do their work in relation to one another rather than as isolated, well-bounded ideas. To the concepts of ownership and appropriation, she adds theft, borrowing, sharing, belonging (rather than belongings), identification and self-realization. Concepts in such 'constellations' both work together and 'work upon one another' (Strathern, this volume, pp.27, 29). Strathern argues for the intellectual value of looking at what happens when concepts reach their limits, at which point other concepts emerge from the shadows. Taking a concept to its limit means finding the concept's possible extent or reach, rather than searching for its 'essence'. The trope of 'shadow concepts' suggests a temporal and conceptual foregrounding and backgrounding of concepts that are always present, and thus always potentially in play, rather than thinking of concepts as bounded essences belonging to alternative or opposed systems. The essays in this volume push the concepts of ownership and appropriation to their edges in the interest of seeing the shadow concepts that emerge.

There are other shifting elements to consider. The established anthropological view of property as relations between persons with respect to things has worked well, but it can also be considered more dynamically. Humphrey and Verdery (2004) have recently questioned the analytic clarity of persons, things and relationships. This goes beyond relativizing: building on the extensive discussion of personhood in anthropology, they question the often-assumed boundedness and stability through time of social persons. They suggest instead that stable and bounded persons are culturally and historically particular, the result of the development of censuses, naming practices and written registers that fixed people to particular territories (2004:6–7). In some instances persons may appear unitary as a result of close ties between personal or group identity and personal or culturally significant things – that is, as a result of their actions in making property claims (cf. Radin 1982; Carpenter *et al.* 2009). The issue of social personhood in relation to ownership and appropriation is prominently highlighted in this volume by Katie Glaskin, Nicholas Long, Tamara Kohn and Rosemary Coombe.

Humphrey and Verdery (2004:7–8) also point out that conventional discourses of property *rights* privilege the rights in a thing over the nature or 'thingness' of the thing itself, a particularly critical oversight in relation to new forms of property where an appreciation of materiality is often vital for understanding how ownership works. Finally, they problematize the idea of 'relations', asking, 'What kinds of relations does a property analysis include?' (2004:8).

Because the tendency has been to presume that persons and things are recognizable and separate, establishing a property relation means overcoming while affirming that separateness: some persons are united with the thing as against other persons, who are excluded from it. But how about 'relations' of consubstantiality … in which persons and things are not seen as clearly bounded and separate but as participating in one another? Is that a 'property relation'? (Humphrey and Verdery 2004:8)

This suggests a need to rethink property in more complex and dynamic terms that do not reify persons, things or relations. The papers in this volume therefore extend the area of recent anthropological theorizing, which has been dominated by the term *property*, by shifting the focus from property and property relations to notions and acts of owning and appropriating which precede, underwrite and inform property relations. They do this by reconsidering four key areas: social personhood; ownership as social communication and symbolic action; the significance of materiality for new forms of ownership; and the interplay between ownership and appropriation on the one hand, and larger political and economic structures on the other.

Personhood and Peoplehood

How does someone who owns become a social person with a culturally specific capacity to own? Like property, personhood is not a natural category, but a cultural and historical creation (e.g. Carrithers *et al.* 1985). Charles Taylor (1985:257) suggests that in Western philosophical terms, 'to be a person in the full sense you have to be an agent with a sense of yourself as an agent, a being which can thus make plans for your life, one who also holds values in virtue of which different such plans seem better or worse, and who is capable of choosing between them'. Individuals only acquire full social personhood after a long period of development (Taylor 1985:257), and there is considerable cross-cultural diversity in the characteristics that constitute a social person and in the processes through which social persons are created (e.g. Fortes 1987; Geertz 1973; Jackson 1998, 2005; Lienhardt 1961; Marriott 1989; Overing and Passes 2000; Reisman 1977; Strathern 1988, 1992a, 1992b). Particularly prominent has been the work of Marilyn Strathern (1988), who has argued that persons in Mount Hagen in the Papua New Guinea Highlands are not distinct, bounded individuals but are instead 'partible' in the sense that they are constituted by the social relations in which they participate over time. Thus personhood itself emerges as a process.

Property is prominent in discussions of personhood in Western philosophy, and many scholars have considered it vital for the development of full personhood. Kant, for example, argued that property is crucial for human agency and for full political participation (Ryan 1984:86–88). Hegel (1967) similarly maintained that property makes a key contribution to the self, a point taken up by the nineteenth-century philosopher Thomas Green (1941), who focused on the contribution that ownership makes to ethical development, the growth of will, and a sense of responsibility (cf. Maurer and Schwab 2006:6). In more recent decades writers have considered the creation of more individualistic forms of social being, and what Macpherson (1962) has called 'possessive individualism'.

These considerations of the significance of things to the development of persons gain particular salience in the case of some forms of property, for example human organs and heirlooms. The legal scholar Margaret Radin (1982) took the position that such things, which are particularly constitutive of persons, must be excluded from the market and should be understood as non-fungible, incommensurable and inalienable. More recently Kristen Carpenter *et al.* (2009) have extended Radin's position from persons to people (or from personhood to peoplehood) by arguing that 'certain lands, resources, and expressions are entitled to legal protection as cultural property because they are integral to group identity and cultural survival of indigenous peoples' (2009:1028; but for a critique, see Busse 2009: 364–5).

In this volume Glaskin, Long, Kohn and Coombe consider the dynamic processes central to personhood and relationships between personhood and ownership. Their contributions direct our attention to subjectivity, intersubjectivity and the creation of subject positions through processes of appropriation and the claiming of ownership. For example, based on research among Aboriginal peoples in Western Australia, Glaskin documents how changes in ideas about intellectual property are linked to changes in social personhood, and how both intellectual property and personhood are constituted intersubjectively.[3] In examining the temporality of persons over the life cycle she finds that social persons include living people as well as the recently dead, who are remembered as individuals, and longer-dead people who collectively become part of what Aborigines call 'country'. It is the recently dead who reveal ritual elements to the living in dreams, and those dreams become the basis for ownership claims, some of which are increasingly individual rather than collective.

In their chapters Marilyn Strathern and Taihakurei Durie also address relations between personhood and ownership. Strathern describes how respect for things is a route to self-realization and dignity in a boarding school. And Durie's discussion of land ownership and appropriation in New Zealand describes how Maori decide legal issues, including ownership, in terms of concrete social relationships rather than abstract norms. Those social relationships depend to some extent on predecessors and geneaology, but also on where people live and how they participate in day-to-day community life. Personhood therefore emerges as a fluid developmental process created through on-going social action. At the same time Maori subjectivity, like that of many other indigenous peoples, includes a social and spiritual connection to the land, focused on belonging and 'having a place to stand' (*tūrangawaewae*). In these terms continuity of contact with land and social community is the basis for Maori understandings of who they are and how they belong in the world.[4] Nicholas Long argues for attending to the subjectivities of persons involved in similarly processual acts of appropriation and ownership. He does this through an ethnography of *anak berprestasi* (literally, 'achieving child') in Indonesia. Like beauty queens, sports stars and spokespersons, such people work hard to be appropriated and to become icons. The result is a relationship of 'mutual possession' with the social or political entities that they represent, and Long suggests that this relationality is at the core of appropriation and that 'appropriation is an act which can reveal a pre-existing mutual possession'. While he considers such appropriation in terms of Foucault's concept of governmentality, he also shows that this provides only a partial picture because it ignores the subjectivities of the people who are appropriated and their potential to act in what Sartre called 'bad faith'.

In contrast Kohn's chapter is concerned with the subjectivities of people who are appropriating rather than being appropriated. She looks at identities forged through 'inter-culturality' in the practice of aikido. This is practice both in the anthropological sense and in the more pedestrian sense of physical training. Aikido students appropriate bodily movements and ways of being, thus creating an embodied subjectivity. They do this through an act which they describe as 'stealing with their eyes' from their teachers' demonstrations. Such subjectivities are authenticated intersubjectively through, among other things, geneaologies of teachers traced back to Morehiei Ueshiba, the founder of aikido.

While the papers by Glaskin, Long and Kohn focus on subjectivities and intersubjectivities of individual actors, Coombe describes how cultural identities and political agencies – what some have termed *peoplehood* (Carpenter *et al.* 2009; Lie 2004) – are constituted through communicative acts of ownership and appropriation. Coombe starts from the position that collective identities do not simply exist before the law, but are in some instances created in relation to law and in relation to subject positions defined by legal regimes and negotiations. National and international structures thus often present indigenous peoples with a kind of double bind. Their own forms of sociality are seen as cumbersome or unacceptable by those with whom they negotiate, and hence kin groups, language groups, tribes and other forms of indigenous social organization become corporations and other kinds of legal entities. Following such transformations, they are often no longer indigenous (or different) enough for the people or structures with which they are negotiating, and they then become simply one of many legal entities.[5] Coombe describes such processes in terms of Foucault's concept of governmentality to capture the sense in which the engagement of indigenous peoples with processes of property and ownership represent both opportunities and means of defining and controlling indigenous peoples. This point is also illustrated in Durie's paper where he identifies the relationship between Maori kin groups and new legal bodies (such as tribal authorities) as an area that would benefit from anthropological study.

Ownership as Social Communication

Ownership as social communication or symbolic action – as processes of on-going assertions and claims – is well documented in several chapters in this volume. Glaskin, for example, describes ownership claims made on the basis of dreams in which ritual knowledge is revealed by the recently dead, and Coombe and Strang describe claims and counter-claims to cultural property and water respectively. In her discussion of 'Xavier borrowing' (which she borrows from Wendel 2007), Strathern draws attention to the moral orders which determine the meanings of communicative acts of ownership and appropriation. In certain contexts (for example, kinship relations) when someone asks for something, it is very difficult to refuse. This is 'Xavier borrowing', where to ask for something includes the assumption that it will be given. But whether one calls this 'borrowing' (with its temporal element) or 'theft' (with its overtones of aggression and finality) depends on the moral order that pertains and its internal assumptions about persons and social relations.

Howard Morphy's chapter characterizes Yolngu art objects as statements about ownership, as ways of 'demonstrating rights' and making claims. But they are also produced for trade and exchange, and for Yolngu there is no clear separation between the two purposes. Significantly, Yolngu do not see wider use of their art as appropriation by national legal structures or by Western art worlds. Instead, they comprehend art as a form of action in the world. Such an approach to art stands against reification of art and art objects by acknowledging and emphasizing the social relations and social agency through which representational objects are produced. Intelligible symbolic action, including understanding an action as appropriation, is formed intersubjectively in relation to ideas about personhood and agency.

Adam Kaul, in his account of tourism in the village of Doolin in County Clare, discusses the role of place names and changing historical narratives, and highlights the processes of appropriating and controlling discourses that underwrite ownership and appropriation of place. Place names reflect local histories of power, and the stories that are told about Doolin – by locals, tourists and government agencies – are a form of 'narrative emplacement'. Rather than overt claims to ownership, the communicative acts through which appropriation takes place involve reworkings of history. They reflect shifting power dynamics as the control of tourism is removed from local people by centers of power at the county, national and transnational levels.

Colin Filer and Michael Lowe describe a long and complex history of land appropriation and ownership in a small area of Papua New Guinea, in which there have been multiple, conflicting and shifting claims and assertions to ownership over the course of a century. The details of those claims and assertions shed light on a critical and much debated point in Papua New Guinea and elsewhere: the relationship between types of land ownership and socio-economic development. According to Filer and Lowe, the oft-cited distinction in Papua New Guinea between land that remains under customary ownership and land that has been alienated from customary owners is not the critical issue in understanding development successes and failures. Instead, they argue for a 'double movement' – the partial alienation of customary land and the partial customization of alienated land. Echoing Coombe's point that claims of ownership can serve to create cultural identities, they argue that this double movement creates new forms of authority, society and individual and group identity in each place where it occurs.

Materiality and New Forms of Property

The concern with original ownership, with how previously unowned things come to be owned, is neither simply of historical interest nor merely an abstract consideration. As Frederic Jameson (1990) showed, the expansion of property claims into new and sometimes unexpected areas of human life is a characteristic of late capitalism (see Busse 2009), and James Boyle (2002) has compared the recent extension of property rights into the public domain with the fifteenth- and sixteenth-century process of enclosure through which the physical commons became private property (see also Bollier 2002). The chapters by Strang, Minnegal and Dwyer, and Wilmore and Upreti deal explicitly with the materiality of new forms of property in their examinations of water, fishing quota and the radio spectrum.

Strang adopts a phenomenological approach to understanding claims to, and conflicts over, ownership of water in Australia. The materiality of water – its fluidity and the difficulty of containing (or enclosing) it – means that, despite efforts to commodify it through the creation of 'virtual' volumetric allocations, water is much more difficult to turn into property than land or material culture. In this sense water has much in common with fish and game animals. Because standard legal ideas about property are ill-suited for thinking about the ownership of water, this opens the possibility of other kinds of ownership based not on legal rights but on knowledge, identity, aesthetic and emotional attachments to place, and imaginative and physical engagement with the environment. As Strang points out, these constitute subtle but important countermovements in what has been an intensive drive towards the privatization of previously common resources.

Minnegal and Dwyer's chapter explores the changing realities of fish and fishers in South Australia. They are interested in the phenomenology of the materiality of fish and the subjectivities of fishermen. The story that unfolds is about the effects of the introduction of individual transferable quotas in the Australian fishing industry. Against that backdrop, they try to understand how fish are imagined by people in the fishing industry and how 'the imagination of fishermen is being reconfigured by the imposition of management strategies that ... translate the uncertainties inherent in macro-level biological and economic systems into lived experience' (p. 197). While 'wild' fish are similar to water in that they are not spatially fixed, fish stocks, unlike water, have been commodities for a long time. What is new is the commodification of the *idea* of fish – what Minnegal and Dwyer call 'paper fish' or 'virtual fish'. In contemporary fishing fishermen move between trying to find and catch fish, and acquiring and holding the needed quotas. The effect of this new form of property is not better fisheries management, but rather changes to personhood and selfhood as trust and cooperation are replaced by coercion and competition. Minnegal and Dwyer characterize this erosion as a movement from probabilistic risk to existential uncertainty.[6] But as both Minnegal and Dwyer's and Strang's chapters illustrate, enclosures or reconfigurations of resources, and what Von Benda-Beckmann *et al.* criticize as the 'fetishization' of private property rights (2006),[7] have generated an array of countermovements. These have also served to encourage governmental efforts to regulate and reduce private property rights, a trend which Hann describes as a new 'double movement' enabling a 'reassertion of Society' (2007:310).

The interplay between state authority and grassroots countermovement is visible in Wilmore and Upreti's examination of the allocation of frequencies within the radio spectrum in Nepal. Despite the spectrum's particular and peculiar materiality – its intangibility and invisibility – ideas about this relatively new form of property are based on ownership being vested in the state which allocates and regulates frequencies through commercial licences – i.e. by treating them as state property. The allocation of a limited number of radio frequencies, however, is the result of social arrangements rather than the inherent physical properties of the radio spectrum itself, since technological innovations have made it an inexhaustible resource.

Another way of talking about this is in terms of rivalrous and non-rivalrous resources (Boyle 2002). A rivalrous resource is one where one person's ownership precludes ownership by someone else – 'if I use this tree to make my canoe, you cannot'. Non-rivalrous resources, on the other hand, are those where one person's ownership or use does not preclude another's. The radio spectrum, as Wilmore and Upreti point out, appears to be a rivalrous resource merely because that is how it is socially and politically organized. But given its actual non-rivalrousness, the radio spectrum could be treated as a commons, and they argue that this would allow for significantly more benefits in terms of the dissemination of information.

This point is analogous to arguments put forward by writers such as Lawrence Lessig (2008) and Michael Brown (1998, 2003). They make use of the non-rivalrousness of intellectual property and cultural expression to argue against restricting access to them on the grounds, for example, that someone's performance or consumption of a piece of music does not stop someone else from performing or listening to it. While this argument for a cultural and intellectual commons is certainly true with respect to the inherent qualities of intellectual property or cultural expression, it ignores the fact that it is the commercial or cultural significance of intellectual property that determines whether it is rivalrous or non-rivalrous. Non-rivalrous things become rivalrous when their exclusive use by a particular community is a key element in that people's identity or their ability to make a living. Performing a piece of music that is critical to a people's identity or their economic viability does not stop them from performing it, but it does mean that the music is no longer unique or exclusive to them. The materiality of property in itself, then, is not the whole story, but, as Minnegal and Dwyer, and Wilmore and Upreti demonstrate, the subjectivities and social arrangements interacting with materiality are critical.

Diverse Property Regimes and the State

A theme that runs through all of the chapters in this volume concerns the role of the state, and other national and transnational political and economic structures, in matters of ownership and appropriation. As Ostrom (1990) has made clear, the management of 'the commons' continues to raise important questions about whether the most effective governance of both people and resources can be achieved through private or collective forms of ownership. In effect, systems of governance serve to mediate property relations and, recursively, systems of property relations define 'who owns the state'. As Alexander (2004:253, 254) observes, privatization entails 'the separation of persons and things from the state' and a 'relational absence'. Thus a shift in the ownership of key resources, such as water, to private elites and transnational networks, coupled with more individuated visions of personhood, not only raises questions about 'who owns the state?' but also about the conceptual viability of the state and even, in ideological extremes, 'society' itself. Inevitably such debates are entangled with issues of both social and ecological sustainability, underlining a reality that property relations are not just social but also environmental relations.

Several of the contributions to this volume highlight ideological divergences in which state-imposed forms of property relations are at odds with subaltern notions of ownership. The examples given by Long and Kaul can be read as local case studies set against the backdrop of the appropriative power of the state, while Minnegal and Dwyer's account documents people's attempts to come to terms with the state's power to promulgate a new regulatory regime and a new form of property that facilitates that regime, and Strang's chapter highlights the relationships between ideology, ownership and ecological sustainability.

Durie's paper on the appropriation of Maori land by the Crown addresses the role of the state most directly. Beginning with the observation that property rights are cultural constructs and that there is nothing universal about them, Durie outlines the differences between English and Maori conceptions of property rights. Maori ownership is communal, although there are individual use rights with respect to particular resources rather than to particular pieces of land. But the right to use depends on contributing to the community, and abstract rights must be backed up by actual use and occupation (*ahi ka*). This contrasts with English ideas about ownership that start with enclosed pieces of land and do not include a requirement either to occupy that land or to contribute directly to the immediate community, a situation that Durie characterizes as reflecting a social transition from community consciousness to state controlled capitalism (this volume). The differences between Maori and English understandings of property and ownership, and the realities of colonial political arrangements in New Zealand, have led to a history of conflict, violence and dispossession of Maori from their lands.

There is a sharp contrast with the situation in Papua New Guinea described by Filer and Lowe, where (sometimes violent) conflict over land results from different and competing ideas about property and ownership. But whereas in New Zealand Maori are a minority that struggles to assert its rights within a postcolonial settler society, in Papua New Guinea both indigenous custom and English common law have made up the country's underlying law since its independence in 1975, and there is a multitude of indigenous peoples and a diversity of property regimes.

Conflicts between indigenous communities and larger settler societies have underlined the need to consider cultural diversity in notions of ownership, and anthropology's translatory skills have been critical in the development of new legal forms that attempt to encompass cultural differences. In Australia, for example, anthropologists have been closely involved in the development of new laws attempting to bring indigenous and non-indigenous systems of law together, most specifically in relation to land and sea rights (Hamilton 1982; Morphy and Morphy 2006; Strang 2000).

An ethnographically based process of translation has also been useful in generating new thinking about ownership within anthropology, and a cross-cultural exchange of theory is readily evident in this volume. As several chapters in this volume illustrate (and as can be seen in other analyses, e.g. Strathern 1988, 1999), indigenous forms of ownership are often explicitly processual in their form, encouraging anthropologists to explore the fluidities of personhood, relationships and things, and challenging the more static or ethnocentric constructs sometimes imposed at a state level.

In discussing radio frequencies in Nepal, Wilmore and Upreti also write about the relationship between the state and civil society. They note the importance of information, such as that provided by radio, for achieving social and economic development goals, and the lack of practical recognition of this by the Nepalese government, which instead focuses on uncontrolled competition and privatization of the radio spectrum. This raises the question of the purpose of property regimes (which are, after all, social conventions) in a neoliberal world in which wealth production through putatively free markets is understood as an end in itself, and the equally important question of who has the power to decide the answer to that question.

The chapters in this volume are organized into three sections: Subjects, Personhood and Peoplehood; Materiality and Immateriality; and Ownership as Social Communication. Taken together, they represent both continuity with, and a re-visioning of, previous anthropological treatments of property. By seeking the edges rather than the essences of concepts such as personhood, social action and agency, materiality and power relations, the collection reconfigures our understanding of these concepts and the ways in which they work together, work on one another and work against each other. Because their conceptualization is rooted more in the everyday lived experiences of people than in abstract legal structures, the result is a more dynamic and processual understanding of property, ownership and appropriation.

Notes

1. *Notes and Queries* (1967:149–51) lists eight types of property – real estate, household and occupation equipment, personal effects, ritual objects, stock, usufruct rights, rights in persons, and 'other forms of incorporeal property' – and five types of rights – rights of use, rights to control the use or disposal of property by others, rights of disposal, rights to derive an income from use of property by others, and 'rights to be described as the titular owner of property without further benefits'.
2. The idea of property as 'a bundle of rights' was originally put forward by the comparative legal scholar Henry Maine in his 1861 book *Ancient Law* (see Hann 2005:111). While static, Maine's conception drew attention to the potential for multiple interests (multiple and diverse rights) in the same thing. In her paper in this volume, Veronica Strang describes alternative notions of ownership based on social identity, mythology, knowledge, engagements, usage, historical association, and emotional ties, rather than rights *per se*.

3. For an earlier formulation of intellectual property as intersubjectively constituted see Simon Harrison (1992).
4. According to Durie, Maori do not accept that one can be an absentee landlord, taking rent but not giving to the community.
5. This problem is central to wider debates about 'biculturalism' versus 'multiculturalism', in which there are concerns that, in the latter case, the particular status of indigenous people is removed through their repositioning as just another 'stakeholder' or 'interest group'.
6. See also Durie (this volume) who notes that the first settlement of an historical grievance between the Crown and Maori consisted of fishing quotas, a new form of property right under the Quota Management System that regulates fishing in New Zealand.
7. Critiques of neoliberalism with regard to property build, of course, on Polanyi's classic deconstruction of 'the great transformation' in notions of property, and its observation that this separated property and social relations (1944).

References

Alexander, C. (2004), 'Value, Relations and Changing Bodies: Privatization and Property Rights in Kazakhstan', in K. Verdery and C. Humphrey (eds), *Property in Question: Value Transformation in the Global Economy*, Oxford, New York: Berg, pp. 251–73.

Bales, K. (1999), *Disposable People: New Slavery in the Global Economy*, Berkeley: University of California Press.

Bollier, D. (2002), *Silent Theft: The Private Plunder of Our Common Wealth*, New York and London: Routledge.

Boyle, J. (2002), 'Fencing Off Ideas: Enclosure and the Disappearance of the Public Domain', *Daedalus*, 131(2): 13–25.

Brown, M. (1998), 'Can Culture be Copyrighted?' *Current Anthropology*, 39(2): 193–222.

Brown, M. (2003), *Who Owns Native Culture?* Cambridge: Harvard University Press.

Busse, M. (2008), 'Museums and the Things in Them Should Be Alive', *International Journal of Cultural Property*, 15: 189–200.

Busse, M. (2009), 'Anxieties about Culture and Tradition: Property as Reification', *International Journal of Cultural Property*, 16: 357–70.

Busse, M. and Whimp, K. (2000), 'Introduction', in Whimp, K. and Busse, M. (eds), *Protection of Intellectual, Biological and Cultural Property in Papua New Guinea*, Canberra: Asia-Pacific Press, pp. 1–28.

Carpenter, K., Katyal, S. and Riley, A. (2009), 'In Defense of Property', *The Yale Law Journal*, 118: 1022–125.

Carrithers, M., Collins, S. and Lukes, S. (eds) (1985), *The Category of the Person: Anthropology, Philosophy, History*, Cambridge: Cambridge University Press.

Cartwright, A. (2001), *The Return of the Peasant: Land Reform in Post-communist Romania*, Aldershot: Ashgate.

Committee of the Royal Anthropological Institute of Great Britain and Ireland (1967), *Notes and Queries on Anthropology*, London: Routledge and Kegan Paul.

Coombe, R. (1998), *The Cultural Life of Intellectual Properties*, Durham: Duke University Press.

Eidson, J. (2006), 'Cooperative Property at the Limit', in F. Benda-Beckmann, K. von Benda-Beckmann and M. Wiber (eds), *Changing Properties of Property*, Oxford: Berghahn, pp. 147–69.

Engels, F. (1972) [orig. 1884], *The Origin of the Family, Private Property and the State: In Light of the Researches of Lewis Henry Morgan*, New York: Pathfinder Press.

Firth, R. (1939), *Primitive Polynesian Economy*, London: Routledge and Sons.

Fortes, M. (1987), *Religion, Morality and the Person: Essays on Tallensi Religion*, Cambridge: Cambridge University Press.

Garnsey, P. (2007), *Thinking About Property: From Antiquity to the Age of Revolution*, Cambridge: Cambridge University Press.

Geertz, C. (1973), 'Person, Time and Conduct in Bali', in C. Geertz, *The Interpretation of Culture*, New York: Basic Books, pp. 360–411.

Geismar, H. (2005), 'Copyright in Context: Carvings, Carvers, and Commodities in Vanuatu', *American Ethnologist*, 32: 437–59.

Geismar, H. (2008), 'Cultural Property, Museums, and the Pacific: Reframing the Debates', *International Journal of Cultural Property*, 15: 109–22.

Gluckman, M. (1965), *The Ideas of Barotse Jurisprudence*, New Haven: Yale University Press.

Green, T. (1941) [orig. 1895], *Lectures on the Principles of Political Obligation*, London: Longmans Green and Co.

Green, T. (1978) [orig. 1885–1888], 'The Right of the State in Regard to Property', in C. Macpherson (ed.), *Property: Mainstream and Critical Positions*, Toronto: University of Toronto Press, pp. 101–18.

Hamilton, A. (1982), 'The Unity of Hunting-Gathering Societies: Reflections on Economic Forms and Resource Management', in N. Williams and E. Hunn (eds), *Resource Managers: North American and Australian Hunter Gatherers*, Canberra: Australian Institute of Aboriginal Studies.

Hann, C. (1998), 'Introduction: the Embeddedness of Property', in C. Hann (ed.), *Property Relations: Renewing the Anthropological Traditions*, Cambridge: Cambridge University Press, pp. 1–47.

Hann, C. (2005), 'Property', in J. Carrier (ed.), *A Handbook of Economic Anthropology*, Cheltenham: Edward Elgar, pp. 110–24.

Hann, C. (2006), *'Not the Horse We Wanted!' Postsocialism, Neoliberalism and Eurasia*, Münster: LIT.

Hann, C. (2007), 'A New Double Movement? Anthropological Perspectives on Property in the Age of Neoliberalism', *Socio-Economic Review*, 5: 287–318.

Harrison, S. (1992), 'Ritual as Intellectual Property', *Man* (n.s.), 27: 225–43.

Hegel, G. (1967) [orig. 1821], *The Philosophy of Right*, translated by T.M. Knox, Cambridge: Cambridge University Press.

Hirsch, E. and Strathern, M. (eds) (2004), *Transactions and Creations: Property Debates and the Stimulus of Melanesia*, New York: Berghahn Books.

Humphrey, C. (1983), *Karl Marx Collective: Economy, Politics and Religion on a Siberian Collective Farm*, Cambridge: Cambridge University Press.

Humphrey, C. (2002), *The Unmaking of the Soviet Life: Everyday Economy after Socialism*, Ithaca: Cornell University Press.

Humphrey, C. and Verdery, K. (2004), 'Introduction: Raising Questions About Property', in K. Verdery and C. Humphrey, *Property in Question: Value Transformation in the Global Economy*, Oxford: Berg, pp. 1–25.

Jackson, M. (1998), *Minima Ethnographica: Intersubjectivity and the Anthropological Project*, Chicago: University of Chicago Press

Jackson, M. (2005), *Existential Anthropology: Events, Exigencies and Effects*, New York: Berghahn Books.

Jameson, F. (1990), *Postmodernism, or, The Cultural Logic of Late Capitalism*, London: Verso.

Kalinoe, L. and Leach, J. (eds) (2004), *Rationales of Ownership: Transactions and Claims to Ownership in Contemporary Papua New Guinea*, Wantage: Sean Kingston.

La Fontaine, J. (1985), 'Person and Individual: Some Anthropological Reflections', in M. Carrithers, S. Collins and S. Lukes (eds), *The Category of the Person: Anthropology, Philosophy, History*, Cambridge: Cambridge University Press, pp. 123–40.

Leach, J. (2004), 'Modes of Creativity', in E. Hirsch and M. Strathern (eds), *Transactions and Creations: Property Debates and the Stimulus of Melanesia*, New York: Berghahn Books, pp. 151–75.

Lessig, L. (2008), *Remix: Making Art and Commerce Thrive in the Hybrid Economy*, New York: Penguin Press.

Lie, J. (2004), *Modern Peoplehood*, Cambridge: Harvard University Press.

Lienhardt, G. (1961), *Divinity and Experience: The Religion of the Dinka*, Oxford: Clarendon Press.

Lienhardt, G. (1985), 'Self: Public and Private, Some African Representations', in M. Carrithers, S. Collins and S. Lukes (eds), *The Category of the Person:*

Anthropology, Philosophy, History, Cambridge: Cambridge University Press, pp. 141–55.

Locke, J. (1980) [orig. 1690], *Second Treatise of Government*, edited by C. Macpherson, Indianapolis: Hackett Publishing Company.

Macpherson, C. (1962), *The Political Theory of Possessive Individualism: Hobbes to Locke,* Oxford: Clarendon Press.

Macpherson, C.B. (1978), 'The Meaning of Property', in C.B. Macpherson (ed.), *Property: Mainstream and Critical Positions*, Oxford: Basil Blackwell, pp. 1–13.

Malinowski, B. (1935), *Coral Gardens and Their Magic*, London: Allen and Unwin.

Marriot, M. (1989), 'Constructing an Indian ethnosociology', *Contributions to Indian Sociology* (n.s.), 23: 1–39.

Maurer, B. and Schwab, G. (2006), 'Introduction: the political and psychic economies of accelerating possession', in B. Maurer and G. Schwab (eds), *Accelerating Possession: Global Futures of Property and Personhood*, New York: Columbia University Press, pp. 1–17.

Mauss, M. (1990 [1925]), *The Gift: The Form and Reason for Exchange in Archaic Societies*, W.D. Halls (trans.), London: W.W. Norton.

Morgan, L. (1974) [orig. 1877], *Ancient Society, or Researches in the Lines of Human Progress from Savagery through Barbarism to Civilization*, edited by E. Burke Leacock, Gloucester: Peter Smith.

Morphy, H. and Morphy. F. (2006), 'Tasting the Waters: Discriminating Identities in the Waters of Blue Mud Bay', *Journal of Material Culture,* 11(1/2): 67–85.

Moutu, A. (2009), 'The Dialectic of Creativity and Ownership in Intellectual Property Discourse', *International Journal of Cultural Property*, 16: 309–24.

Ostrom, E. (1990), *Governing the Commons,* Cambridge: Cambridge University Press.

Overing, J. and Passes, A. (eds) (2000), *The Anthropology of Love and Anger: The Aesthetics of Conviviality in Native Amazonia*, New York: Routledge.

Polanyi, K. (1944), *The Great Transformation*, New York: Farrar and Reinhart.

Posey, D. (2004), *Indigenous Knowledge and Ethics: A Darrell Posey Reader*, edited by K. Plenderleith, New York: Routledge.

Proudhon, P.-J. (1970) [orig. 1840], *What is Property? An Inquiry into the Principle of Right and of Government*, translated by B. Tucker, New York: Dover Publications.

Radin, M. (1982), 'Property and Personhood', *Stanford Law Review*, 34(5): 957–1015.

Recht, J. (2009), 'Hearing Indigenous Voices, Protecting Indigenous Knowledge', *International Journal of Cultural Property*, 16: 233–54.

Reisman, P. (1977), *Freedom in Fulani Social Life: An Introspective Ethnography*, translated by M. Fuller, Chicago: University of Chicago Press.

Rose, C. (1994), *Property and Persuasion: Essays on the History, Theory, and Rhetoric of Ownership*, Boulder: Westview Press.

Rose, C. (2004), 'Economic Claims and the Challenges of New Property', in K. Verdery and C. Humphrey (eds), *Property in Question: Value Transformation in the Global Economy*, Oxford: Berg, pp. 275–95.

Ryan, A. (1984), *Property and Political Theory*, Oxford: Basil Blackwell.

Strang, V. (2000), 'Not So Black and White: the Effects of Aboriginal Law on Australian legislation', in A. Abramson and D. Theodossopoulos (eds), *Mythical Lands, Legal Boundaries: Rites and Rights in Historical and Cultural Context*, London: Pluto Press, pp. 93–115.

Strang, V. (2005), 'Water works: Agency and Creativity in the Mitchell River catchment', *The Australian Journal of Anthropology*, 16(3): 366–81.

Strathern, M. (1988), *The Gender of the Gift: Problems with Women and Problems with Society in Melanesia*, Berkeley: University of California Press.

Strathern, M. (1992a), *After Nature: English Kinship in the Late Twentieth Century*, Cambridge: Cambridge University Press.

Strathern, M. (1992b), *Reproducing the Future: Essays on Anthropology, Kinship and the New Reproductive Technologies*, Manchester: Manchester University Press.

Strathern, M. (1999), *Property, Substance and Effect: Anthropological Essays on Persons and Things*, London: Athlone Press.

Strathern, M. and Hirsch, E. (2004), 'Introduction', in E. Hirsch and M. Strathern (eds), *Transactions and Creations: Property Debates and the Stimulus of Melanesia*, New York: Berghahn Books, pp. 1–18.

Taylor, C. (1985), 'The Person', in M. Carrithers, S. Collins, and S. Lukes (eds), *The Category of the Person: Anthropology, Philosophy, History*, Cambridge: Cambridge University Press, pp. 257–81.

Van Meijl, T. (2009), 'Pacific Discourses about Cultural Heritage and its Protection: An Introduction', *International Journal of Cultural Property*, 16: 221–32.

Verdery, K. (2003), *The Vanishing Hectare: Property and Value in Postsocialist Transylvania*, Ithaca: Cornell University Press.

Von Benda-Beckmann, F., Von Benda-Beckmann, K. and Wiber, M. (2006), *Changing Properties of Property*, Oxford and New York: Berghahn.

Wendel, J. (2007), 'Making and Unmaking Possessive Individual: "Xavier borrowing" at a Catholic Mission Pacific Islands Secondary School', *Anthropological Forum*, 17: 269–83.

Ziff, B. and Rao, P. (eds) (1997), *Borrowed Power: Essays on Cultural Appropriation*, New Brunswick: Rutgers University Press.

Part One
Subjects, Personhood and Peoplehood

–2–

Sharing, Stealing and Borrowing Simultaneously

Marilyn Strathern

Abstract

This chapter reflects on certain styles of anthropological reasoning. The crux is in the title: concepts do their work in relation to other concepts. Yet the terms themselves do not tell you about the relations between them. I invert commonsense understanding that these three must refer to different actions, in order to make another difference, singling out one from the other two. Such analytical choices are at the heart of descriptive endeavour.

This volume asks anthropologists to look specifically at acts of owning and appropriating, with a focus on activities typifying the everyday. Nothing could be more mundane than people standing in a queue or school children losing their things. That two English lawyers have discerned fundamental ideas about property in these acts encourages the anthropologist to take equal liberty. The focus is the activity of 'borrowing'. Insofar as borrowing implies taking for a time someone else's property, far from blurring it reinforces the notion of property rights. So if there are situations in which it is not appropriate to talk about property regimes, then is it appropriate to talk about borrowing? It all depends, it seems, on the company that concepts find themselves in. An initial inspiration here is a particular Pacific Island invention that appears to circumvent the implications of thinking in terms of property; as we shall see, it circumvents consequences entailed in other conceptualizations as well.

Introduction

Imagine yourself at a boys' boarding school, and taking great effort to keep your things together. There are lockers, but if it is clothing that has to hang out to dry, you can't put it there. It's just a personal article of clothing, but look at the boy beside you sitting down and cutting holes in the fabric to make it less attractive to thieves. This is how Wendel (2007) describes what was called (in English) 'borrowing' by boys at Xavier High School on Chuuk, Micronesia, in the 1970s.[1] Whether pencils from other students or food from the staff dining hall, borrowing was so entrenched that staff and students alike called it 'Xavier borrowing' – though at different moments it could also be thought of as sharing or as stealing. But, as Wendel drily remarks (2007:271), if one is not to render definitions meaningless, 'A material object cannot be "shared", "stolen" and "borrowed" simultaneously'. They got conflated, he says, because, against the Jesuit Fathers' attempts to control the boys' behaviour, the students valued the circulation of objects. Separating out sharing, stealing and borrowing, each implying clear notions of possession, were precisely attempts to exert control.

Such acts of owning and appropriating typify the everyday. I take up Wendel's point about the kinds of relationships people set up between words and things, in what to them can be the most ordinary of situations, as a means of talking more generally about concepts that anthropologists draw on in analysis. Definitions enable the writer to control his or her descriptions. Do we follow the missionary Fathers who would have supported the view taken by some students that borrowing was, strictly speaking, mistreatment of 'someone's belongings', or do we fall in with the person who was trying to explain to an outsider about sharing in the dorm: 'That's why we steal from each other because we, like, we share. But we don't call it stealing but ... borrowing' (Wendel 2007:272, 270)? And if we go with the first, do we gloss – as glossed in the records of the Student Council – 'belongings' as 'property', or do we make more of the fact that the second speaker does not evoke the concept (property) at all?

What anthropological reasoning[2] might we bring to these equivocations? One provocation is evident: concepts do their work in relation to other concepts.

I

Ordinary Behaviour and an Unordinary School

The concept of property is inevitably going to shadow any intention to leave it behind. So let me start with the very idiom we might want to get away from, and a remarkable example from a lawyer of something familiar to anthropologists, exemplifying large concerns, theoretical fields even, through everyday things that seem at the outset of little consequence.

The everydayness of acts comes from their routine or unremarked nature. So for the English nothing could be more mundane than standing in a queue, although they can be trained for it. The lawyer Gray (n.d.:39)[3] observes that 'much of the educational world of the child involves endless standing in line at school'. It is not only the discipline of the queue that attracts attention, but everything that queuing tells us about legal order. The queue is more than a society in miniature following, as others have observed, the rules of distributive justice; specifically, Gray argues, it performs many of the functions of property.

If the queue implies a certain organization of time, waiting being rewarded by each place-holder shuffling up to assume priority, queuing behaviour draws on a primitive canon of property jurisprudence in the Anglo-American tradition, the rule of first possession, as one might see 'in any children's playground' (Gray n.d.:13). He points to the willingness to suffer – as in tired feet – as a surrogate for rights asserted through labour; to the ownership of the moving space that the queuer occupies as being, in effect, a time-bound occupancy as understood by the term 'estate'; to certain limited ways of sharing, gifting or selling the commodity time creates. Interlopers and queue-jumpers in effect commit an assault on privacy, the right to peaceful enjoyment of one's property (property in time spent), within the common law understanding of what it means to disregard personal dignity.[4] 'The normative structure of the queue silently underscores the point that the ultimate property relates to human dignity – the reinforcement of a life-enhancing self-propriety' (ibid.:41, italics removed). Of course, the queue does not always work quite as imagined. Yet it seems most like property in mirroring the latter's systematic deception, the notion that on a daily basis 'we all participate in a mutual conspiracy of property talk, allowing ourselves to believe … that proprietary analysis betokens a stable, ordered structure of entitlement to the goods of life' (ibid.:36). All kinds of informal adjustments are made so that property appears intact, queues appear to be fair and public norms endure.

I have dwelt on Gray's paper for two reasons. There is anthropological interest in tracing habits of thinking across social fields, here the law finding legal precepts in a queue. Then there is the provocative fact that this lawyer weaves in and out of the terms 'property' and 'ownership', although neither is to be conflated with 'possession'.[5] In adopting or eschewing certain concepts, the anthropologist in turn is likely to look for material with which to construct a systemic, or ethnographic, view of the world of concepts within which each [concept] exists. A second lawyer (Cooper 2007), for example, has recently deployed 'property' in tandem with 'belonging', and in a context that has also received ethnographic attention (Stronach and Piper 2008). Her aim is to see what these terms can tell us about a particular kind of community; it is a happy circumstance that it is a boarding school.

Nobody would suggest that the school, Summerhill in Suffolk, England, was an ordinary one. Founded in 1921 it is run as a 'child democracy', its core being the School Meeting where staff and students together agree on the rules.[6] The Meeting is also a forum to which children take complaints about others and where disputes are adjudicated. However, ordinary things go on as well, such as children standing in queues waiting for a teacher's attention or taking turns to jump into the swimming pool. One interest of the school for our present purposes is that the children have at times been explicitly trained in the practices of private property.

Property is a problem. 'Law 37: You can't swap, sell or buy Magic Cards without someone from the Swindling Committee [being present]'; lending money is outlawed; 'petty theft' is a nuisance that demands practical management (Stronach and Piper 2008:14, 16, 12). But property is also a solution. What interests the lawyer is the way in which the notion of private property was promoted in Summerhill to engender care for both personal and collective things. The school's founder had difficulty getting the children to treat tools properly, and suggested at a Meeting that they should introduce 'a possessive element' throughout (Cooper 2007:627). Pupils should take responsibility by making things – and spaces – their own. This form of respect was to become a route to self-realization and dignity.[7] One corollary is that much 'mischievous behaviour', especially theft and vandalism, takes place against a backdrop of expectations about property – indeed Cooper (2007:647) argues that '[o]wnership provides [such mischievous behaviour] both the means and terrain'. This is no less true of borrowing. Restrictions have to be put on 'children's ability to sell, loan or give away their possessions', on selling clothes, and among younger children on borrowing one another's belongings. There is on-going need for rules.

Cooper observes that most prohibitions are anchored less in the notion of a foundational property holder than in the exercise of the collective membership of a self-governing body, appeals being made to fairness and necessity. In fact, the 'rhetoric of ownership and property ... intersects a social system within the school ... where the productive capacity of spaces and things is ... largely determined by an agenda of governance – by belonging rather than belongings' (ibid.:637). Belonging is not, in her account, in simple antithesis to property. On the one hand, property interests 'blur into' non-propertied ones, where rights and permissions are based on membership rather than 'prior possession'; on the other hand, belonging is part of an overall 'property regime' in the school that combines 'elements of both private and more communal systems' (ibid.:626). Rather than dismissing the notion of property, Cooper instead shows how the school invites us to extend our conceptualization of it. In other words, beyond issues of privacy and control, we should understand property as here being organized round relations of belonging. The distinctive way in which Summerhill marshals communal or collective interests allows one 'to explore the work performed by property practices *within* [its] community' (ibid.:627, my emphasis). Thus 'an emphasis on individual ownership and possession' is doing 'a lot of community work' (ibid.:637). Indeed, it is an explicit Summerhill ethos that life entails, simultaneously we might say, the individual exercise of choice and collective forms of identification. Personal projects of self-expression and autonomy are fostered by the familial atmosphere that the children find in the school.

This account alerts us to the way in which, for the actors, concepts form distinct constellations. The observers (of the queue, of the community) are clearly grouping the concepts they use. The queue, Gray suggests, does much of the work that property does; Cooper's Summerhill analysis is about the concept of property being put to work within a community. I now return to the school I began with, where it is the concept of 'borrowing' that seems to have a lot of work to do, and where 'sharing' appears as a distinct 'community' ethic. This school is not run as a democracy.

Borrowing Things

Like Summerhill, Xavier High School on Chuuk, founded by American Jesuits in 1952, makes room for reflection and self-criticism, yet is altogether more conventional in its authority structure. Without the Summerhill example to the contrary, however, one probably would have not have thought twice about the distance teachers keep from pupils. From the outset its Student Council was separate from the Faculty, i.e. staff, Meeting.[8] The distance was felt particularly by the Pacific Island pupils in terms of meals (eaten apart) and food ('qualitatively different' (Wendel 2007:276)). In fact the provision of food was a constant target of the boys' complaint. Stealing from the food supplies of the teachers (the Jesuit priests) was at once a lark and a form of retribution.

It seems that, in their thieving escapades, students were reacting both to the control that the teachers tried to impose and to feeling demeaned about how they had to eat. Raiding the kitchens was part revenge, part an assertion of self-esteem. Wendel, who had taught at the school while doing fieldwork there, describes this as negative kinship: the teachers were in no sense kin, and reinforced this when they did not share their food. However, boys also stole from one another, although taking/losing things did not become widely labelled as 'stealing' until consumer goods and pocket money became plentiful. Even then, it was ambiguous, to teachers and students alike, as to what taking other boys' things meant. Now, one could not assume kinship among the latter either – indeed they hated being lumped together as 'Micronesians' when they came from such diverse islands. Nonetheless the boys did come from similar backgrounds, where those living in close proximity were habituated to helping themselves to one another's personal possessions. And if one was asked for something it was very difficult to refuse. Indeed, the very utterance of the request could imply that the thing was already given and, once asked for, was likely to be taken off and not seen again. What became known as 'Xavier borrowing' was exactly that. Wendel (2007:282) quotes a Pohnpeian student to this effect: 'They borrow things from someone and never return it. This borrowing is called "Xavier borrowing"'.

To follow Gray one might have insisted that a crucial element in the notion of borrowing is that of a time-share, so that return is usually built in.[9] You have in your possession someone else's property for a period, and when money is involved probably mark the interval by paying interest. At the same time the English term 'borrowing' may be used in informal or casual contexts, including situations where no return is intended. The point is that for as long as it is embedded in property discourse, borrowing exists within a nexus of concepts to do with what kind of title, or right, of ownership passes with possession. In this discourse borrowing contrasts with purchase, where title is bought; or with inheritance, where it is bestowed; or with gifting, where title is handed over. Borrowing only transfers possession, not ownership. At Xavier to borrow with no intention of returning the article may also be done when there is no asking either.

In Anglo-American property language, taking – with no return or without asking – would be in distinct contrast to 'sharing', which implies an invitation to enjoy or a prior right to a joint portion of, someone's title in something. However, at a time when the idea of cultural practice began to take hold, new teachers would be inducted into the ways of Xavier school by being told that 'Xavier borrowing' specifically reflected 'Micronesian culture'. It could be left uncertain whether a property discourse was in play or not. Borrowing and sharing were elided: 'Micronesians are used to sharing' (Wendel 2007:279) was one explanation for Xavier borrowing. Sharing referred to practices among students, and seemed to play back some of their own usage, as in the case of the new boy who assumed that at school things such as pencils would be shared between friends. The term is of course often used by anthropologists in decidedly non-property contexts, indeed in antithesis to property ownership, a point to which I return.

Teachers took different positions on occasion, as did pupils. There seems to have been considerable effort to prevent borrowing, including Xavier borrowing, when it was likened to theft. Paralleling some of the Summerhill preoccupations, taking things was a constant source of debate. Training was needed! In the words of a Micronesian teacher, 'Some kind of strict measure seems necessary to teach and train the boys to respect other's rights and properties' (statement from Faculty Meeting [Wendel 2007:274; original punctuation]). One Student Council meeting in 1960 spent a lot of time discussing how to discourage students from 'borrowing' one another's soap. While, following Cooper, the reasons included the sheer inconvenience of it, the fact that soap had cost someone money was a prime consideration. At the same time there was also an inclination to forbearance, a sense that 'Xavier borrowing' somehow captured a mode of sociality among the Pacific Islanders that otherwise eluded the organization of relationships by the school hierarchy.

The students will have been familiar with hierarchy and rank. Perhaps the issue was to do with the way in which power was exercised. Think of the troublesome thieving from the Fathers because they did not share their food. Almost certainly it would not be an egalitarian but a nurturing (parental) or redistributive (chiefly) form of 'sharing' that the students might have expected. Indeed, when in later years they had money it was often food that students bought to give to friends. Power from having things to dispose of accrued to those who could thus share – in the sense of sharing out – their wealth. The kind of pocket money boys started with was one source of power differentiation (Wendel 2007:280), precisely to the extent that it enabled the possessor to spend on creating and sustaining relationships. Taking other people's money deprived them of that capacity; it was almost an injury.

So what about trying to make items of apparel worthless – like cutting holes in fabric, a ruse that apparently failed – so that no one would want them? Not all the boys were prepared to put up with the kind of casual taking of personal possessions that sometimes went on between friends. In any case these items were worn underneath other clothes, and would not have conferred the value that being seen wearing someone else's clothing might have carried. Perhaps some of the connotations of borrowing came from other practices. When concepts appear to the observer to form constellations that work together, they may also be working upon one another. Thus when a boy regarded borrowing someone's underwear without asking as stealing, was he comparing the act with other forms of injury? It was not depriving him of the wealth by which to make relationships, nor of the agency of giving something rather than having it taken, and yet I suspect an indignity of sorts was being inflicted. If huge efforts were made to hide the clothes, then the owner revealed just how very much he did not want them to be taken – he was making himself vulnerable to attack by exposing what he put value on. The 'attack' might have no more motive than showing how the owner could be outwitted, an element enjoyed by the raiders on the school kitchens.

This may be a somewhat Melanesian reading on my part. When persons deploy things to enhance their spheres of influence, they are in effect enlarging or extending their potential agency (Gell 1998), thus exposing themselves to the extent that it (their agency) matters to them; theft is an attack on that extended person. If that reading applies here, and I have the raiders in mind, the degree to which the victim can be provoked to extreme measures is likely to be watched with great interest – even to the point of the perpetrators relishing the severity of punishment.

In any event, for a while in Xavier's history it seemed that the terms stealing and borrowing provided reference points for people at the school to think about different modes of sociality. There was overlap in the views held by particular teachers and particular students, and they changed through time. Nonetheless, when views were ascribed to roles, teachers and students were polarized. Both were concerned about how things circulated, but deployed different constellations of concepts to express this concern. I infer that teachers used a concept of property to hold fast to the meanings that things carried, where indignity is compounded by failure to recognize proprietorship. Whether or not they used a property-derived vocabulary, students may well have added a different indignity altogether, namely the kind of effect one can have on persons through restricting their capacity to be effective in relationships. Stealing in the first case is an assault on property rights and the proprietary relationships upon which (in this view) social order rests; stealing in the second is designed to injure, to create a victim and, however mild, constitutes an act of aggression.

We can now rewrite Xavier borrowing. The Fathers would no doubt be correct in discerning the excuse contained in boys' appeals to cultural difference, as well as the charity in their own;[10] however I speculate[11] on what might not have been particularly obvious, a 'cultural' reason indeed. Maybe the pupils needed a term that in effect took the aggression out of 'stealing'. In fact this might even make the term and concept of 'borrowing' a *concession* to the new world order (the culture) introduced by the Jesuits (cf. Wendel 2007:273).

I wonder if in those early days the boys were not responding to a perception that casual violence was inappropriate in the school context: to go around accusing people of stealing all the time would be an equally aggressive thing to do. (By contrast, stealing from the Fathers was not casual at all, and seems to have had a provocatively aggressive undertone.) Among the boys, if the label 'borrowing' conceded to the demands of school life, the situation it may well have averted was inciting other students to the kind of retaliatory action expected from someone who has been injured. 'Borrowing' would then work as a peaceable substitute, that might – but need not – do some of the injurious work of thieving while saving the face of the victim otherwise compelled to defend his person. Amidst all that talk about things going missing and the ambiguities of what borrowing meant, borrowing may sometimes have been intended as counterfeit theft. But it avoided the social consequences of publicly conceptualizing the act as such.

So for all that 'Xavier borrowing' was linked to practices of sharing supposed to have come from people's home areas, the speculation I offer is that if we consider it instead in relation to stealing or theft we encounter another truth altogether. This is in some sympathy with the papers (Sykes 2007) among which Wendel's account appears, which emphasize the internal critiques that grow up with new moral orders.[12] It was, then, because of the success of the school's governance procedures that pupils internalized a need to deflate their interactions, leaching out of them something of which the school authorities were hardly aware. What they could well have brought from home, in the early days at least, were all the aggressive connotations of taking things unasked, never to be returned. To call such acts 'borrowing' side-stepped the consequences of admitting injury.

Whatever constellations of concepts the boys came with, school experience was bound to rearrange them.

II

It is to my embarrassment that the postulate that concepts do their work in relation to other concepts is one that I have to be reminded of having aired in like manner nearly twenty-five years ago. Forgetting is only really an embarrassment to the extent that at the time of writing one hopes to have created something that can be built on – hardly possible if one has forgotten what it was. However, perhaps forgetting has its part to play as well. For the reminder is in a recently published paper by Corsín Jiménez and Willerslev (2007), and I want to follow their argument about displacement and the work it does in anthropological description and re-description.

Shadowing the account of (more or less) mundane practices given here are theoretical concerns about ownership and appropriation that have long preoccupied anthropology. Consider, then, just how we might think of the relations set up between concepts at the very moment when the notion of 'relation' itself comes to seem problematic. Corsín Jiménez and Willerslev caution against attempting to 'relate' everything by creating a single conceptual space within which every concept can be fixed, as the Jesuit Fathers tried to do through a kind of matrix of terms. Instead, the authors' interest is in what happens when concepts reach their limits, and when the concepts that have been stalking them – for they have been there all the time – at that moment emerge from the shadows. The metaphor will become evident in a moment. Meanwhile I keep with the vocabulary of 'relations'.

Now what the Jesuit teachers were trying to do is salutary for the anthropologist. Theirs was, so to speak, an indigenous (Euro-American) effort to take a systemic view by sorting out the definitions. Before thinking about how social theorists might deploy concepts to do with the nexus of appropriation that I have identified as sharing, stealing, borrowing, it has seemed important to the anthropological endeavour to accumulate a little observational insight into how these concepts circulate in ordinary life. In Corsín Jiménez and Willerslev's words (2007:537, emphasis omitted), 'we might do more justice to ethnography if we attend to its own moments of re-description and look to see how indigenous concepts find residency in their own accounts'. By this they mean both that concepts always live with others (other concepts) *and* that there are (socially, culturally) different indigenous ways of so living. Those ways can be recovered from people's own re-descriptions, as we might apprehend the Xavier boys' adaptations to school life.[13] Taking Corsín Jiménez and Willerslev as theoretical guides also means following them, some little way at least, into Siberia.

General Models and a Particular Case

The authors hope to develop alternatives to prevalent styles of anthropological reasoning that presuppose laying out concepts in a grid or matrix. No matter how subtle the perception of ambiguity, a matrix invites focus on the essence of meaning. A kind of movement may be imagined from the mingling of essences, which leads to writers referring to concepts being blurred or unsettled or transgressed or contaminated. The movement Corsín Jiménez and Willerslev have in mind is quite different, prompted by the Spanish philosopher Triás from whom, as they say, they borrow. Triás's interest is in taking concepts to their limits. Rather than searching inward for its essence, looking outwards one considers a concept in terms of its possible extent or reach. At its limit a concept forces a re-description of everything it has delimited up to then, for it is here that 'concepts capture their own shadow and become something other than what they are' (Corsín Jiménez and Willerslev 2007:538).[14]

As we have seen, the concept of private property gave Summerhill children endless experimental moments in seeing how far it could be applied – like the boy who claimed a corner of the grounds because he had cut all the nettles away from it.[15] The same concept (private property) also gave a means of expression to mischief such as thieving and vandalism. If, however, the moment came at which property were to be conceived *as* theft, we could say it had captured its own shadow. The response of a Summerhill teacher to a child who had damaged his bedroom with a machete was, 'It is his to use but not to wreck' (Cooper 2007:635, emphasis removed). Perhaps the boy was responding to the fact that, taken to one extreme, rules about personal commitment and care that are part of the English school's overt ideology of property also have a shadow: they are simultaneously rules about personal choice and individual self-expression.[16] At its limit, everything is re-described.

Similar examples could be drawn from the Micronesian school,[17] but I hold back until Siberia has been introduced. In referring to a shadow, Corsín Jiménez and Willerslev are drawing on an explicit notion through which Yukaghir hunters from northeastern Siberia attribute to all physical entities a side (the 'other side') on the very edge of visibility. Although they resemble the things they outline, shadow-images are 'things that are never just themselves, but always something else as well' (2007:528). The authors apply the notion to areas of economic life to do with ownership, sharing and theft.

One of the objects of their exercise is a critical grasp on the way some anthropologists have differentiated economic regimes based on ownership from those based on sharing, as though the relations between them afforded a stable matrix of possibilities. Definitions are always going to run into equivocations. But – echoing Cooper – rather than refining or abandoning the analytical vocabulary, they point to other ways in which these terms can retain or be extended in their usefulness. For what is open to anthropological re-description is the parallel between them. This includes the possibility of a temporal movement – flipping from one mode into what has shadowed it all along – that obviates any overt 'relationship' as such.[18] What will turn out to be interesting in any particular movement is a matter for ethnographic investigation.

Yukaghir production forms a dual economy. The protocols of elk hunting are conducted through an ethic of sharing, whereas trapping for sable fur evokes norms of ownership. But each apparently distinct sociality is the invisible shadow of the other: 'a visible institution or practice is never simply identical with itself but always carries with it its invisible double or shadow, which can turn back upon it so that one crosses over and becomes the other' (2007:528–9).

The kinds of egalitarian claims that accompany the distribution of elk meat, often justified in terms of kinship obligations, lead to demand sharing where one can ask for anything and take without expecting to make a return. However, elk hunting also leads to dependency on outsiders for fuel and ammunition, and here people are caught up in just the kinds of unequal relations and necessary debts that characterize sable trapping. When it comes to sable fur, rights to individual ownership feed into transactions with Russian traders with whom trappers are always in some kind of debt. One way of overcoming the uncertainties of these relationships is to flip into alternative mode, and treat the trader as a compassionate friend and kinsman to whom things may be given for nothing. The contrast between debt relationships and sharing relationships, Corsín Jiménez and Willerslev (2007:533–4) insist, is not here usefully conceptualized as a co-relation between alternative systems. Rather, either may be visibly 'foregrounded' while, as the shadow of the other, either may be momentarily obscured as its invisible 'background'.[19] A concept only works in displacement and is always there to effect further displacement.

It would be a pity if this theoretical mode could be interpreted as simply offering the shadow-image in the place of other analytical metaphors, so that anything could be seen as the shadow of something else, and the anthropologist would continue to set up (a matrix of) contraries and then find concepts trailing their opposites. The model holds more power than that. It suggests that the anthropologist look for co-presence, look for what in any particular social configuration is 'always there'. But it would have to be a co-presence of creative potential, so that it was able to turn what had been visible into the shadow of another form, summon another world.[20] I say 'look for' because the anthropologist at this juncture has to be ethnographer; there can be nothing *a priori* about the journeying together of concepts and shadow concepts. Corsín Jiménez and Willerslev are clear that the ethnographer's focus must be on indigenous preoccupations. One of the entities, for example, that seems always there in Yukaghir thought is theft. It is as though it stalked everyday intentions, lying in waiting to upset hunting for meat or trapping for furs alike. However, to take their model to its own limit, does theft or stealing work as a shadow concept in this Siberian material?

Taking something for nothing is theft, which is how the authors suggest that trading sometimes appears; each party tries to outwit the other. But then again hiding meat is also theft;[21] all acts of sharing take place against the possibility of keeping things to oneself. Yet I am not sure if stealing carries sufficient creative or potentive force to itself effect a switch of worlds. When it appears, it does not bring with it an economy of theft or a world of thieves. Nor is it suddenly revealed that all trapping is stealing[22] or that all sharing is a form of private consumption. The terms are not reversible. If 'theft' is not itself an index that tells you in any clear way which world you are in, then perhaps it should not be isolated as a distinct concept, that is, as a concept made distinct by having a shadow. Rather, it is theft that is differentiated by those worlds. Theft of sable is regarded as theft of private property, as Yukaghir treat it, while what is being stolen when meat is secreted away is not private property, but the expectations of others to share in the food. This might suggest to the ethnographer that, however theft works as a concept in English, one might be cautious about describing its conceptual status in Yukaghir.

Evidence that 'theft' works as a concept with a shadow in English, or at least in some English-speaking situations, comes from the schools. I return to the high school in Micronesia. Suppose I re-described my comments about borrowing in tandem with stealing in the light of the Siberian model. Rather than a relationship between terms, we could instead propose that borrowing and stealing are each other's shadows. Certainly there seems to be a sense in which all Xavier borrowing is also theft. Despite the different usages by teachers or students, I take it as relevant that this is a reversible[23] description that can be held (at times) by anyone at the school. The same range of behaviour that is called borrowing can also be called stealing. Perhaps what turns the one into the other are the limits of people's tolerance for one another's intentions, or the extremes to which people can be induced into passivity or provoked to retaliation. However, I started with three terms, not two – borrowing, stealing *and* sharing. Bringing sharing back in also brings me to my conclusion.

Borrowing Persons

Stopping children borrowing from one another seems a hazard of boarding school management. But no one ever thought in Summerhill, as teachers seem to have done at Xavier, that borrowing reflected a cultural background away from school and a habituation to 'sharing'. In fact borrowing was not given a great deal of work to do in the English school, certainly not in the way property was. However, in Summerhill, theft was very definitely one of the other sides of property. So while theft was also a problem in both places, as we saw with Yukaghir, not all thieving is of the same kind. That theft loomed large at Xavier was perhaps because what was stolen was not only private property; pupils also stole things that should or could have been shared. So how does sharing here qualify or modify the shadow-image that borrowing casts for stealing, and stealing casts for borrowing?

If borrowing's shadow is theft, can it also have a second shadow? Can borrowing, specifically 'Xavier borrowing'– taking without return and often without asking – simultaneously be shadowed by sharing? It would seem the case that what was observed for stealing was true a second time: the same range of behaviour that is called borrowing can also be called sharing. In this case what turns the one into the other is the extent (the limit) to which claims could be made for cultural exceptionalism. So that what was given an exceptional name within school, *Xavier* borrowing, also marked off certain acts as having exceptional origins in the students' backgrounds outside school. Yet the latter understanding could be turned back into its school-based version at any time by teachers or students saying that 'cultural' distinctiveness was irrelevant to judging behaviour in school or, conversely, that this kind of borrowing was a school tradition.

Xavier borrowing can be analysed, then, as an invention that played off different conceptual worlds against one another. Borrowing could translate equally well into the protocols of private property as it could into imagined norms of collective living so-called. In local idiom[24] these conceptual worlds were conjured up as the difference between development and culture, between modernity and tradition, between individual and communal modes of sociality. They were worlds that encompassed but also lay beyond the school. A relational model might suggest that 'Xavier borrowing' mediated between them. However, since neither world existed quite as people described, it is perhaps closer to the imaginative work being done here (Corsín Jiménez and Willerslev 2007:539; cf. Battaglia 1994:641) to say that, in having a shadow in common (namely, borrowing), it was possible for the actors to hold at bay the totalizing displacement of one these conceptual worlds by the other. The boys did not have to choose between them. Either could instead be displaced by, be shadowed by, what went on in the school.

Sharing and stealing each has the potency to summon these polarized worlds. I cited in the case of stealing the two types of theft; we can discern two types of sharing too. There is the exceptionalism of 'culture' and its purportedly sharing ethos, and there is the beckoning milieu of developers and elites in which school-leavers hope to share. Yet within the confines of the school, at least as I have argued, both stealing and sharing are accompanied by the shadow of borrowing. That is, it is borrowing that got the students simultaneously out of and into both the worlds these other concepts summoned. This indirection is, I suspect, highly functional. Presumably the boys had to learn to grow up in both at once. 'Xavier borrowing' would appear to be a creative and potent equivocation that allowed them to do so.

There is one more comment to make. Let me push the concept of borrowing, and specifically 'Xavier borrowing' with its double shadow evoking at once tradition and modernity (as the school vernacular has it), to one last limit. Suppose one thought of borrowing persons.[25] Is this not in a sense what the institutions of modernity do, finding recruits for their societal and progressive endeavours? Is not one of the equivocations in the boys' position to do with the displacement of their mothers and fathers[26] by the school's teachers, who have to be both mother and father? Is there a sense in which the boys are borrowed, from their parents as it were, to further the purposes of the school?

The concept of borrowing, as I am extending it, is inflected by Moretti's account (n.d.) of residential affines who contribute to the welfare of the landowning group they live with. Refugees from war, their own land now useless to them, it is not that they reside only for a while, it being unlikely they will ever return, but that their origins are elsewhere, that is, their (kinship) origins in other people. When the owners to whom one has to attend are not one's own mothers and fathers, they must be positively induced to afford continuing nurture and care. And isn't one of the problems at Xavier, and similar institutions, not that the children have new or surrogate parents, but that their parents and relatives at home no longer comprise an unambiguous source of nurture?[27] They can even be rendered irrelevant. What looked like a set of relationships the pupils have to keep in balance gets re-described as no balance at all.

Xavier borrowing indeed – it is the boys who have been taken without return! I do not mean that no advantage flows back home, but that as persons produced by their origin place they cannot return. Their education and aspirations, the opportunities the school provides, displace the originating sources of creativity and fertility. The vernacular talks about this source as traditional culture; I prefer the more immediate notion of parental nurture, for it acknowledges the persons from whom they have come. This is the sense in which the students cannot return, for they cannot go back to the persons they came from. They have become dependent on the school and on the school teachers for inducting them into a new world. And for the period they are there, taking their place in the queue, they are entirely dependent on the school as an institution with a mission to fufil, that is, their education. The teachers must (be persuaded and cajoled to) feed them. At the same time they 'feed' the school in so far as they are essential to the school's modernizing project. The school is proud of its successful graduates.

There is no way of expressing this appropriately in English. There is in effect no concept of 'borrowing persons', and among English-speakers not much acknowledgement of what could be at stake in displacing parental nurture. But if the anthropologist were to turn the 'borrowing of persons' into a concept, then it has already cast something of a shadow. I would expect to find it (the visible form of the shadow) precisely in the way the school deals with success and failure, and the way pupils are expected to contribute to the school's achievements.[28] This highly visible part of school life everywhere is routinely, mundanely even, encountered as a school's justification for itself. Yet if Chuuk is like anywhere else in the Pacific, from the boys' point of view success at school is rather more than about careers. It is about whether the students are going to find a world ahead of them that is going to live up to world they have left behind. Will these borrowed persons be able to share in the fruits of that new world or were they stolen from other kinds of lives to no purpose?

Acknowledgements

The University of Auckland must be thanked for the generosity of the Hood Fellowship, and Mark Busse and Veronica Strang both for the inspiration of their theme and for many courtesies. I am grateful to those who have shared their papers with me, and to Karen Sykes for sending me the collection from *Anthropological Forum*; I appreciate the opportunity of seeing a personal account of Summerhill by Danë Goodman. Davina Cooper, Alberto Corsín Jiménez, Daniele Moretti, Almut Schneider, Ian Stronach and John Wendel kindly commented on an earlier draft, and the paper has benefited from the interest of colleagues at the University of Kent and the Federal University of Minas Gerais, Brazil.

Notes

1. At this time consumer goods were altering the range of possessions available, the articles in question being underwear, newly the rage.
2. Within legal debate, Rose's (1994) famous chapter on crystals and mud in property law suggests that contrasting modes of engagement with others leads to an oscillation (between cases, over time) between crystal clear rules and procedures and muddying equivocations introduced by discretion-laden understandings and interpretations.
3. My thanks for permission to cite this unpublished paper; date and page numbers here refer to a draft.
4. 'The demoralization cost which the normative order seeks to avert is, in large measure, the injury inflicted upon the psyche of the queuer by disrespectful encroachments upon a special zone of autonomy' (Gray 2007:41).

5. Note the common law distinction between ownership and possession; ownership being invested in an intangible right can take the form of overlapping or sequenced (turn-taking) entitlements in a way that possession does not.

6. Compulsory lessons is not among them, and the school has consistently attracted attention as the very opposite of the rule-bound body it is, surviving many studies, and many official attempts to close it down. Summerhill is 'an almost perfect panopticon, incapable of secrets ... a total institution with boundaries both invisible and powerful ... [where the] Meeting scrutinizes breaches of the culture and legislates for and against transgressors' (Stronach and Piper 2008:1). Stronach and Piper's focus was quite elsewhere than property relations, so the way these creep into the account is interesting.

7. One of the long-argued philosophical justifications for property; Radin (1993) is cited by Cooper for the manner in which she links this to personhood.

8. Wendel's article ranges over different periods in the school's history. I follow his usage in referring in general to 'Jesuits', primarily priests or Fathers, who ran and taught at the school; from time to time non-ordained teachers were also attached.

9. 'Borrow', once a noun in English, referring to a pledge or security, is nowadays only found as a verb. It has both the sense of taking an item on credit, on the understanding of returning it, and of deriving an intangible, such as authority or language, from another rather than holding it by inherent right. In the latter sense, the compilers of the OED remark that the implication that adoption is only temporary is often dropped. Thus Ziff and Rao (1997) 'borrow' as a title for their book the title of a painting (Joane Cardinal-Schubert's *Borrowed power*). It is this latter sense that Sykes (2008) takes to a different kind of limit from that explored here, in referring to the creative work of borrowing as a means of eliciting new images and new relationships.

10. The Jesuits were aware that theft carried aggressive overtones: according to a 1964 textbook they thought there was a crucial difference between taking things from within 'the group' [of kin] and from non-kin, the former being iniquitous ('theft'), the latter positively praiseworthy ('stealing' appears to be the label, but this is the only juncture at which the term is differentiated from theft) (Wendel 2007:274). Similar in-group/out-group analyses were found in attempts to comprehend indigenous legalities in Papua New Guinea at the time. I must note the point because it runs counter to the analysis I am giving here, and to my usage of the term 'theft' [not differentiated from stealing] that attempts to follow the way it was used in tandem with 'borrowing' at Xavier High School.

11. I speculate; this is not in Wendel's text. One source of speculation is familiarity with a different quarter of the Pacific, Melanesia and in particular the Papua New Guinea Highlands.

12. Though my speculation does not require taking on the social criticism entailed in the concept of the possessive individual, a theme of the volume.

13. Martin (2007), writing on Tolai (Papua New Guinea), gives the example of betel nut, a stimulant that is a prime focus for informal commensality. (Before it became an accepted way of earning money, Xavier pupils would as casually reach into one another's betel bags as ask for a share.) Aspiring men of the Tolai elite may cut themselves off from the expectations of others by cutting themselves off from this popular form of 'sharing'. They avoid the endless cycles of everyday reciprocity, less concerned about being asked for betel than training themselves not to ask others.

14. A non-relational move. In an earlier version of their article they referred to this as a moment of conceptive potential.

15. It came to a School Meeting because the open space he had 're-coded' as a possession seemed excessive. In the end his right of possession was recognized (Cooper 2007:633).

16. Commitment, care, choice, preference: see Cooper (2007:637–8).

17. Sykes (2007:221) refers to Xavier borrowing as taking reciprocity 'to its limits', making 'the difference between borrowing and theft ... increasingly hard to define'.

18. Compare Wagner's (1978, 1986) disquisition on the oscillation between the literal and figurative formation of concepts.

19. The quotation marks note Corsín Jiménez and Willerslev's location of these terms in comparison with Battaglia's (1994) foreshadowing of a shadow of a kind – she deploys the apparent paradox of 'invisible foregrounding'. However, her subject matter is not concepts as such, but all the history, affect and past and future intentions that invisibly accompany the circulation of things (and see Demian 2004).

20. As it in turn became visible, it was able to turn what had been visible into its own shadow.

21. This was a more prominent theme in an earlier version of the paper the authors kindly sent me than in the published article.

22. Unless one takes the interests of spirits into account.

23. 'Reversibility is ... the conceptual name we give to the *ayibii* [Yukaghir 'shadow']: the name the concept takes when it captures the shadow at the moment it reaches its limit' (Corsín Jiménez and Willerslev 2007:539).

24. Local to the English language, Micronesia, international schooling, Jesuits and pupils, and so forth.

25. This does not come out of the blue. It was stimulated by an unpublished paper by Daniele Moretti (n.d.) on the Hamtai of Papua New Guinea, for which I am most grateful, space preventing me from going into detail.

26. I don't know if the terms carried a resonance of ownership for Micronesian islanders as they do in much of Melanesia.
27. That is, the continuity is broken: home has changed, kin are no longer all-encompassing. I am sure people would not present it to themselves in this way, and in any event these suppositions would need to be ethnographically nuanced. Sykes (2001) provides a striking account from matrilineal New Ireland where fathers' duties of paternal nurture focus on the provision of school fees as a statement of fatherhood.
28. This falls outside the account of Xavier High School that is my source; I was therefore very pleased that John Wendel thought the idea of 'borrowed persons' rang true (pers. comm., 6 viii 08).

References

Battaglia, D. (1994), 'Retaining Reality: Some Practical Problems with Objects as Property', *Man* (NS), 29: 631–44.

Cooper, D. (2007), 'Opening up Ownership: Community Belonging, Belongings, and the Productive Life of Property', *Law and Social Inquiry*, 32: 625–64.

Corsín Jiménez, A. and Willerslev, R. (2007), 'An Anthropological Concept of the Concept: Reversibility among the Siberian Yukaghirs', *Journal of the Royal Anthropological Institute* (NS), 13: 527–44.

Demian, M. (2004), 'Seeing, Knowing, Owning: Property Claims as Revelatory Acts', in E. Hirsch and M. Strathern (eds), *Transactions and Creations: Property Debates and the Stimulus of Melanesia*, Oxford: Berghahn, pp. 60–82.

Gell, A. (1998), *Art and Agency: An Anthropological Theory*, Oxford: Oxford University Press.

Gray, K. (n.d.), 'The Legal Order of the Queue', unpublished paper, 2007, University of Cambridge.

Leach, J. (2003), *Creative Land: Place and Procreation on the Rai Coast of Papua New Guinea*, Oxford: Berghahn Books.

Martin, K. (2007), 'Your Own *Buai* [Betel Nut] You Must Buy: The Ideology of Possessive Individualism in Papua New Guinea', in K. Sykes (ed.), 'Interrogating Individuals: The Critique of Possessive Individualism in the Western Pacific', *Anthropological Forum*, 17: 269–83.

Moretti, D. (n.d.), 'Ecocosmologies in the Making: New Mining Rituals and the Owned Environment in Two Papua New Guinea Societies', unpublished paper, 2008, University of Cambridge.

Radin, M. (1993), *Re-interpreting Property*, Chicago: University of Chicago Press.

Rose, C. (1994), *Property and Persuasion: Essays on the History, Theory and Rhetoric of Ownership*, Boulder: Westview Press.

Stronach, I. and Piper, H. (2008), 'Can Liberal Education Make a Comeback? The Case of "Relational Touch" at Summerhill School', *American Educational Research Journal*, 45: 6–37.

Sykes, K. (2001), 'Paying a School Fee is a Father's Duty: Critical Citzenship in Central New Ireland', *American Ethnologist*, 28: 5–31.

Sykes, K. (ed.) (2007), 'Interrogating Individuals: The Critique of Possessive Individualism in the Western Pacific', *Anthropological Forum*, 17: 213–308.

Sykes, K. (2008), 'The Value of a Beautiful Memory: Borrowing, Imitation and Learning to Make a Malanggan Mortuary Sculpture in New Ireland', conference presentation, University of Cambridge.

Wagner, R. (1978), *Lethal Speech: Daribi Myth and Symbolic Obviation*, Ithaca: Cornell University Press.

Wagner, R. (1986), *Symbols that Stand for Themselves*, Chicago: University of Chicago Press.

Wendel, J. (2007), 'Making and Unmaking Possessive Individuals: "Xavier Borrowing" at a Catholic Mission Pacific Islands Secondary School', in K. Sykes (ed.), Interrogating Individuals: The Critique of Possessive Individualism in the Western Pacific, spec. iss. *Anthropological Forum*, 17: 269–83.

Ziff, B. and Rao. P. (eds) (1997), *Borrowed Power: Essays on Cultural Appropriation*, New Brunswick: Rutgers University Press.

On Having Achieved Appropriation

Anak Berprestasi in Kepri, Indonesia

Nicholas J. Long

Abstract

This chapter takes up the volume's overall project of developing a dynamic and processual theorization of ownership and appropriation by analysing the experiences of Indonesian schoolchildren who dreamed of representing their province in a national debating tournament. In doing so, they actively competed to be appropriated as figureheads that would be emblematic of both the aspirations and the achievement potential of their home region: the newly formed province of Kepri,[1] which encompasses approximately 3,200 islands in the waters between Sumatra and Borneo, just to the south of Singapore. Although it had been fervently wished for, it rapidly transpired that the appropriation was transacted in bad faith by both the children and their province. This leads me to argue for the crucial role of human subjectivity in determining both the dynamics and the trajectory of the appropriative relationship. Such a recognition not only enhances our understanding of this specific case, but also carries broader significance for any anthropological study of the appropriation of people.

Appropriating People

In law, 'just appropriation' is defined as 'the ways in which a person can come to own a natural resource that was previously not (privately) owned' (Attas 2005:9). By contrast, the 'dishonest appropriation of property belonging to another' is classified as theft (Jefferson 2006:533). Operating within these parameters, anthropologists have produced many excellent accounts of the social processes and cultural logics by which certain entities might be appropriated (justly or unjustly) into new property regimes (see Godelier 1979; Ingold 1987; Root 1996). However, a different notion of appropriation features in disciplines such as architecture and literary theory. This perspective, strongly influenced by the work of Paul Ricoeur, sees appropriation as a situation in which a text, broadly

Figure 3.1 A group of *anak berprestasi* carrying trophies and decorated with sashes bearing the name of 'Kepri Province'.

understood, has its meaning actualized for the present reader: 'as appropriation, interpretation becomes an event' (Ricoeur 1981:185). Ricoeur's work parallels the legal and economic usage of 'appropriation' to the extent that it that makes one's own what was initially alien, but this is understood in terms of semantic meaning rather than natural resources.

A number of consequences can follow from the successful appropriation of a text. Following the connotations of appropriation's Latin root *proprius*, which denotes stability and assuredness, Strong (1996:125) suggests that 'I have appropriated something when I have made it mine, in a manner that I feel comfortable with, that is in a manner to which the challenges of others will find little or no significance'. Similarly, Hertzberger (2001:170) argues that the appropriation of built structures stems from 'invest[ing] so much care and dedication that they become part of you, absorbed into your own personal world'. The affective and political attachments that such appropriations foster facilitate dispositional control over the text's meaning: 'a text is politically appropriated when its reader can shamelessly use it to do something, to further an argument or position ... The text can be called on as an authority in an argument or struggle' (Strong 1996:125). We thus see two overlapping approaches to appropriation in the literature: one concerned with property, and one concerned with the legitimate determination of meaning. Indeed, one can imagine how a text might come to be appropriated twice: first it is stolen, then it is read, interpreted and commandeered by the thief.

This chapter concerns cases in which individuals are selected as figureheads of a broader entity – their town or their province – through having performed themselves as somehow exemplary or exceptional. They are people who embody particular normative values, be that youth, beauty and morality (as in many beauty contests) or, as in my principal ethnographic example of school debaters, 'achievement'. Although such people do not (usually) become the literal property of the entity that is endorsing them (the state, for example), they are embroiled in precisely the kind of appropriative processes described by Ricoeur, Hertzberger and Strong. People recruited to act as public symbols are constructed and disciplined in such a way as to ensure that the state feels it has made them its own: it feels comfortable with them, has a monopoly over their meaning, and can use them to do something or advance its own position. The mechanisms by which this might be done are manifold. Inappropriate individuals are screened out. Those who are selected are themselves subject to symbolic refashioning such that they come to embody the normative values or messages that the state wishes to evoke. In some cases this process is visited very obviously upon the appropriated person, as when figureheads find themselves under obligation – either tacit or stated explicitly in a contract's 'morals clause' – to refrain from activities that might dilute or contradict the messages they have been chosen to convey (Kressler 2005). Moreover, the process of competing to be selected leads to contestants self-fashioning in advance in order to symbolize the meanings that the state wants to be expressed. In each case, the person's capacity to symbolize is circumscribed, channelled and elaborated in specific directions according to the agenda of the state. It is therefore no coincidence that much of the current anthropological literature on figureheads and emblems – such as beauty queens or exemplary children – describes the process of their construction as one of 'inscription', 'conversion into a text', or indeed 'appropriation' (e.g. Ahmed-Ghosh 2003; McGranahan 1996).

Whilst in broad agreement with these authors' attention to appropriation, I would nevertheless question the unilinear and transitive terms in which this process is described. Appropriation figures as an extractive and transformative act visited upon a passive object or person, the analytical status of which is analagous to that of an inert natural resource. But just as the fluid material properties of water lend distinct qualities to its capacity to be appropriated and owned (Strang, this volume), so the properties of human subjectivity and agency need to be factored into any account of the appropriation of people. Aside from the fact that appropriation might be desired and actively solicited, once appropriation has taken place the human capacities for affectivity, doubt, cynicism and bad faith can bedevil both appropriator and appropriated. This requires analysts to pay close attention to the ethnographically specific ways in which the subjectivity of an appropriated person both changes and is changed by the dynamics of the appropriation process.

In other words appropriation is not just a condition or an act, but an ongoing and evolving relationship between two entities. This characterization highlights how the form of 'ownership' that appropriation establishes could usefully be thought of, in Gabriel Tarde's terms, as *la possession réciproque*, or 'mutual possession' (see Candea 2010). For Tarde this was the force which held all relations in any kind of 'society' together.[2] Thus:

> I possess my government, my religion, my police, as well as my specific human type, my temperament, my health; but I also know that the ministers of my country, the priests of my cult or the policemen of my district count me in the number of their flock, just as the human type, if it were to personify itself somewhere, would see in me no more than one of its particular variations. (Tarde 1893:43)

Despite its ubiquity Tarde nevertheless admitted that 'mutual possession' was far from intuitive to the (European) cultures in which he was writing. 'All of philosophy so far has been premised on the verb *to be*,' he argued. 'From the principle *I am*, it is impossible to derive, with all the subtlety in the world, any existence besides my own; hence the negation of external reality. But if you postulate *I have* as the fundamental fact then that which is *had* as well as that which *has* are both given as inseparable' (Tarde 1893:43). If a culturally emplaced philosophical *habitus* usually works to solipsistically stifle consciousness of 'mutual possession', one might nevertheless envisage concrete social situations in which an awareness of this relationality is brought acutely to the fore. A case where a person has been appropriated as an emblem of a region or state would be exactly such an instance. However, it is rarely the case that simply anybody can be appropriated as a figurehead: the process is typically premised on a pre-existing 'mutual possession' that allows the person to function as a legitimate symbol of that entity. Consequently more is at stake in the concept of 'mutual possession' than an awareness of the relational constitution of entities. Rather, appropriation can be seen as a process in which 'mutual possession' can be worked over and reflected upon by both parties, potentially causing it to be understood and to operate in novel ways. As such, the subjectivities of those who have been appropriated offer a powerful ethnographic vantage point from which to think not only about 'appropriation', but also about questions of politics, citizenship and regional belonging.

An Achieving Archipelago

Shortly after Indonesia declared independence, the Riau Archipelago (what is now Kepri) was annexed to and administered from a portion of mainland Central Sumatra known as Riau Daratan. This fostered great resentment in the islands. In 1998 when President Suharto fell from power and Indonesia began a complex decentralization process that saw increasing power delegated to the provinces, politicians and activists in Kepri called for the archipelago to separate from Riau Daratan and become a fully autonomous province within the Republic of Indonesia (Faucher 2007). This was finally achieved in July 2004. As with other instances of decentralization in post-Suharto Indonesia, the movement was embedded in claims of ethnic sovereignty. Although Kepri's proximity to Singapore had long made it an attractive site for domestic migrants, rendering it one of the most ethnically diverse provinces in Indonesia (Lyons and Ford 2007), official discourse (which identifies each province with a particular ethnocultural identity) designates it 'Malay'.[3] Activists drew on this discourse to argue that Kepri should be governed by Malays, as had been the case in the precolonial sultanate – and in stark contrast to the Riau Daratan government, which was dominated by other Sumatran ethnic groups.

Though couched in the language of ethnicity, the analysis that supported these arguments spoke of sustained economic inequality between mainland and archipelagic Riau, with the intimation that Malays (and others) in Kepri were suffering as a result of neglect and (ethnocultural) discrimination. Drawing direct comparisons with Dutch rule, many framed the relationship in terms of 'colonialism': *penjajahan* in Indonesian (as are all further local terms) (Sumanti Ardi 2002:70). Riau Daratan is a wealthy region due to its substantial oilfields, but informants told me that such affluence should have been paralleled by recent developments in Kepri. The 1980s and 1990s had seen a great economic boom in the archipelago following its incorporation into the Indonesia-Malaysia-Singapore Growth Triangle (IMS-GT). Industrial parks combining 'world-class' Singaporean management expertise with the ready availability of cheap land and labour led companies from across the Asia-Pacific to outsource clothing, electronics and semi-conductor production to Kepri, in particular the island of Batam. Meanwhile the island of Bintan was selected to host a luxury international beach resort with revenue shared between Indonesia and the Singaporean management. This period also witnessed a boom in Singaporean tourism to Kepri's towns, fuelled by the prospect of cheap shopping, eating, and the ready availability of prostitution and drugs. This was itself a consequence of the IMS-GT. As hotels and industrial parks sprang up in Kepri, the region's reputation as 'developed' (*maju*) led to levels of migration that far exceeded the actual job opportunities available. Many were left stranded in poverty and/or forced to operate within a 'shadow economy' (Lindquist 2008).

For the long-term residents of Kepri the IMS-GT also failed to bring prosperity, but rather fostered a sense of 'being on the margins' (Ford and Lyons 2006). Most of the Riau islands lay outside the borders of the growth triangle and saw no benefits from its introduction. Even in the urban centres many Riau Islanders found it difficult to compete for jobs with migrants from elsewhere who were arriving better educated and willing to work for lower wages. Meanwhile profits from the IMS-GT were either channelled straight to the central government or taken by the administration in Riau Daratan to spend on projects on the Sumatran mainland. In neither case was the money reinvested in educating or training Riau Islanders so that they had the skills required to take advantage of the new opportunities available. Kepri's citizens diagnosed their province as suffering from a 'human resources crisis'.

The question of how to improve 'human resources' (*sumber daya manusia; SDM*) has therefore been a matter of considerable public and political concern ever since provincial independence. Administrators have adopted a multi-pronged approach to the problem, one particularly prominent element of which has been an effort to inculcate 'achievement values' within the population. *Prestasi* (achievement) has been a major trope in contemporary Indonesia ever since the technocratic turn to modernization theory in the 1970s (Budiman 1979), and the contemporary school citizenship syllabus reiterates and underscores the national duty of citizens to make themselves high achieving by 'searching out opportunities for *prestasi* and approaching these with due preparation and enthusiasm' (Departemen Pendidikan Nasional 2003:19). A key source of inspiration was the American psychologist David McClelland, who had argued that the cultivation of a psychological 'need for Achievement' (referred to as *n* Achievement) amongst the population was the key to a society's economic prosperity (McClelland 1961). Kepri administrators and intellectuals elaborated on this further, citing McClelland directly in their arguments that *n* Achievement needed to be fostered in Riau Malays from an early age in order to stave off competition from migrants and allow businesses to grow (e.g. Fakhrunnas 2004:106; e.g. Suwardi 2002:68).

A crucial instrument in their strategy was the public competition or *lomba*. Typically targeted at children or young adults, such contests are so ubiquitous in Kepri that they dominated the weekly schedules of most of the families I knew in the fieldsite for this research, the provincial capital of Tanjung Pinang. When friends from other parts of Indonesia came to visit, they expressed great surprise that so many contests were being held in a town that was so small. Nevertheless these activities fit very well with the aims and aspirations of the nascent province. The prospect of the positive affects and material opportunities that stemmed from being a champion were understood to provide 'motivation' for the populace at

Figure 3.2 An *anak berprestasi* from Kepri Province.

large (Long 2007:96–9). As an official from the Tourism Department explained, 'champions become models for their classmates. Their classmates will see that they have won the prize, and that will give them motivation to be more disciplined so that they can win a prize in the competition next year. It is an excellent socialization strategy.' This view was further entrenched by champions' frequent appropriation as public symbols in the media and in political rhetoric. Sulaiman, a café owner, collected newspaper clippings about *anak berprestasi*, or high-achieving children, and used them to coax his daughter into performing better at school. One term when her marks were steadily declining, Sulaiman asserted it was because there had been relatively few profiles of *anak berprestasi* in the papers that month.

As well as being a technique through which to inculcate achievement values in the population, identifying high-achieving children and appropriating them as symbols of the province also served to demonstrate that Kepri was capable of producing high-quality human resources itself. This both legitimized the new government in the eyes of its citizens, and proved to detractors in the rest of Indonesia that Kepri was deserving of its status as an autonomous province. However, for this latter function to be truly effective, it was necessary for the children to achieve – or at least hold their own – alongside competitors from elsewhere in the country. People appropriated to represent their province in this way are at once discursively elaborated as the embodiment of normative self-optimizing values *and* as agents whose performance in the national contest will either ratify or undermine the narrative of Kepri as an achieving archipelago. Thus when a team from Kepri performed well in the national Qur'an Reading Contest (MTQ), reaching joint eighth rank overall, the head of the Department of Religion was unequivocal in his delight. 'We are in the top ten provinces in Indonesia,' he declared to a packed stadium. 'Extraordinary (*luar biasa*)! Now all the other provinces in Indonesia must acknowledge that we are *berprestasi* and they must take us seriously as rivals'.

But what if one loses? A bad performance would not only thwart the *anak berprestasi*'s expectations of themselves, it would also thwart the expectations of the government and the public at large. Under these circumstances, fundamental dimensions of human subjectivity – doubt, disbelief, mistrust – complicate the appropriative relationship. To understand the implications of this requires thinking about the cultural logics by which Riau Islanders explain achievement and the social experience of representing one's home region in an interlocal competition.

Achieving Achievement

The psychologist Carol Dweck (1999) identified two theories of the self that underpin American achievement discourses. One sees the ability to achieve as a function of fixed innate attributes such as 'intelligence' or 'talent'. The other stresses the capacity of anybody to achieve through sufficient diligence and hard work. Though both logics circulate in Kepri, it is the latter that is promoted most widely. A stock narrative in newspaper accounts of *anak berprestasi* is that they had previously been 'lazy' and performed very badly; motivation and discipline were the cornerstones of success.

However, my informants also placed great emphasis on how the qualities of 'the self' were intertwined with environmental factors. School quality was evaluated in terms of its 'facilities' (*fasilitas*), not because of the educational opportunities facilities provided, but because of their subtle psychological influence on motivating students to achieve. One pupil explained that 'if the people of Kepri want to improve our human resources, we need to improve the local public schools by, for example, renovating broken and damaged buildings, buying new chairs, tables, and many other things that are needed for the teaching and learning process. This will automatically increase the competency of students because they are motivated to study harder.' In the imaginations of parents and students, Kepri fared worse than other regions in Indonesia because its schools were dirty, with uncomfortable furniture and stained unpainted walls. The exception was Batam, which as a by-product of the IMS-GT had a cluster of private schools operating to 'international standard' curricula and employing Singaporean staff. However, facilities on other Riau islands were feared to be 'the worst in Indonesia'.

It was not just the material environment that was considered to have a formative influence on students' motivation and capacity to achieve. Unkind, fierce or unprofessional teaching staff were frequently indicted as 'demotivating' students, a point which resonates with the broader public concern over human resources. As many frustrated parents explained, local teachers and education officials were usually island-born (*orang pulau*) and had learned how to teach in the years when Kepri was not yet aware of 'modern educational standards'. Wealthier schools had tried recruiting directly from Jakarta, only to find that no teacher was willing to move to Kepri on the salary they were offering. This epitomizes the paradox faced by Kepri's residents. They need their human resources to be improved, but the only people willing to help them do this are people they consider to be human resources of low quality.

Framing the problem of achievement in this way constructs an important and deterministic relationship between the performance of the citizen and their home town or region which, through its administrative policies, facilities and human resources, delimits that citizen's capacity for *prestasi*. There is a parallel with recent Melanesian ethnography that has stressed the creative potential of land (Leach 2003). Creations, which may include pigs, crops, trees and people, are extensions not of labour but of the land itself. Their mobility and detachability render them 'land that moves' – which is always associated with that originatory land until and unless they become attached elsewhere (Strathern 2009).[4] In Kepri the sense of having been created 'regionally' involves many factors – not least the decades of neglect by the Riau Daratan government – and is activated by contexts in which the region defines the person. Bearing in mind that Indonesian contests structurally reflect administrative regions (Tenzer 2000:102–105), the competition context can do exactly that. The participant is a creation of a region, and as such its extension. But one can have been created badly and it is precisely this fear that Kepri youngsters feel when they are appropriated as a 'high-achieving' local champion.

The *anak berprestasi*'s appropriation by the provincial government is thus problematic because of the mutually possessive relation on which that act of appropriation is premised – that of being a regional 'creation', someone whose personhood (and by extension their capacity for achievement) is the product of having been raised in and moulded by a province of a certain kind. If that province is filled with facilities of a poor standard and teachers of a low human resource quality, this gnaws away at the achiever identity that the appropriation is supposed to endorse.

The Lomba Kompetensi Siswa

Early in my fieldwork, my neighbour, Fatimah, reported that some students from her school were taking part in the Kepri branch of the LKS (*Lomba Kompetensi Siswa* – or Students' Competency Competition). This was a national tournament for vocational school students incorporating over fifty subcategories of contest, from foreign languages to cabinet making. Fatimah invited me along, suggesting that I might enjoy the chance to travel to Batam, and that my presence might lift the children's spirits. Many, she reported, would be very nervous and the novelty of a Western presence might distract them.

Having been actively involved with Indonesian schools debating earlier in my studies (Long 2006), I decided to follow the team representing Tanjung Pinang in the English language debating competition. The team was composed of four Chinese students – Teddy, Clarissa, Martina and Bella – with a Malay girl, Sarimah, as the reserve. The team had been selected amidst ambitious aspirations that students from Tanjung Pinang might make it into the top five teams in Indonesia. Teddy added that he didn't mind if he was ranked lower, provided Kepri beat Riau Daratan, its former 'colonizer'. Explaining that he felt a loyalty to his province that was 'non-ethnic', he told me that he hoped success in the LKS would do two things. It would show the rest of Indonesia that Kepri's independence had been worthwhile and had enabled its human resources to flourish. Secondly, it would send a clear message to everyone in Kepri that Chinese and other non-Malays were committed to their province and able to bring it glory and *prestasi*. He was perhaps remembering an incident where a Chinese girl had won a contest to be the 'face of Kepri' in tourism brochures, only to find her victory declared illegitimate by certain Malay organizations (Long 2007). Since his parents and teachers stressed that no such discrimination existed in the meritocratic domain of education, Teddy was keen to make the most of the opportunities the LKS presented. He viewed his current appropriation by educational authorities in the town, and his potential future appropriation by the entire province, as a means to affirm both the provincial commitment to human resource quality and his own legitimacy as a symbol of the region.[5]

On paper the team looked strong enough to carry out these hopes. Teddy and Martina had been school champions in their respective junior high schools, while Bella and Clarissa were top of their classes in English and ranked highly in other subjects. Nor was there a problem of motivation: when they were selected, the children were delighted – in Teddy's words, 'almost crying with excitement'. But different tears were shed in the first training session. Fadli, their coach, described how Martina had trailed off crying only twenty seconds into a five-minute speech, whilst Clarissa had arrived at the session with her father, demanding to be withdrawn. Their anxiety was that their English would never stand up against that of the students from Batam, and they would suffer a humiliating defeat.[6]

Fadli tried to instil confidence in the team through an intensive training regime, but their regional insecurity quickly resurfaced at the tournament itself. During the opening speech, while the presiding official was explaining how the LKS would improve human resource quality by providing opportunities to compete 'at the highest level' and exhorting pupils to 'do your best and be a winner!', members of the audience were furtively talking amongst themselves, predicting which teams would triumph. A journalist from a local newspaper approached the Tanjung Pinang squad, asking what their expectations were. Fadli, dutifully echoing the opening speech, said that they would try their best and hopefully win. The journalist raised his eyebrows incredulously. 'Surely it's not likely that Tanjung Pinang stands a chance at the English debate competition,' he remarked. 'After all, Batam is an industrial city with close links to Singapore. It has so many international schools!' Hearing this reactivated the latent anxieties within the team. The next day they reported they had barely slept, kept awake by the fear they would be beaten.

> *Teddy:* I thought 'there's no chance we can win if we go to Batam, they'll all be much better than us.' ... But I thought that it was still nice to be able to go travelling to Batam, we could go to the malls and see what Batam was like for free. But then I also thought 'well, going to Jakarta would be nice too. I've never been to Jakarta...' But I still didn't think we would win... The ones that scared me were Batam Business School, because they came in, and that fat boy, he was so scary, he had really good English and I know that he really wanted to win, and they were wearing those waistcoats, and really smart stylish clothes, and we were just in our uniform, and I thought 'oh no, we will lose...'
>
> *Fadli:* Yes, and SMK Kartini [an expensive school in Batam] wore clothes that were extremely fashionable, and yet I was surprised it was their speeches that were the worst of all.

Tanjung Pinang were ultimately declared undefeated champions. That this was a surprise result for all concerned, the Tanjung Pinang students included, illuminates the reasoning by which regions' relative prospects are computed. When high-quality human resources are believed to be generated by structural factors that in

Figure 3.3 Students from Kepri encounter a team dressed in fashionable blazers at the national debating finals in Jakarta.

turn reflect the geopolitics of a region (foreign direct investment from Singapore, levels of industrialization, etc.) it seems impossible that Batam, blessed with all the benefits of the IMS-GT, could lose. This perception is further entrenched by a reading of the symbols of developed (*maju*) lifestyles, such as fashionable clothes, that carry an associative, rather than causal, logic of achievement.

A similar sense of 'achievement geography' prevailed when I accompanied the team to the national finals in Jakarta. The tournament convenors explained that new provinces such as Kepri were unlikely to succeed in the LKS because their new governments were inexpert in allocating appropriate funding and training. Regional hierarchies also structured coaches' and speakers' expectations regarding their competitive performance. Teddy expressed his delight at being drawn against Southeast Sulawesi for his first debate, confident that this Eastern Indonesian province would 'probably not be very good'. The team from Bali, which has a major tourist industry and ready access to native English speakers, were stunned to find themselves beaten by West Sumatra in the octo-final; their coach brokenly confessed he had no idea how he could explain this to the education office back home. But such occurrences underscore the risk and unpredictability inherent in contests: although they may serve to perform and re-affirm expected rankings, they can also overturn them. This was also observed when Kepri, after a successful performance in the preliminary rounds, were ranked seventh overall and best in Sumatra. Nobody was more surprised or delighted than Teddy: 'I thought at the national level we would definitely lose, because these were the best students from all over the country from provinces like West Java and Jakarta and everywhere and they'd definitely be really good but it turns out we were pretty good too. I was very surprised!'

Though eliminated in the quarter-finals by Jakarta (the tournament favourites and eventual victors), individual speaker rankings brought further surprises as Martina was revealed as the tenth best speaker of the tournament and Teddy the sixth. The students could return to Tanjung Pinang happy with their *prestasi* and the name they had built for Kepri.

So far, the story appears to endorse the meritocratic principles that McClelland (1961) argued distinguished an 'achieving society'. The Kepri students possessed a strong desire to perform well – and did. Moreover their appropriation overturned a system of regional cataloguing that would classify them as extremely mediocre purely by dint of geographic prejudice. Yet a few months afterwards all funding was cut for Kepri's English debating activities. The vocational school teachers' union pooled funds to stage a small provincial contest in 2007, selecting a squad of four speakers to represent Kepri at the national level, hoping this would induce the government to grant them funding. The authorities remained firm. Education officials explained this was a simple matter of cashflow: their budget was limited and sending students to competitions in other parts of Indonesia was very expensive. Difficult decisions had to be made, and they had to prioritize activities that were in keeping with the province's identity (predominantly 'cultural' contests centred around 'traditional' Malay dance, drama and poetry) or in which the province was likely to succeed. Fadli and I visited the provincial office several times, hoping to persuade the department that the previous year's *prestasi* suggested Kepri stood a very good chance of victory, but Ibu Mardiana, the official we spoke to, was unconvinced:

> This province is not good at English language yet. It has never won anything for English language, and perhaps we should invest the money in things we are good at and can win. Your vocational school kids aren't that good. When have our vocational schools ever been champions in English debating? I've never heard of such a thing, and if it had happened, I would definitely have heard of it. Sixth rank is not champion. Sixth rank doesn't earn prize money for the province, does it? So what is the use? Our vocational schools are still extremely ordinary!

Returning home, Fadli glossed the situation with a single phrase: 'This poor province... (*Kasihan provinsi ini...*)'

When the students heard, they were disappointed, but also angry. Yusuf, one of their friends and a fellow debating enthusiast, said he was 'shocked' by the bureaucrats' attitude. 'It's as if they don't even care,' he protested. Teddy simply said this made him 'realize how bad Kepri was':

> I used to think I liked living in Tanjung Pinang, but not now. The government is so bad, they don't know how to organize things well. I didn't realize that before, but I see it now. When I'm older, I would like to help my province to improve, but I don't want to just be stuck here if it's like this. I think I would rather live in Java or abroad.

Indeed, this did represent a turning point for Teddy. Where he had once thought of going to university and learning skills to enter the Kepri civil service, he has now moved to Batam, where he works in a bank in an effort to save money to fund studies in Singapore or Australia. 'It is something that I have to do,' he explained when I met him in 2009. 'I have to stay here until I can make enough money to leave. But once I've gone, I will not come back to Kepri.' This stance can hardly be attributable solely to the saga of the LKS. But, as Teddy himself is quick to concede, it was in his fall from grace as a champion debater that he began to perceive and relate to the province in a completely new way. This speaks very cogently to the question of appropriating people, because it exemplifies the shifting nature of the relationship between students and Kepri as achievement is allocated, as they are appropriated as *anak berprestasi*, and as they find themselves in 'good faith' or 'bad faith' vis-à-vis this achiever identity.

Achievement in Bad Faith

I use 'bad faith' here in Sartre's sense of an evanescent condition with which consciousness can affect itself, in which the subject strives to constitute itself in the mode of what it is not (Sartre 2003:90). It thus involves a duplicity in which 'I must know in my capacity as deceiver the truth which is hidden from me as the one deceived ... and this not at two different moments [...] but in the unitary structure of a single project' (ibid.:72). This project is not static but dynamic, its trajectory being determined by a range of social and psychological factors. Bad faith may be simply a fleeting evanescence, or it may be a durable condition in which it is possible to live permanently as an escape from the anguish engendered by a realization of humankind's true state, which for Sartre is a radical freedom in which individuals are always free to make their own choices and must therefore carry ultimate responsibility for their actions.[7]

He gives the illustration of a café waiter who is living in bad faith. This waiter, 'a little too precise, a little too solicitous' (ibid.:82) is, Sartre concludes, adopting procedures to maintain himself in bad faith, aiming to realize himself as being a waiter through gestures taken as an 'analagon':

> What I attempt to realize is a being-in-itself of the café waiter, as if it were not in my power to confer value and urgency upon my duties and the rights of my position, as if it were not my free choice to get up each morning at five o'clock or to remain in bed... Yet there is no doubt that I *am* in a sense a café waiter – otherwise could I not just as well call myself a diplomat or a reporter? But if I am one, this can not be in the mode of being-in-itself. I am a waiter in the mode of *being what I am not* (Sartre 2003:83).

This model is of theoretical interest to anthropology because it applies most palpably in contexts where social discourses induce the subject to self-fashion in various ways that reach beyond what s/he fundamentally considers him or herself to be. Unlike Sartre I am not concerned here with whether this selfhood is intuited to be a radical existentialist freedom, or something very different – such as a regional creation. Rather I am interested in using his account of 'bad faith' as a productive metaphor for the awareness and reflexivity of an individual or population towards their self-fashioning, an awareness that stems precisely from persistently trying to constitute themselves as something they are not. This opens up a conceptual space – the mentality of governmentality, so to speak – where the subject evanesces between bad faith and either 'cynicism', in which the deception is admitted (I am not really an achiever, my province is bad and I do not trust the judges who gave me that title) or 'good faith', in which one fully believes one's conceit (I am an achiever, I am a credit to my province, my province has the ability to create a high-quality human resource). It is this vacillatory domain, and all the social meaning it generates, that might be productively explored by the anthropologist.

'Kepri province' seeks to appropriate *anak berprestasi* as evidence of its being successful – but their bad faith is in evidence when they glory in their selection, and even express aspirations to be in the top five teams in Indonesia whilst simultaneously being wracked by anxiety that they will be utterly defeated by children from neighbouring Batam. They adopt procedures – statements, dispositions – to enact the role of the high-achiever: ambitious, confident, extraordinary. This is the person they have been told they are and that, through the social valorizations outlined earlier, we have established they aspire to be. Yet this is conflated in a single project of subjectivity with the knowledge that they are regional creations – that they have been named as *luar biasa* (extraordinary) but that they are, as Ibu Mardiana was later to reiterate, *sangat biasa aja* (extremely ordinary). They can only feel comfortable in their *prestasi* within the region by which it was allocated – although even here they may feel that the result was unprofessional, and the *prestasi* not a reflection of meritocracy so much as luck (Long 2007:98). Elsewhere local discourses of themselves as remarkable are trumped by the associative logic of 'achievement geography', marking a fundamental alienation from, and disappointment in, the appropriating region that the *anak berprestasi* believes will hamper his or her performance.

In reality the unpredictable nature of a contest puts all these assumptions on the line to generate its own new hierarchy of ability in a specified domain – allowing bad faith to evanesce towards a good faith in the achiever identity as it is ratified through the 'objective' and nationally endorsed measures of results and scores. Hence as the students defeat teams from Batam, and then provinces such as Southeast Sulawesi or Aceh – a process which culminates in their high rankings – they come to believe that they might actually be *berprestasi*. Moreover, through their bodies and minds, created by Kepri (and more specifically Tanjung Pinang), the province and town become equated with the capacity to achieve. On their return both their schools and the media enlisted the results as evidence that Kepri does indeed have excellent human resources, holding the young debaters up as exemplars to their peers. This fosters regional pride within the team, and delight in outranking Riau Daratan, the province that held them back for so long.

Having begun their journey constructed as extraordinary, but convinced of their own ordinariness, the team returned home genuinely *berprestasi,* viewing this in good faith – only to be told that funding for debating was being withdrawn because they are too ordinary. As funding cuts knock on the door, Ibu Mardiana is all too willing to suspend the ideological illusion of a high-achieving province. Kepri's human resources are poor, she says, they cannot cope with English language and are better off sticking to Malay dance. While this decision was doubtless influenced by the ethnonationalist sentiments surrounding the province's formation, it is indicative of regional rather than ethnic politics. Although this particular debating team was all-Chinese, the province usually fields mixed teams, whilst champions in 'Malay cultural contests' are frequently non-Malay. The issue seems to be not who should be allowed to achieve, but literally what is capable of being achieved by the people living in the Riau Archipelago. For all that the students tried to throw off the shackles of a hampering regionalism, provincial administrators viewed their *prestasi* with cynicism and still saw them as overdetermined by a conceptualization of the province that their own *prestasi* was supposed to have overturned. For the students, this merely demonstrated that the provincial government was 'very bad, with poor human resources' (*sangat jelek, dan SDMnya jelek*). When they left the LKS, other provinces were beginning to whisper that Kepri was a province to watch out for, with great human resources and high-potential students. Yet ironically, by achieving this and winning a victory for regional identity, the students came to feel more divorced than ever from the Kepri they went there to represent.

Conclusion

The case study of the LKS offers a powerful insight into the subjectivity of appropriated people. The Kepri debaters' internal state varied wildly, from paralyzing doubt over the legitimacy of their appropriation as *anak berprestasi*, to a genuine conviction in their aptitudes, to a crushing disappointment once provincial officials revealed that they considered the appropriation to have been unsuccessful and a poor use of money. Framing this in the Sartrean vocabulary of bad faith, good faith and cynicism provides a vocabulary through which it is possible to track similar processes in any case where a person is appropriated. As I outlined at the beginning of the chapter, appropriated people have their capacity for symbolization realigned to accord with the aims of the appropriating entity. This realignment is exactly the kind of self-fashioning that stands to be bedevilled by sentiments of bad faith, a point that is rendered especially crisp by the notion of self as regional creation that can be detected in Riau Islanders' accounts of their achievement. If *anak berprestasi* are an extension of Kepri, mutually possessed by it and thus hamstrung by the very same flaws it contains, it is easy to see how they might fashion themselves as high-achieving human resources in bad faith. However, similar dynamics, where the appropriated person fails to recognize themselves in the language and behaviour of their appropriator, could apply to any situation where an emotionally complex and reflective human subject is appropriated. Questions of whether, when and how good faith in appropriation is maintained thus emerge as much more salient research questions than is suggested by accounts that describe the appropriation of people as an inscription of normative values onto a passive and docile human being. As with other papers in this volume, therefore, I argue it is essential that appropriation should be theorized as a dynamic process. To do so complements Kohn's ideas on how a focus on processes of appropriation can enhance our study of identity (this volume). For Kohn's informants – practitioners of the martial art *aikido* – appropriations of ways of moving and training gained meaning when they were put together in a history – a narrative of their own projects of enskilment and self-making. I would strongly endorse this position, but qualify it by emphasizing that such histories are often inseparable from accounts of the dynamics of people's own appropriation over time. For example, it was the fact that the Kepri debaters were 'dropped' by the Education Department just as they truly believed themselves to have truly mastered the skills of debating that made that situation particularly traumatic, subverting the narratives that both the debaters and the government would have wanted to deploy.

A processual model also has implications for how we should think about the form of ownership on which the appropriation of people is frequently premised:

Tarde's mutual possession. Given that subjectivities are never static, and follow their own – often turbulent – trajectories, appropriation can allow for new understandings of one's own efficacy and identity, and by extension of the relationships of mutual possession in which one is engaged. When the Kepri debaters were in bad faith, the facts of mutual possession were felt to be traumatically constraining, but when they returned home successful, they were entirely convinced that they were genuinely high achieving and that their province had enabled them to be so. The relationship was now not one of shame but of pride – a situation that was quickly reversed when the appropriative relation was terminated by the Education Department. Thereafter, the fact that the provincial gaze did not correspond with the students' views of themselves meant they no longer felt obliged to be mutually possessed by it, slicing through their civic pride and leaving them with little compunction about relocating themselves – and their human resource potential – elsewhere. Thus a retheorizing of how people are appropriated is not only of theoretical interest. The ethnographic tracking of the appropriation process and its intersections with human subjectivity is also of immense practical relevance in understanding today's world. For, while the trajectories of appropriated people may generate achievements and accomplishments that appear to further state aims, their final disposition towards their appropriator stands to mould them as social and political actors for many years to come.

Acknowledgements

The research on which this chapter was based was funded by the ESRC and sponsored by the Indonesian Institute of Sciences (LIPI) and Universitas Riau. I would like to thank Sharyn Graham Davies for her enthusiastic collaboration in putting together the panel in which this paper originally featured, and Mark Busse, Matei Candea, Chris Hann, Leo Howe and Veronica Strang – as well as seminar audiences at Brunel, LSE and Manchester – for their many helpful comments on earlier versions of the text. All names are pseudonyms and all italicized local terms are in modern Indonesian.

Notes

1. A contraction of 'Kepulauan Riau', which translates as the Riau Archipelago.
2. Tarde's own conception of 'a society' was extremely broad, including the body, an atom, or a solar system: any entity which is composed of multiple other

entities mutually possessing each other. For further discussion see Candea (2010).

3. Self-identified Malays only comprised 40 per cent of the province's population in the 2000 census (Ananta 2006).

4. Such a logic is by no means exclusive to Melanesia. Gray (1998) traces a similar logic of what he terms 'consubstantiality' in the Scottish Borders, where the identity of particular families is inextricably linked with – and rhetorically substitutable for – that of the farms in which they live. Strang (pers comm.) reports that residents of Northern Queensland similarly see the land as 'growing them up'. 'Being grown up' was also the idiom used by Freeman's (2010) informants in Ethiopia to describe the effects of NGO activities. This Ethiopian example resonates particularly well with the Kepri material, since it suggests that what is producing the person is not just 'the land', but rather a regime of governance as deployed in space and time.

5. There are parallels here with numerous studies that have described how individuals or groups that are appropriated as 'representative', 'authentic', or 'quintessential' of a particular region may gain agency to pursue their own political agendas, at the same time as being heavily circumscribed by the appropriator's discourse (e.g. Adams 1995; Cole 2007; Shepherd 2002). What I would underscore, however, is that the scope for individual agency relies heavily on the dynamics and the stability of the appropriation – pointing once again to the importance of developing a more processual approach to the concept.

6. Here there is an instructive contrast with Kohn's analysis of *aikido* practitioners (this volume). She found that, through training, aikidists were able to absorb and appropriate new 'ways of moving and being that may become intrinsic to one's own cultural life and personal embodied identity as well as to the stories that people tell of themselves'. However, this presumes a sense of selfhood in which one's capacity to learn and master aikido techniques is open-ended. By contrast, the notion that Kepri selves had their capacities trammelled by structural and geopolitical factors meant that, within these early training sessions, the debaters found themselves unable to absorb the techniques they were being taught, and/or failed to have faith that these could now be part of their 'personal embodied identity'. Questions of political and regional subjectivity thus seem to affect not only the ways in which people are appropriated (the focus of the present paper) but also their capacity to appropriate skills and knowledge. This is important to note, since the two concerns are, clearly, mutually informing.

7. Although 'bad faith' has negative overtones in popular parlance, I am using it as a morally neutral analytical concept in this discussion.

References

Adams, K.M. (1995), 'Making-up the Toraja? The Appropriation of Tourism, Anthropology, and Museums for Politics in Upland Sulawesi, Indonesia', *Ethnology*, 34: 143–53.

Ahmed-Ghosh, H. (2003), 'Writing the Nation on the Beauty Queen's Body: Implications for a "Hindu" Nation', *Meridians*, 4: 205–27.

Ananta, A. (2006), 'Changing Ethnic Composition and Potential Violent Conflict in Riau Archipelago, Indonesia: An Early Warning Signal', *Population Review*, 45: 48–68.

Attas, D. (2005), *Liberty, Property and Markets: A Critique of Libertarianism*, Aldershot: Ashgate.

Budiman, A. (1979), 'Modernization, Development and Dependence: A Critique of the Present Model of Indonesian Development', in G. Davis (ed.), *What Is Modern Indonesian Culture?* Athens, Ohio: Ohio University Centre for International Studies.

Candea, M. (2010), 'Anonymous Introductions: Identity and Belonging in Corsica', *Journal of the Royal Anthropological Institute*, 16: 119–37.

Cole, S. (2007), 'Beyond Authenticity and Commodification', *Annals of Tourism Research*, 34: 943–60.

Departemen Pendidikan Nasional (2003), *Kurikulum 2004: Standar Kompetensi Mata Pelajaran Kewarganegaraan Sekolah Menengah Atas Dan Madrasah Aliyah*, Jakarta: Balitbang Depdiknas.

Dweck, C.S. (1999), *Self-Theories: Their Role in Motivation, Personality and Development*, Philadelphia: Psychology Press.

Fakhrunnas, M.A. Jaffar (2004), 'Riouw Anno 2204', in A. Tasman, G. Lontar, F. Jabbar, M. Zaini, Olyrinson, M. Kafrawi and H. Kafrawi (eds), *Pertemuan Dalam Pipa: Cerita Dari Riau*, Jogjakarta: Logung Pustaka and Akar Indonesia.

Faucher, C. (2007), 'Contesting Boundaries in the Riau Archipelago', in H. Schulte Nordholt and G. van Klinken (eds), *Renegotiating Boundaries: Local Politics in Post-Suharto Indonesia*, Leiden: KITLV Press.

Ford, M. and Lyons, L. (2006), 'The Borders Within: Mobility and Enclosure in the Riau Islands', *Asia Pacific Viewpoint*, 47: 257–71.

Freeman, D. (2010), 'The Morality of Development: Pentecostalism and NGOs in Southern Ethiopia', Senior Research Seminar, Department of Social Anthropology, University of Cambridge, 26 February 2010.

Godelier, M. (1979), 'The Appropriation of Nature (1)', *Critique of Anthropology*, 4: 17–27.

Gray, J. (1998), 'Family Farms in the Scottish Borders: A Practical Definition by Hill Sheep Farmers', *Journal of Rural Studies*, 14: 341–56.

Hertzberger, H. (2001), *Lessons for Students in Architecture*, Rotterdam: Uitgeverij 010.

Ingold, T. (1987), *The Appropriation of Nature: Essays on Human Ecology and Social Relations*, Iowa City: University of Iowa Press.

Jefferson, M. (2006), *Criminal Law*, Harlow: Pearson/Longman.

Kressler, N.B. (2005), 'Using the Morals Clause in Talent Agreements: A Historical, Legal, and Practical Guide', *Columbia Journal of Law and the Arts*, 29: 235–59.

Leach, J. (2003), *Creative Land: Place and Procreation on the Rai Coast of Papua New Guinea*, Oxford and New York: Berghahn.

Lindquist, J. (2008), *The Anxieties of Mobility: Migration and Tourism in the Indonesian Borderlands*, Honolulu: University of Hawai'i Press.

Long, N. (2006), 'Debating Democracy: School Debaters Struggle against Social Norms to Promote Change', *Inside Indonesia*, 88: 33–4.

Long, N. J. (2007), 'How to Win a Beauty Contest in Tanjung Pinang', *Review of Indonesian and Malaysian Affairs*, 41: 91–117.

Lyons, L. and Ford, M. (2007), 'Where Internal and International Migration Intersect: Mobility and the Formation of Multi-Ethnic Communities in the Riau Islands Transit Zone', *International Journal on Multicultural Societies*, 9: 236–63.

McClelland, D.C. (1961), *The Achieving Society*, Princeton: D. van Nostrand.

McGranahan, C. (1996), 'Miss Tibet, or Tibet Misrepresented? The Trope of Woman-as-Nation in the Struggle for Tibet', in C.B. Cohen, R. Wilk and B. Stoeltje (eds.), *Beauty Queens on the Global Stage: Gender, Contests and Power*, New York and London: Routledge.

Ricoeur, P. (1981), *Hermeneutics and the Human Sciences: Essays on Language, Action and Interpretation*, Cambridge: Cambridge University Press.

Root, D. (1996), *Cannibal Culture: Art, Appropriation and the Commodification of Difference*, Boulder: Westview Press.

Sartre, J.-P. (2003), *Being and Nothingness: An Essay on Phenomenological Ontology*, London and New York: Routledge.

Shepherd, R. (2002), 'Commodification, Culture and Tourism', *Tourist Studies*, 2:183–201.

Strathern, M. (2009), 'Land: Intangible or Tangible Property?' in T. Chesters (ed.), *Land Rights*, Oxford: Oxford University Press.

Strong, T.B. (1996), 'Nietzsche's Political Misappropriation', in B. Magnus and K.M. Higgins (eds), *The Cambridge Companion to Nietzsche*, Cambridge: Cambridge University Press.

Sumanti Ardi (2002), *Amuk Melayu Dalam Tuntutan Provinsi Kepulauan Riau*, Pekanbaru: Unri Press.

Suwardi, M.S. (2002), 'Pendidikan Kewirausahaan Sebagai Upaya Pemberdayaan Orang Melayu', in Isjoni Ishaq (ed.), *Orang Melayu: Sejarah, Sistem, Norma Dan Nilai Adat*, Pekanbaru: Unri Press.

Tarde, G. (1893), *Monadalogie et Sociologie*, Chicoutimi: Bibliothèque Paul-Émile-Boulet de l'Université de Québec à Chicoutimi.

Tenzer, M. (2000), *Gamelan Gong Kebyar: The Art of Twentieth-Century Balinese Music*, Chicago: University of Chicago Press.

–4–

Appropriating an Authentic Bodily Practice from Japan

On 'Being There', 'Having Been There' and 'Virtually Being There'

Tamara Kohn

Abstract

This chapter aims to contribute to an established yet growing literature that burgeoned from the mid 1990s (including works by Clifford 1997; Gupta and Ferguson 1997; Moore 1996 etc.) on how identities are continually forged through mobility and 'inter-culturality'. Multiple influences from near and far fashion individual identities, particularly in what Bauman has called our 'heterophilic age' (1997:55). So my aim here, to explore ideas about processes of appropriation in the context of martial arts training, is part of a larger project that explores the possibilities of an internal diversity that individuals may attain through the discipline of leisure practice. To understand the way that people may appropriate and come to feel a sense of developing ownership over new ways of moving, interacting, training etc., one must move with people beyond boundaries of home and place.

Introduction

Most studies of disciplined practices have tended to be located in the arts' respective homelands: for example, Alter on Indian wrestlers in India (1992), Wacquant on American boxers in Chicago (1995), Cox on Zen arts in Japan (2003). Thus they have not fully questioned the degree to which ideas of self, culture and society may be transformed through embodied 'foreign' cultural practice in different locales. Zarrilli's detailed study of Kalarippayattu martial artists in South India (1998) does consider briefly how a few Keralan instructors have exported the art and 're-elaborated' the craft for a new public with different demands in different cultural locales and at different historical moments.

The practice itself and the subjectivity it helps create are not static, but rather open to manipulation and interpretation in the interplay between the constantly altering horizons of individual subjectivities; the interplay between the metaphors, images, and representations of the body culturally available; the interpretation of the body, experience and practice articulated by individual masters; and the socio-political and economic environments. (ibid.: 241)

My own inquiry attempts to demonstrate how this interplay works for practitioners of the Japanese martial art of aikido – a practice that is comparatively young (created by one founder out of other martial forms in the early twentieth century), but which has spread its wings a lot further than the Keralan art to become one of the most popular martial arts in the world with teachers and centres of training in over forty countries. My questions of mobility and identity crafting therefore go beyond the study of the art's exportation out of Japan (and the different audience needs that the practice must address in different locales to be successful) to question how aikidoists traverse the world literally and virtually to harvest ways of training and reacting from masters that they can then consciously and unconsciously cultivate for themselves in private and public ways. They actively 'body forth' the worlds they choose to live in (Jackson 1989:136), even if there are ideas of regional and national character of practice and apprenticeship that interact with this process.

Strauss's (2005) study of the transnational practice of yoga is another example of a fine ethnography dedicated to the understanding of how body practices travel, with particular attention paid to the methods involved in such study and how social communities form around practices rather than locales. The feeling for the training that comes through the writer's own practical understandings of the focal body art form informs Strauss's work as well as most of the ethnographies listed above. I concur with Cox, who convincingly argues that the researcher's own experience of training is a necessary prerequisite for providing access to the 'aesthetic value' of martial arts practice (2008), and for some ethnographers this phenomenological stance, this 'empathetic understanding' (cf. Jackson 1989) is indeed primary to accessing (and then interpreting and relating) the sensuality of any practices that are taken into the body. For example, Lindsay's study of his own interactions with a 'hand drumming' teacher and his observations of his growing 'practical understanding' of the practice (1996) articulates some sensibility of the rhythm and 'flow' of that practice and the presence and absence of the body to the drummer in the performative moment. And yet one might ask how this drumming and the ethnographer-drummer's consciousness of it travels through different social, cultural and bodily spaces.

Technologies of the body (such as drumming, dancing, sport, martial training, etc.) in the Foucaultian sense are practices of self-making (1988), and yet they are also produced and manipulated through movement that takes the body in and out of different meaning-rich environments. Environment has long been recognized as a key ingredient in the process of personal enskilment, and Palsson (1994:901) reminds us that a holistic view of such a process must look beyond the physical requirements of training and the relationship between the teacher and student, to include the larger community that supports it. The case provided here in this chapter draws from the contemporary intercultural world of Aikido, a single practice with shared origin (from Japan), with its practitioners moving through environments in a range of different ways and expressing disparate ideas of best path for its practical appropriation.

Aikido

Aikido was developed in the 1920 and 1930s by Morehei Ueshiba (O Sensei) and based upon the judo, jujutsu, sword and spear techniques that he studied in his youth, as well as his spiritual training. O Sensei became a devotee of a new religion called Omoto-kyo that biographers have suggested shaped a growing concern in his writing and teaching for developing a path of 'universal harmony' through aikido. The name 'aikido' was designated by the founder during the Second World War and has been variously defined and translated as 'the Way of

Figure 4.1 Aikido uses the energy of the attack to pin or throw the assailant. Photo: Gary Payne.

Figure 4.2 Instructor from Japan demonstrating with the author at a seminar in Australia. Photo: Tony Smibert.

Harmony of Spirit' or 'the Way of unifying with life energy' or 'the Art of Peace'. Aikido is a non-competitive martial art in which one uses the energy of an attack to pin or throw the attacker. It includes the 'principles of harmony' more generally found in traditional Japanese arts, and it also explicitly encourages students to cultivate 'self-realization' through discipline (see Kohn 2003, 2007, 2008; Yuasa 1993). In the 1950s and 1960s a number of O Sensei's disciples travelled and then resided in various countries in Europe, the Americas and Australia to establish the art. Various 'hard' and 'soft' styles of aikido are now hugely popular around the globe with many thousands of practitioners.

Popular writing on aikido would suggest that the founder's idealistic path is being followed through the work of his disciples, and yet there are also many fissures and tensions that manifest at both organizational levels as well as at the primary bodily level in terms of ideas of *how* to train and with whom. This chapter begins to tease out some of these, with particular reference to global practitioners' different proximities to Japan and/or Japanese mastery. Such variance will demonstrate the need to account for mobilities, real and imagined, when attempting to identify processes of bodily appropriation, ownership and enskilment.

Over the past two decades I have trained with various master teachers (and their students) around the world – movement that fits both my migration experience (I've lived and worked now in three different continents) as well as my own 'learned' ideas of best practice for serious students of the art (a view that is sometimes but not always shared). Many encounters with aikidoists from a variety of backgrounds suggest that understandings and fantasies of 'Japaneseness', acquired or developed through martial training as well as the discourses that surround the training, are negotiable and changing, depending on national, local and personal experience. 'Traditional Japanese martial art' training, wherever it takes place in the world, allows absorption of ways of moving and being that may become intrinsic to one's own cultural life and personal embodied identity as well as to the stories that people tell themselves and others.

The stories collected from aikidoists that position them within the Japanese martial arts global community seem to emanate from three locations: positions of 'being there', 'having been there' and 'virtually being there'. The first set of stories emerge in the process of living in and training in Japan as foreigners – people who are presently, in effect, pilgrims from the Western world to a perceived Mecca of the aikido world (cf. Coleman and Eade 2004). The second come from students and teachers in Western dojos who reflect on and make use of their past experiences of studying aikido in Japan; the third come from people who have never been to Japan, but refer to their training and other culture-rich experiences with their first or second generation Japanese masters in the West. I have found myself in all these three camps at different times: for many years I studied aikido in the UK and US with Japanese masters as well as with 'Western' teachers, some of whom had trained in Japan and some of whom had not. I then had the opportunity to spend six weeks of research leave training and conducting fieldwork in Japanese dojos, and now in Australia I train with some reference in my mind and my body to my experiences in all of these places. For most senior students and teachers, reference to the path of learning and genealogies of teachers are central to situating oneself in the aikido world (as is often the case at professional conferences for international colleagues positioning themselves in the academy[1]). It is within the contexts of mobility and relationships with other practitioners that embodied appropriations of ways of moving and training are given meaning, both in terms of an individual's processual sense of enskilment as well as self-making, and then these intangible properties are (or are not) capitalized upon in different ways.

To take a new practice into the body is to appropriate through action a self-enhancing way of reacting, moving and interacting with other bodies. It also often involves the consumption of tools that support the training – the special outfits, the wooden weapons, the popular literature, the ritual objects for the training space, etc. Appropriation and consumption inhabit similar but not identical territories. Consumption involves a personal and often a bodily acquisition of things and ideas that one selects by choice, often dictated by fashion, and that helps produce a sense of self-distinction (Bourdieu 1977). Csordas (1990) elaborates on Bourdieu's notion of *habitus* (1977) to frame the process of embodiment as a methodological paradigm – as a type of self-awareness that allows for the reconstitution of self through creative change. In contemporary aikido practice around the world, on the performative surface level, the art is embellished with the 'embodied' casings of a particular cultural history. This casing (or 'wrapping' as Hendry's (1995) study of Japanese 'culture' has called it) can include the costume and practice space that envelops the practitioner which includes: the *kamiza* ritual shrine on the mat that features a photo of the Founder; the calligraphy that decorates many dojos; formal rituals of respect on the mat space; and the wearing of the *hakama* (the divided skirts once worn by samurai). The casing can also include the Japanese vocabulary that names the art's techniques: one needs to learn to recognize these terms in order to perform the actions they name, and yet the words need not be meaningful beyond this surface association.

Figure 4.3 Visiting foreign students in Iwama dojo, Japan – often called the birthplace of aikido.

The wrapping of 'Japaneseness', while fascinating and challenging for newcomers to the practice, and avidly *consumed* by many of them, sometimes fades in its importance (or at least fades in its presence in reflections on the meaningfulness of training) as aikidoists become more experienced. Committed practitioners seem to demonstrate less attentiveness to consuming these performative cultural casings and more to the *feeling* of connection to subtle embodied movements that they appropriate from their teachers. These can then be possessed or 'owned'– felt to be part of oneself and one's own personal practice and knowledge. They can also be appropriated for the self and then passed on to future training partners, sometimes quite unselfconsciously and at other times strategically. Through the reflections of aikido students and teachers (and also drawing on my own experiences) this chapter illustrates how these bodily appropriations are performed and conceived, and how such conceptions attend to ideas of authority and authenticity based on practitioners' own mobilities and the proximity of Japanese bodies and places.

In Japan: Stealing and Losing through Training – Some Ideas on 'Being There'

In December 2007 and January 2008 I spent six weeks training in Hombu dojo, which is located in Shinjuku in central Tokyo. Hombu dojo means literally the 'home' dojo. It is a five-storey building housing three dojo training spaces. Hombu has roughly 1,300 members and an average of 300 students attend daily classes. The thirty instructors who teach at Hombu are listed at the time of writing on the dojo's website. All are men, although many women train (indeed 'women's classes' were held during the week, as well as special children's classes, and a significant number of women train in the mixed classes).[2] This 'World Headquarters' of the Aikikai Foundation oversees the accreditation for dojos in over forty countries. Foreign students comprise around twenty per cent of the active membership and the majority of these are male. Most of the foreigners I met in Hombu were aikido pilgrims who came to Japan specifically to train in aikido, and most had stayed and supported themselves with local jobs – teaching English, working as editors and translators, working for companies. They either came daily to a range of different teachers' classes, or they 'followed' only one or two teachers. Some trained in Hombu for some classes and then attended other 'local' dojos elsewhere in Tokyo. The biggest turnout at Hombu was for the 6.30 a.m. class taught every day by the 'Doshu' – the head of the Aikikai and the grandson of the founder.

In social moments before and after classes as well as in cafés and restaurants after training, I informally interviewed a range of foreign students (some were there for a few weeks, some would stay for several years, and some had made

Japan their home for many years). The interviews explored their experiences of training in Japan and how these compared with their previous experiences elsewhere. I also took notes on my own experiences and thoughts while training in Japan, on group discussions and on embodied un-vocalized interactions that I interpreted as being meaningful (as an 'insider') on and off the mat. Many of the students I interviewed spoke in different ways about the high level of commitment, authenticity, 'everydayness' and joy in their training at Hombu. Some commentators isolated what they recognized as special in the ethos of training. Joe,[3] an American married to a Japanese woman with three children and ten years of residence in Tokyo, told me: 'There's a different quality here – we can train daily with fifth and sixth dans and there is no ego, no training partners trying to teach you, no bashing people for the sake of it'. This comment therefore compares what is experienced at Hombu with a series of 'problems' Joe associated with his past training. A comment from Phil, another American, focused on the quality of instruction: 'The teachers are just all so awesome'. The 'awesomeness' is, in Phil's mind, set against his only previous experience in a small remote dojo in the American mid-West with relatively inexperienced teachers and little contact with more established dojos and instructors.

Yet Phil also warned me (as others had) to stay away from the 'old man corner' in Hombu, where elderly (and exceptionally fit) Japanese men apparently like to give foreign students a hard time. 'Stay over at this end', he said to me, 'you don't want to get yourself injured in old man corner like I did when I arrived'. Needless to say I followed his advice for a little while, and then eventually ventured forth where I found the 'old men' to be exceptionally kind in their training with me. 'Hmm, that's interesting. Maybe it's just the young blokes they are testing,' Phil mused when I reported this, and I think that is likely to be the case as it fits well with Japanese masters' own reflections on their early years of training, when they often recall the ordeals they survived as young apprentices when the more senior students would test them on the mat. Alas, Phil's gut reaction to the unexpectedly hard treatment by these men was suspicion of anti-Western sentiment.

'Being there' in Hombu involved marvelling at special features of the training. The ambient qualities of sound, talk and silence were recurrent themes in students' reflections. Enthusing in the changing room after a particularly energetic class, Sharon said 'the silence is still so special to me – just the slapping of mats during class – there's just such a connection in every class through the silence that just doesn't happen at home where people just never stop talking and analysing every movement instead of just training.' Yet some responses revealed a tension between the joy of such quality practice and students' feelings about their lack of ability to fit into Tokyo and Hombu life more generally: 'I'm a nowhere man in a nowhere land, but I do feel that the mat and dojo is a refuge in this city,' said Tim from the UK. Tim learned a Japanese expression which, for him, explained why the dojo was a refuge – 'Goen – Aikido Goen'. He was given a translation of *goen* as 'kinship', but the word could more accurately be translated as 'auspicious synchronicity of connection', or a sort of tacit and fortuitous understanding.[4] All three translations could support Tim's feeling that, no matter what happens outside, in the dojo he was at home with a group of others who shared a sense of purpose and aesthetic appreciation for aikido.

Interestingly, however, a sense of comfort, refuge and 'being at home' away from 'home' does not entail a sense of ownership over the social or physical space of Hombu dojo for foreigners. The travelling martial artist owns the body transformed by appropriating new ways of training, but he may not feel he 'belongs' or socially 'owns' the foreign environment in which his body trains.

Iain, for example, was less than enamoured with the social scene in Hombu dojo, even if he loved the training: 'The Japanese never really get too close to us foreigners in the dojo even after many years'. His friend Ali from Malaysia tried to make sense of a similar feeling of being an outsider by qualifying the particular training culture at the dojo: 'Hombu is just too busy a hub with so many teachers and students that you find most folk just come in, train hard, then leave – so it's hardly a place to hang out'. Such non-belonging was expressed by Signe from Holland as a sense of 'ordeal' (her term) coupled with a sense of opportunity. When she felt drained by the effort to support her aikido training in Japan (through paid translation work and teaching English language classes), she focused on her own body and its changes – changes in shape; a deeper understanding of aikido techniques; a sharper reaction to others on the mat – and she showed me how she wrote about these in her diary, complete with diagrams. Her writing, she said, is a useful form of self-therapy, but she imagined that it would also be an invaluable tool in the future as reading it would offer a gentle jog on her memory that she said she would be able to use for her own training when she returned home. The 'tools' of appropriation were both her bodily senses and the reflexive notebook that recorded how changes in reactivity and knowledge were effected through daily practice.

The minutiae of bodily coping in a foreign world involved, for these foreign students, acting appropriately in infinite and subtle contexts that extended well beyond the practice mat, including: speaking and interacting politely (cf. Hendry 1995), managing sweat, eating with chopsticks (cf. Cox 2008), and negotiating busy city traffic on a bicycle. These are learned behaviours, cultural performances that are produced out of particular contexts. Once away from Japan the contexts that produced and required them are generally absent or certainly less frequent, so they can fade in bodily memory or may be actively 'switched off' when they are not in their right place. Michael Herzfeld recently narrated a lovely story about the embodiment of culturally rich gestures of head-bowing respect that he unconsciously picked up and used in Thailand and which he then automatically performed with his body as he arrived late to a formal meeting in Italy, to the bafflement of his audience: it was neither understood nor useful (see Herzfeld 2009). Similarly polite chopstick use in eating noodles in Japan would not necessarily migrate well to a dining establishment in England, where chopsticks are to be found for 'Asian food' consumption, but slurping and shovelling might be seen as uncouth. Perhaps we could say that these learned behaviours are more often borrowed than appropriated – they are perceived as tools of survival, rather than tools of self-making for temporary visitors in foreign lands.

The repetitive martial training on the mat, however, leads to more repetitive training on other mats far away. Indeed the reason many foreigners see the dojo and mat as a 'refuge' in a strange city is because the forms practiced there are shared and familiar (cf. Kohn 2001, 2007), even if they involve a slightly different style of teaching and learning. This learning on the mat is seen as a cumulative and collaborative forging of the body and 'self' in very lasting ways, as the body thus shaped is imagined always to be able to summon whatever it has learned from within the self as it reacts to an attack or to a throw situated on any training mat (or, practically, in any street environment). The body becomes a vessel moving in and through places and non-places (*á la* Auge 1995). It has appropriated thousands of ways of reacting to other bodies that may attack it – some elements are recognized and remembered and named (e.g. 'this is Osawa Sensei', 'this is Masada'), but generally they are not. In the end the movement, the reaction to the attack, is fully appropriated – and the 'authored' bodily contributions made along the way lose their distinctiveness over the years.

Ways of Appropriating Practical Bodily Knowledge

What seems to draw some of these people to train and stay as long as possible in Japan is a feeling that something special is available there that they will be able to take away as a part of themselves, even if the social environment can be tricky to negotiate. The heart of that special something, expressed occasionally in words but most clearly expressed in the silence of training that characterizes Hombu and other 'traditional' training environments (in and out of Japan), is in the *way* the self becomes transformed through the training. It lies in the embodied notion that once past the early stages of training, students no longer learn techniques, but elaborate on their understanding of them and the principles that shape them. They learn to 'steal' fragments of movement from a teacher's demonstrations with their eyes and through bodily contact, through the feel of the movement. It is the responsibility of the student to take from the teacher's demonstration and training, not for the teacher to give. If we use the term 'appropriation' here, appropriation may be seen as stealing, as taking surreptitiously with the eyes and body. This is an accrual that is ordinary and accepted, and associated with everyday interactions, as Strathern (this volume) explains in relation to 'Xavier borrowing'. What people take they then try to hold onto with repetitive bodily training with others who are simultaneously stealing what they perceive from the same performance. When a teacher demonstrates a technique, students watch what he is doing and how he is moving, but then when he finishes and it is time to practice with a partner, the keenest students often rush to find the student who was used in the demonstration to train with him because they have recognized the power of bodily transmission. The student who *felt* the throw is seen as being in the best position to have captured a holistic experience that the eyes cannot see and that might be physically absorbed. All the senses get to work on this process of appropriative embodiment that extends well beyond visualization: it is achieved best through what Damasio calls a 'somatosensory modality' that includes touch, muscular awareness, pain, temperature and sound that may or may not be consciously experienced (2000: 318–19).

The notions of 'theft' and 'transmission' are common in traditional martial discourse as is a more tactile concept of 'absorption'. A Japanese master in California told me that serious students need to 'absorb what (they) steal through the skin' through many years of daily training that is felt through physical contact with others on the mat. The quality and sincerity of the training environment facilitates that process. A person achieves their unique selfhood by incorporating into their own aikido body the many pilfered ingredients from these Masters. And of course the Masters from whom this knowledge is stolen haven't lost anything from this taking. Appropriation in this case (as in numerous other contexts of embodied apprenticeship) is not a process of depriving others of something they had. It becomes, instead, part of a positive and culturally informed learning process. The many who appropriate the same technique from the same performance may take away different treasures since the eyes and body so often pick up different clues. Appropriating any bodily practice is hence quite a different process to appropriating an object – a painting, a bracelet, a house – that can only be in one place at a time. But this intangible fission of bodily knowledge doesn't happen without some contestation of values. In a later section I will consider how the politics of aikido national and world communities interacts with such embodied processes of appropriating skills. First, however, I want to consider how ideas about bodily appropriation may be qualified by traditional Zen philosophies of practice.

A discourse that speaks of martial artists as adding to their bodily knowledge by stealth (by stealing with the eyes and practising with the body) can ironically coexist with a very different discourse of subtraction and deletion. Repetitive training can be understood as a path that allows one to reveal something that already lies within. A number of teachers make reference to Zen and *budo* (martial ways) discourse to explain to their students how the training process is a polishing or forging process – a sloughing off of excess. To train hard is to begin to reveal the perfect sword, stone or spirit that already lies within (see Kohn 2008:147). And this metaphorical framing presents a conundrum of course – to be able to appropriate (steal) and to drop away (lose) at the same time requires one to accommodate some degree of conceptual contradiction, but the two processes can still be seen to work together. Over coffee after the Doshu's morning class, Mark from Philadelphia told me that he has 'a lot of really bad habits that stop ... [him] from learning. When I just concentrate on the way Sensei moves through space and look at the whole throw and try to *capture the feeling* I have watching him, then some of those sticking points I have disappear – even if just for a short while'. So by stealing he can then polish his own stone. Another way of reconciling contradictions is demonstrated by Marie who commented after a particularly tiring session in Hombu:

> When I'm really tired, I tend to just see that Sensei is doing, like, *uchikaitenage*, and I just do what I always used to do in my dojo back home rather than see something new he is giving me. I really have to slap myself at times like this and say 'hey – I didn't come all this way to just stay still' and then I have to let go of my old ways to, like, open my eyes wide to be able to take it in properly and work on taking those little gifts that are right there in front of me.

So here by sloughing off (or at least suspending) the old, Marie's eyes become open and clear enough to permit her to steal the new. In the comments from Tokyo made above, a sample of foreign students reflexively consider their own bodily engagement with their present training experiences, sometimes comparing this with other past training environments in other countries that are held to be different. Sometimes they focus on atmospheric qualities that they feel enhance their training, and sometimes the 'gifts' they feel they receive through such an environment come with a price on and off the mat – the occasional pain and discomfort of feeling outcast, even when every effort is felt to have been made (in one example) to date local girls or to become fluent in the Japanese language.

What is accrued and taken into the self from the training is not something that can be isolated – it is located in a feeling of value, a sensation of training quality, the recognition of a plethora of teaching mastery available, that is experienced and absorbed into the body and then carried through life as long as sustenance is offered through continued training. None of the foreign students interviewed in Japan considered the kudos or authority that 'having been there' would offer upon their return to Europe, America or Australia, focusing instead on the ups and downs of their present transformations with occasional reference to their past experiences.

Back at Home: The Commodification of Appropriated Bodily Knowledge

In the north of England I trained with people from a range of social backgrounds who often travelled further for aikido than they ever did for family holidays or work. They travelled for special seminars taught by visiting and established masters in the UK and the European continent. Some (generally more senior) students and teachers flew to camps in California or Southern or Eastern Europe or to special events in Japan. The sense of progressing through the art and providing credentials and achieving status through a genealogy of training experience with Japanese masters or *Shihan* is common. The most famous living *Shihan* were, in their early days, students of O Sensei, but this generation is ageing and gradually awarding *Shihan* status and responsibility to their most senior students. Teachers who have the experience to do so may commodify their aikido history: they may use it in different ways to attract new students and advertise their dojos (their training clubs) on the web or in advertising flyers and posters.

Most websites have a link where the instructors' credentials and experience is provided. For example, a dojo chief instructor in Greece lists a very elaborate personal history that begins with her aikido training at a very young age in a local dojo in England, and includes attendance at camps taught by famous travelling instructors. In her teens she moved to Japan to train in Hombu for several years and the site lists all the 'legendary *Shihan*' active then as well as naming the 'uchi-deshi' (live-in students) who were her 'training partners' then and who, she adds, are 'now senior teachers at Hombu dojo'. Thus she demonstrates that she wasn't just seeking a bit of Japanese experience, but that she selected her training partners (or vice versa) to forge her body through physical daily training with students who themselves aspired to become masters.

The narrative continues with a period of apprenticeship with a master in the US and then enumerates the development of her own teaching profile and black belt promotions back in Europe. The commodification of expertise achieved through mobility and contact with particularly 'known' aikido bodies in and out of Japan is clear in this woman's biography. She fosters the local and the global nature of her aikido history simultaneously. The potential students who visit the website most likely know nothing about what her different teachers' aikido practice was actually like, what four years of daily training in Japan might feel like, or what it might produce in the visiting student's body, but they are encouraged to imagine that such a broad range of serious study would provide a teacher with great breadth of accumulated knowledge of and commitment to the art.

Similarly a weekend course in Australia opened its on-line advertising flyer by saying: 'Classes will be taught by a number of senior instructors whose wide range of backgrounds will provide attendees with a valuable spectrum of Aikido interpretations'. It then lists each (Australian) instructor's 'credentials', based on the year their training in aikido began (only listed if this was some time ago), experience of travel to train, particularly to Hombu, and a list of major *Shihan* there and elsewhere who they have trained 'under'.

Both of these examples are classic forms of presentation that reveal a particular philosophy about the way in which a body art path can be usefully traversed. However, they are both about people who run their own dojos that are independent from the major *Shihan* who they might once have studied with. The global and mobile nature of aikido training for senior students/teachers in this position thus produces a rich cocktail of diverse influences and stylistic potential.

The More Authentic Past

Western aikidoists who trained in Japan many years ago occasionally flag a perceived 'authenticity' in the training they underwent 'back then' that they imagine does not exist in the present day. 'Having been there' at a special time in the past becomes a source of storytelling to other aikido enthusiasts, a source of identification of self (through memories), as well as an advertising point for dojo websites and recruitment. The Western teachers who present these credentials in these advertisements are assumed to be conduits of the training quality they would have been able to appropriate in Japan. The authenticity of such appropriation is thus seen to be embedded not just in the place of practice, the style of interaction and the names of famous teachers, but in the time of training – a time (past) of greater authenticity and rigour. In California, Barry, who trained in Japan as a young man said:

> One year of proper training back in the 70s with those guys couldn't be achieved with even ten years of training nowadays. They pushed you like nobody's business and didn't worry about being sued! I established my core aikido from that time. I hear that now they never show *koshinage* (hip throws) in Hombu dojo because they fear hurting any of the foreign students!

While his evidence of present training in Japan is based on hearsay it becomes through this narration part of a competing field of understanding about how the body is transformed through perceived 'foreign' and more or less 'authentic' practice.

The recalled past in a foreign land is often seen to be more rigorous than the present and more apt to reveal remarkable experiences ('Yamaguchi Sensei could actually hold a person down with only his big toe!') as well as transferable tips for practice. Bruce shared his memories of Hombu many years ago, recalling how he had 'brought back' from one Hombu teacher a particular way of executing a throw while simultaneously protecting his 'centre' in a way he'd never encountered before. To his surprise he found that another teacher in his local organization had picked this up from him and then started teaching that particular move to his own students and 'got the credit for it'. He was quick to add with a good-natured laugh that 'it's all good' and he doesn't really mind. However, this story adds yet another dimension to the understanding of how 'having been there' may result in movement learned in the past becoming objectified, commodified and then reconfigured in terms of its heritage. In this case a new version of a technique becomes objectified by the travelling aikidoist who has, through his own bodily practice, harvested and then imported it from Japan to his home country, but it can then be easily appropriated by another with its 'authentic' origins lost in time.

The More 'Traditional' Silence

Ideas about processes involved in the art's embodiment are expressed in very different ways for different individuals in different places. Some Japanese and other masters outside Japan have successfully transported the embodied philosophies of 'stealing' and 'transmission' and 'polishing' into their Western dojos, and some of their students have reproduced such principles in their own teaching. To steal effectively they are encouraged to engage in discussion 'through the inside' (Irie Sensei, pers. comm. 2009).

Discussion 'through the inside' is achieved through sensitive body contact with training partners, rather than through spoken conversation or processing movements and intentions through the conscious translating mind.[5] For some, this sort of learning with the eyes and the body is the only way to train. It creates an intensity of practice sensation – the sharp slapping of the *tatami* (practice mat), inhalations and exhalations, occasional soft sounds of whispered pardons (*sumimasen* or 'excuse me'), the swishing of *hakama* on the cloth cover of the *tatami* – and the continuous swirling soft focus movement in the practitioners' peripheral awareness of all the other bodies training around them.

In America and Europe and Australia, however, there are many dojos where aikido technique is endlessly explained and described and analysed verbally on the mat. Students then expect to be 'taught', and wait for explicit instruction that is only partly embodied. This leads to students often repeating such verbalizations in their training, correcting one another, stopping the flow, standing around, arguing over what they saw their teacher do, or just chatting to each other. Those accustomed to such banter are still practising the art of aikido and progressing along a learning path, but the notion of bodily 'appropriation' is no longer about a surreptitious stealing with the eyes and body, and ideas of bodily appropriation and personal development aided with metaphors of, for example, 'polishing one's own stone' are supplanted instead by an intellectualizing filter that stops the flow of training, or places it into a different ambiance of mentalized physicality. 'American students like to think things through and confirm what they see with questions,' said Stan, an experienced teacher in California. 'They don't trust their own bodies to really mimic what they see in front of them and want to check it with you first.'

The majority of practitioners in the West never visit Japan, but conceive of their own personal embodied transformations in relation to ideas of Japaneseness and the authentic 'true' training afforded by a close connection to particular Japanese master(s) who teach in the West. This entails ideas of loyalty to a single master (*Shihan* or *Sensei*), and corresponding relations of rank and respect between students, as embodied in the Japanese *senpai/kohai* relationship (the relation between the senior mentor and junior protégé). Here, authenticity (not unlike that which is located in past encounters with aikido training in Japan) is connected to the genealogy of teachers past. But it is also located in an idea that the living disciples of the founder who left Japan long ago (in the 1950s and 1960s) to spread the art to the Americas and Europe and beyond would preserve in its purest form the spirit of aikido. In San Diego there were several Japanese students who had travelled to California to be live-in *uchideshi*[6] for Chiba Sensei because they felt that his aikido more closely embodied the founder's art than anything they could find in Japan. Several of his students commented that they have no need to travel to Japan, as they cannot get better training anywhere else in the world than their own dojo. One of his senior students advertises this sentiment in his list of credentials on a California dojo's website by underlining his black belt and teaching qualifications with a statement that he 'studied under T.K. Chiba *Shihan* his whole career'. This, then, is a noted and important qualification for many in the world aikido community, and one that relates to another way of thinking about appropriation – less as a process of bodily *bricolage* and more as a process of apprenticeship in which long-term commitment and dedication is a significant commodity affording another path for progression in the art.

Appropriating a Master and His Practice: 'Virtually Being There' with the First Generation Disciples in the Global Ecumene

There are some Japanese *Shihan* who migrated to the West more than forty years ago, and who have become master teachers with whom students remain for long periods of time. The teacher's authority, far from Japan, stems both from his demonstrated daily practice and the quality of his students. This creates a lattice of organizational and artistic expertise that is designed to carry the art into the future, and, significantly, expresses the master teacher's embodiment of his Japanese past with O Sensei and other key teachers in Japan.

These 'special' teachers completely live their practice, having an autotelic existence unlike that of the majority of aikido teachers, who generally have other jobs (either from desire or necessity), and whose identities are thus multiple. The position of these top-ranked martial masters is unusual in a Western context, where their prime 'occupation' doesn't fit comfortably within the occupational structures that more generally provide status within the host society. Yet in the martial arts community they are hugely respected and their every move and word repeated and revered. They hold court over a large body of students who train in their respective local dojos. The aikido they demonstrate in large summer and winter camps is mulled over and replicated in other dojo contexts. Their ideas and opinions are supported by their followers, and these followers are supported and taught/led (and awarded promotions) by them. In this way masters act as icons to students (within the global community of aikidoists), forming relationships of mutual responsibility. Masters still maintain ownership and authority over 'authentic' practical knowledge, but this knowledge is communally cared for by the most senior students who then 'teach' what they have learned to junior students at local dojos. The distinctiveness of a particular master's training is avidly protected by his devoted caretakers as a precious resource that must stay safely in the fold.

This sort of dedication to a single master pays off for the student with a deep sense of connection to a short but prestigious lineage and an elite cohort of contemporaries. It also permits the construction and maintenance of an organization with a strict syllabus, grading criteria, rules of membership, payment, insurance etc., which serves to uphold the position of the leaders, and their ownership of knowledge within the community. Senior students can leave their local teacher(s) to start their own 'satellite' dojos, but the ultimate control and authority is held by the organization, with the *Shihan* at its helm backed by the World Headquarters of Aikido in Hombu. Students are protected and nurtured in this space, but their bodily appropriations are also somewhat confined and face a 'danger of "ossification": the hardening of attitudes' that lead to students not being encouraged to take seriously any alternative way of doing the same techniques (Goldsbury 2000). Students that feel such confinement and leave such teachers gain a degree of independence and the freedom to roam the 'aiki-wilderness', find another teacher, or start something new, but in doing so they lose their authority gained by association with this traditional elite. A major question circulating now among some Japanese *Shihan* in the West and their disciples is concerned with what will happen to the art and its supporting structures when these now aging samurai in the West are gone. Will this most 'authentic' (Japanese) practice be preserved? And who will own this knowledge? The questions demonstrate quite clearly that both the *Shihan* and their students believe there may be something in the Japaneseness of the transmission from a single master that may not easily be replaced. Elders in the multicultural family that have spent the past forty years studying their teacher's every move will find that the art's continuity depends on stepping out of a position of appropriative mimicry into a position of generative creativity. The authenticity of martial training is in its ability to adapt and change, and ownership will only come to those who can make that final shift.

Conclusion

The divisions between spatial and temporal qualities associated with 'being there', 'having been there' and 'virtually being there' are anything but clear cut. Some foreign students in Hombu dojo in Japan are as devoted to one *Shihan* as those just described with a single master abroad. Some who trained in Japan years ago have left the art completely and look back at the training with anything but rosy glasses. Others had a youth of movement and variety before settling on a single teacher. The majority of students who train in local dojos around the world probably feel no need to experience *Shihan*-level instruction at camps in their country or abroad, and just enjoy the regular exercise and social belonging to a local club. While there is huge diversity, there are also clear patterns in the way in which bodies may appropriate culturally laden ways of being.

To study how appropriation and ownership works in this embodied socio-cultural world of practice, we have considered how individual bodies have been taught to move along paths of learning in the art of aikido (e.g. through stealing with eyes, or tempering the perfect sword within the body with hard repetitive training). Practice, however, is not just about what an individual does with her body in order to turn new technique into something she can lay claim to for herself. It is also about how she interacts with other teachers and students in the social and political environments where such training takes place. Identities are shaped through individual positioning within the formal social structures of authority that shape and limit students' options. The perceived undeniable authenticity and commitment of the first generation of Japanese masters abroad, for example, affords these men a particular claim of ownership over specialized knowledge as well as the means by which that knowledge is transmitted to their students. The hierarchical structures of authority within their dojos are rigorously maintained even if some individuals challenge them, and they promote a continued genealogical and cultural connection to Japan.

Identities of relatedness to Japan (real, remembered or imagined) are linked to authority over knowledge in the aikido world that an individual might travel widely for or earn through a lifetime of dedication to one master. 'Foreign' practical knowledge is fully appropriated within the body when a way of throwing moves from what is remembered from a particular teacher at a particular time is transformed into something owned and produced naturally in a repertoire of technique. Such knowledge may also be commodified by teachers in different ways to attract students. Identities are forged from practice as well as from ideas about how such bodily appropriation works best: by stealing, borrowing, absorbing, polishing, learning with one master or with many, and then transmitting it all to the next generation of practitioners in the intercultural spaces of training. The illustration of aikido demonstrates that it is impossible to isolate bodily appropriation and ownership from questions of authenticity, tradition, enskilment, consumption, commodification and authority.

Acknowledgements

I am grateful for the Early Career Research grant from the University of Melbourne that supported my trip to Japan in Dec 2007–Jan 2008 as well as for the patience and help offered by the teachers, staff and students of Hombu dojo. I want to thank the editors of this volume, Veronica Strang and Mark Busse, as well as Adam Kaul and Bill Birnbauer, for their helpful comments on drafts of this chapter.

Notes

1. I have been guilty of this in accounting for myself as an aikidoist and as an anthropologist – mostly obliquely through humorous memories and gossip, but a public positioning nonetheless.
2. A number of foreign visitors have commented on the 'sexist tradition' of Hombu where only male teachers instruct despite the presence of very skilled female students (some of whom train at Hombu but teach in their own dojos outside). While I won't include issues of gender in this discussion, I mention this here in order to apologize to the reader for the use of 'he' in reference to Japanese Shihan throughout. This is because the Shihan I include in my descriptions are indeed all men, although there are now a few female non-Japanese Shihan in the aikido world.
3. Respondents' names have been changed to preserve anonymity.

4. Thanks to Carolyn Stevens for this contextually sensitive translation of the Japanese term.

5. The distinction between 'showing' and 'telling' in pedagogic practice is beautifully illustrated in Strang's (2000) article on performative representations of indigenous landscape. In the aikido case, the audience immediately practices together – 'showing to' extends to a much more embodied 'doing with', and this sensory cocktail is what is distinguished so markedly from 'telling and asking'.

6. An *uchideshi* is a live-in student who attends all classes, attends to his teacher's wishes and needs and looks after the dojo, and who is seen as an apprentice to a particular teacher.

References

Alter, J. (1992), *The Wrestler's Body: Identity and Ideology in North India*, University of California Press.

Auge, M. (1995), *Non-Places: Introduction to an Anthropology of Supermodernity*, London and New York: Verso.

Bauman, Z. (1997), *Postmodernity and its Discontents*, Cambridge: Polity Press.

Bourdieu, P. (1977), *Outline of a Theory of Practice*, Cambridge: Cambridge University Press.

Clifford, J. (1997), *Routes: Travel and Translation in the late 20th century*, Harvard: Harvard University Press.

Coleman, S. and Eade, J. (eds) (2004), *Reframing Pilgrimage: Cultures in Motion,* London: Routledge.

Cox, R. (2003), *Zen Arts: An Anthropogical Study of the Culture of Aesthetic Form in Japan*, London: Routledge Curzon.

Cox, R. (2008), 'Thinking through Movement: Practicing Martial Arts and Writing Ethnography', Unpublished presentation, American Anthropological Association meetings, San Francisco.

Csordas, T. (1990), 'Embodiment as a Paradigm for Anthropology', *Ethos*, 18(1): 5–47.

Damasio, A. (2000), *The Feeling of What Happens: Body, Emotion and the Making of Consciousness*, London: Vintage.

Foucault, M. (1988), 'Technologies of the Self', in L. Martin, H. Gutman, and P. Hutton (eds), *Technologies of the Self: A Seminar with Michel Foucault*, Amherst: University of Massachusetts Press.

Goldsbury, P. (2000), 'Aikido and Independence: On Not Finding One's True Master', *Aikido Journal*, 119, accessed 2/2010 at http://www.aikidojournal.com/article?articleID=480.

Gupta, A. and Ferguson, J. (1997), *Culture, Power and Place: Explorations in Critical Anthropology*, Durham and London: Duke University Press.

Hendry, J. (1995), *Wrapping Culture: Politeness, Presentation and Power in Japan and Other Societies*, Oxford: Oxford University Press.

Hendry, J. (2005), 'Japan's Global Village: A View From the World of Leisure', in J. Robertson (ed.), *A Companion to the Anthropology of Japan*, Oxford: Blackwell.

Herzfeld, M. (2009), 'The Cultural Politics of Gesture: Reflections on Embodiment of Ethnographic Practice', *Ethnography*, 10(2): 131–52.

Jackson, M. (1989), *Paths towards a Clearing: Radical Empiricism and Ethnographic Inquiry (African Systems of Thought)*, Bloomington: Indiana University Press.

Kohn, T. (2001) '"Don't Talk – Blend": Ideas about Body and Communication in Aikido Practice', in J. Hendry and B. Watson (eds), *An Anthropology of Indirect Communication*, London: Routledge.

Kohn, T. (2003), 'The Aikido Body: Expressions of Group Identities and Self-discovery in Martial Arts Training', in N. Dyck and E. Archetti (eds), *Sport, Dance and Embodied Identities*, Oxford: Berg.

Kohn, T. (2007) 'Bowing onto the Mat: Discourses of Change through Martial Arts Practice', in S. Coleman and T. Kohn (eds), *The Discipline of Leisure: Embodying Cultures of 'Recreation'*, Oxford: Berghahn.

Kohn, T. (2008), 'Creatively Sculpting the Self through the Discipline of Martial Arts Training', in N. Dyck (ed.), *Exploring Regimes of Discipline: Ethnographic and Analytical Inquiries,* Oxford: Berg

Lindsay, S. (1996), 'Hand Drumming: An Essay in Practical Knowledge', in M. Jackson (ed.), *Things as They Are: New Directions in Phenomenological Anthropology*, Bloomington: Indiana University Press.

Moore, H. (ed.) (1996), *The Future of Anthropological Knowledge*, London: Routledge.

Palsson, G. (1994), 'Enskilment at Sea', *Man*, 29: 901–27.

Strang, V. (2000), 'Showing and Telling: Australian Land Rights and Material Moralities', *Journal of Material Culture*, 5(3): 275–99.

Strauss, S. (2005), *Positioning Yoga: Balancing Acts Across Cultures*, Oxford: Berg.

Wacquant, L. (1995), 'Pugs and Work: Bodily Capital and Bodily Labour among Professional Boxers', *Body and Society*, 1(1): 65–93.

Yuasa, Y. (1993), *The Body, Self-Cultivation, and Ki-Energy*, New York: State University of New York Press.

Zarrilli, P.B. (1998), *When the Body Becomes All Eyes: Paradigms, Discourses and Practices of Power in Kalarippayattu, a South Indian Martial Art*, Oxford: Oxford University Press.

–5–

Dreaming in Thread

From Ritual to Art and Property(s) Between

Katie Glaskin

Abstract

This chapter draws on an indigenous Australian case study concerning Bardi people of northwest West Australia. The discussion focuses on *ilma*, a genre of public ritual, and one Bardi man's transformation of one of the component parts of this genre into artworks. An important dimension of the ritual is that its intersubjective constitution as a form of property emerges from within Bardi social relations, and these reflect a relational form of personhood. I explore whether the (apparent) transition from rights embedded in a 'society' to those exercised by the 'individual' entail other kinds of transformation. A closer examination of these issues illuminates the relationship between property, persons and intersubjectivity, and the property(s) between, and reveals that transformations in both property and persons appear to be taking place in this context.

Introduction

In June 2006 a group of Bardi singers and dancers from the remote community of One Arm Point in Western Australia became the first indigenous Australians to perform at the historic site of Stonehenge, England. They performed *ilma*, a genre of public performance that involves three elements: song, dance and ritual objects the dancers carry, all of which are separately called *ilma*, as is the genre of 'open', unrestricted performance they collectively make. The use of the one term to refer to the different elements as well as to the whole performance is one indication that the elements of *ilma* in important senses represent the other elements: they belong together, and in this sense, are 'the same' (see Morphy, this volume).

Ilma are understood as being revealed by spirit beings in dreams rather than being the individual creation of the person who dreams them. In some cases a dream may be corroborated by others who have had the same dream or who have dreamt complementary elements of the overall *ilma* (so it is possible for one person to 'get' the design in a dream, while another receives the accompanying song). The dreaming of ritual elements, the wider group validation of this as ancestral revelation, and the subsequent incorporation of dreamt material into ritual has been widely reported in Australian ethnography (e.g. see Dussart 2000:139–76; Glaskin 2005; Kaberry 1939:257; Keen 2003; Keogh 1989; Marett 2005; Myers 1986; Poirier 2005; Tonkinson 1970). With respect to *ilma*, the individual is not seen as responsible for creating the 'new' ritual nor its constitutive elements, but they do retain important responsibilities for the dreamt ritual, including oversight of its performance. In terms of 'ownership' some ambiguity is created by the simultaneous denial of agency/authorship on the one hand, and responsibilities held towards the ritual on the other. This ambiguity is also connected with the main issue on which I focus in this chapter: the transformation in property relations that occurs when one element of a ritual genre undergoes commodification separately to the other elements of that ritual form, and separately to most persons within whose society that ritual is generated and performed. In considering the processual elements of this, I am interested in thinking through the intersubjective dimensions of property and the relationship between property and personhood that may be co-implicated in this transition.

In this I begin from the basis that property is inherently relational, that it involves a person or persons exercising rights and obligations with respect to things in relation to others. Thus we can talk about property as 'a form of sociality', as Harrison (1992:235) does, and highlight the interrelational and intersubjective dimensions of property thus understood (Durie's chapter in this volume similarly underscores these relational dimensions of property with respect to Maori lands and resources). Harrison argues that intellectual property is particularly 'distinctive' in terms of its social dimensions, since 'its objects have no existence except on the plane of intersubjectivity. They presuppose a shared universe of information and meaning, and depend on that universe not only for their value, but for their very reality' (1992:235). Thus one of my arguments here is that when those things that are constituted intersubjectively as a form of property are removed from one social context into another, the property(s) of the thing itself is transformed.

Scholars differ about what constitutes property and persons, and about the relationship between property and personhood (e.g. see Humphrey and Verdery 2004 and Radin 1982 for some overviews). If property is understood as rights that certain persons hold over things in relation to other persons, then, as Radin says, this 'necessarily implicates the nature of the entity to which they accrue' (1982:957). The development of Western capitalism coincided with the development of the modern notion of the individual in Western society (Lindholm 2007[2001]:19–41), and the possessive individualism that followed (Macpherson 1962) is symptomatic of this market economy. Broadly speaking, such 'individual' personhood contrasts with a 'relational' personhood, which itself has different forms and emphases (see, for example, Conklin and Morgan's (1996:667) distinction between 'structural-relational' and 'processual-relational' forms). In thinking about property in terms of a subject-object (or person-thing) orientation (Humphrey and Verdery 2004:6), we need to keep in mind that the distinction between persons and things is not necessarily apparent in all contexts (Glaskin 2009), and that 'both things and people undergo constant change' (Strang, this volume). I remain mindful that ideas concerning ' "person," "thing," and "relation" ' vary (Humphrey and Verdery 2004:6), as do the relations that give rise to rights in 'things', both material and immaterial, corporeal and incorporeal, that may be understood as relations of property. Here I take the view that an important dimension of *ilma* prior to their commodification is that their inter-subjective constitution as a form of property emerges from within Bardi social relations, and that these reflect a relational form of personhood.

The importance of kinship in indigenous Australian societies is well estab-lished. Classificatory kinship (the extension of kinship terminology and associated behaviour to non-biological kin) means that everybody in the known social universe is classed as a 'relative' of some kind and treated accordingly, although some relatives are closer than others. The extent to which a person's life is co-constituted through their relationships with others within these dense social networks of kinship obligations has led some anthropologists to describe indigenous Australian personhood in terms similar to those that have been used in Melanesia, in which persons are described as 'dividuals' rather than individuals (e.g. Redmond 2005). While I have reservations about the use of the term 'dividual' in the Australian context, indigenous Australian forms of personhood are aptly described as relational, in contrast to the individual model of personhood that is now prevalent in Western societies (Glaskin 2008a). Austin-Broos (2009) has appropriately described the situation that many indigenous Australians in remote regions currently experience as one in which the colonial process involves a transition from a kinship-based economy to a market-based economy. She argues that this is a process which itself involves an 'ontological shift': 'the passage from which the human subject is first and foremost a relative (kin) to one in which the subject becomes a market individual' (2009:6). As *ilma* enter into a market economy, and as Bardi are drawn more intensively into these economic relations, a question that similarly emerges is whether this shift in property relations is accompanied by shifts in concepts of personhood. I am thus interested in exploring whether the (apparent) transition from rights embedded in a 'society' to those exercised by the 'individual' entail other kinds of transformation, and I argue that a closer examination of these issues can reveal a more nuanced understanding of the relationship between property, persons and intersubjectivity – and of the property(s) between.

Ilma as **Property**

Ilma are a public genre of dreamt ritual, meaning that there are no restrictions concerning who may see the *ilma* performed (in terms of gender or age). As already noted, an important aspect of *ilma* is that they are considered to have their genesis in dreams. This understanding of *ilma* provenance is intimately related to Bardi conceptions of personhood. Like many indigenous Australians, Bardi hold that before birth, they exist as pre-existing spirit-beings emplaced in country, called *raya*, that may become instantiated as persons. Other spirit beings inhabit country too: *ingarda*, which are similar to *raya*, but inhabit different locations; important creator beings, who made the country and gave humans laws to follow; dangerous spirit beings of various kinds; and the spirits of the old people who have passed away and returned to their country. In this cosmology Bardi persons exist as spirits before birth and continue to exist as spirits after death. One of the important ways through which these various spirits are understood to communicate with people is in dreams; hence the appearance of a deceased person or a *raya* in a dream is understood as an actual visitation by that spirit being (see Glaskin 2005, 2006, for further discussion of this). Generally speaking, though, it is only *jarlngunggurr*, those persons who are considered to have extraordinary powers, who have ceremonies or ceremonial elements revealed to them in dreams. This revelation may occur in dreams through dream travel, being taken to a metaphysical location by a *raya* or other spirit being and 'shown' what is emplaced there, or through the appearance of a *raya*, a deceased person or other spirit being in the dream. Revelation from named deceased persons implies something about the relationship between the living person and the deceased person that is not immediately evident in revelations from less personalized categories of beings, and this is something that I explore further as my discussion progresses. For expedience I refer to nocturnal revelation by spirit beings, which includes deceased persons, as ancestral revelation, since deceased persons are ultimately assimilated into country as unnamed spirit beings, the 'old people' who inhabit the country (Glaskin 2006; see Munn 1970).

It is significant that because of their ancestral origins *ilma* are not thought of as having been individually 'created'. This contrasts with other Bardi song genres, in which individual creativity and authorship is recognized (Glaskin in press). In cases where deceased persons reveal *ilma* in dreams, the deceased persons are considered as metaphysical agents of revelation, rather than authors or creators of the *ilma*, in my understanding. In the case of Billy Ah Choo's *ilma*, discussed below, what is revealed through the *ilma*, and through the metaphysical agency of the deceased man old Wiggan, are significant aspects of Wiggan's life and his experiences after death. Old Wiggan himself is not considered to have 'made' the *ilma*, rather to have 'shown' them to the dreamer, Ah Choo.

Keogh described *ilma* as a cognate of the *nurlu* song genre of the West Kimberley. He says that within this genre the person who receives the songs in dreams '"owns" those songs, dances and dance paraphernalia' (Keogh 1989:3). He explains what is meant by 'ownership' in this context, as meaning that the person who dreams the *ilma* 'has rights over their use and display, and performances cannot be staged without his permission and participation' (1989:3). The person who dreams the *ilma* has the initial responsibility to 'bring them out' – to publicly reveal these to other Bardi people – the means through which such dreamt material ultimately enters a broader communal domain. Dreamt material is tested, as is the right of the person to 'bring them out' (Metcalfe 1970–1). While the person who dreams the *ilma* has responsibilities towards that dreamt material, their authentication as ancestral revelation is intersubjectively constituted, and this also means that the broader community retains a certain interest in these and in their performance, transmission and reproduction over time.

Thus the apparent paradox – that *ilma* remain associated with the name of the person who dreamt them long after that person dies, even as individual creativity is denied in the act of jural authentication of their other-than-human origins – is not such a paradox after all. Rather it reflects the ambiguities that arise from the intersubjective dimensions of *ilma* in their constitution as a form of intellectual property, and the responsibilities held by the person who dreams them. Here we begin to get at something of the property(s) *between* kinds of property that are often characterized either as 'communal' or 'individual'. People speak of 'Billy Ah Choo's *ilma*', 'old Muju's *ilma*' or 'old Ruby's *ilma*' (and see Robinson 1973:221), but there is necessarily a wider social dimension to them being regarded as *ilma*, as ancestrally revealed, in the first place. This is evident in the 'testing' of newly dreamt *ilma*, which is part of the process of constituting them as a form of property. In Kopytoff's (2007[1986]) terms, we can think of the *ilma* as having a cultural biography that begins with an individual's dream, but the dreamt *ilma* at this stage is perhaps not even then a 'thing'. Through memory, a person's perception of their subjective nocturnal experience is translated into something that others can apprehend. Since memory is itself both biologically and culturally formed (Solms and Turnbull 2002:140,146), what is dreamt and remembered is understood as an *ilma* and rendered recognizably as such (to those others who validate it). Its emergence as a perceptual category '*ilma*' is already intersubjective.

When the person who dreamt the *ilma* dies, someone else 'takes them over', assuming the responsibility for their performance, and it is in such cases that issues may arise as to who has rights in relation to the *ilma*. Among Bardi primary rights in country are typically gained through patrifiliation, with secondary rights gained through matrifiliation, marriage and through *nimalj*, in which patrifiliates grant usufructuary rights to resources in their own estate to specific persons. In contrast rights to *ilma* do not appear to be predictably inherited through descent from the person who dreamt them, although an ideology of patrifiliation or of close genealogical reckoning informs people's claims to rights over *ilma* once the person who has dreamt them passes away. I say 'appear' because, at the time of my research, only three sets of *ilma* were contemporarily being performed: Ah Choo's *ilma*, which I discuss further below; a set that was 'new' and had not been fully accepted and incorporated by broader Bardi society; and a set for which responsibility had been taken after death by the dreamer's sister's son. There were older sets of *ilma*, sets remembered by the name of those who dreamt and managed them, that were no longer performed. In one such case a brother had taken over the responsibility of the *ilma*. I suspect that the apparent lack of unambiguous rules about inheritance of the *ilma* is associated with the fact that *ilma* are mainly dreamt by *jarlngungurr* (persons having supernatural powers to heal or perform sorcery) rather than by *umbarda* (ordinary persons) (Glaskin 2008b). Since only a small number of people are considered to have these powers, there are not usually many people at any given time dreaming new *ilma*, and sets of *ilma* over time are clearly identified with a limited number of people who have dreamt them. As far as the postcolonial ethnographic record and oral history reveals, many *ilma* have a fairly ephemeral quality, reflected in an apparently limited inheritable trajectory of *ilma* custodianship following the death of the person who dreamt them. This may be related in part to the suspension of certain *ilma* performances following the death of persons who become particularly identified with their performance (as has occurred in one case at least). That individual *ilma* do not seem to persist for that long through time – the oldest set of *ilma* at this stage probably being Bill Ah Choo's, dreamt in the late 1960s and early 1970s – is likely to be a refraction of their intersubjective constitution as 'things' of value in the first place, of the temporal contexts in which they socially emerged and in which they are enacted.

From Ritual to Art and Transitions Between

The *ilma* performed at Stonehenge belong to a canon that is well known amongst Bardi and Jawi peoples. These *ilma* were dreamt by Billy Ah Choo, and concern the life and death of the Bardi man, Henry Wiggan. Although there are *ilma* in existence other than these, Ah Choo's *ilma* hold a special place for Bardi people. Billy Ah Choo's *ilma* were dreamt during a time of rapid social transition and upheaval. The mission on Sunday Island to which many Bardi people had been drawn from 1899 onwards was closed down in 1962, after which most of the Bardi (and Jawi) people from the mission were relocated to Derby. Bardi and Jawi who were relocated during that time lived in town camps on the edge of the marsh at Derby, and oral history accounts indicate that this was also a time of considerable social dislocation. By these accounts people were deeply unhappy living in Derby, and they sought to return to their own country (Robinson 1973:191–2; Glaskin 2002:97–9). In the movement to return to their own country, people who are today referred to as 'leaders' of Bardi people emerged, and these included Billy Ah Choo and Tommy Thomas who were also ritual leaders (Robinson 1973:257). It was during this period that Billy Ah Choo dreamt the *ilma*, saying that Wiggan had brought them to him in dreams. Robinson says that it was in 1967 that 'the old man came to Billy in a dream' (1973:221–2), some four years after old Wiggan's death in December 1963. Robinson says that 'by September 1968, the *ilma* were made up of nine segments, most of which were accompanied by dance sequences' (1973:222). (A more recent – although still provisional – count of Billy Ah Choo's *ilma* during my fieldwork identified some twenty-six or twenty-seven different segments). Billy Ah Choo and Tommy Thomas began the larger Bardi movement to return to their own country in 1969, and in 1972 the Bardi and Jawi community on the Bardi mainland at One Arm Point was formed.

The commercial performance of *ilma* can be dated to 1969 when Billy Ah Choo and others performed them at the Derby Boab festival with the encouragement of the then Department of Native Welfare, which supported the performance of traditional dances during this celebration (Robinson 1973:224). Robinson reports that 'they later took the ceremony to Broome, where they organized their own performances with Broome Aborigines, charging admission fees to tourists from the "Centaur" which was returning from a voyage to Singapore' (1973:224). These early performances evidently fostered the view that *ilma* had value, not just to other Bardi and Jawi, but also to non-indigenous others. Unlike the Yolngu art context that Morphy discusses in his paper (this volume), it was a considerable time after colonization before Bardi performed *ilma* commercially; similarly to the Yolngu case it is clear that Bardi also see these performances as an important means of communicating their culture to others. *Ilma* have been commercially performed since the late 1960s in numerous contexts, though not always without issue amongst Bardi people themselves.

In 1997 the performance of Billy Ah Choo's *ilma* at an indigenous cultural festival held in Bardi country at One Arm Point elicited a number of contentions over who had the rights to perform these *ilma*. The primary contentions were between descendants of the man who had dreamt them (Ah Choo's descendants), and the descendants of the man who, when deceased, was said to have revealed these *ilma* in dreams to him (old Wiggan's descendants). This opposition was rooted in an ontology in which persons have an existence prior to human instantiation and after physical death, and thus it was that serious questions could be raised about whose descendants had rights to the *ilma*. The descendants of old Wiggan felt themselves to be the rightful 'owners' of the *ilma*, which concerned events in Wiggan's life, and they felt that the members of Ah Choo's family, who performed the *ilma,* should have sought their permission to perform them at this event. There were also tensions amongst different branches of Ah Choo's descendants about rights to perform the *ilma* and about whose permission was required to do so, and these also drew on issues concerning who had the closest genealogical links to Billy Ah Choo and who were the better and most consistent performers of the *ilma,* thus upholding Bardi tradition. These contentions over who has rights to perform the *ilma* are indicative of their status *as* property. Alongside these issues there were also tensions surrounding Roy Wiggan's production of *ilma* as stand-alone artworks for the commercial art market.

In the distant past *ilma* were made of natural materials such as vines, bark, feathers and native cotton. Sometime during the mission days at Sunday Island (from 1899 to 1962), and certainly by the late 1940s, these 'totems' (as they are often referred to in English) were being made from tin (Glaskin in press). Contemporary *ilma* are made from lightweight plywood, which is cut into various shaped pieces, painted and affixed to a wooden cross, allowing the dancer to hold the *ilma* at the cross's join, so that it faces outwards to the audience during the performance. Long nails are hammered into the board at intervals and threaded with different coloured wools or cotton string; many *ilma* are completed with the addition of tufts of cotton wool around the perimeter.

Since 1991 Roy Wiggan, old Henry Wiggan's son, has been making and selling *ilma* as artworks. As an artist, he has achieved significant success, contributing works to eighteen exhibitions (including some solo exhibitions); his work is represented in fifteen major Australian art collections (Short Street Gallery 2009). The initial momentum for the commodification of the *ilma* came from Lord Alistair McAlpine, who commissioned Roy to make *ilma* for tourist performances in Broome and Kooljaman (Cape Leveque). In 2000–2001 Australian City Properties Pty Ltd donated this collection of *ilma* – some 1016 objects which had been made by Roy (with assistance from his sons) – to the National Maritime Museum of Australia (Commonwealth of Australia 2001). These are described by the Museum as 'multimedia polychrome works of wood and dyed yarns' (ibid.); elsewhere they are described as string sculptures. Roy has continued to produce *ilma* since, all the while maintaining that these new *ilma* are revealed to him in dreams, usually (although not always) by his father, old Wiggan, the same deceased man who revealed *ilma* in dreams to Billy Ah Choo.

Roy has long been critical of the commercial *ilma* performances mounted by other Bardi people on the grounds that those who perform them only do so when there is monetary recompense to be gained, and he contrasts this with the old days when *ilma* were regularly performed for the community, arguing that other Bardi have 'lost their culture'. Information concerning Roy and the *ilma,* which is fairly regularly reproduced on various websites with little variation, has it that it is *because* of this abrogation of culture by his own people that Roy himself decided to sell the *ilma* as artworks, so as to promote and make his culture known.[1] Thus Roy's own commodification of *ilma* is intimately associated in his own accounts of why he began to make and sell *ilma*, with his own sense of individual isolation: as he would render this, the lone upholder of an authentic tradition amidst general cultural decay, as clearly articulated in his interview with journalist Philip Adams (Australia Adlib 2003). Notwithstanding these criticisms of other Bardi people, during the period 1994–9 (at least) I also heard a number of Bardi people discuss Roy's production of *ilma* for the commercial market in critical terms. While economic jealousy associated with how much money was made from the *ilma* cannot be discounted, there was a more pressing issue for the senior people who spoke to me about this. Many of them felt that if these *ilma* were being revealed to Roy in dreams, then his responsibility was to 'bring them out' properly to the rest of the Bardi community with all three components – the material representation (the 'totem'), the dance and the song. The material *ilma* were not, in the first instance, conceptually considered as being dissociable from other constituent parts.

Roy's criticisms of Bardi who perform *ilma* commercially, and other Bardi people's concerns over his production of *ilma* for the commercial art market, have a long and complex interpersonal provenance. This is an apt point to consider the issue of intersubjectivity and its relationship to intellectual property in the context of what was occurring when Billy Ah Choo dreamt his *ilma*, and the relationship between him and old Wiggan, who revealed the *ilma* to him in dreams.

In her discussion of Voloshinov's (1973) inquiry into the 'basic reality of language', Merlan says that 'he eventually concludes that its basic nature lies in verbal interaction' (2005:176). Voloshinov's point, as Merlan describes it, is that 'basic orientation of subjects towards interaction … [is] its basic starting point' (2005:177). Subjectivity similarly implies interaction and intersubjectivity: that 'the social self is a subject to others and a subject to himself only through others' (Rorty 2007:43). Our subjectivity is formed experientially, in relation to others who also experience themselves as subjects. Regardless of whether the societies in which we live emphasize individual or relational forms of personhood, intersubjectivity is an essential component of our identity and experience.

Leaving aside emic explanations about dream visitations at this point, I would like to suggest that Billy Ah Choo's experiences of old Wiggan coming to him in dreams can be understood in terms of the relationship between the two men. Amidst the social grounding of people's lives, some social relations are more significant than others in a subject's formation. Amongst indigenous Australians growing up in remote communities, these are likely to be related to significant kin relations and to persons who are important processually through one's life-cycle, and this is evident in the relationship between the two men considered here. Old Henry Wiggan was Billy Ah Choo's *gara* (mother's brother) (Robinson 1973:221,

313);[2] he was also Billy Ah Choo's *jawul*, responsible for putting Billy Ah Choo through Law (male initiation rituals). *Jawul* is a term used reciprocally between the person going through Law and his ritual guardian who is often his mother's brother. Throughout his life the young man has reciprocal responsibilities towards his *jawul*, which include, among other things, providing him with his favoured portions of any turtles and dugongs caught. As I was told, Billy Ah Choo was 'Henry Wiggan's nephew and *jawul*, he was looking after Billy Ah Choo and so when Henry Wiggan died all those *ilma* went back to Billy Ah Choo'.[3] Arguably as Billy Ah Choo's *jawul,* old Wiggan played an important relational role in the constitution of Billy Ah Choo's identity in life, and through the dreams of Wiggan coming to Ah Choo and revealing *ilma*, continued to do so after his death. Additionally the ongoing reproduction of this canon of *ilma* continues to commemorate the relationship between the two men, even as their descendants contest who has primary rights to these *ilma* after their death.

Discussing the idea of intellectual property (in her example, Malanggan carvings), Strathern has argued that 'there is nothing particularly "intellectual" about the fact that the image, like the words of a song or the design of an ornament, is a mental one' – arguing that such knowledge is embodied knowledge, that the distinction between the mind and body in this regard is artificial, and that 'the knowledge in question is the memory' (2005:151). It is memory that holds images and so on, in people's minds. She notes that 'the image that is eventually reproduced will be negotiated from various anticipated claims on it' (ibid.). This confirms the importance of considering the intersubjective dimensions of both mind and memory in the reproduction of property that is often referred to as 'intellectual property'. Since *ilma* as intellectual property are relationally constituted, they can be seen to reflect important elements of Bardi personhood. This is evident in terms of the understanding of their provenance (ancestral revelation through dreams), but also in terms of what they depict. Thus as I contend below, different *ilma* through time, examined in historical context, also provide an important opportunity to see changes in emphasis in personhood which might be understood as coinciding with some of the changes in property relations that the commodification of *ilma* as artworks also apparently signal.

Property and Persons

In general terms Billy Ah Choo's *ilma* are concerned with events that took place in old Wiggan's life, particularly those events that occurred when his raft drifted a long way out to sea. The *ngaarri ilma* is different in that it is also concerned with his experience after death. The term *ngaarri* is used to refer to spirits of the deceased, most usually to those who have recently died. The *ngaarri ilma* performances vary according to who dance them, but have in common that they are performed by a lone male who portrays the role of a recently deceased person trying to learn the dances of the dead. However, because the *ngaarri* is only learning, he cannot keep time; the sticks he uses to dance with splay out at awkward angles, and threaten to trip him and make him fall over. This *ilma* is danced in an extremely humorous manner to elicit maximum audience amusement.

The *ngaarri ilma* is different to others I have seen performed in a number of respects. It is the only *ilma* that is not accompanied by a 'totem', a design; the *ngaarri's* hands are necessarily occupied with the thin sticks with which he must learn to dance. Principally this is a performance in which the dancer's individuality is displayed in a focused way. Other *ilma* are all performed by a number of dancers: three, four or more dancers all perform similar movements in time together. The *ngaarri* alone is covered in white ochre, signifying his ghostly status. This is the only *ilma* that is overtly humorous. Finally this is the only *ilma* I know of that represents, in some way, the experiences of the deceased.[4]

As the *ngaarri ilma* shows, *ilma* reflect aspects of Bardi personhood and can, I think, also reveal something of changing emphases in this over time. An interesting juxtaposition in this regard is between the *ngaarri ilma* and an *ilma* that Roy Wiggan's father, old Wiggan, himself dreamt when he was still alive.[5] This latter *ilma* concerned Roy's brother, in his existence as a *raya* (spirit child) prior to his birth. In this *ilma* the *raya* who are not incarnated as humans, who still exist only as spirit children, miss Roy's brother, who has left them in order to be instantiated as a human. Roy has commented on this, saying that: 'those *raya* that he left behind they sort of, they really missed him... We danced that when I was a young boy. That was that *raya*, saying they were sad that he's gone'.[6] This *ilma* mirrors the human collective experience of death: the loss of one of the group's members and the experience of that loss. In this *ilma*, though, the absence of the individual is marked *in comparison to* the community of spirit beings (and from their perspective). Conversely, the *ngaarri ilma*, while referencing the communal – the community of spirits into which the deceased is not yet integrated – highlights the lone individual, and it is the individual's perspective that is accentuated.

These two *ilma* could be taken as simply having different emphases that accord with Bardi understandings of the processes of becoming and un-becoming human, of the transitions between spirit and human realms. Equally, I argue, the *ngaarri ilma* could also be seen as reflecting a transition correlating with the time in which the Sunday Island mission was closed and Bardi came to live in the town of Derby – a place unfamiliar to them that was not their country, and where the psycho-social stability of the community was arguably disrupted (Robinson 1973; Glaskin 2002). The lone figure of the *ngaarri* trying to learn the dances of the dead highlights individual experiences. Although the *ilma* performance in itself can be masterfully funny, I suggest that part of what makes this *ilma* so humorous, too, is that it strikes a deep experiential chord associated with the dislocation people felt when they were exiled in Derby. The *ngaarri* – a ghostly figure uncertain of his moves – dances alone. Thus one reading of this lone figure is that it suggests (or intimates) the beginnings of an intercultural constitution of a differently oriented form of personhood, one that begins to shift in emphasis from the relational towards the 'individual'.

This is an apt point at which to return to Roy's production and commodification of the *ilma* as artworks, in which this transition towards an individual orientation can arguably be seen: the production of only a part of the genre separated from its other parts, the separation of the *ilma* from a communal performative dimension, and the separation of Roy himself in certain ways from other Bardi people. As he becomes the individual artist, both for himself and for the artworld, this distancing is reflected in his criticisms of other Bardi people who perform the *ilma*, which are also extended to Bardi culture more generally. I suggest that what is occurring here is the emergence of a kind of possessive individualism, in which Roy assumes the moral grounds for his own actions (Robbins 2007:302), in which he represents his production of *ilma* as exerting 'a sense of responsibility for trying to change and author new forms of representations' (Hirsch 2007:236), emerging as a self-conscious possessor of his own culture, monitoring others' deportment (to paraphrase Sykes 2007:222).

The Property(s) Between

Lord Alistair McAlpine's commissioning was an important impetus for Roy's initial production of a large number of *ilma*, arguably launching him on the pathway to his artistic career. Thus, it is interesting to briefly consider the fate of these commissioned *ilma*, which is somewhat different to those specifically produced for the art market and which are unambiguously collected as such. Unlike the commercial artworks produced since, the one thousand *ilma* held by the National Maritime Museum of Australia arrived without documentation of the 'stories' associated with them. This has been an ongoing issue for the museum, which has sought to rectify this through various means, and it is still actively working on trying to have these *ilma* documented. Documenting mainly relies on Roy's information as the producer of them: unlike *ilma* that are brought out among the community and embodied performatively, the 'stories' for these *ilma* remained 'unknown' to most other members of the Bardi community. The implication is that Roy is getting older, and should he die without the 'stories' for these *ilma* having been recorded, then they may remain 'lost'.

A contrary perspective to the view that Roy alone can provide the 'stories' for these *ilma* emerged in relation to a mooted project concerning an appraisal of these in heritage terms. At that time Roy had declined to be involved, but some other Bardi people had reportedly asserted that they could provide the details of the *ilma* as required for documentation.[7] This can be understood as meaning at least two things: firstly, that *ilma* iconography, even that which may be comprised of apparently 'new' elements, remains interpretable to other Bardi people. Secondly, and as its corollary, the idea of 'speaking for' these can be understood in an indigenous context such as this as an evident assertion of some kind of proprietary rights over these *ilma*. In this sense it is clear that it is not the material artefacts that are claimed as property, but the intellectual property in *ilma* as a genre. These particular *ilma* (as material artefacts), then, have a complex social history, moving as they have out of the ambit of wider Bardi involvement in them, but with an apparent potential to be brought back in. This reflects a Bardi reassertion of these *ilma*'s missing dimensions, wider community involvement in the constitution of their meaning. Morphy (this volume) writes that in Yolngu artworks the addition of figurative images 'fill[s] in a gap in interpretation of the images that in Yolngu ceremonial contexts is performed in dance and song'. In the case of these *ilma,* this 'gap in interpretation' is yet to be filled and will rely on documentation in order to do so.

Earlier I argued that the removal of things that are constituted intersubjectively as a form of property from the social context in which they are generated transforms the property(s) of the thing itself. By 'property' here I mean the attributes of the thing, but these attributes are fundamentally related to the thing as a form of property: on who has claims to it, in what contexts, and from what basis. Roy's creation of the material *ilma* separate to the other elements of their genre excludes other Bardi from the grounds of their production. As Bardi assertions concerning possible documentation of the one thousand *ilma* reveals, though, this exclusion remains contested, as does Roy's autonomy in his production of them, and the autonomy of those 'things' that he made, the *ilma* themselves. Their properties, in that sense, remain contingent on the relational contexts in which they are embedded: as ritual, as art or as stored museum piece. It is to the context of their commodification as artworks, though, to which I lastly return.

Gell says that 'artworks are never just singular entities; they are members of categories of artworks, and their significance is affected by the relations that exist between them' (1998:153). *Ilma* as stand-alone artworks are not, at this point, completely disembedded from *ilma* as a genre of 'open' ritual: it is this 'tradition' which vests the artworks with something of their value and meaning. Significantly, though, they are not authenticated as ancestral revelations by the Bardi jural public, who are excluded from their co-production; rather, their 'authentication' comes from within the framework of the Western art market, which construes these as desirable artworks. Part of this desirability, beyond the aesthetic value they might otherwise immediately hold for a non-Bardi viewer, is arguably the attachment of significant value to the ancestrally revealed origins the artist claims for the *ilma*. After all, this makes them 'traditional'. This commercial orientation on behalf of the artist also signifies a different emphasis in relationality, one which emphasizes the individual and individual action over the jural public, and shifts towards a differently constituted intersubjectivity in which non-indigenous persons, who buy and promote the *ilma*, play an important symbolic and constitutive role – implicitly and at times explicitly 'authenticating' them as having dreamt ancestral provenance. The *ilma* can thus be mapped over time as having different relational emphases reflective of intersubjective and intercultural engagements, some of which may dialogically shift the grounds of being over time.

The performance of *ilma* as public ritual suggests a communal dimension – rights embedded in a society – and Roy's production of *ilma* as artworks with an individual dimension. Further examination of these issues has revealed that ownership is not so clearly vested in the society or the individual in these different contexts. The cosmological authentication of *ilma* provenance relies on the intersubjectively constituted agreement of others that this is indeed the case. Even as it is the individual who dreams the *ilma*, *ilma* necessarily have a corporate dimension that is implicated not just in their ritual performance, but in their status and acceptance as *ilma* in the first instance. In Annette Weiner's terms the cosmological authentication of dreamt innovative material serves to 'link individuals and groups with an authority that transcends present social and political action' (1992:4). Thus *ilma* become property – a valuable and contested property – by virtue of the relations through which they are constituted. Dussart has similarly argued in the Warlpiri context that dreamt material that becomes incorporated into a ritual context is 'a commodity jointly held, if not jointly controlled' (2000:173). Taking dreamt *ilma* out of the context of becoming ritual takes them also out of the ambit of being a 'commodity jointly held'. Yet in the case of Roy's production of *ilma* for the art market, I would argue that an important intersubjective element to their overall constitution and acceptance remains. This is oriented differently vis-à-vis a Western art world and purchasing public that implicitly accepts the ancestral provenance of the *ilma*, reading value into these origins. This in turn reflects a different orientation towards others and towards being-in-the-world. If we understand personhood, like intellectual property, to be constituted intersubjectively, then transformations in both property and persons appear to be taking place in this context. Speaking of Kopytoff's work, Appadurai says that 'the commodity is not one kind of thing rather than another, but one phase in the life of some things' (1986:17). The production of *ilma* as artworks may be understood as 'one phase' in the life of *ilma* as 'things', but insofar as it constitutes the *ilma* as a different kind of 'thing', it is arguably a phase that represents a 'longer term shift' in the 'social history' of *ilma* in general (Appadurai 1986:34). In my view this longer-term shift can also be understood as reflecting some broader transitions amongst Bardi, an 'ontological shift' (Austin-Broos 2009) from a more relational form of personhood towards the kind of possessive individualism required to participate in the Australian market economy.

Acknowledgements

The research on which this paper is based would not have been possible without the support at various times of the Kimberley Land Council, the Australian National University, the Berndt Foundation at the University of Western Australia, and most especially, the many Bardi and Jawi persons who have shared so many aspects of their lives with me. James Leach and Alex King convened the session that first elicited this paper, and I am most grateful to them; and to Veronica Strang, Mark Busse and Chris Hann, who provided very useful comments on earlier drafts of this paper. Any shortcomings herein remain my own.

Notes

1. It is noteworthy here that Roy has previously recorded at least one CD of sung *ilma* for commercial release.
2. MB here also being structurally equivalent to MMBS and MFZS.
3. Fieldnotes, 2/7/97.
4. This view is formed on the basis of the *ilma* contemporarily performed and those no longer performed but remembered, as well as on an analysis of the field tapes of *ilma* recorded by Toby Metcalfe in 1970 and 1971 (Metcalfe 1970–1), and those recorded by Ray Keogh in 1983 which are held at the Australian Institute of Aboriginal and Torres Strait Islander Studies in Canberra (Keogh 1983). There is just one *ilma* recorded by Ray Keogh in 1983, which 'belonged to' old Muju (preceding Billy Ah Choo's *ilma)*, which is explained by Keogh's informant (on tape) as being 'Muju's first corroborree that he produced because of Sambo's spirit coming to him and singing to him, while he was dead, you know, he could hear this in the grave' (A13452, Field tape T83/47).
5. Ray Keogh recorded Roy singing this *ilma* in 1982; I have not heard of this *ilma* from other Bardi people.
6. Ray Keogh Field Recordings A13450, T83/45, recorded 7/6/83, held at AIATSIS.
7. A. de Hoog, pers. comm., 20 August 2009.

References

Appadurai, A. (1986), 'Introduction: Commodities and the Politics of Value', in A. Appadurai (ed.), *The Social Life of Things: Commodities in Cultural Perspective*, Cambridge: Cambridge University Press, pp. 3–63.

Austin-Broos, D. (2009), *Arrernte Present, Arrernte Past*, Chicago: University of Chicago Press.

Australia Adlib (2003), 'Ilma, Painting, Dance: Roy Wiggan', available from: http://www.abc.net.au/arts/adlib/stories/s902638.htm, accessed 31/10/07

Commonwealth of Australia (2001), available from: http://www.anmm.gov.au/webdata/resources/files/00-01AnRep.htm, accessed 4 December 2008.

Conklin, B. and Morgan, L. (1996), 'Bodies, Babies, and the Production of Personhood in North America and a Native Amazonian Society', *Ethos*, 24(4): 657–94.

Davies, M. and Naffine, N. (2001), *Are Persons Property? Legal Debates about Property and Personality*, Aldershot: Ashgate.

Dussart, F. (2000), *The Politics of Ritual in an Aboriginal Settlement: Kinship, Gender, and the Currency of Knowledge*, Washington, DC: Smithsonian Institution Press.

Gell, A. (1998), *Art and Agency: An Anthropological Theory*, Oxford: Oxford University Press.

Glaskin, K. (2002), 'Claiming Country: A Case Study of Historical Legacy and Transition in the Native Title Context', PhD dissertation, Department of Anthropology and Archaeology, Australian National University, Canberra.

Glaskin, K. (2005), 'Innovation and Ancestral Revelation: The Case of Dreams', *Journal of the Royal Anthropological Institute*, 11(2): 297–314.

Glaskin, K. (2006), 'Death and the Person: Reflections on Mortuary Rituals, Transformation and Ontology in an Aboriginal Society', *Paideuma*, 52: 107–26.

Glaskin, K. (2008a), 'Anatomies of Self and Relatedness', paper presented at the European Society for Oceanists conference, Verona, 11 July 2008.

Glaskin, K. (2008b), 'Dreams and Memory: Accessing Metaphysical Realms in the Northwest Kimberley', *Journal of the Anthropological Society of South Australia*, 33: 39–73.

Glaskin, K. (2009), 'Towards an Understanding of Human-Humanoid Robot Relations in Contemporary Japan,' paper presented at the University of Western Australia Anthropology seminar series, Perth, Western Australia, 16 October 2009.

Glaskin, K. (in press), 'On Dreams, Innovation and the Emerging Genre of the Individual Artist', in R.I. Lohmann (ed.), *Creations: Imagination and Innovation, Anthropological Forum, Special Issue*, 20(3): 251–267.

Harrison, S. (1992), 'Ritual as Intellectual Property,' *Man*, 27(2): 225–44.

Hirsch, E. (2007), 'Looking Like a Culture,' *Anthropological Forum*, 17(3): 225–38.

Humphrey, C. and Verdery, K. (2004), 'Introduction: Raising Questions about Property', in K. Verdery and C. Humphrey (eds), *Property in Question: Value Transformation in the Global Economy*, Oxford: Berg, pp. 1–25.

Kaberry, P. (1939), *Aboriginal Woman, Sacred and Profane*, London: Routledge.

Keen, I. (2003) 'Dreams, Agency, and Traditional Authority in Northeast Arnhem Land', in R.I. Lohmann (ed.), *Dream Travelers: Sleep Experiences and Culture in the Western Pacific*, New York: Palgrave Macmillan, pp. 127–47.

Keogh, R.D. (1989), '*Nurlu* Songs from the West Kimberley: An Introduction', *Australian Aboriginal Studies*, 1: 2–11.

Keogh, R.D. (1983), Field Tapes A13450 T83/44–49, Recorded 7/6/83 at Mamabulanjin, Broome, Canberra: Australian Institute of Aboriginal and Torres Strait Islander Studies.

Kopytoff, I. (2007) [1986], 'The Cultural Biography of Things: Commoditization as Process', in A. Appadurai (ed.), *The Social Life of Things: Commodities in Cultural Perspective*, Cambridge: Cambridge University Press, pp. 64–91.

Lindholm, C. (2007) [2001], *Culture and Identity: The History, Theory and Practice of Psychological Anthropology*, Oxford: Oneworld Publications.

Macpherson, C.B. (1962), *The Political Theory of Possessive Individualism: Hobbes to Locke*, London: Oxford University Press.

Marett, A. (2005), *Songs, Dreamings and Ghosts: The Wangga of North Australia*, Middletown: Wesleyan University Press.

Merlan, F. (2005), 'Explorations towards intercultural accounts of socio-cultural reproduction and change', *Oceania Special Issue*, 75(3): 167–82.

Metcalfe, C.D. (1970–1), Bardi Public Corroborees, Culture Heroes, and Narratives, Field Tape No.5, Canberra: Australian Institute of Aboriginal and Torres Strait Islander Studies.

Morphy, H. (2008), *Becoming Art: Exploring Cross-Cultural Categories*, Sydney: University of New South Wales Press.

Munn, N. (1970), 'The Transformation of Subjects into Objects in Walbiri and Pitjantjatjarra Myth', in R.M. Berndt (ed.), *Australian Aboriginal Anthropology*, Perth: University of Western Australia Press, pp.141–63.

Myers, F. (1986), *Pintupi Country, Pintupi Self: Sentiment, Place, and Politics among Western Desert Aborigines*, Washington, DC: Smithsonian.

Poirier, S. (2005), *A World of Relationships: Itineraries, Dreams, and Events in the Australian Western Desert*, Toronto: University of Toronto Press.

Radin, M.J. (1982), 'Property and Personhood', *Stanford Law Review*, 34(5): 957–1015.

Redmond, A. (2005), 'Strange Relatives: Mutualities and Dependencies Between Aborigines and Pastoralists in the Northern Kimberley', *Oceania Special Issue*, 75(3): 234–46.

Robinson, M.V. (1973), 'Change and Adjustment Among the Bardi of Sunday Island, North-Western Australia', MA Dissertation, Department of Anthropology, University of Western Australia, Perth.

Robbins, J. (2007), 'Afterword: Possessive Individualism and Cultural Change in the Western Pacific', *Anthropological Forum Special Issue*, 17(3): 299–308.

Rorty, A. (2007), 'The Vanishing Subject', in J. Biehl, B.Good and A. Kleinman (eds), *Subjectivity: Ethnographic Investigations*, Berkeley, University of California Press, pp. 34–51.

Short Street Gallery (2009), 'Roy Wiggan: Artist Information', http://www.shortstgallery.com.au/artist.php?id=5, accessed 15 July 2009.

Solms, M. and Turnbull, O. (2002), *The Brain and the Inner World: An Introduction to the Neuroscience of Subjective Experience*, New York: Other Press.

Strathern, M. (2005), *Kinship, Law and the Unexpected: Relatives are Always a Surprise*. Cambridge: Cambridge University Press.

Sykes, K. (2007), 'Interrogating Individuals: The Theory of Possessive Individualism in the Western Pacific', *Anthropological Forum*, 17(3): 213–24.

Tonkinson, R. (1970), 'Aboriginal Dream-Spirit Beliefs in a Contact Situation: Jigalong, Western Australia', in R.M.Berndt (ed.), *Australian Aboriginal Anthropology: Modern Studies in the Social Anthropology of Australian Aborigines*. Nedlands: University of Western Australia Press, pp. 277–91.

Voloshinov, V.N. (1973), *Marxism and the Philosophy of Language*, trans. L. Matejka and I.R. Titunik, New York and London: Seminar Press.

Weiner, A. (1992), *Inalienable Possessions: The Paradox of Keeping-While-Giving*, Berkeley: University of California Press.

–6–

'Possessing Culture'

Political Economies of Community Subjects and their Properties

Rosemary J. Coombe[1]

Abstract

The proliferation of collective claims made in cultural and proprietary terms demands a critical understanding of the political economies of community construction in order to understand ownership as a process through which property-holders are constituted as social actors and as political agents. The legal and political conditions under which culturally self-defined communities emerge to make possessive legal claims include neoliberal governmentalities, environmental regimes, intellectual property and cultural policy initiatives, as well as indigenous rights discourses which converge in many parts of the world to encourage collective needs and aspirations to be expressed in terms of community property rights. Exploring ethnographic examples from Latin America, it becomes clear that the global conditions under which collective holders of culturalised property claims have assumed greater agency and voice are diverse and their objectives contradictory. The communities empowered via recognition of their traditional knowledge, their intangible cultural heritage, or their traditional cultural expressions are situated at the intersections of old regimes of power and attachment, emerging forms of governmentality, and new imaginaries of social justice.

Introduction

Assertions of cultural property and proprietary claims premised upon cultural grounds have proliferated dramatically in the last decade (Brown 2005; Coombe 2009b). Globally, as more and more peoples bear or possess cultural distinction for new ends, legal discourses and international policies ground their claims (Coombe *et al.* 2007; Coombe 2007b; Comaroff and Comaroff 2009). Holders of cultural properties are emerging to make unique claims under the auspices of international treaties and conventions, 'soft law', customary law and human rights norms. These collectivities and their social movements often stress grassroots priorities, local needs and place-based values but their activities are shaped by the activities of external actors, foreign institutions, global networks of influence, transnationally circulating policy instruments, and international norms and fields of publicity – as well as new forms of capital accumulation (Verdery and Humphrey 2004). In this essay, which draws upon my own ethnographic work in international policy arenas as well as the fieldwork-based studies of other anthropologists, I will sketch the contours of a distinctive field of transnational politics in which, concomitantly, cultural properties are asserted and new political identities and agencies are forged.[2]

In these processes of political articulation, communities are freshly 'imagined', traditions are 'invented' as innovative and generative foundations for investment, planning and development and 'cultures' proliferate in legal guise. We need to explore the legal and political conditions under which culturally self-defined communities emerge to make possessive legal claims, considering the kinds of leverage these legal and political conditions enable, as well as the constraints they impose. In short, I argue that we must critically acknowledge the political economies of community construction in order to understand ownership as a process through which property-holders are constituted as social actors and as political agents.[3] Neoliberal governmentalities, environmental regimes and activism, and indigenous rights discourses converge in many parts of the world to encourage collective needs and aspirations to be expressed in terms of community property rights. I will be particularly concerned with the conditions under which collective holders of culturalized property claims have assumed greater agency and voice, arguing that these global conditions and forces are diverse and their objectives often contradictory.

While neoliberalism has spread throughout the world, it has done so unevenly and inconsistently (Kingfisher and Maskovsky 2008). Neoliberal governmentality profoundly 'shapes cultural realms in the production and affirmation of diversity through the commodification of difference' (Perreault and Martin 2005:193). Yet it seldom operates entirely in conditions entirely of its own choosing (Radcliffe 2005); its mandates are interpreted and reworked by the subjects it enables who may subvert the opportunities it opens up for new ends (Bondi and Laurie 2005). As John Clarke suggests, neoliberalism as an analytic category is best approached 'as an assemblage of technologies, techniques, and practices that are appropriated selectively, that come into uncomfortable encounters with "local" politics and cultures, and that are mobile and connective (rather than "global")' (2008:138). Although neoliberalism may be present everywhere, it is not necessarily everywhere dominant, but is engaged in processes of articulation with other political-cultural projects. These include alternative development and citizenship struggles as well as social agencies that may resist neoliberal strategies of depoliticization. Indigenous peoples have been particularly savvy in reworking indigenous and human rights discourses, in particular, to challenge neoliberal agendas and the subject positions they demand (Santos and Rodriguez-Gravito 2005) even while they take advantage of the forms of recognition that neoliberal regimes of governance, such as those of environmentalism, afford them.

After demonstrating these points using ethnographic studies from Latin America, I will clarify the theoretical concept of governmentality with which I am working, exploring its potential and its limits for understanding the heightened significance of community identities and proprietary claims under neoliberalism, particularly through a new emphasis upon intellectual and intangible cultural properties. Recognizing that community is a controversial analytic category, I argue that theoretical criticisms of the concept nonetheless need to attend to the political fact that collectivities so designated have assumed new significance as property-holding social actors. These developments take place in a transnational political field in which foreign agents figure significantly in the processes through which culturally identified collectives politically emerge as property holders and rights claimants.

Some Communities and Their Properties

Recent Latin American studies illustrate the globalized terrain on which new political agencies are forged as well as the transnationally oriented tactics through which properties are asserted. Mary Weismantel (2006) explores the emergence of the contemporary political significance of the 'ayllu' in Andean regions, a term often glossed as 'community' in Andean studies. Only a decade ago the term was considered by anthropologists to mark a form of cultural homogeneity and continuity that betrayed an essentialist form of Orientalism. It has nonetheless become central to indigenous activism, resistance and political legitimacy in Colombia, Ecuador, Peru, Bolivia and Chile. For most of the latter half of the twentieth century the ayllu was accepted as a group sharing an identity based in descent, residence and ethos with social institutions and cosmologies that served spiritual, economic and political functions. Romanticized in its preconquest form by Peruvian intellectuals, it has long served to voice aspirations for distinctively Andean cultural futures.

Weismantel (2006:89) recalls that anthropologists 'described the ayllu, reified it, and then abandoned it' under shifting fashions of academic discourse. Meanwhile the ayllu became central, first to environmental advocates seeking communities for sustainability and biodiversity projects, and more recently to an anti-racist, anti-colonialist and non-Western political process of forging new visions of indigenous liberty and autonomy. No longer an isolated closed corporate community (if it ever was) the ayllu is now promoted as a political vehicle for greater representation in national societies, new forms of citizenship, and decolonizing economic strategies. Moreover, it is expressly deployed in an overtly anti-capitalist politics that insists upon the continuing significance of gift exchange and collective ownership of means of production as a means to protect indigenous peoples against the predations of white society (ibid.:94–5). Cultural survival is one objective of ayullu movements, but so is the maintenance of material livelihood, political autonomy and national influence. Although attachments to tradition and its protection are characteristic of movement rhetoric, these possessive rights claims are nonetheless mobilized to project distinctive futures as alternatives to modern forms of development.

Geographers Andolina, Laurie and Radcliffe, moreover, show that this concept is transnationally over-determined in the Andes (2005; 2009). Focusing on the ayllu-based social movement in Bolivia, they illustrate how it has taken advantage of new ethnodevelopment policy frameworks championed by banks, development aid groups and NGOs. This dynamic is typical of new articulations between culture and development in the Andes through which subaltern actors have networked globally to put pressure on domestic authorities (Bebbington 2001). The Bolivian ayllu movement, Andolina *et al.* suggest, is 'emblematic of increasingly common transnational processes where multi-scalar changes in political visions, language, policies and funding flows converge to reconstruct identities' (2005:679). Both indigenous social movement platforms and multilateral development interventions in the Andes have converged around an image of culture as discrete and holistic (Radcliffe *et al.* 2002), but they deploy this imagery for distinctive ends.

Whereas language had historically predominated over local territory as political identity markers amongst Andean peoples in Bolivia, Ecuador and Peru, the influence of international indigenist movements, human rights, environmental and grassroots development NGOs, and global policy frameworks put new emphasis upon local territoriality, customs and heritage in the constitution of subjects who then demanded greater autonomy, direct participation, promotion of their languages and cultures, greater socio-economic equity and self-determination in development planning (Andolina *et al.* 2005:681–2). States and official development institutions selectively appropriated international indigenous rights concepts when re-crafting agendas for neoliberal development and governance. Many Latin American states adopted a multiculturalist or plurinational discourse to accompany new forms of decentralization while development industries adapted the concept of social capital to target indigenous social organization. The indigenous subject position was paradoxically localized and transnationalized in the process.

Ayllus have precolonial origins in Bolivia and many survived the revolution with lands and community structures intact. They are defined by limited direct democracy in communal assembly, systems of collective work and community service. Historically they provided indigenous peoples with a collective identity, a spiritual base, 'and economic security through land rights, (non-capitalist) reciprocal exchange and collaborative labour' (ibid.:684). Nonetheless, the vast majority of peoples obtained access to state benefits and social security through peasant federations who were the state's privileged interlocutors. Through the weakening of the state and the growing intervention of transnational actors, the ayllu became a national political subject in the late 1990s.

In less than two decades, community-level ayllus were named and championed as the region's authentic cultural base for legitimate grassroots political and economic activity as class and union politics were denigrated as external colonial impositions (ibid.:686). Foreign NGOs such as the Andean Oral History Workshop, Oxfam America and the European-Union sponsored Campesino Self-Development project played an important role in this process. Their interests meshed in affirming ethnicity over class and promoting collective rights for interlocutors defined culturally by local customs and territories. In this they adopted and promoted principles of indigeneity enshrined by the ILO Convention 169, an early international indigenous rights instrument which 'identified peoples according to maintenance of tradition and attachment to local territories' (ibid.:688) while recognizing communal property and customary justice systems. Ayllus, it appears, were the only spatially appropriate authorities to fit the bill; they became more self-conscious about their cultural identities and their cultural properties as a consequence.

As the Bolivian state instituted decentralization strategies that demanded popular participation, communities were registered as political actors and encouraged to legalize title to their original community lands. In a political context in which Bolivia was being lauded as simultaneously democratic, neoliberal and multicultural, the ayllu movement was finally embraced by the state. No doubt this was influenced by foreign investment needs and development bank desires to avoid negative publicity from overt harm to indigenous peoples. Indigenous traditional knowledge and communal social practices were perceived as valued 'social capital' in projects that endorsed the projection and assertion of localized ethnic identities. Ethnodevelopment, embraced by transnational networks of NGOs, bilateral agencies and multilateral institutions committed to indigenous rights, was new to Bolivia in the 1990s. It was modelled on the perceived success of indigenous peoples' confederations in Ecuador, where nationally linked, culturally based community actors have gained considerable autonomy, influence and wealth through their management of external investments (Radcliffe and Laurie 2006a, 2006b; Rhoades 2006; Perreault 2003). Like their Ecuadorian counterparts the Bolivian ayllu movement sought to constitutionalize territorial and cultural property rights and jurisdiction over community justice systems.

If for development agencies in the Andes indigenous culture is a form of social capital that can be treated like an asset, for indigenous movements culture is the basis for a successful politics of anti-colonialism (Radcliffe *et al.* 2002). Like its counterparts in Colombia, Peru and Ecuador, with whom they have established relationships of solidarity, the Bolivian ayllu movement sees itself as engaged in a project of decolonization. All of these groups have become increasingly politicized as part of transnational movements, opposing the expansion of the Free Trade Association of the Americas, for instance, and offering new visions of 'counter-modern' development (Gow 2008) based on indigenous rights to possess and develop traditional knowledge grounded in cultural heritage.

Indigenous identity parameters to some extent line up nicely with neoliberal objectives; concepts of social capital, grassroots empowerment and good governance may correspond to cultural difference, local institution building and traditional leadership practices (Andolina *et al.* 2005:698). Ayllu development platforms overlap with neoliberal agendas to the extent that the reactivation of Andean structures of production, reciprocity and collective labour are galvanized for boosting exports of 'ayllu value-added products' (ibid.:695), ecologically sound agriculture and local empowerment through community-based bicultural education. On the other hand their import-substitution policy, practices of self-reliance, opposition to free trade agreements, resistance to mining and oil extraction and growing linkages to other indigenous peoples in anti-capitalist movements suggest that these community-based indigenous movements have their own agendas.

These processes have been explored more locally. In *The Ecological Native* (2005), for instance, Astrid Ulloa explores the global legal and political economic conditions under which the indigenous peoples of Colombia's Sierra Nevada de Santa Marta (SNSM) constituted themselves as cultural communities and political interlocutors from 1992 to 2003 in national, transnational and international political networks that include political entities at various scales, multilateral institutions, NGOs and environmental social movements. In 1992 Colombia was internationally recognized as especially high in biodiversity in the global environmental talks resulting in the Rio Declaration that called for the implementation of sustainable development programmes for biodiversity 'hotspots'. These policies promised an unprecedented flow of research and funding into hitherto remote areas in many parts of the world to the benefit of many peoples previously marginalized relative to the state. Under the auspices of the Convention of Biological Diversity (CBD), international influence on the Colombian government emphasized the need to recognize the knowledge, territories and resources of indigenous peoples (Ulloa 2005:102). Such UN-sanctioned international environmentalist politics arose simultaneously with international indigenous rights movements in the early 1990s, enabling peoples newly recognized as global actors to propound new visions of their relationships to the places that sustained their lives and livelihoods.

Indigenous or ancestral territory, as distinguished from the Western concept of land and property (Nasaday 2003), was deployed to project a novel understanding of culturally distinctive peoples' collective proprietary interests into the international political sphere. The cultural politics of the indigenous peoples of the SNSM were dialectically articulated with global environmental policies; the historical continuity of their collective traditions of territoriality was rhetorically forged through a spectrum of power that extended from local government offices to transnational activist networks. This political strategy deployed a vocabulary that skilfully wove discursive threads from human rights, indigenous rights, sustainable development and environmentalist narratives. Indigenous peoples claimed their traditions as the source of globally relevant knowledge that enabled them to exercise environmental responsibilities with concomitant rights to exercise control over their territories and resources as legitimate and alternative forms of sustainable development. Such alternatives 'allow culture to serve as the coordinating political principle for environmental management and conservation strategies' (Ulloa 2005:75). This was a strategic means to recover control over territory regarded as an ecologically, politically and symbolically significant place and, concomitantly, to regain possession of natural resources and cultural heritage. This process is widespread in the Southern Americas. Gabriela Valdivia (2005) and Margrita Sertje (2003) observe analogous forms of collective culturally based political subjectivities emerging amongst black and indigenous populations in the Ecuadorian and Colombian Amazon respectively, as they became familiar with global discourses, transnational agencies and approved self-governance structures.

Indigenous organizations such as the Cabildo Territorial Council (CTC) in the SNSM represent their territory and its characteristics as integral to their cultural identities. Such territory, they are careful to maintain, is not empty land, a container for the provision of environmental resources, the common heritage of humankind, nor potential private property. Instead it is a place in which harmony is maintained by indigenous peoples as stewards of an integrated, inalienable, cosmologically defined and spiritually animated realm following principles that are now articulated by the SNSM as 'The Original Law'. Such customary law is asserted to legitimate ancestral ownership and to ground indigenous rights as well as the state's recognition of their plan for the management of the resources of their territory based upon the traditional knowledge they are acknowledged to possess. Thus they:

> project an image of themselves in the national and international media as ecological indigenous peoples whose great care for nature is based on their ancestral wisdom from

which the 'younger brothers' should learn. Their strategies include seeking relations and support from NGOs, environmental organizations, human rights organizations, anthropologists and public figures who can help publicize their concerns about their cultures and territory. Indigenous peoples have a clear awareness that their cultural identity has been affected by the importance of the SNSM's status as one of humanity's heritage sites due to its biological and cultural diversity. This linkage has become an important political strategy for publicizing their status as autonomous indigenous peoples. (Ulloa 2005:72)

Throughout the Americas in the last two decades, assuming an ecological ethnicity has been a means to appeal to transnational NGOs and social movement networks for new forms of support ranging from financial assistance to transnational political alliances. In so doing indigenous peoples established new relationships with transnational indigenist movements and other social movements, building coalitions with peasants and workers that enabled them to press for new visions of citizenship and interculturalism resulting in new forms of democratization (Ulloa 2005:16; see also Asher 2009; Gow 2008; Gustafson 2009; Rappaport 2005; Wilshusen 2003). Moreover:

they have also brought transnational agents into the local political process in an effort to integrate their strategies of modern science and planning, expert knowledge, sustainable management of natural resources, and the idea of territory ... Indigenous policy proposals and political activities find a focal point in the idea of indigenous autonomy that has reshaped the terms of public discourse about nature, environment and ecology and formed the political context in which struggles over competing conceptions of nature, territory and property are taking place. (Ulloa 2005:216)

Such struggles are entailed by the fact that indigenous empowerment has come at a price; ironically, the neoliberal regimes of power such as the environmentality (Agrawal 2005) or eco-governmentality 'in which they are now enmeshed increasingly demand that they perform as free and autonomous agents in western terms in order to position their lands, resources and knowledge as values in environmental markets' (Ulloa 2005:16).

As many scholars have noted, the new multilateral institutions that regulate the environment such as the Global Environmental Fund (the funding body for the CBD) do so in neoliberal terms that construct biodiversity as a world currency subject to international surveillance and scientific control. The CBD recognition of indigenous and local communities' traditional knowledge as relevant to the conservation of biological diversity, for example, is embedded in a neoliberal regime that defines the latter as a 'resource' for humankind best valued through market mechanisms (McCarthy and Prudhon 2004). Hence the emphasis upon securing access to and sharing benefits from the development of useful genetic resources into (patentable) goods and the emphasis on market-based intellectual property mechanisms to ensure these.

Under such conditions, indigenous peoples may find their practices and knowledges transformed into forms of exploitable commodified expertise. They may be encouraged to treat their territory as environmental capital best developed for eco- and ethno-tourism, their resources as the basis for eco-products, and their collective identities recognized as disembedded political entities – self-interested agents capable of approaching their lands and resources instrumentally and contractually (they may also be completely ignored if the political and economic costs of dealing with them are deemed too onerous, as Cory Hayden (2003a, 2003b) has illustrated). Non-indigenous parties may desire secure indigenous rights and sovereignties predominantly to provide the certainty necessary for creating legally binding market transactions; intellectual property is promoted as a vehicle to further these ends. Not surprisingly, however, some indigenous peoples now use the vocabularies of Western intellectual property systems in new ways.

Colombian indigenous peoples were amongst the first in the world to insist that their traditional environmental knowledge and the genetic resources in their territories were their own collective intellectual properties (Ulloa 2005:46–7), effectively controlling research in their territories, asserting the priority of their own customary law for protection of their knowledge and traditions, contesting the intellectual properties granted to others based on appropriations of their own perceived cultural properties, and calling, along with other indigenous peoples, for a global moratorium on bioprospecting (see essays in Florez 1998). Whether we see indigenous peoples' collective identities and proprietary claims as evidence of a subaltern cosmopolitanism or counter-hegemonic globalization (Eudaily 2005; Goodale 2006; Santos 2002; Stewart-Harawira 2005), or as harbingers of neoliberal investments in ethno-incorporation (Comaroff and Comaroff 2009), we cannot deny that more and more communities are heavily invested in culturalized futures.

While indigenous people have become increasingly savvy in navigating the new terrains that neoliberalism and an emerging human rights discourse present, they have done so in a fashion that has attracted scholarly criticism. Such criticism fails to reflect upon the structurations of the legal and policy fields in which these assertions are calculated interventions. Allegations of essentialism (strategic or otherwise), recognitions of social construction (not appreciated as creative political agency), citing inventions of tradition (which are implied to be evidence of inauthenticity), and accusations of primitivism or misguided romanticism levelled at contemporary assertions of collectivity reveal a profound lack of sensitivity to the stakes at issue for many peoples and the political economies in which they are situated (Doane 2007). They may also unintentionally serve to undermine subaltern political objectives (Briggs 1996; Hale 2006).

Many debates about the wisdom of protecting traditional knowledge, intangible cultural heritage, or other cultural properties also reveal a lack of knowledge of the social movements and struggles in which possessive and/or proprietary claims to cultural resources are made (Coombe 2005). Arguably some anthropological treatments of the collective identities that emerge in indigenous politics have been too quick to situate and reduce these identities to figurations in Western discourses that demand certain essential positionings for natives, thereby reducing indigenous activity to a kind of *induced agency* (Veber 1998:387). Assertions of indigenous cultural content in a peoples' identity and aspirations thus becomes evidence of strategic image management or self-Orientalism, preempting the possibility that other ways of life and cultural resources drawn from other histories might provide resources for an effective contemporary political subjectivity. Anthropologists might instead pose more pertinent questions. What kinds of recognition and redistribution are being offered to peoples who choose to occupy spaces of collective subjectivity that they define culturally? What political opportunities does this afford them and what political limits do they thereby face?

A critical ethnographic exploration of this new political economy, I would suggest, might attempt to accomplish three objectives. First, such an analysis would address the local needs and desires of actors engaged in transnationally linked social movements that inspire claims to cultural goods. Second, it would delineate the interpellation of market-based subjectivities that seek to naturalize possessive relationships to culture as a development asset or other resource. Finally it would interrogate the relationship between these. In the Ecuadorian and Bolivian Andes, for instance, control over and possession of traditional knowledge as a new form of property seems to figure *simultaneously* in neoliberal desires to locate 'social capital' and invest in its (market-based) futures *and* in rights-based struggles for recognition, differentiated citizenship and negotiated autonomies from state powers. State and market-based pressures to produce developmentally appropriate culture greet those who struggle to articulate political aspirations for culturally appropriate development (Laurie *et al.* 2005; Andolina *et al.* 2009).

Systems of intellectual property, rolled out to extend market mechanisms into an ever-wider range of cultural activities, produce new social differentiations, as do rights recognizing indigenous autonomy for the purpose of incorporating peoples as 'active self-governing market subjects' (Bondi and Laurie 2005). Assertions of collective patrimony may be read by banks and development agencies as rational, instrumental, proprietary behaviour, but they may also figure in political projects that reterritorialize, re-embed and re-enchant concepts of community and culture. Neoliberalism may aspire 'to foster globalization, marketization and entrepreneurship', but paradoxically as investors of diverse kinds seek local partners, they seem to incite the articulation of '*diverse* sites of community' (ibid.:27; emphasis mine) that emphasize communitarian subjectivities, social solidarities and collective citizenship (Andolina *et al.* 2009).

Governmentality's Agents

Under neoliberal conditions, social theorists assert, a new form of governmental rationality is emerging that focuses on 'the organization of self-regulating and self-managing communities' (Bennett 2002:142) constituted through the new programmes that make them administrable (Rose 1999:189). This is a shift in government that recognizes collectivities as new kinds of persons (Clarke 2008) and invests them with new responsibilities as 'self-governing' actors (Ong 2006). Not surprisingly social groups involved in this new field of engagement learn to project their needs and aspirations in the languages of self-governance and identity assertion that both economic markets and international political arenas increasingly demand.

Governmentality is a concept particularly relevant to the study of cultural property because the concept allows scholars to attend to the ways in which 'culture has often been both the object and the instrument of [the] governmental policy that regulates social life' (Bratich *et al.* 2003:6). Foucaultian anthropologists suggest that technologies of subjectification and the management of resources for identity construction are important means by which social behaviour is effectively managed (Inda 2005:10). Under neoliberal conditions the work of governmentality is often done not only by states, but by so-called NGOs whose agencies validate new forms of knowledge and recognize expertise held by newly empowered subjects (Rose 1999). As we have seen, these newly empowered subjects increasingly constitute themselves by asserting a possessive relationship to territories and resources which they seek to protect, to conserve, to sustain, to manage (and sometimes to trade), encouraged and sometimes incited by a host of laws and policies.

Scholars of cultural property have neglected a fundamental tenet of legal anthropology – namely, that identities do not exist before the law but are forged in relation to law and the subject positions afforded by legal regimes and policy negotiations (Hirsch and Lazarus Black 1994; Mertz 1994). This is one aspect of the Geertzian (1983) observation that law creates the facts it purports merely to recognize, and the Marxist position that a possessive subject is called forth by forms of capital accumulation as a matter of legal ideology and consciousness (Collier, Maurer and Suarez-Navez 2001). Governmentality scholars, moreover, ask that we consider the encouragement and support of subjectivities in such ways that these come into alignment with the diverse objectives of regulation.

For example, numerous parties have engaged in lengthy international political negotiations over the best means to protect traditional knowledge, innovations and practices (hereinafter traditional knowledge). So-called indigenous and local communities embodying 'traditional' lifestyles are understood in global policy circles to make substantial contributions to the preservation of biological diversity through the cultural specificity of their traditional knowledge, but are unfortunately excluded from the benefits that accrue from the use of their knowledge and innovations in commerce. For our purposes the veracity of this narrative is not as important as its political consequence: the massive efforts invested in righting this perceived wrong through the deliberations around new proprietary entitlements and the local aspirations that attach to these negotiations.

Although they are *not* uniformly popular, variations on intellectual property rights such as legislative amendments to copyright, trademark, geographical indication and trade secret protections as well as new forms of intangible property protection have been recommended as solutions to the injustices perceived to follow from a lack of recognition and compensation for the use of traditional knowledge. Proposals aim to ensure adequate benefit sharing with communities in the Global South, that communities provide prior informed consent for the use of their knowledge about environmental resources, that patents based upon biological resources disclose places of origin to enable communities to detect instances of 'biopiracy', and that local customary law is respected, so as to prevent practices of corporate misappropriation. Representatives of states, NGOs and indigenous peoples convene regularly to discuss these issues at World Intellectual Property Organization (WIPO) meetings to draft provisions to protect genetic resources, traditional knowledge, and traditional cultural expressions (Coombe 2009a). Simultaneously UNESCO steers international deliberations about the best protocols for implementing the Intangible Heritage Convention, brought into force in 2006 to recognize community rights in a broad new range of expressive cultural forms. In all of these ongoing policy-making efforts, I would suggest, norms and subjects are co-produced and co-evolve (Reardon 2005).

Under neoliberal conditions distinctive forms of subjectification may therefore be accomplished by the devolution of the management of cultural resources to distinctive collectivities who are encouraged to adopt possessive bearings towards them pursuant to policies promoted by the CBD, UNESCO and WIPO (amongst others). Population groups are arguably 'subjectified' as communities while their practices are objectified as traditional knowledge, traditional cultural expressions or intangible cultural heritage, proprietary forms over-determined by international legal requirements and institutional demands. Simultaneously global and regional indigenous rights norms legitimate collective possessive claims (al Attar *et al.* 2009) that support new forms of sovereignty, alternative forms of development and distinctive cultural futures. Community may serve diverse purposes.

Community Subjects, Foreign Parties and Indigenous Politics

Community is a term that has long attracted controversy in anthropology and the social sciences (Amit and Rapport 2002; sources cited in Creed 2006b). One caution against the romance of community came via critical ethnographic studies of community-based natural resource management policies and regimes that proliferated in the 1990s (Agrawal and Gibson 2001; Brosius 1997; Brosius *et al.* 1998). These scholars reminded us that community was a highly naturalized and normative term. They insisted that widespread preoccupations with 'mythic' communities – small, harmonious, integrated, isolated groups using locally evolved norms to manage resources sustainably – were dangerous fictions that blinded policy-makers to internal divisions, local politics and multi-scalar strategic alliances. Policies that required a suitably 'corporate' property-owning social group as a precondition for extending rights and directing investments, they feared, would exclude many of the world's disadvantaged (Li 1996). Indigenous or tribal groups might be privileged by this discourse while other populations of the rural poor would be further marginalized. In many parts of the world, people indigenous to a region were not formed into bounded groups with a clear sense of territorial possession (Li 2000; Tsing 1999). The extension of new forms of culturalized community properties might thus create distributional inequities.

A governmentality perspective, however, is less concerned with communities as 'natural' social actors and more concerned with the realities such mappings propound and the practices and identities thereby put into play. Rather than positing or refuting the positivity of communities, we might attempt instead to maintain an emphasis upon community-making processes, recognizing that 'communities, states and NGOs are mutually implicated in relations laced with power' (Li 2005:445). Communities will be formed, co-opted and constituted as possible loci of demand for and opposition to governmental projects in engagement with state institutions, particularly when making proprietary claims where the state is a necessary interlocutor.

Scholarly debates about communities in environmentalist politics reached an impasse early in the twenty-first century. It became apparent that the evocation of community in community-based natural resource management furthered diverse and often diverging agendas. Conservationists hoped to involve local people in transnational conservation and resource management as a means of protecting biological diversity. Development organizations (driven in part by past criticisms) aimed to promote local participation. Activists hoped to empower local groups, and indigenous peoples aspired to new forms of recognition and political rights based on their cultural knowledge (Brosius *et al.* 1998:158–9). Many scholars unfortunately ignored these diverse agencies and their objectives. Instead they scrutinized the fictions of community, territory and tradition used to accomplish these ends. But if advocates could be accused of using these concepts romantically, critical scholars appeared to glorify their own critical and ironic stance towards 'social construction' – reducing genuine political dilemmas, environmental needs and local aspirations to philosophical problems of 'essentialism' and its perceived dangers (ibid.:159–60). Anthropologists realized that social constructivist critiques served to obscure complex politics and inadvertently undermined subaltern struggles while supporting developmentalist agendas (Brosius *et al.* 2005). With such hindsight we might seek to avoid these same quandaries in our studies of emerging community property holders and their collective cultural claims.

One volume of anthropological essays posits community as 'an obsession' that has 'become ubiquitous in the way we talk and think about life in the twenty-first century' (Creed 2006a:3), primarily because of the proliferation of social engineering projects that focus on the community as the appropriate vehicle and target for change. Nonetheless if community-based governmentalities have multiplied, actors who resist such projects *also* constitute themselves as communities, as do those who assert claims to resources that recognition as a community may secure (ibid.:3). For instance, despite earlier theoretical hesitations about using the community concept in his research in rural Thailand – due to its capacity to romanticize group social life – Peter Vandergeest now admits that he finds it unavoidable, 'because it allows activists and scholars to discuss forms of place-based collective action' (2008:208) that are not appropriately described using other categories of analysis. As he acknowledges, communities figure as social actors with distinctive capacities in global commodity chains and NGO activist networks in ways that were inconceivable just two decades ago. Nonetheless, I would agree with Creed (2006a:6) that we should use the concept to focus analysis 'rather than [as] simply an empty category of heuristic or descriptive convenience', recognizing that it is doing distinctive forms of political and legal work.

Emerging global norms demand that communities provide consent for the use of knowledge and resources, reflect upon tradition and consider their practices as forms of heritage. International laws and international institutions call for communities to exercise particular powers and propose that they hold particular types of properties. Where peoples have no institutions to engage in these negotiations and/or where states have not implemented laws to recognize them, 'communities' will nonetheless be located. Early anthropological studies of bioprospecting and alleged biopiracy (Berlin and Berlin 2004; Greene 2004; Hayden 2003a, 2003b) illustrated the politics of community performativity, strategic entrepreneurialism, as well as the perverse consequences that ensued when traditional knowledge was objectified and community reified in the absence of legal frameworks of recognition. Corporations, NGOs and development agencies bearing obligations to secure consent for the use of traditional knowledge or to secure community participation when designating heritage properties will inevitably find communities at some scale who are prepared to bargain. Questions of who represents communities are inevitable, but they are not necessarily insurmountable (Rosenthal 2006). We can anticipate that states will increasingly recognize new forms of community to decentralize government powers and responsibilities, meet international responsibilities and attract new forms of investment. In short communities are rarely wholly homegrown but increasingly forged in encounters with foreign agents.

Communities form in contexts and for purposes of engagement with other institutions; they will present themselves in the fashion that attracts powerful interlocutors at different levels of power (Li 2000). They may be assisted by actors such as NGOs, who may be more adept at deploying rhetorics that enamour metropolitan audiences to 'peripheral' causes and community violations. This is certainly the case with respect to the culturalization of property rights. International institutions and NGOs clearly play important roles in the process of mobilizing communities to claim rights to cultural resources and to claim resource rights on cultural grounds. Both indigenous peoples and other so-called local communities have strategically used their new role in biodiversity politics, for example, as a means to effect an institutionalization of their territorial and political rights while calling international attention to their dispossession (Escobar 2008).

We might accept that communities are made, not found, and that the culturalized localities we see emerging are globalized sites that invoke an armoury of transnational institutions and agencies – without thereby prejudging their capacities as political vehicles. The ethnographic studies examined earlier illustrate a political terrain in which discrete communities embracing culturally distinctive identities emerge in concert with transnational activities, interests and investments. NGOs have been crucial in focusing indigenous movements on cultural issues and rights to difference, consolidating their political and organizational processes around cultural identities centred in tradition under the larger legal and political umbrella of self-determination. Proprietary demands for territories, resources and control over knowledge and heritage have been central to these struggles. In these political processes the cultural attributes on which they ground their claims become a constitutive part of their political identities, even when these distinctions were not historically matters of political significance (Escobar 2008; Hvalkof 2006). The collective values they hold as communities also become increasingly significant in their political projections.

Conclusion

Cultural difference has become an important resource in transnational struggles for recognition, redistribution, and economic and political investment, as well as the basis for establishing new rights and new properties. The communities empowered via recognition of their traditional knowledge, their intangible cultural heritage, or their traditional cultural expressions are situated at the intersections of old regimes of power and attachment, emerging forms of governmentality and new imaginaries of social justice. In some areas of the world they may map nicely onto historical forms of identity, solidarity and communal attachments, but in others they may be constituted using borders that reiterate colonial divisions of power, further exacerbate local relations of social inequality, isolate and contain peoples, and depoliticize their struggles (Li 2007). State powers may instantiate new forms of collective subjectivity for purposes of discipline, surveillance and appropriation. NGOs may find traditions and recognize communities where they are most comfortable. Aid and lending institutions may continue to 'locate culture' in areas they perceive as having the requisite social capital to engage in collective entrepreneurship (Bebbington 2004). However, we may also find recently 'capacitated' communities making new demands on states, international courts and multilateral institutions for legal recognition, political autonomy and respect for customary law, to limit and enjoin extractive development projects, to oppose trade agreements and reinterpret intellectual property regimes, while engaging in new forms of coalition building and articulating new forms of citizenship and means of democratization. The articulation of cultural properties figures in most of these struggles.

Possessive cultural claims emerging from biodiversity conservation and sustainable development have in some places been linked to emancipatory discourses on minority rights, democracy, new types of citizenship and social justice struggles. In others they have led to new forms of exploitation and disenfranchisement. The same range of political consequence should be anticipated for the proliferation of culturalized property claims that will ensue in the near future as governments enact law and policy to meet their commitments under new international legal instruments. While neoliberal governmental practices may seek to attach groups to the kinds of heritage that can most easily be managed as commodifiable resources, they do not necessarily succeed in so doing: 'it is important to look not just at the forms of collective and individual identity promoted by practices of government, but also at how particular agents negotiate these forms – how they embrace, adapt, or refuse them' (Inda 2005:11).

Ultimately, the 'friction' (Tsing 2005) produced when the subjectifications of governmentality come up against and potentially ignite new forms of struggle offers promising new avenues for anthropological inquiry. Governmental activities may originally have been designed to manage and control so-called local communities so as to incorporate them more completely into regimes of state and market citizenship. However, to the extent that these subject-positions become encoded as indigenous ones, they also invite local communities thus subjected to reflect upon their historical practices and to express their appeals in the normative discourses that global indigenist movements afford, articulating new limits to neoliberal governmentality in the process (Coombe 2007a). Processes of community formation and cultural proprietorship are processes of political articulation. New legal and political economies of property are transnational, sometimes inconsistent, usually dynamic and often socially generative. Diverse forms of sociality are clearly imagined and engendered by the interpellation of communities to serve needs for neoliberal governmental engagement just as they will be by expectations for collective management of cultural property. Governmental subjectivities may also be diverted and deployed in movements for livelihood security, political autonomy, territorial rights and distinctive forms of citizenship through indigenist movements that skilfully invite cultural difference to be performed as a place of unique responsibilities requiring distinctive sovereignties. The propriety of owning culture thus promises to continue to be the subject of academic controversy and political vitality.

Notes

1. The author wishes to acknowledge the Stellenbosch Institute for Advanced Study (STIAS) for providing resources and support for this research, and Nicole Aylwin and Lisa Norton for research and bibliographical assistance. She thanks Ilana Gershon for superb commentary and constructive criticism.
2. The legal geography I map in this essay is most pertinent to an international and transnational political arena in which indigenous identities are recently emergent, revitalized, and often contested. It may be less salient where indigenous identities have long been recognized by state powers and established by treaty relationship, but even in these situations, peoples are variously located and those less privileged by historical circumstance may look beyond the state for political leverage.
3. I use a similar framework to explore the construction of community subjects with particular emphasis upon intellectual property rights and policy in a complementary paper that draws upon different ethnographic examples (Coombe 2010).

References

Agrawal, A. (2005), *Environmentality: Technologies of Government and the Making of Subjects*, Durham: Duke University Press.

Agrawal, A. and Gibson, C. (2001), 'The Role of Community in Natural Resource Conservation', in A. Agrawal and C. Gibson (eds), *Communities and the Environment*, New Brunswick, NJ: Rutgers University Press, pp. 1–22.

al Attar, M., Aylwin, N. and Coombe, R. J. (2009), 'Indigenous Cultural Heritage Rights in International Human Rights Law', in C. Bell and R. Patterson (eds), *Protection of First Nations' Cultural Heritage: Laws, Policy, and Reform*, Vancouver: University of British Columbia Press, pp. 533–83.

Amit, A. and Rapport, N. (2002), *The Trouble with Community: Anthropological Reflections on Movement, Identity and Collectivity*, London: Pluto Press.

Andolina, R., Laurie, N. and Radcliffe, S.A. (2009), *Indigenous Development in the Andes: Culture, Power and Transnationalism*, Durham: Duke University Press.

Andolina, R., Radcliffe, S. and Laurie, N. (2005), 'Development and Culture: Transnational Identity Making in Bolivia', *Political Geography*, 24: 678–702.

Asher, K. (2009), *Black and Green: Afro-Colombians, Development and Nature in the Pacific Lowlands*, Durham: Duke University Press.

Bebbington, A. (2001), 'Globalized Andes: Livelihoods, Landscapes and Development', *Ecumene*, 8: 414–36.

Bebbington, A. (2004), 'Social Capital and Development Studies 1: Critique, Debate, Progress?' *Progress in Development Studies*, 4: 343–49.

Bennett, T. (2002), 'Culture and Governmentality', in J. Bratich, J. Packer and C. McCarthy (eds), *Foucault, Cultural Studies and Governmentality*, New York: SUNY Press, pp. 47–66.

Berlin, B. and Berlin, E. (2004), 'Prior Informed Consent and Bioprospecting in Chiapas', in M. Riley (ed.), *Indigenous Intellectual Property Rights: Legal Obstacles and Innovative Solutions*, Walnut Creek: Alta Mira Press, pp. 341–63.

Bondi, L. and Laurie, N. (2005), 'Introduction', in N. Laurie and L. Bondi (eds), *Working the Spaces of Neoliberalism: Activism, Professionalisation and Incorporation*, Malden, MA: Blackwell Publishing, pp. 1–8.

Bratich, J., Packer, J. and McCarthy, C. (2003), 'Introduction', in J. Bratich, J. Packer and C. McCarthy (eds), *Foucault, Cultural Studies and Governmentality*, New York: SUNY Press, pp. 1–16.

Briggs, C.L. (1996), 'The Politics of Discursive Authority in Research on the "Invention of Tradition"', *Cultural Anthropology*, 11: 435–46.

Brosius, J.P. (1997), 'Endangered Forest, Endangered People: Environmentalist Representations of Indigenous Knowledge', *Human Ecology*, 25: 47–69.

Brosius, J.P., Tsing, A. and Zerner, C. (1998), 'Representing Communities: Histories and Politics of Community-based Resource Management', *Society and Natural Resources*, 11(20): 157–68.

Brosius, J. P., Tsing, A. and Zerner, C. (2005), 'Introduction: Raising Questions about Communities and Conservation', in J.P. Brosius, A.L. Tsing and C. Zerner (eds), *Communities and Conservation: Histories and Politics of Community-Based Natural Resource Management*, Walnut Creek, CA: Alta Mira Press, pp. 1–34.

Brown, M. (2005), 'Heritage Trouble: Recent Work on the Protection of Intangible Cultural Property', *International Journal of Cultural Property*, 12: 40–61.

Clarke, J. (2008), 'Living with/in and without neoliberalism', *Focaal – European Journal of Anthropology*, 51: 135–47.

Collier, J., Maurer, B. and Suarez-Navaz, L. (2001), 'Sanctioned Identities: Legal Constructions of Modern Personhood', *Identities*, 2: 1–27.

Comaroff, J. L. and Comaroff J. (2009), *Ethnicity Inc*, Chicago: University of Chicago Press.

Coombe, R. (2005), 'Protecting Traditional Environmental Knowledge and New Social Movements in the Americas: Intellectual Property, Human Right or Claims to an Alternative Form of Sustainable Development?' *Florida Journal of International Law*, 17: 115–36.

Coombe, R. (2007a), 'The Work of Rights in the Space of Neoliberal Governmentality's Limits', *Anthropologica*, 49(2): 284–9.

Coombe, R. (2007b), 'Legal Claims to Culture in and against the Market: Neoliberalism and the Global Proliferation of Meaningful Difference', in E. Darian-Smith (ed.), *Ethnography and Law*, Aldershott: Ashgate Publishing, pp. 95–115.

Coombe, R. (2009a), 'First Nations' Intangible Cultural Heritage Concerns: Prospects for Protection of Traditional Knowledge and Traditional Cultural Expressions in International Law', in C. Bell and R. Paterson (eds), *First Nations' Cultural Heritage: Rights and Reconciliation*, Vancouver: University of British Columbia Press, pp. 313–62.

Coombe, R. (2009b), 'The Expanding Purview of Cultural Properties and their Politics', *Annual Review of Law and Social Sciences*, 5: 493–512.

Coombe, R. (2010), 'Cultural Agencies: The "Construction" of Community Subjects and their Traditions', in M. Biagioli, P. Jaszi, and M. Woodmansee (eds), *The Making and Unmaking of Intellectual Property*, Chicago: University of Chicago Press (forthcoming).

Coombe, R., Schnoor, S. and Ahmed, M. (2007), 'Bearing Cultural Distinction: Informational Capital and New Expectations for Intellectual Property', *University of California Davis Law Review*, 40: 891–917.

Creed, G. (2006a), 'Reconsidering Community', in G. Creed (ed.), *The Seductions of Community: Emancipations, Oppressions, Quandaries*, Santa Fe: School of American Research, pp. 3–22.

Creed, G. (ed.) (2006b), *The Seductions of Community: Emancipations, Oppressions, Quandaries*, Santa Fe: School of American Research.

Doane, M. (2007), 'The Political Economy of the Ecological Native', *American Anthropologist*, 109(3): 452–62.

Escobar, A. (1998), 'Whose Knowledge, Whose Nature? Biodiversity Conservation and the Political Ecology of Social Movements', *Journal of Political Ecology*, 5: 53–82.

Escobar, A. (2008), *Territories of Difference: Place, Movements, Life, Redes*, Durham, NC: Duke University Press.

Eudaily, S. (2005), *The Present Politics of the Past: Indigenous Legal Activism and Resistance to Neoliberal Governmentality*, New York and London: Routledge.

Florez, M. (ed.) (1998), 'Biological and Cultural Diversity: Challenges and Proposals from Latin America,' special issue of *Beyond Law: New Work on Law and Social Change from Latin America*, 6(18 and 19): 1–219.

Geertz, C. (2000) [1983], *Local Knowledge: Further Essays in Interpretive Anthropology*, New York: Basic Books.

Goodale, M. (2006), 'Reclaiming Modernity, Indigenous Cosmopolitanism and the Coming of the Second Revolution in Bolivia', *American Ethnologist*, 33(4): 634–49.

Gow, D. (2008), *Countering Development: Indigenous Modernity and the Moral Imagination*, Durham, NC: Duke University Press.

Greene, S. (2004), 'Indigenous People Incorporated? Culture as Politics, Culture as Property in Pharmaceutical Bioprospecting', *Current Anthropology*, 45: 211–37.

Greenhouse, C. (2010), 'Introduction', in C. Greenhouse (ed.), *Ethnographies of Neoliberalism*, Philadelphia: University of Pennsylvania Press, pp. 1–12.

Gustafson, B. (2009), *New Languages of the State: Indigenous Resurgence and the Politics of Knowledge in Bolivia*, Durham: Duke University Press.

Hale, C.R. (2006), 'Activist Research v. Cultural Critique: Indigenous Land Rights and the Contradictions of Politically Engaged Anthropology', *Cultural Anthropology*, 21: 96–120.

Hayden, C. (2003a), *When Nature Goes Public: The Making and Un-making of Bioprospecting in Mexico*, Princeton: Princeton University Press.

Hayden, C. (2003b), 'From Market to Market: Bioprospecting's Idioms of Inclusion', *American Ethnologist*, 30: 359–71.

Hirsch, S. and Lazarus-Black, M. (eds) (1994), *Contested States: Law, Hegemony and Resistance*, New York: Routledge.

Hvalkof, S. (2006), 'Progress of the Victims: Political Ecology in the Peruvian Amazon', in A. Biersack and J.B. Greenberg (eds), *Reimagining Political Ecology*, Durham: Duke University Press, pp. 195–232.

Inda, J. (2005), 'Analytics of the Modern: An Introduction', in J.X. Inda (ed.), *Anthropologies of Modernity: Foucault, Governmentality, and Life Politics*, Malden: Blackwell Publishing, pp. 1–20.

Kingfisher, C. and Maskovsky, J. (2008), 'Introduction: The Limits of Neoliberalism', *Critique of Anthropology*, 28(2): 115–26.

Laurie, N., Andolina, R. and Radcliffe, S. (2005), 'Ethnodevelopment: Social Movements, Creating Experts, and Professionalising Indigenous Knowledge in Ecuador', *Antipode*, 37(3): 470–96.

Lemke, T. (2002), 'Foucault, Governmentality, Critique', *Rethinking Marxism*, 14(3): 49–64.

Li, T. M. (1996), 'Images of Community: Discourse and Strategy in Property Relations', *Development and Change*, 27: 501–27.

Li, T.M. (2000), 'Articulating Indigenous Identity in Indonesia: Resource Politics and the Tribal Slot', *Comparative Studies in Society and History*, 42: 149–79.

Li, T.M. (2005), 'Engaging Simplifications', in J.P. Brosius, A. Tsing and C. Zerner (eds), *Communities and Conservation*, Walnut Creek, CA: Altamira Press, pp. 427–58.

Li, T.M. (2007), *The Will to Improve: Governmentality, Development and the Practice of Politics*, Durham: Duke University Press.

McCarthy, J. and Prudhon, W.S. (2004), 'Neoliberal Nature and the Nature of Neoliberalism', *Geoforum*, 35: 275–83.

Mertz, E. (1994), 'A New Social Constructionism for Sociolegal Studies', *Law and Society Review*, 28: 1243–65.

Nasaday, P. (2003), '"Property" and Aboriginal Land Claims in the Canadian Subarctic: Some Theoretical Considerations', *American Anthropologist*, 104(1): 247–61.

Ong, A. (2006), *Neoliberalism as Exception: Mutations in Citizenship*, Durham: Duke University Press.

Perreault, T. (2003), 'Changing Places: Transnational Networks, Ethnic Politics, and Community Development in the Ecuadorian Amazon', *Political Geography*, 22: 61–88.

Perreault, T. and Martin, P. (2005), 'Geographies of Neoliberalism in Latin America', *Environment and Planning A*, 37: 191–201.

Radcliffe, S. (2005), 'Neoliberalism as We Know It, but not in Conditions of its Own Choosing', *Environment and Planning A*, 37: 323–9.

Radcliffe, S. and Laurie, N. (2006a), 'Culture and Development: Taking Culture Seriously in Development for Andean Indigenous People', *Environment and Planning D: Society and Space*, 24(2): 1–18.

Radcliffe, S. and Laurie, N. (2006b), 'Indigenous Groups, Culturally Appropriate Development and the Socio-Spatial Fix of Andean Development', in S. Radcliffe (ed.), *Culture and Development in a Globalizing World: Geographies, Actors, and Paradigms*, London and New York: Routledge, pp. 83–106.

Radcliffe, S., Laurie, N. and Andolina, R. (2002), 'Indigenous People and Political Transnationalism: Globalization from Below Meets Globalization from Above?' available at http://www.transcomm.ox.ac.uk/working%20 papers/WPTC-02-05%20Radcliffe

Rappaport, J. (2005), *Intercultural Utopias: Public Intellectuals, Cultural Experimentation, and Ethnic Pluralism in Columbia*, Durham: Duke University Press.

Reardon, J. (2005), *Racing to the Finish: Identity and Governance in an Age of Genomics*, Princeton: Princeton University Press.

Rhoades, R. (2006), 'Linking Sustainability Science, Community, and Culture', in R.E. Rhoades (ed.), *Development with Identity: Community, Culture and Sustainability in the Andes*, Wallingford, UK: CABI Publishing, pp. 1–16.

Rose, N. (1999), *Powers of Freedom*, Cambridge: Cambridge University Press.

Rosenthal, J. (2006), 'Politics, Culture and Governance in the Development of Prior Informed Consent in Indigenous Communities', *Current Anthropology*, 47: 119–42.

Santos, B. (2002), *Toward a New Legal Common Sense*, 2nd edn, London: Reed Elsevier.

Santos, B. and Rodriguez-Garavito, C. (2005), 'Law, Politics and the Subaltern in Counter-hegemonic Globalization', in B. Santos and C. Rodriguez-Garavito (eds), *Law and Globalization from Below*, Cambridge: Cambridge University Press, pp. 1–26.

Sertje, M. (2003), 'Malocas and Barracones: Tradition, Biodiversity and Participation in the Colombian Amazon', *International Social Science Journal*, 174: 561–71.

Stewart-Harawira, M. (2005), *The New Imperial Order: Indigenous Responses to Globalization*, London: Zed Books.

Tsing, A. (1999), 'Becoming a Tribal Elder and Other Green Development Fantasies', in T. Li (ed.), *Transforming the Indonesian Uplands: Marginality, Power and Production*, London: Harwood, pp. 159–202.

Tsing, A. (2005), *Friction: An Ethnography of Global Connection*, Princeton: Princeton University Press.

Ulloa, A. (2005), *The Ecological Native: Indigenous Peoples' Movements and Eco-Governmentality in Colombia*, New York and London: Routledge.

Valdivia, G. (2005), 'On Indigeneity, Change and Representation in the Northeastern Ecuadorian Amazon', *Environment and Planning A*, 37: 285–303.

Vandergeest, P. (2008), 'New Concepts, New Natures?' in J. Nevins and N.L. Peluso (eds), *Taking Southeast Asia to Market*, Ithaca: Cornell University Press, pp. 206–24.

Veber, H. (1998), 'The Salt of the Montana: Interpreting Indigenous Activism in the Rain Forest', *Cultural Anthropology*, 13: 382–413.

Verderey, K. and Humphrey, C. (eds) (2004), *Property in Question: Value Transformations in the Global Economy*, Oxford: Berg.

Wade, P. (1997), *Race and Ethnicity in Latin America*, London: Pluto Press.

Weismantel, M. (2006), 'Ayllu: Real and Imagined Communities in the Andes', in G. Creed (ed.), *The Seductions of Community: Emancipations, Oppressions, Quandaries*, Santa Fe, NM: School of American Research, pp. 77–100.

Wilshusen, P. (2003), 'Territory, Nature and Culture: Negotiating the Boundaries of Biodiversity Conservation in the Colombian Pacific Coast Region', in S. Brechin, P. Wilshusen, C. Fortwangler and P. West (eds), *Contested Nature: Promoting International Biodiversity with Social Justice*, Albany: SUNY Press, pp. 73–88.

Part Two
Materiality and Immateriality

–7–

Cultural Appropriation

The Honourable Sir Edward Taihakurei Durie KNZM

Abstract

This chapter examines the cultural dimensions of property rights in New Zealand. It considers how competing perceptions of property have contributed to conflict from the beginning of contact between Maori and Pakeha. Introducing the different legal regimes, it uses examples to stimulate thoughts on a theory for customary property law and management.

Introduction

This chapter considers the cultural dimensions of property rights in the context of Maori and Pakeha relationships. 'Maori' are native New Zealanders, a term usually contrasted with 'Pakeha' or non-native New Zealanders especially of English descent. The opinions are based on personal experience dating from 1974 as a Maori Land Court judge, later as chief judge of that Court and chairman of the Waitangi Tribunal, and thereafter as a High Court judge and a commissioner of the New Zealand Law Commission. The relevance of the Maori Land Court is that it has overseen the administration of Maori land from its establishment in 1862 to convert customary tribal tenure to individual ownership. The Waitangi Tribunal came much later in 1975, after protestations over the treatment of Maori people past and present. It was to hear Maori claims that government laws and policies were or are inconsistent with the promises to Maori in the Treaty of Waitangi, a treaty proposed by the British to secure British sovereignty. On proven claims the Tribunal recommends appropriate action to government to provide relief and to prevent further prejudice in future. The High Court is a superior court in the legal system and the Law Commission is a statutory body promoting the review and reform of New Zealand law after considering, amongst other things, the Maori world-view.

Accordingly while the chapter is based on observation rather than research, the observations relate to an experience in legal institutions each with a role in managing cultural difference. Those observations are supported in turn by an upbringing that sharpened the recognition of cultural disparities. As a youngster I had regular access to my *marae* or tribal meeting place with its distinctive *whare runanga* (meeting and sleeping house), *kauta* (cookhouse) and *wharekai* (dining hall). It was next to the family homestead and was the focal point for my *hapu* (tribe) of Tahuriwakanui which is of the Ngati Kauwhata *iwi* (tribal group) of the district of Manawatu.

Beyond the *marae*, however, Pakeha predominated in what was a prosperous farming district. The *hapu* had been displaced by a massive influx of settlers from the 1870s, and the original bush and swamp had long been converted to pasture. My education in Maori *tikanga* or law was therefore less than that available to others of predominantly Maori districts.

On the other hand my grandfather was one of a number of Maori who had maintained a role in tribal leadership. He also had a national role in forming and administering official policy in relation to Maori land. The early exposure to both Maori policy and the dominant Pakeha society introduced me to different perspectives at an early age. The cultural differences, of which most Pakeha were ignorant given their preponderant numbers, regularly confounded the popular and earnest expressions of goodwill and there was rarely a true meeting of minds. For example, Maori would frequently resist proposals that local authorities (Councils) genuinely considered of benefit to Maori, because Maori could see the implicit racism or paternalism. The Council's condemning of scores of small *whare* (single room houses) around the several rural *marae* in the early 1950s, accompanied by the introduction of state rental homes in town for Maori and generous loan and later family benefit arrangements for new home building in town, illustrates as well the official aversion to the Maori rural and communal living.

This compounded the urban migration to which the sudden rise in crime and truancy has been attributed. World economics is usually blamed for this international phenomenon, but there were other factors at play in New Zealand. This is a small country and I suspect the main movement initially was to local towns rather than distant cities. Frequently, as in Manawatu, it was not difficult to get to work from rural areas when Maori worked mainly in the factories of secondary industries on the outskirts of town, on arterial roads and railways, or in agricultural contracting. In many cases these people shifted as a result of the antipathy of town planning to rural *papakainga* or Maori settlements.

Cultural contrasts were also plain from moving from an all-Maori boarding school to a nearly all-Pakeha university hostel. At university the law curriculum was mono-cultural, New Zealand history was not taught, and a small academic clique faced opposition in seeking to introduce Maori studies. The ignorance of Maori land losses through questionable land purchases and confiscations to punish so-called rebels (to which I will refer again) were particularly distressing for Maori students. They had grown up knowing of these things and were witness to the anguish and alienation of their elders. Several of those students bore heavy burdens of resentment as a result and would shape their careers to the promotion of change.

Maori land law had a special interest for me because during the 1960s the government proposed to further integrate Maori land ownership with the general law. This was the major Maori issue of the time. My family was affected because amongst other things it introduced death duties for the large landholders for the first time without the time given to Pakeha to engage in estate planning. While still a student I was charged with arguing the issue before the Maori Affairs Select Committee of Parliament. However, the topic had more than a parochial interest for me. Studies of law and society and of economic history gave me cause to reflect on the role of property law in shaping the cultural and economic future of peoples, throwing into relief the threat posed to Maori culture from the ongoing subversion of customary land law. Effectively Maori land had become an illusory asset. Indeed I think it is still an illusory asset today. For notwithstanding that Maori trusts and incorporations now contribute substantially to the national economy, there is no significant benefit to the Maori communities as dividends are dissipated in increasingly small shares to people who left the community long ago.

Another 1960s concern was the absence of Maori from senior positions in the national and district offices of what was then the Department of Maori Affairs. This department strongly influenced the formation of Maori land policy and had a direct role in Maori land administration. There were also no Maori judges on the Maori Land Court. When I was appointed as a judge of that Court after a period in private legal practice, I was the first Maori to hold such office (and at age thirty-four, by far the youngest). It seemed tragic to me that although many Pakeha judges and officials had worked conscientiously alongside Maori they could never do for Maori as Maori could do for themselves had they been given a chance. I for one had grown up in a family with a proven record in land management, but who remained beholden to the Department and the Court. It seemed obvious that transient Pakeha officials, no matter how well intentioned, were no match for those whose commitment to land and people was hereditary, bound not by the principles of public administration but by the bonds of consanguinity. There was simply a chasm between the values of the bureaucracy and English law and the community values of the ancestral legal order on which the Maori leaders of that time still relied.

This chapter will consider how competing perceptions of property have contributed to conflict from the beginning of contact between Maori and Pakeha. It will then introduce the different legal regimes, using examples to stimulate thoughts on a theory for customary property law and management. I begin, however, with the current political scene and the prospects for reform.

Political Context

Following the National Elections of November 2008 Mr Key, the leader of the successful National Party, sought a relationship agreement with the recently constituted Maori Party. It was unusual that a new party with a narrow focus (it had formed only in 2004 and primarily to represent Maori interests) should have had the early success that it had. In its second election it had secured five of the seven parliamentary seats reserved for Maori, notwithstanding the previous domination of those seats for most of the previous century by the Labour Party, a major party in New Zealand politics.

While the agreement had long-term prospects for the National Party, the desire for dialogue could be seen as presaging a genuine interest in Maori perspectives, especially since Mr Key did not need the support of the Maori Party to form a government at the time. Citing his party's manifesto, Mr Key stressed his belief that his party 'shares many values with Maori including especially the recognition of property rights'.

That was a significant statement given that both parties were aware of the different views between Maori and Pakeha over what could be held as a private property right. Behind the search for a common policy were Maori concerns about the previous government's highly contentious Foreshore and Seabed Act 2004 by which, in the Maori view, their customary property rights had been denied. With the commercialization of inshore seas for aquaculture, and the threat to beach access through exclusive seafront developments and sales to foreigners, Maori claimed an interest in the foreshore and seabed as unalienated customary lands. In the popular perception of the general law, those same areas were presumptively government land held for the public benefit. The issue of who owned the foreshore and seabed was taken to the Maori Land Court, but a preliminary question of whether the Maori customary interests had in fact been extinguished had first to be determined in the general courts.

In the general courts the Court of Appeal determined that the operation of law had not extinguished such interests as Maori might have. This led the government of the day to enact the Foreshore and Seabed legislation to constrain the rights of Maori to proceed through the courts. Instead all would be resolved through negotiations where government would maintain a controlling hand.

The government's response led to a substantial Maori protest march, the resignation of a Maori Minister from the Labour Government and her formation of the independent Maori Party. In the light of that background Mr Key was asserting that his party, like the Maori Party, is passionate about respecting property rights. He inferred that the principle of the determination of property rights is quintessentially a judicial matter, one founded on rights rather than political convenience. Accordingly in the subsequent relationship agreement of

16 November 2008, there was express provision for a review of the previous government's Foreshore and Seabed Act 2004. In the following year I was appointed to chair the review panel.

However, the real issue was not about property rights as ordinarily understood in New Zealand law (bearing in mind that New Zealand law derives from and substantially replicates English land law). The substantive issue was about the different cultural perceptions of what property rights might be. This was reflected in the relationship agreement (and also in the review panel's terms of reference) in that the review was to consider not the ownership in terms of standard New Zealand law, but whether the Act 'adequately maintains and enhances *mana whenua*'. '*Mana whenua*' or tribal authority over customary territory, whether land or water, invokes customary land management responsibilities to ensure that the resource, including the associated plant and wildlife, is protected for future generations. '*Mana whenua*' then, is different from 'ownership', notwithstanding that generally Maori land rights have been equated with rights of 'ownership' as understood in ordinary New Zealand law.

That leads back to the main point. While both of New Zealand's founding cultures are passionate about property rights and expound the need to respect them, they differ on what those rights are. The issues then are whether the current political climate presents a fresh opportunity to close the gap in cultural comprehension, and whether, to make the best of any such opportunity, the debate should have the benefit of dispassionate anthropological advice.

I come then to summarize the history of clashing cultural conceptions of property rights and to consider the depth of feeling that this history has engendered.

The History of Culture Clash

I will illustrate the cultural clashes over property rights in four time slots, from 1820–60, 1860–1960, 1960–2000 and from the year 2000. I will focus on how those clashes inform the distinctive ideologies on land appropriation and management.

1820–60

The popular view is that Maori sold the greater part of New Zealand between 1820 and 1860. Yet subsequent Maori conduct suggests that Maori understood the transactions quite differently from sales. Records also indicate that Maori had a distinct and complex view of these transactions. Although the colonial state was not formed until 1840, 1820 is relevant since government provided retrospectively for transactions made by speculators or residents who arrived from and after that time. However, the record suggests that Maori may have viewed these transactions like licences to occupy, conditional on ongoing benefits passing to the associated *hapu*. Tribes had been known to allocate space to persons outside of the tribe in the past as a result of inter-tribal marriages in many cases, but also out of competitive urges to strengthen the tribe. Pakeha, with their access to new foods, goods and technology, became highly valued as a result. But in the Maori way the underlying ancestral ownership remained with the tribe. In Maori traditions people came from the earth mother, and each child was born of the earth which was carried forward in the woman's womb. Thus '*whenua*', meaning 'land', means also the 'placenta', conceptualizing of a filial relationship between the people of a place and their land. The local tribe was called the '*tangata whenua*' or the people born of the land where they lived.

The Maori world-view could not therefore treat land as a tradable commodity. The present issue, however, which is relevant to the integrity of many land transactions, concerns the point at which Maori comprehended and accepted a trade in land on Pakeha terms. The facts relied upon to support a presumption of early change are not as probative as first appears. For example, the survey and fencing of the affected land need not have established a sale in the minds of the affected Maori when it could equally prescribe the area of occupation rights. Nor is survey and fencing evidence of the assumption of exclusive occupation rights when it was necessary to fence in the stock that Pakeha introduced. For the lack of significant animals before the Pakeha came, Maori had no customary need to fence their gardens and the introduction of animal husbandry was not seen as imposing an obligation on Maori to fence the animals out, but an obligation on the Pakeha to fence their animals in.

There are also settler reports of Maori pillaging homes (according to custom in retaliation for a wrong) when those whom they had placed on the land moved away and when strangers, who were in fact purchasers, took their place. Maori 'licences to occupy' were meant to be personal to the occupants with a direct nexus between the occupier and the tribe holding the ancestral rights in the district. Similarly Maori demanded further payments from purchasers which presumably would establish the necessary connection between the newcomer and those with the ancestral rights; or Maori asserted their interest by occupying parts of the subject land or by helping themselves to stock and crops. There are also records of settler complaints of overbearing Maori conduct as though Maori were presuming to own the settlers as well. From the Maori view, however, the settlers were subject to tribal law and authority.

The traditional economic order was based on gift exchange, a form of transacting known to many tribal societies in different forms. Its extensive use amongst Maori has been thoroughly explored by the late Professor Raymond Firth in his pioneering works on Maori economics. Elements of gift exchange survive today in the monetary gifts or koha at inter-tribal gatherings and in the generous feeding of guests, but it was formerly central to everyday survival.

The important aspects of gift exchange for present purposes are, first, that the gifts imposed powerful obligations on receivers to respect and to respond generously to the donors in the future and, secondly, that at heart was the cementing of ongoing relationships between peoples. The ethic has continued. I was frequently acquainted as a judge with accounts of 'meetings of assembled owners', the statutory process by which the many owners in Maori lands could respond to proposals for the use of their land. Often the owners rejected the best offers, in immediate commercial terms, favouring other offers that presaged a continuing relationship, like joint working arrangements for local Maori work groups and management training for those achieving educational grades.

Gift exchange, the incorporation of fresh blood into the tribe, the spiritual connections of land and people and the presumption that relationships would be determined by tribal law, infer either that Maori comprehended the 'sales' as other than 'sales', or that they would not have accepted the settler view of the transactions until it was patent that the Maori world had been displaced. Acceptance of that would presumably have been grudging, given only after the settlers flooded the land in greater numbers than Maori could have foreseen, or after the major wars of the 1860s and 1870s had ended with defeat, land confiscation, treason and murder trials, hanging and imprisonments. The real issue then is not about the capacity to comprehend but the necessity to concede.

From 1840 to 1860, with some short exceptions, government maintained the pre-emptive right to purchase Maori land. Government, aware of the earlier Maori challenge to the preceding purchase claims, wrote into many of the purchase deeds that Maori had wept over the land and now had left it forever. But did Maori truly pack their bags and head down the road after a tearful farewell to the land? I doubt it. I am not aware of eyewitness accounts for such scenes. Many of the government purchase deeds are for sales so large that a province could be covered by a small number of them, and so extensive as to involve a host of *hapu*, not a small group of wailers. I think the greater evidence is that Maori simply stayed on in their homes on lands that were eventually cut out for them as reserves.

The government's pre-emptive right of purchase was written into the Treaty of Waitangi earlier mentioned. It was a critical part of government policy that the on-sale of land would fund colonization and development costs. It had also been decided that Britain would not annexe New Zealand without the consent of the Maori chiefs, a strategy that would give moral force to Britain's later claim to exclusive sovereignty. The consent document was the Treaty of Waitangi. In terms of the text in English Maori ceded sovereignty in return for guarantees that their property would be secured to them for so long as they wished. In addition there was a Maori text for the Maori signatories – but it was not a direct translation of the English. One reason was the difficulty of conveying English law concepts like 'sovereignty' and 'sales' to a people whose beliefs could not countenance either central control or land alienation.

The result was that in terms of the Maori text Maori ceded a right of national governance (or '*kawanatanga*', a transliteration coined for the purpose), but specifically retained their traditional authority to manage their own lands, homes and people. That could only have strengthened their argument that their land dealings should be governed by their own law. From the 1870s governments dismissed the Treaty as having no legal significance, but it was consistently significant for Maori. From the 1970s as a result of continuing Maori protests and the initiative of an outstanding Maori politician, government has acceded to its recognition for prescribed purposes. Today the Treaty has considerable influence in the development and administration of national policy and many attribute the 'Waitangi process' as initiating much closer understandings between Maori and Pakeha.

One has also to consider the resilience of cultural norms. New Zealand social history is marked by Pakeha predictions that Maori would die out and Maori strategies to maintain their identity and culture. The strength of those movements would provide the base for a cultural renaissance that probably peaked in the 1990s. Accordingly, although Maori custom has changed outwardly, inwardly it is noteworthy for its adherence to the underlying ancestral values.

So, for example, in 1967 government enacted legislation to hasten the final assimilation of Maori land and general land tenures. Maori protested through land occupations culminating in a nationwide land march that is now seen as a defining moment in New Zealand history. There followed an amending Act of 1974 to strengthen the place of Maori values in the law affecting Maori land and a further consolidating and amending Act to the same end in 1993.

Further, while governments never acceded to the Maori interpretation of the land transactions, Maori never conceded the reality of their ancestral associations with areas that have long passed to Pakeha hands. Eventually, in the 1970s, the New Zealand Maori Council secured a provision in resource management laws compelling planners and developers to have particular regard to the relationship of the Maori people with their ancestral lands. It was symptomatic of the period that even then it took judges and planners many years to develop any real appreciation of how this law should be applied.

Later the distinction between cultural and formal ownership would be advanced in the context of artefacts then owned by New Zealand collectors and museums, so that when Maori artefacts were proposed for exhibition in the United States in the 1980s (the 'Te Maori exhibition'), *hapu* and *iwi* secured the cultural right to be actively involved on all matters relating to their dispatch and display. As a result the exhibition was an outstanding success. Maori brought their culture to the world in a way that government could not.

The survival of the Maori ethic at home in the 1980s can also be illustrated by reference to a land transaction between Maori following the Tarawera volcanic eruption of 1886. The lands of a particular tribe of the Rotorua district had been so affected by ash that the tribe was forced to leave. They moved to lands allocated to them by a tribe of the Hauraki district. The Maori Land Court, which from 1865 was determining the ownership of such land as then remained in Maori hands, came to award title of the Hauraki land to the individual members of the Rotorua tribe on the basis of their occupation. Following the practice of the Maori Land Court the land was vested in those persons as the absolute owners of an indefeasible state title.

Eventually the Rotorua people returned to their own district and, notwithstanding the land's high value, applied to the Maori Land Court in the 1980s to have the land returned to the Hauraki people. As the Rotorua people were no longer contributing to the Hauraki district or living on the land, it was seen to be consonant with custom that the title should be restored to the people with the ancestral connection.

1860–1960

The large numbers of Pakeha who had taken up lands allegedly purchased lay behind the outbreak of war in 1860. Following on from the wars in North Auckland and Wellington, it was the third war between Maori and imperial troops, but this one was explicitly connected to the failure of Pakeha to comprehend or accept Maori views on land rights. Also, where the previous fighting had been local, this war would affect the whole country and would engender a Maori distrust of Pakeha that continued well into the 1960s.

The settlement of Taranaki lands around New Plymouth had already caused much local fighting, but settlers were pouring in and there was no realistic prospect that the Maori view of those transactions would be acknowledged. The next question was whether government could pick and choose the Maori to deal with on any further transactions and whether it was right to treat with a few sellers without the approval of the leading tribal figures.

In Taranaki in 1860 the question came to a head when the Governor sought to acquire yet more land at nearby Waitara. When the paramount leader, Wiremu Kingi, opposed the further alienation of land, the governor dealt with a lesser chief at Waitara in respect of that person's particular interest. It was then that the supporters of Wiremu Kingi took to arms. A number of other leading *rangatira* or chiefs in other parts of the country, seeing that they could be similarly affected, came out in support and the war rapidly assumed a national character.

The war spread throughout the North Island and did not finally end until twenty-one years later with the invasion of Parihaka on the western slopes of

Mount Taranaki. The people of Parihaka sought not only to hold on to the few lands left for them, but to maintain an independent political authority for the district without outside interference. It should be noted here that Maori have never had the semi-independent reservations akin to those of native North Americans. The military invasion of Parihaka, and the trial and incarceration of its leaders for treason, highlighted a further misunderstanding about land rights. In the English system land titles confer maximum freedom of use to landowners, subject only to specific statutory provisions in the national interest. In the Maori system, the right to use the resources of a district, be they land or water, is so burdened by social obligations to the *hapu* and by ancestral values about the protection of resources, that individual rights cannot be severed from the political authority of the *hapu*, or the *iwi* in some cases, to maintain overall control.

It is not just the twenty-one-year duration of the war that tells of the passion about land rights and customary autonomy. At the height of the war there were 18,000 imperial troops in addition to the colonial militia. That is small compared with, say, the 146,000 American combat troops in Iraq at 2008, but it was large for its day compared to other countries where British forces were fighting. The historian Jamie Belich has reckoned that in terms of the comparable native populations, the 18,000 Imperial troops in New Zealand would have equated with 50 million troops in India.

The lessons of the war are imperfectly remembered, however, for government continues to deal with tribes in the same way as that which led to the wars. Effectively the war began in 1860 because government handpicked the persons they chose to deal with and rejected the people's choice. Currently under what is seen as a process for the settlement of the Treaty of Waitangi claims, government is negotiating with tribes to provide a measure of compensation for the tribe's historic losses, often requiring the tribes to aggregate for that purpose so that the process can be managed at a reasonable economic scale. But with whom does the government negotiate given that there has never been a comprehensive scheme for the establishment and recognition of tribal authorities? The necessary process is indicated in the United Nations Declaration on the Rights of Indigenous Peoples (UNDRIP) of 2007, which refers to the right of such peoples to determine the structures of their institutions in accordance with their own procedures (article 33.2) and, in a comparable context, the duty of states to treat with indigenous peoples through such institutions (article 32.2). In fact government treats with such members of the tribe as government considers appropriate before the aggregated *hapu* have established their own structure, raising the prospect, and giving rise to allegations, of picking and choosing to the government's own advantage.

1960–2000

The period from 1960 may be summed up in a work by New Zealand anthropologist Dame Joan Metge, who describes Maori and Pakeha as 'talking past each other'. By 1960 Maori owned about ten per cent of their original lands, practically all in individual ownership by then and so fragmented through successions that cases of more than a hundred of owners in one title were now common, almost entirely because property ownership had come to be defined in Pakeha terms.

Again from the outset of the period it appeared that little had been learnt from the previous cultural clash. In 1960 the government produced a report on Maori land (the Hunn report), proposing amongst other things compulsory acquisition of the small fragmented shares. The report's rationale was that 'everybody's land is nobody's land'. It mattered not that each land share was indicative of identity, or of a *turangawaewae* or 'place to stand' in Maori thinking – a significant view given the vast loss of land and the extensive urban migration that followed from the early 1950s.

Once more there were conflicting views on land rights. Another form of cultural warfare followed. As already mentioned it was marked by unlawful occupations and demonstrations, including the 1975 'Maori Land March' from the far north of the North Island to Parliament at the island's southern tip. There were all the anticipated consequences of police intervention and arrests.

However, the protests were effective and led to significant changes in legislation. Restrictions were imposed on the alienation of Maori land. Further in 1975 the Treaty of Waitangi was written into statute law for the first time and the Waitangi Tribunal was established to inquire and report on claimed breaches. That led later to settlements in recognition of past losses, settlements that presaged the marshalling of assets, this time in tribal control.

Treaty settlements, which I introduced earlier, are now invariably with district *iwi* with regard to their land losses. The first, however, was a 1992 national settlement in respect of fisheries. Interestingly, this settlement used a newly created property right in the form of fish quota under the Quota Management System to compensate for the loss of fishing rights guaranteed under the Treaty of Waitangi. The settlement gave Maori a substantial stake in the national fishing industry. Previously, neither Maori nor English law had conceived of a property in fish before the fish had been caught.

However, despite this activity government still seemed no wiser about the fundamental difference between Maori and Pakeha property rights. For change in that respect one had to await the new millennium.

From 2000

The need to think twice about the Maori perception of property rights arose after a Court of Appeal decision on rights to the foreshore and seabed in 2003. The foreshore and seabed claim, already introduced in this chapter, was nothing new. Long before government came, Maori asserted claims to water, harbours, rivers, lakes, foreshores, estuaries, seabeds, reefs, rocks (including those submerged at low tide) and mudflats. Prior to 1840 Maori had fought to control such resources and there was no question in Maori law that they could be the subject of proprietary rights. The first whalers found they had to pay to take on fresh water or to use harbours. Use rights of such resources had also been intricately allocated.

While the private ownership of harbours, rivers and related resources was not provided for in the general New Zealand law, tribal ownership with private use rights was normal in Maori law and Maori claims to such areas were before the Maori Land Court from the 1870s and before the general courts by the 1920s. The claims were argued at all court levels and some lasted many years as a result. The best known foreshore case, in relation to a vast tract known as the Ninety Mile Beach, ran six years from 1957 to 1963. Court proceedings in respect of the country's second longest river, the Whanganui river, lasted over twenty years from 1938 to 1958.

The claims to water-related natural resources are unsurprising. Although land would become increasingly important, Maori traditionally thought in terms of resources and, given the comparative dearth of animal life and plantation crops, fresh and salt water had provided the main resources for the harvesting of food – fish and water fowl. It is telling that the first claims heard by the Waitangi Tribunal related to these resources, not to the land. They concerned the two main harbours of New Zealand's largest city, Waitemata and Manukau, the reefs off the Taranaki coast and Kaituna river.

However, until the Court of Appeal case of 2003 the public had no need for concern. The courts had not generally conceded to a Maori conception of property rights in terms of resource use. The position appeared to change with the 2003 decision, even though the court's requirements for proving a continuing foreshore right were extremely limiting. This leads back to where this discussion began: the Foreshore and Seabed Act 2004, the Maori protest, the formation of the Maori Party, the 2008 election and the government decision to work co-operatively with the Maori Party and to revisit the property issues involved.

The Differences in the Property Regimes

I do not propose to labour the distinctive attitude of tribal peoples to land. The broad concepts are common to indigenous peoples in many places and should be well known. The focus here is on particular aspects that demonstrate different values. The customary Maori interest in land is in belonging not owning. The fact that my father farmed the land now in my name, his mother before him and her mother before her, and that the antecedents on our *whakapapa* (family tree) can be named for the preceding twenty-five generations back to about 1350, tells me who I am and how I belong in the world. I stand on the land and look to the river from the cliff near to where the family home once stood. I look behind me to the *marae* beside the church, to the paddocks tended by generations of the family and beyond to the *urupa* (cemetery) on an adjoining cliff face overlooking the point where Ngati Kauwhata first entered Manawatu. I am then comfortable with my allotted space on earth. 'Property' is farthest from my mind for the experience is spiritual. I have a place in eternity.

The land also defines relationships. The record of who has what in the surrounding blocks supplies the lateral connections in the *whakapapa* and defines how we are all related. It serves to bind us and to internalize a sense of duty to nurture one another. Sitting in my urban room amongst legal texts I think of land rights, but on the land I think of (not of) rights but of duties, duties to the dead, the living and the generations to come.

I think, for example, of my grandfather who on his farm had some forty children pass through his care, so that the income that passed to him from the farm was largely spent on others. I now live away from the part that passed to me and it is farmed within the family, but I collect no rent. The old people did not accept that one could be an absentee owner, taking rent from the land, but not being there to give to the community. Those of the family who use the land on the other hand have contributed for years, rebuilding the family *marae* and so on. It is not the individual right to receive that is important then, but the duty to support the community.

The ethical and spiritual considerations of land ownership apply also to chattels, the implements and ornaments of old. In many families the greenstone passes through the woman's line and is seen to bear the life-force of those who held them before, while implements and weapons pass through the men. These bear the *hau* (breath) of those who once wielded them or who, in fashioning them for a particular use, gave them life. They are not owned, but held for the family generally or for preferred descendants depending on the case.

As in general New Zealand law thoughts can be possessed, as captured in stories, sayings, songs and incantations. Recently in a settlement with the government over its historic losses, another tribe with whom I am connected sought government recognition of its 'ownership' of a particular *haka*, a posture dance that school groups and sports teams throughout New Zealand have become accustomed to performing. Then not just ancient items but modern songs may be seen to belong to a particular community. A documentary was screened recently in which a popular Maori entertainer described the criticism he received for singing the Maori version of a Western pop song that had become the signature song of a tribe to which he did not belong.

First, it should be noted that it is frequently not the composer who is seen to own the work but the composer's tribe. Second, the recognition of this form of property right appears to be consistent with Maori protocols for recognizing individual contributions for the benefit of a wider group. The important thing is to acknowledge the composer and the composer's people, and to respect their gift for the benefit of all the tribes. While different practices will apply in different contexts, the recognition of proprietary interests in compositions seems to have more to do with maintaining the protocols of respecting the various tribal groups than in defining the commercial boundaries of exclusive use rights. The circumstances are always various however. In the Land Court, for example, songs have been sung as an assertion of occupation rights.

This is not to say that there are no exclusive rights. Long-term use maintained to the present is the usual basis for recognizing exclusive rights of resource use within the tribal group. There may be a right to catch a particular type of fish at a particular spot at a particular time of year for example, the foundation for which is simply popular recognition of an ongoing use over a long period, made stronger if the user can point to, say, his father and his father's father as having done the same. We see elements of this today in the Pakeha community as well in the assertion of white-baiting rights at particular river spots. These rights may be seen as exclusive, but in the Maori case the right is invariably conditioned by the duty to contribute to the common good of the tribe as occasion requires. I think that is a significant difference that goes to the heart of Maori communalism and Pakeha capitalism.

Even seating arrangements at the *whare runanga* or tribal meeting house can give rise to a form of proprietary entitlement. I refer to practices distinct from those with the backing of ritual such as the allocation of spaces for the leading tribal speakers or the *kai karanga* on formal occasions, or when visitors claim the right to locate themselves at the foot of the carved wall posts that depict their ancestors. The fact that a particular matriarch has regularly sat at a particular location at the less formal family gatherings, for example, can create an expectation that grows with time that that place is rightfully hers. It seems a small point, but to me it illustrates the dependence of customary proprietary rights on popular acknowledgement of ongoing use and occupation. It needs emphasis because it is not always appreciated how much the Maori Land Court altered custom through its rules of succession, as will later be explained, by creating an uncustomary class of absentee owners in Maori Land titles. It also needs emphasis because even today, in the Treaty settlement process, governments remain concerned to protect the perceived voting rights of persons who are never seen on the home *marae*.

In Maori custom rights grew cold and disappeared if they were not regularly exercised, and their resuscitation depended upon a long-term reoccupation in person.

It seems important then to avoid a fundamentalist view of what constitutes a *hapu* or *iwi*, and to avoid the oversimplification of customary relationships. It is tidy to say that a tribe is composed of the descendants of the eponymous tribal ancestor, but the reality is more subtle. A tribe is characterized by descent, but it is not defined by it. Similarly it must be stressed that property rights are cultural constructs, no matter how trite or obvious that observation is, and that real distortions and grievances are likely to follow if the property rights of one culture are interpreted within an alien property framework. In New Zealand the failure to recognize and uphold that view left the owners of Maori land, as statutorily defined, with an unworkable title system and has so removed the asset base of the tribes as to undermine customary leadership and the customary tribal institutions.

Another feature of custom is that use rights are defined in terms of access to resources rather than as rights to defined parcels of land and, consistent with that, access was not given for all purposes and for all times. For example, one might have the right to fish from a particular spot for mullet when the mullet are running. Someone else may have the right to fish from the same spot for *kahawai* at another time. One may have the right to the berries from a tree and another to take parts of the tree to fashion implements. This contrasts with the English system following land enclosures about 300 years ago, when a single proprietor could have the title to all the resources within a defined land parcel. A further distinction is that the ownership of defined parcels under the English tenure system does not carry with it obligations to support others of the local community (although they may be rated by a local authority). In fact under the customary system there is no direct right to the land at all, but only conditional rights of habitation and specific and prescribed rights of access.

It follows from the foregoing that the determination of property rights should be undertaken by the people of the culture concerned according to their own processes. This is critical. To force one people's culture into another people's law is cultural appropriation. UNDRIP was designed to prevent this. History, and policies and practices that continue to this day, show the real dangers in the appropriation of cultural rights by outside actors. Not only may those from outside the culture be influenced by their own cultural biases in the interpretation and application of the customary law, but they are likely to ask the wrong questions, to subvert the cultural processes by which issues are decided and to remain ignorant of the nuanced way in which decisions are made by the people of the culture concerned.

To illustrate the point I refer to one of the many issues that arose from a statutory direction to the Maori Land Court to determine successions to interests in Maori land 'in accordance with Maori custom'. The question was whether as a matter of custom *whangai* (adopted children) succeeded to their birth parents or their adoptive parents. *Whangai* were common within Maori communities, children being used to strengthen ties between the various branches of the extended family or between generations and because children tended to be seen as the children of the whole extended family and not just of particular parents.

Based upon the minutes of the proceedings and the eventual decisions of the Pakeha judges, the judges appear to have assumed that there were only three options, that *whangai* should succeed to birth parents, their adoptive parents or both. They plainly sought a single rule for every situation, on this issue as on a host of others. It seems obvious, however, on this issue as in many others, that there is no single rule. Indeed, to ask for the rule is to ask the wrong question. One must search rather for what is *tika* or right for the particular case. Did the *whangai* live mainly with birth parents or the adoptive parents? Was this a case where the children just happened to live with the adoptive parents for convenience or was there a larger purpose involved? What is the blood relationship between the birth and adoptive parents? Was the purpose of the adoption to maintain a family connection or to secure an heir for a childless couple? Was there an agreement between the parties at the time? What was the effect on the siblings? And so on. In reading over past records it seems to have been a regular happening in the Maori Land Court that the Court would look for a simple rule to govern all cases where the people would look for what was *tika* or right, that is, for what seemed to give substantive justice having regard to all the circumstances of the particular case. Consistent with this the Maori word for their law is '*tikanga*', which is simply the noun form of the adjective '*tika*', describing that which is fair, right or just.

Unfortunately tribal leaders themselves became conditioned by the Court's practice of hunting for neat prescriptive rules that circumvent the need for a comprehensive appreciation of Maori society in order to fathom the justice of a case. While there were scathing criticisms of the Court decisions (most judges finding that *whangai* succeeded to their adoptive parents) it seems to have been assumed by later Maori leaders that there was in fact a rule. Perhaps unwittingly they were giving credence to the foreign system that the Court introduced. It is telling that they could not then agree on what the rule was and so assumed instead that the rule must vary from tribe to tribe.

That was the position when recently, to receive a share of certain fisheries assets following a settlement between Government and Maori on the allocation of fishing rights, the tribes were required to establish entities having regard to certain statutory criteria, including a provision that each tribe should decide for itself whether or not *whangai* should be included as tribal members through their adoptive parents. Unsurprisingly there was no agreed settled rule within the tribes as well. Truth was, there never was that neat and simple single rule that the judges so earnestly sought.

Nor did judges accommodate the custom that rights could grow cold and be lost if persons remained away from their lands for too long. The principle was expressed in terms of *ahi ka*, or of keeping one's fires upon the land. However, the judges substituted simple rules of succession like the rule that children were entitled to succeed to the land interests of both parents. That rule was problematic from the moment that persons were recorded as owners on the Court's titles for it was common that persons married outside of their tribe and shifted to the tribe of their partners. They became absentee owners as did their children and the remoter issue. Today absentee ownership is the most common form of ownership on Maori Land Court titles notwithstanding that absentee ownership is incomprehensible in customary terms.

As a further caution against a fundamentalist view of Maori tribes as comprised of all descendants and of only descendants, I mention the practice of 'incorporation' – the process of recruiting persons in order to strengthen the tribal group. These could be persons who could themselves convert their latent or inchoate interests to membership by establishing contact with the *hapu* on the basis that they or their forebears had been part of the *hapu* in previous years. They could be persons whose antecedents in fact never resided with the *hapu* in question, but who have genealogical connections nonetheless (most Maori having genealogical links to several *hapu*). They could be persons who married into the tribe. And they could also be persons with no blood or marital links at all.

It has been common since last century for people to encourage Maori with links to their district to settle there, contributing to the local *hapu*, notwithstanding that they or their immediate antecedents were in fact raised somewhere else, and especially if they have some needed skill. However, this form of recruitment has not in fact been limited to relatives or to Maori. From first contact there have been many examples of the attempted or actual incorporation of Pakeha, as was described earlier with reference to the land transactions between settlers and Maori from about 1820. Evidence to the Waitangi Tribunal in relation to a North Auckland claim demonstrates the competition amongst the *hapu* to secure Pakeha when Pakeha traders came with their array of new goods and skills. The issue was whether the resulting land transactions should be seen as sales or as use right arrangements. However, the evidence also demonstrates the Maori practice of incorporation.

For example, a North Auckland *hapu* sought to secure a saw-miller seeking timber for ship spars, showing where he could build a house, build a mill and extract timber from a forest. On paper the trader drew a diagram depicting the areas and the natural boundaries of coastline and creeks. As described earlier there could be different views of the sort of transaction that was intended. According to the paper the saw-miller was buying the land and all the resources within the natural boundaries, but it was feasible that in the *hapu*'s view the saw-miller had only a conditional use right. Interestingly a Pakeha contemporary, Frederick Manning, would unwittingly confirm these perspectives in a book of his experiences that lampooned how Maori attached different values to different classes of Pakeha. There are other Pakeha descriptions of the practice throughout Polynesia and there are many accounts of significant working relationships between *hapu* and Pakeha individuals in later years.

Conclusion

Anthropological analysis and other studies of custom would assist the reform of Maori land law today. It would assist too in reviewing the administration of Treaty claim settlement assets and the construction of tribal authorities for the management of tribal affairs, especially in terms of cultural matching, the ethic of ensuring a fair relationship between formal structures and tradition. Cultural matching is also important in considering options for the resolution of disputes outside the Maori Land Court or the general court system and under the aegis of tribal authorities.

A professional consideration of Maori property interests would also advance the current debates in respect of the foreshore and seabed, rivers, lakes, geothermal fields and freshwater springs. The ownership of water is particularly critical. I have already suggested that it was the water-based resources that provided the main source of food for Maori and that these resources had special significance for that reason. Also, as earlier observed, it was presumed that land issues would dominate the business of the Waitangi Tribunal when it was established in 1975. In fact the first several claims to be heard related to water resources and the first major settlement concerned fisheries.

Presently this country has a major job to do in relation to property interests and asset administration and we will need sound research to ensure that this time the distinctive cultural variables are better appreciated and understood.

–8–

One Hundred Years of Land Reform on the Gazelle Peninsula

A Baining Point of View

Colin Filer and Michael Lowe

Abstract

People who write about customary land in Papua New Guinea commonly make the observation that it accounts for ninety-seven per cent of the country's surface area. If they are right, then the 'bare facts' of land tenure have not changed since Independence in 1975. In fact they are wrong, but the appearance of a static division of space continually motivates a debate about what (if anything) should be done about the 'mobilization' of customary land to facilitate 'rural development'. Behind the ideological trappings of this argument, we find a rather curious double movement: on the one hand a substantial increase in the proportion of 'customary' land which is subject to specific forms of modern property right; and on the other, a simultaneous increase in the area of 'alienated' land subject to successful rental claims by customary landowners. In this chapter we investigate one case of this double movement on 'alienated' land claimed by the Kakat Baining people of East New Britain to illustrate some of the contradictions embedded in arguments about the relationship between 'land mobilization' and 'rural development'.

Introduction

The common starting point for academic debate about land reform in Papua New Guinea (PNG) is the observation that ninety-seven per cent of the country's land area is 'under' customary ownership, while the remaining three per cent has been 'alienated' from its customary owners. The proponents of radical reform argue that the institutions of modern capitalism can only thrive on the tiny proportion of land which has been alienated, and this proportion therefore needs to be expanded (Gosarevski *et al.* 2004; Jones and McGavin 2000; Lea 2002). One defence of custom then claims that development has taken place and can be made to accelerate on the vast area of land which has not yet been alienated, so there is no inherent contradiction between a process of land reform and the basic principle of customary ownership (Fingleton 2005; Ploeg 1999; Ward 1981). A second defence of custom takes aim at any kind of land reform which supports a foreign or capitalist model of 'development' and therefore threatens to create a class of landless citizens (Anderson 2006; Lakau 1997). The appearance of a stalemate in this policy domain may be ascribed to a lack of indigenous ownership over the reform process itself (Levantis and Yala 2008) or to the power of a class of smallholders whose attachment to customary land is part of the Australian colonial legacy (Fitzpatrick 1980; MacWilliam 1988). But whether or not the participants in the debate believe that some amount of customary land ought to be 'mobilized for development', they all seem to share a common assumption that complete or partial alienation of land is a one-way street, and that traffic along this street has either been blocked by an inappropriate or dysfunctional institutional framework, or else successfully opposed by a coalition of national political interests.

When the Commission of Inquiry into Land Matters observed in 1973 that '[a] lienated land comprises only 2.8% of the total land area of Papua New Guinea' (PNG 1973:46), it relied on evidence contained in the government's register of freehold and leasehold land titles. It can be argued that the proportion of alienated land has declined since then because areas of customary land that have been freshly alienated are more than offset by the areas of alienated land whose official records have been lost or stolen. On the other hand the loss of alienated land can also be represented as the continuation of a trend already established during the period of the first Somare government (1972–7), which returned 220,000 hectares of 'vacant government land [almost one per cent of PNG's land area] to the original customary owners in areas of land shortage' (Fingleton 1982:119). If this trend is accepted as a fact, then it looks like the radical reformers have an even harder task ahead of them because we cannot simply say that 'nothing has changed' over the last thirty-five years. Yet the current debate is still framed by mutual acceptance of the 97:3 ratio. In 2008 the Australian government aid agency could still observe that 97 per cent of PNG's land is 'customary', 2.5 per cent is 'public' and 0.5 per cent is 'freehold' (AusAID 2008:4). Perhaps the desire to preserve this 'fact' against the sweep of history reflects a genuine belief that nothing much *has* changed over the last thirty-five years and hence to underline the argument that *something needs to be done* to 'make land work', even if it is not just the acquisition of more public land or the creation of more freehold titles. Be that as it may, our argument is that relatively small movements in the frontier separating parcels of alienated land from the vast unregistered hinterland of custom are only one aspect of a much bigger double movement which involves *the partial alienation of customary land* and *the partial customization of alienated land.*

This movement takes different forms in different parts of the country. In this paper we investigate its manifestation in the vicinity of Lassul Bay on the north coast of the Gazelle Peninsula in East New Britain Province. East New Britain has a special place in the history of PNG's land policy debate because the Tolai people who constitute the dominant ethnic group in that province were at the forefront of the movement to restore colonial plantations to national and local ownership during the late colonial period (Chowning *et al.* 1971; Grosart 1982; Grosart and McColl 1975). The struggle for land in their densely populated corner of the Gazelle Peninsula has remained a major subject of ethnographic inquiry and a major influence on the course of national policy in the postcolonial period (Fingleton 1985; Kean 1998; Lowe 2006; Martin 2006). However, in this paper we turn our attention to the much bigger, but far less densely populated area traditionally occupied by the Baining people, where the struggle for land has not been a major subject of ethnographic inquiry, but where the double movement of property rights has taken its own distinctive form. This will enable us to see how the creation of a hybrid space with fuzzy boundaries is not just the result of people competing for access to a scarce resource, nor simply the reflection of a grander contest between the forces of 'custom' and 'development'. What appears at first sight to be a double movement in the ownership of land is revealed at the local scale as a sequence of transactions and appropriations, attachments and detachments, possessions and dispossessions, in which land is only one of several 'things' at stake.

The Lassul Bay Landscape

Lassul Bay is located along the north coast of the Gazelle Peninsula, about sixty kilometres west of Rabaul. The communities around Lassul Bay are counted amongst the twenty-one wards of the Lassul-Baining Local-Level Government (LLG), which is one of three LLGs which make up the Gazelle Open Electorate or District. The indigenous people of this area are generally known as the North Baining or Kakat Baining – one of five Baining populations who speak distinct but related languages and occupy most of the mountainous interior of the Gazelle Peninsula as well as some parts of the coastal zone.[1] Their traditional territory extends across the northwestern part of the peninsula, including most of the area represented by the Lassul-Baining and Inland Baining LLGs. Nevertheless, the Baining people now constitute a minority of the population in the Gazelle District.

Figure 8.1 shows the spatial division of the coastal zone around Lassul Bay into numerous blocks of alienated land with a customary 'hinterland' to the south and east of them. In this case at least, most if not all of the records pertaining to ownership of the alienated land parcels are still held by the Lands Department in Port Moresby. Most of these are freehold titles, suggesting that they were alienated under the German colonial regime before the First World War, although part of the area covered by these titles has since reverted to state ownership. The minority of leasehold titles (Portions 41, 45, 796, 800 and 803) may have been created after the Australian government secured a League of Nations mandate to administer the Territory of New Guinea in 1921. Most of the alienated land titles in the area, including the five leasehold titles, currently belong to an agribusiness company, New Guinea Islands Produce, which local people know by the name of its marketing subsidiary, 'Agmark'.

The lines that clearly separate the space of alienation from the space of custom in this area have no counterparts in the division of the local population. The area shown on Figure 8.1 contains all or part of five council wards, each of which is subdivided into a number of census units whose names are shown on the map, but there is no official map which shows the spatial boundaries of these political units. In that sense they are simply groups of people who are periodically distinguished by the conduct of a census and whose political interests are officially represented by different councillors in the Lassul-Baining LLG whose headquarters are located on the shores of Lassul Bay.

The North Baining people have their own way of dividing the coastal zone into fairly large territorial units, which Fajans calls 'districts', separated by the major rivers which flow north into the Bismarck Sea. In precolonial times the residents

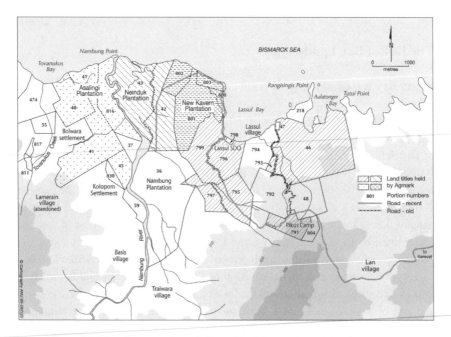

Figure 8.1 Map of census units and alienated land titles in the vicinity of Lassul Bay.

of a single 'district' did not form a unified political entity because raiding and fighting took place both within and across their boundaries (Fajans 1997:16), but these territorial units have become more like political and religious communities since the Catholic mission entered the area and turned them into 'parishes'. So Lan is not just the name of a village and a larger council ward, it is also the name of a district or parish that stretches from the Nambung River in the west to the Karo River in the east, and all of the Baining people who live between these two rivers regard themselves in some sense as members of a single community. Most of the families in this community maintain houses, gardens and cocoa blocks in several different parts of the parish, so the division of the local Baining population between council wards and census units is both artificial and unstable. The Baining settlements which now comprise Pikus Camp, Lassul village and Traiwara village have all been established as outposts of Lan village within living memory, but Lan village itself has never been more than a loose cluster of hamlets. As some of its residents have recently moved east towards the Karo River, it is now divided between the original area of settlement, known as 'Lan 1', and the newer area, known as 'Lan 2'. A similar process of dispersal has resulted in the division of both Lassul and Traiwara villages into two spatially discrete groups of hamlets.

While the population of Lan parish is officially divided into three council wards, each with its own elected councillor, the physical boundary between one ward and the next is only recognized as such when it coincides with the boundary between two blocks of alienated land that belong to different plantations. Thus the boundary between Traiwara and Lassul wards appears to follow the northern and eastern boundaries of Nambung Plantation (Portion 36) until it reaches the point at which a wedge of customary land separates Portion 36 from Portion 797 of Lassul Plantation. Beyond that point the three Baining councillors have no evident interest in delineating or protecting the boundaries between their jurisdictions. Even the boundaries between alienated and customary land have become increasingly porous as Baining people have occupied (or reoccupied) parts of the Nambung, Lassul and Seeberg plantation lands that have not been commercially managed for many years.

Very few Baining people have been formally employed as plantation workers since the end of the German colonial period, so the bulk of the population now resident on the four plantations in the area which are still counted as distinct census units (New Kavern, Neinduk, Nambung and Asalingi) is the residue of a plantation workforce recruited from other parts of PNG. Some of the Sepik and Highland labourers formerly employed on Nambung plantation came to an arrangement with the Bainings of Traiwara ('Dry Creek') village which enabled them and their families to settle on customary land and establish cocoa blocks along the upper reaches of the Nambung River.[2] The Sepik settlement is located on the western side of the Nambung River, but its inhabitants are evidently counted as part of Traiwara census unit because that census unit contains the customary owners of the land in question. Even where this type of settlement has been established, the social division between the Baining and non-Baining sections of the local population now seems quite clear, and there is little evidence of intermarriage between the two groups except where non-Baining children or adults have previously been adopted by Baining families.

In Baining terms the area west of the Nambung River, including Asalingi plantation, belongs to Nangas district or parish, and we might therefore infer that the people with strongest claims to customary ownership of most of this territory are concentrated in Nangas village, which is not shown on Figure 8.1, because its hamlets are located west of Tovanakus Creek. Baining people form a majority of the population in Basis village and part of the population of Kolopom Settlement, but many of these people have migrated to this area from other Baining communities in the mountain ranges to the south. The timing of this migration and the degree of their integration with the Nangas 'community' has not been established. The non-Baining population of Kolopom ward, including the settlement of Bolwara, includes a substantial number of Tolai people, Duke of York islanders, and members of other ethnic groups who were formerly employed as plantation workers in the area but who managed to acquire blocks of land from the customary owners. This helps to explain why the local councillor is himself a Tolai, but the history of land transactions in this ward has also been a bone of contention with the Baining population of Lan parish because of the long history of antagonism between Bainings, Tolais and Duke of York islanders. Recent census figures suggest that people who identify themselves as Bainings account for about half of the thousand or so people who currently reside in the area shown on Figure 8.1.

The Double Movement in History

Our own interest in the history of this area stems from the conduct of a social baseline study that was triggered by plans to build an industrial facility on the shores of Lassul Bay. If these plans are implemented, then the double movement will take a new turn, but we shall see that there have already been several turns along the road that leads to the present state of affairs. From the point of view of the indigenous Baining population, the history of this area over the last century or so is a history of land lost and partially reclaimed. We get a clear sense of this from a version of recent history recounted by three senior Baining men of Lan parish in 2007.

According to the local census book one of our Baining informants was born in 1950, and he says that he was born and brought up in a Baining settlement on land now occupied by Lassul 'Sub-District Office' (Portion 798). The story goes that the Australian colonial administration told the inhabitants to vacate this settlement to make way for the new government station, but failed to offer any compensation for their loss. The residents supposedly moved to Lan village, but after a short while (three years or so), a group of ten men from that village jointly founded the settlement now known as Lassul 1 on the eastern shore of Lassul Bay within the boundaries of Portion 794. It is said that Traiwara village was established shortly afterwards, also by a group of ten men from Lan village, at a time when Nambung Plantation was owned or managed by a white man called 'Backhouse'. Both settlements are now seen as part of a deliberate strategy to occupy areas that might be vulnerable to colonization by Tolai settlers migrating westwards from around the Catholic mission station at Vunamarita. Our informants did not suggest that they were part of a strategy to reclaim customary rights to land alienated by German planters or Australian colonial administrators over the course of the previous century.

At the time when Lassul 1 was founded, the 'boss' of the Lassul, New Kavern and Neinduk plantations – along with another plantation called 'Cacao' – is said to have been a Chinaman called 'Achok'. Achok apparently had a series of meetings with the new settlers through which it was finally agreed that they would retain the right to occupy and use the land around the settlement and could plant their own coconuts on it. Around the time of PNG's independence in 1975, Achok is said to have 'given' his plantations to a mixed-race man called 'Pauli'. Some years later Pauli moved to Australia and 'gave' the plantations to a Tolai businessman and politician called 'Konga'.

Konga brought a Malaysian logging company into the area, thus causing a lot of damage to local people's land and resources, especially their water supplies and food crops, with little or nothing by way of compensation. Some of the money which customary landowners should have received as royalties was supposedly invested in a trade store on New Kavern plantation, but no more was seen of that money when Konga 'gave' the plantations and the trade store to Agmark after the logging operation had come to an end. One informant (the Lassul ward councillor) claimed that the area of flat land immediately behind Lassul government station was sold by Konga to the Lassul Baining Community Government (as it then was) for K15,000, but the value of this land was reduced when the loggers blocked the channel through which a creek formerly drained into Lassul Bay. Parts of the land in question are now described as a 'swamp' whose waters occasionally flood the government station and adjacent hamlets of Lassul village.

Let us now see how these fragments of oral history square up against the written historical records of the area. These records reach back to the German colonial period, well beyond the memory of anyone living in the area today, but there is one event from that period which still has legendary status for local people.

On 13 August 1904 a Baining man called Tomaria led an attack on the Catholic mission station of St Paul, which was located east of the Karo River in the Baining 'district' of Puktas. Two priests and eight other German missionaries were murdered (Hempenstall 1978:149). At the time of the massacre the missionaries had already been working in the area for eight years and had drawn the attention of Albert Hahl, chief justice and later governor of German New Guinea, to the Tolai practice of raiding Baining territory, killing and eating any adults they could find, then kidnapping and enslaving their children. Tomaria himself was one of the Baining orphans who had been enslaved in this way, but had then been freed by the German administration and returned to the care of the missionaries. While he and his fellow killers were rounded up and shot, the German authorities continued to regard the Bainings as subjects in need of protection from their Tolai neighbours.

The subsequent alienation of Baining land along the north coast of the Gazelle Peninsula could be construed as an act of reprisal for the St Paul's massacre (Rohatynskyj 2001:26), but may also have been intended to create a sort of European 'buffer zone' between the two native populations (Hempenstall 1978:150). Immediately after the massacre, Governor Hahl took a personal interest in the recruitment of German farmers from Queensland to settle in the hillier areas above 400 metres, where it was thought they would be less susceptible to malaria (Sack and Clark 1979:261; Hahl 1980:113). One of the blocks alienated for this purpose included the current Portion 791, and the Baining settlement of Pikus Camp which takes its name from the fig trees planted at that time which are still a prominent feature of the local landscape. By 1914 the hill farm experiment had proved to be an economic failure (Sack and Clark 1979:301; Hahl 1980:118), but coconut plantations had been established all along the coast. In the period before the First World War Baining men were recruited to work on the plantations and to build the network of riding tracks connecting them together. The track from Vunamarita mission station reached as far as Neinduk plantation by 1911 and a track connecting Pikus Camp to the old 'Bolten' plantation (Portion 46) was completed shortly afterwards (Sack and Clark 1979:318, 370).

When the Australian government took formal control of the area in 1921, it promptly embarked on a programme of expropriating German land assets and selling them to new owners in order to secure war reparations. This process was completed by 1927. In the 1930s the names and shapes of plantations in the area were much the same as they are today. One account of plantation society in this period may be found in the memoirs of Margaret Wood (Boys 1993), whose husband Eric was the manager of Neinduk plantation (then owned by W.R. Carpenter & Co.) from 1931 to 1934. She tells us that Lassul plantation (Portions 795–799) was still in operation, although it had been classed as a second rate property when being sold by the Expropriation Board, while the old Seeberg plantation (Portions 48 and 792) and Bolten plantation (Portions 46 and 793) had both been abandoned. It seems that most of the plantation workers at this time were recruited from the mainland of New Guinea, especially from the Sepik region, while the Baining people had retreated into their mountain settlements, and only made occasional visits to the coastal plantations to exchange root crops for tinned meat and salt. We know from other sources that government officials were worried by the evident decline in the Baining population in this period (Fajans 1997:39), and this partly explains the steps taken by the government and the Catholic mission in the late 1930s to gather some of the survivors together in the present villages of Lan and Puktas (Kokopo Patrol Report[3] 2–46/47).

If sickness was already taking its toll on the North Baining population in the 1930s, worse was to come when Japanese soldiers occupied the area from 1942 to 1945. The Bainings were forced to work on construction of a track connecting Rabaul to Open Bay (in the south of what is now the Lassul-Baining LLG area), then forced to carry cargo along it for up to fifteen hours a day (Fajans 1997:41). The Japanese plundered their gardens, consumed all their pigs and chickens, and executed anyone who showed signs of resistance. They were aided and abetted in these activities by some of the plantation workers who had been left behind by the retreating Australians and who now volunteered to join the Japanese native police force (Nelson 2006:340). Several hundred Bainings, including some from the mountainous interior, were confined in a labour camp within the boundaries of Nambung plantation and more than 400 of them apparently died in a dysentery epidemic (Kokopo PR 2–46/47). From a pre-war population of more than 2000 in seven 'Coastal Baining' villages, only 813 were left at the end of 1946 and barely 600 four years later (Nelson 2006:340; Kokopo PR 3–50/51).

In 1946 231 survivors from the pre-war population of Lan village had established a new village called Lassul 'on ground owned by the natives' in Lassul Bay, and a temporary 'native hospital' had been established in the same location (Kokopo PR 2–46/47). A later patrol report tells us that this was indeed the place now occupied by Lassul government station (Rabaul PR 5–64/65). A smaller group of forty-five Baining people from the mountain village of Lamerain (which still exists today) seem to have established a village of the same name on customary land near the boundary of Tovanakus plantation (Portion 474). In 1949 a patrol to investigate the 'Reported Stealing of Coconuts from Plantations at Massaw Bay and Lassul Plantation' found that the people of Lassul village had been selling copra to the manager of Guntershoehe plantation (east of the present site of Lan village), but when he left the area towards the end of 1948 they took to harvesting coconuts from the unoccupied Lassul plantation and selling the copra to Chinese traders (Kokopo PR 5–48/49). By 1952 Nambung, New Kavern, Neinduk and Asalingi plantations were all back in production, but Lassul plantation was still unoccupied.

By this time it seems that the villages of Lassul and Lamerain had both moved from their previous locations. The people of Lamerain were said to be 'moving back to their own native-owned land from their present position on the beach' (in Tovanakus Bay), while Lassul village was said to be 'moving back to its old site ... about 1½ miles from the present village' (Kokopo PR 3–51/52). The new settlement of Lamerain was about '3 miles inland', directly south of Tovanakus Bay (see Figure 8.1), while the people of Lassul seem to have moved to what is now the site of Lassul 1 (on Portion 794) and then moved back to the site of the native hospital (Portion 798). However, by 1955 Lassul village had been 'abandoned' in favour of a new village at Lan, possibly because the native hospital had closed in 1952 (Rabaul PR 5–54/55). There is no indication in the patrol reports that the villagers had been obliged to resettle themselves in order to make way for a new government station and, although a new aid post had been opened on Portion 798 by 1956, a new government patrol post was not established on this site until the end of 1965, replacing the one formerly located on Portion 47 (Rabaul PRs 5–64/65 and 6–65/66). Portion 798 was registered as state land in 1967, but we have not found any record of the process by which it was acquired.

The post-war demographics of these coastal Baining settlements are something of a puzzle. Patrol officers remarked on the preponderance of 'elderly natives' and the shortage of women and children, and one declared in 1950 that Lamerain was 'finished' because there were only 10 children to replace 49 adults (Kokopo PR 3–50/51). But they also record a high incidence of intermarriage between Baining women and plantation labourers, some of whom are said to have taken their wives away on the completion of their labour contracts while others remained in the area and may have been partly responsible for sparking local interest in cocoa production (Rabaul/Raunsimna PRs 4–56/57 and 1–57/58). The subsequent cocoa boom of the 1960s then seems to have encouraged some of the inland Baining people to resettle in the coastal zone, including the area around Lassul Bay, and hence to reverse the former process of depopulation and ethnic dilution.

The villagers of Lan and Puktas began planting cocoa in 1954 (Rabaul PR 1–55/56, Rabaul/Raunsimna PR 1–57/58) and local people still recall that this endeavour was encouraged by the Catholic priest then in charge of Vunamarita mission station. By 1965 a group of Lan villagers was cultivating and processing cocoa on a portion of Guntershoehe plantation which had been 'given' to them by the manager (Rabaul PR 4–64/65). By 1967 Baining villagers had apparently abandoned their former 'policy' of selling wet beans to the local plantations and were shipping or trucking dried beans direct to Rabaul for private sale (Bainings PR 3–66/67; Pomio/Bainings PR 1–67/68). Meanwhile two former members of the local plantation workforce – one a Tolai, the other from the New Guinea mainland – had obtained leases over two blocks of government land west of Tovanakus Creek (Portions 811 and 817) and were hiring local Baining men to plant, pick and process cocoa on these blocks (Rabaul PR 4–64/65; Bainings PR 1–68/69). We do not know when or how these two blocks had been removed from customary ownership, but one government officer felt moved to remark on the absence of any 'feeling that this form of tenure in any way is superior to customary tenure' (Bainings PR 1–68/69). By this he seems to have meant that local Baining villagers continued to expand the area planted to cash crops on their own customary land. In 1969 Lamerain village had 28,000 cacao trees (75 per cent bearing), while Lan village had 40,000 (90 per cent bearing) (ibid.).

Despite these signs of vigorous economic development, the cocoa boom added further impetus to the double movement of land rights. Patrol reports from the 1960s already note the emergence of coastal Baining resentment over the previous alienation of so much land for plantation development and the more recent 'encroachment' of Sepiks, Tolais and Duke of York islanders onto the remaining areas of customary land or the 'native reserves' established by the colonial administration (Rabaul PRs 4–64/65 and 6–65/66). It is hard to tell whether Baining men who were sometimes employed by the owners of alienated land were simply seeking additional income or seeking to reassert their customary land rights. On the other hand the Baining practice of 'leasing' land to non-Baining members of the plantation workforce continued apace. The last Australian officer in charge of Lassul government station says that he was authorizing paper records of such transactions in the early 1970s, but admits the possibility that some of these transactions may have related to parcels of alienated land which Baining people had already 'repossessed' (Ron Brew, personal communication, March 2009).

PNG Lands Department records indicate that the titles to Lassul plantation (Portions 795–9), the former Bolten and Seeberg plantations (Portions 46, 48, 792 and 793) and the area around Pikus Camp (Portion 791), were indeed held by a man called Achok in 1969. Achok's full name was Engelbert Chok Chow and the titles were held jointly with his partner, John Sing Fat Chow.[4] Another branch of the Chow family held the titles to New Kavern plantation. Most if not all of the titles belonging to this family were transferred to Lassul Trading Company in 1970, but the officer in charge of Lassul government station in 1973 believes that Achok was still the real owner of Lassul plantation, while Pauli Aming was merely the manager. According to this informant Joe Backhouse maintained that he had been 'given' Nambung plantation after the Second World War as a sort of reward for his service as the military officer responsible for executing natives found guilty of collaborating with the enemy, but post-war patrol reports do not seem to support this claim. Local Baining people apparently allowed the manager of Guntershoehe and Tovanakus plantations (Jim Swallow) to build a house on a small offshore island east of Lassul Bay, but when he joined the expatriate exodus around the time of Independence, his plan to sell this house to the son of a prominent Tolai political leader (Matthias Toliman) was immediately thwarted.[5] The customary owners are said to have dismantled the whole edifice in the space of a single weekend and removed all the parts to the mainland (Ron Brew, personal communication, March 2009).

In 1985 the land titles held by Lassul Trading Company were acquired by another Tolai politician, Nakikus Konga, who was elected as Member of Parliament for Gazelle Open Electorate in 1987. He probably purchased the titles to Neinduk and Asalingi plantations at the same time. In 1999 he sold all these titles to the company which local people know as 'Agmark'. Agmark thus owns the titles to four of the five local plantations that were operating in the 1930s, along with the abandoned Bolten plantation (Portions 46 and 793) and the abandoned German hill farm around Pikus Camp (Portion 791). For some unknown reason it does not own the titles to the abandoned Seeberg plantation (Portions 48 and 792). One explanation would be that this is the area of land which Achok 'gave back' to the local Baining people.

The recent history of Nambung plantation is still something of a mystery. Local informants say that the titles were sold to a company called Las Ples ('Last Place') some time around PNG's independence in 1975. This company was apparently controlled by Tolai and Sepik interests, and its operations were funded by two K1 million bank loans, one of which was unsecured. Whatever the financial arrangements, the plantation was poorly managed and soon fell into disrepair. That is why some of the labourers began to make encroachments onto customary land outside the plantation boundaries. When local Baining people received a windfall of baitfish royalties in the late 1980s, there were plans to use some of this money to purchase Nambung plantation, but they were evidently unsuccessful.[6] One Agmark manager told us that his company had tried to add Nambung plantation to its local collection, but was unable to complete the transaction because the title is held by the Department of Lands while the Rural Development Bank holds the unsecured mortgage over the property.

In 1990 or 1991 Nakikus Konga entered into an arrangement with Niugini Lumber, a subsidiary of Rimbunan Hijau, to log the 'Konga Freehold and Taraiwara' Timber Rights Purchase (TRP) area (Fajans 1998:20). The records of the PNG Forest Authority relating to this timber concession have not been sighted, so we do not know the precise boundaries of the TRP area, nor the content of agreements that should have been required in order for the logging company to operate on customary land in the Lan 'district'. But we do know that the operation attracted a good deal of negative publicity in 1993 because of the damage caused to 'gardens, houses, cash crops, trees and water sources' (*Times of PNG*, 28 October 1993) and the use of coral from the reef around Malai Point (Portion 803) to fill in part of the swampy area around the log pond on the western shores of Lassul Bay (Portion 800) (*Times of PNG*, 30 December 1993). Officers from the East New Britain Provincial Government conducted an investigation, but it seems that no further action was taken against the logging company. The logging operation apparently came to an end in 1994.

The Double Movement Today

While the records of the PNG Lands Department might seem to suggest a clear-cut distinction between alienated and customary land in this area, the current situation is far more complex. According to Agmark management, the Baining people of Lan 'district' have recently been 'encroaching' on parts of Portions 797 and 799 of the old Lassul plantation land. Observations in the field suggest that this is only the most recent phase in a longer term process of encroachment which extends to several of the other alienated land titles in the area, but it does seem to be a process which has recently gathered additional momentum. Over the same period, former plantation workers and other non-Baining people have continued to 'encroach' onto customary Baining land without necessarily obtaining the consent of the customary owners.

One of the reasons for the current complexity of the land tenure situation is that Baining society, like that of some other Melanesian peoples with very low population densities, traditionally lacked corporate landowning groups with clearly defined boundaries. One could not say that they were 'patrilineal' or 'matrilineal' because they did not have any rules of inheritance. When people died, their personal assets, the products of their own physical labour, were normally destroyed by their grieving relatives (Fajans 1997:21). Since land was in plentiful supply, individuals and families were free to make gardens, hunt wild animals or gather forest resources in any place where they felt safe to do so. It was not very safe to do so in areas near the coast because of the risk of attack by Tolai raiding parties or by other groups of Bainings, but people did occasionally come down to the shore to collect shellfish and saltwater (for its salt content) (ibid.:33). Baining ideas and institutions pertaining to the ownership of land only began to change when Europeans and other Papua New Guineans began taking their customary land away from them (ibid.:47), and later through their own engagement in the cultivation of perennial cash crops or their negotiations with logging companies. While the colonial authorities might have thought that large swathes of Baining territory were effectively 'waste and vacant', the Baining for their part have a well-deserved reputation for refusing to accept that the alienation of customary land can ever be more than a temporary arrangement.

For reasons previously indicated, the old Lassul plantation (Portions 795–9) is the most complex and potentially contested of the landholdings in the area. When direct management of the plantation ceased in the 1980s, the entire labour force left and most of the buildings and facilities were also removed. This encouraged local Bainings to establish temporary food gardens within its boundaries, but for the people of Lassul village in particular, this was little more than a continuation of the arrangements or understandings that had apparently existed for many years about some of the other 'alienated' land portions south of Lassul Bay. Portions 46, 794 and 796 had long been used for food gardens and cocoa blocks, and individual houses (now the hamlets of Lassul 2) had been built on the last of these areas.

During the 1980s and 1990s there was a further movement of people out of Lan village to occupy land along the eastern boundary of Nambung plantation and the southern boundary of the old Lassul plantation in settlements which are now sometimes grouped together under the name of 'Traiwara 2' because they are counted as part of Traiwara census unit. These people then began to establish food gardens and some cocoa blocks in the southern sections of Portions 797 and 795, while people from the original Traiwara village (now 'Traiwara 1') began to establish temporary food gardens in the southern parts of Nambung plantation (Portion 36).

The present decade has witnessed further acts of 'encroachment' on both of these abandoned plantations, along with unprecedented incursions into the southern part of New Kavern plantation (Portion 801), which is still notionally under Agmark management. Aside from food gardens, new cocoa blocks have been planted, and new houses, cocoa fermentaries, chicken and pig pens have been built in their midst. These recent developments are said to have followed a meeting at Lassul government station in 2002, at which local Baining people asked the provincial governor to help them reclaim formal ownership of Lassul plantation. Local people now say that they took the matter into their own hands because the governor failed to keep a promise to 'look into it' and they fear the plantation might otherwise be used in ways that would involve a further influx of 'outsiders' to the area.[7] Provincial authorities are also thought to have promised or planned to purchase New Kavern plantation from Agmark in order to establish a new government station on one part of it (Portions 800 and 803) while turning the rest of it (Portions 801 and 802) over to Lassul village farmers. The periodic flooding of the current government station is cited as evidence in favour of this move.

In 2006 a local Baining leader and provincial public servant, who lives in Traiwara 2 and works in the health centre at Lassul government station, took further steps to establish full control over Nambung plantation. Some of his family members settled around the derelict plantation house, took over management of the cocoa fermentary, and began to plant new seedlings. The small number of former labourers still living on the plantation were then told that all their wet cocoa beans would henceforth be purchased and processed by the local fermentary now under Baining management. The leader justified this action by claiming that

Figure 8.2 The cocoa fermentary at Nambung plantation.

one of his own ancestors had originally sold the plantation land to the Germans, his father had been one of two men who tried (unsuccessfully) to buy it back in 1975, and repossession was now warranted by the years of subsequent neglect and (once again) by the threat of a further influx of 'outsiders' to the area. But this was also represented as a pioneering attempt to prove that local Baining people could successfully manage a plantation in a modern way and therefore qualify themselves to take over the management of the other plantations in the area.

While Agmark managers grumble about Baining acts of 'encroachment', they have not made any attempt to defend their property rights by force, either by deployment of plantation labourers as security guards or by calling for police assistance to evict the squatters. There is no policeman based at Lassul government station and the maintenance of public order in the area rests in the hands of a village court whose magistrates are all senior Baining men. Government agricultural officers from outside the local area have assisted Baining farmers in their recent acts of encroachment. Most of the cocoa harvested and fermented by local Baining farmers, whether on customary or alienated land, is sold to Agmark at a purchasing point located on Portion 800, although Baining farmers complain about the price they receive and sometimes look for alternative ways of getting their product out of the area. Indeed the purchase and export of cocoa grown

Figure 8.3 The labourers' compound at Nambung plantation.

Figure 8.4 The Agmark purchasing point on New Kavern plantation.

Figure 8.5 Noticeboard at the Agmark purchasing point.

by local smallholders is now Agmark's primary economic activity in the area. The old copra-based plantation economy, commemorated by the ancient coconut palms which still dominate much of the alienated landscape, now looks to be dead and buried because the price of copra relative to the price of transportation is too low for anyone to make money out of it.

Conclusion

The double movement of land rights around Lassul Bay has primarily taken the form of a two-way process of 'encroachment' across the legal boundary between alienated land and customary land. The origins of this process can be traced back to the years immediately following the Second World War, when local Baining men first helped themselves to the coconuts growing on Lassul plantation while apparently 'giving' some of their women or their land to plantation labourers from other ethnic groups. Yet with the passage of time there has also been a role reversal in the relationship between 'insiders' and 'outsiders'. For while the outsiders were leading the insiders (and some of their customary land) to the rewards of cocoa production in the 1960s, it is the insiders who now assert control over the work of the outsiders left within the ever more porous boundaries of the old plantation economy.

This agricultural version of the double movement has been accompanied by a more erratic version which involves the distribution of rent from different forms of extractive industry. In the 1980s local Baining people were somewhat taken aback by the government's 'gift' of baitfish royalties that were derived from a marine resource which they had never thought they owned (Turner 1990). Around the same time some of them agreed to sell their customary 'timber rights' to the State because they hoped that logging might bring a form of economic reward that would not offer further opportunities for outsiders to plant cash crops on their customary land (Fajans 1998). The logging operation came and went, the rewards did not meet local expectations, but it was indeed local Baining farmers who made use of the logging tracks to access new land for cocoa production. Now these people face the prospect of negotiating the distribution of 'landowner benefits' from the processing plant which a mining company would like to build on part of the 'alienated space' that is the subject of their agricultural encroachment (*Post-Courier*, 14 August 2008).

All such transactions across the boundary between customary and non-customary spaces or places entail new forms of reflection on the organizing principles of customary ownership (Filer 2007). For example, the government's gift of baitfish royalties and purchase of timber rights were both conditional on the identification of 'clan agents' who could sign receipts and agreements on behalf of the clans which Baining society did not have. The social consequences are neatly but rather sadly illustrated in an undated letter written to the chairman of 'Poiniar Landowner Company' on behalf of 167 members of the 'Luanpracha Clan'.[8] The letter states (in Tok Pisin) that since the logging operation of the early 1990s, 'we have not received any royalties, so now we have a clan'. The letter goes on to make four 'recommendations' in which the demand for the unpaid royalties is linked to a proposal to register clans and their landholdings and appoint 'clan directors' for the purpose of distributing the missing money.

The North Baining people seem to have migrated from a world in which space was not conceived as a transactable good, to one in which it was taken or given or borrowed in asymmetrical transactions with members of other ethnic groups, to one in which it yields rents and royalties which have to be redistributed between the constituent parts of Baining society. That might seem like a one-way street. But behind this appearance of 'development' there is another double movement. On the one hand the Baining have grown more like the other Papua New Guineans who have 'encroached' onto their customary land, and they have done so in the very process of resisting that encroachment. On the other hand the process of resistance has created a stronger sense of Baining identity which conceals the demographic history of inter-ethnic marriage and adoption.

What we have sought to demonstrate in this paper is that the double movement of local property rights – the partial alienation of customary space and the partial customization of alienated space – is liable to create distinctive hybrid forms of authority, identity and society in each of the places where it occurs. The story of Lassul Bay is not just a story about the creation of a hybrid property regime in which modern and traditional land rights are mixed up by a series of ambivalent transactions – 'gifts' which are not really gifts or 'sales' which are not really sales. It is also a story about the peculiar sense of ownership which has emerged from a long history dispossession and repossession. In Australian sporting jargon a player is said to be 'owned' if he or she is dispossessed by foul play that fails to attract a penalty. It seems to us that Baining people think about the ownership of both land and persons in much the same way, for reasons which should now be evident, and this way of thinking about the most fundamental act of appropriation cannot be captured in any classification of specific forms of economic transaction.

Acknowledgements

The authors would like to thank Mark Busse, George Curry, Keir Martin and Veronica Strang for their comments on an earlier draft of this chapter.

Notes

1. The name 'Baining' is itself derived from the word for 'bush people' in the language of the Tolai people.
2. It is not clear that the Bainings freely consented to this arrangement. By one account, the plantation workers began to cultivate the land without consulting the customary owners, and government officers had to mediate an agreement by which no further encroachments would occur without prior negotiation and appropriate payment.
3. Henceforth abbreviated PR. Kokopo PR 2–46/47 refers to Kokopo Patrol Report Number 2 of 1946–47.
4. John Chow had been recorded as the owner of Lassul plantation in 1952 (Kokopo PR 3–51/52).
5. Toliman was a member of PNG's House of Assembly from 1964 until his death in 1973. Lassul Bay was part of his constituency.
6. By one account, the Lan people did manage to purchase a shareholding in the company that owned the title to the plantation (Fajans 1998:20; Turner 1990:43). If so, the fate of this shareholding still remains a mystery.

7. Their greatest fear is a resettlement scheme that would bring more Duke of York islanders to the area.
8. According to Fathers Hesse and Aerts (1996: 27), Luanbracha [sic] is the name of a pond that is recognized as the abode of the dead by all North Baining people.

References

Anderson, T. (2006), 'On the Economic Value of Customary Land in Papua New Guinea', *Pacific Economic Bulletin*, 21(1): 138–52.

AusAID (2008), *Making Land Work – Volume One: Reconciling Customary Land and Development in the Pacific*, Canberra: AusAID.

Boys, P. (1993), *Coconuts and Tearooms: Six Years in New Britain, New Guinea in the 1930's – the Colonial Days*, Auckland: Pat Boys.

Chowning, A., Epstein, A.L., Epstein, T.S., Goodale, J. and Grosart, I. (1971), 'Under the Volcano', in A.L. Epstein, R.S. Parker and M. Reay (eds), *The Politics of Dependence: Papua New Guinea 1968*, Canberra: Australian National University Press.

Fajans, J. (1997), *They Make Themselves: Work and Play among the Baining of Papua New Guinea*, Chicago: University of Chicago Press.

Fajans, J. (1998), 'Transforming Nature, Making Culture: Why the Baining Are Not Environmentalists', *Social Analysis*, 42(3): 12–26.

Filer, C. (2007), 'Local Custom and the Art of Land Group Boundary Maintenance in Papua New Guinea', in J. Weiner and K. Glaskin (eds), *Customary Land Tenure and Registration in Australia and Papua New Guinea: Anthropological Perspectives*, Asia-Pacific Environment Monograph 3, Canberra: ANU E Press.

Fingleton, J. (1982), 'Land Policy in Papua New Guinea', in D. Weisbrot, A. Paliwala and A. Sawyerr (eds), *Land and Social Change in Papua New Guinea*, Sydney: Butterworths.

Fingleton, J. (1985), 'Changing Land Tenure in Melanesia: The Tolai Experience', PhD thesis, Canberra, Australian National University.

Fingleton, J. (ed.) (2005), *Privatising Land in the Pacific: A Defence of Customary Tenures*, Discussion Paper 80, Canberra: Australia Institute.

Fitzpatrick, P. (1980), *Law and State in Papua New Guinea*, London: Academic Press.

Gosarevski, S., Hughes, H. and Windybank, S. (2004), 'Is Papua New Guinea Viable?' *Pacific Economic Bulletin*, 19(1): 134–48.

Grosart, I. (1982), 'Nationalism and Micronationalism: The Tolai Case', in R. May (ed.), *Micronationalist Movements in Papua New Guinea*, Australian National

University Research School of Pacific Studies, Department of Political and Social Change Monograph 1, Canberra: Australian National University Press.

Grosart, I. and McColl, C.F. (1975), 'East New Britain', in D. Stone (ed.), *Prelude to Self-Government: Electoral Politics in Papua New Guinea 1972*, Canberra: Australian National University Press.

Hahl, A. (1980), *Governor in New Guinea*, ed. and transl. P. Sack and D. Clark, Canberra: Australian National University Press.

Hempenstall, P. (1978), *Pacific Islanders under German Rule: A Study in the Meaning of Colonial Resistance*, Canberra: Australian National University Press.

Hesse, K. and Aerts, T. (1996), *Baining Life and Lore*, 2nd edn, Port Moresby: University of Papua New Guinea Press.

Jones, L. and McGavin, P. (2000), *Creating Economic Incentives for Land Mobilisation in Papua New Guinea: A Case Study Analysis of the Formation and Maintenance of Institutions That Assist Mobilisation of Land for Agricultural Uses*, Discussion Paper 77, Port Moresby: Institute of National Affairs.

Kean, P. (1998), 'Power and Development: A Foucauldian Analysis of the History of Economic Development on the Gazelle Peninsula and in the Siki Resettlement Schemes, New Britain, Papua New Guinea', PhD Thesis, Monash University, Australia.

Lakau, A. (1997), 'Customary Land Tenure, Customary Landowners and the Proposals for Customary Land Reform in Papua New Guinea', *Anthropological Forum*, 7(4): 529–47.

Lea, D. (2002), 'Are There Advantages to Maintaining Customary Land Tenure in Papua New Guinea?' *Pacific Economic Bulletin*, 17(2): 42–55.

Levantis, T. and Yala, C. (2008), 'Breaking Away from the Land Policy Stalemate', *Pacific Economic Bulletin*, 23(1): 99–110.

Lowe, M. (2006), 'Smallholder Agrarian Change: The Experience in Two Tolai Communities', PhD thesis, Canberra, Australian National University.

MacWilliam, S. (1988), 'Smallholdings, Land Law and the Politics of Land Tenure in Papua New Guinea', *Journal of Peasant Studies*, 16: 77–109.

Martin, K. (2006), 'After the Volcano: Land, Custom and Conflict in East New Britain', PhD thesis, Manchester, University of Manchester.

Nelson, H. (2006), 'Payback: Australian Compensation to Wartime Papua New Guinea', in Y. Toyoda and H. Nelson (eds), *The Pacific War in Papua New Guinea: Memories and Realities*, Tokyo: Rikkyo University, Centre for Asian Area Studies.

Ploeg, A. (1999), 'Land Tenure and the Commercialisation of Agriculture in Papua New Guinea', in T. van Meijl and F. von Benda-Beckmann (eds), *Property Rights and Economic Development: Land and Natural Resources in Southeast Asia and Oceania*, London and New York: Kegan Paul International.

PNG (Papua New Guinea) (1973), 'Report of the Commission of Inquiry into Land Matters', Port Moresby: Government Printer.

Rohatynskyj, M. (2001), 'On Knowing the Baining and Other Minority Ethnic Groups of East New Britain', *Social Analysis*, 45(2): 23–40.

Sack, P. and Clark, D. (eds) (1979), *German New Guinea: The Annual Reports*, Canberra: Australian National University Press.

Turner, J. (1990), 'Lassul-Bainings (East New Britain)', in C. Filer (ed.), *The Sociology of Baitfish Royalties in Papua New Guinea*, Occasional Paper 6, Port Moresby: University of Papua New Guinea, Department of Anthropology and Sociology.

Ward, A. (1981), 'Customary Land, Land Registration and Social Equality', in D. Denoon and C. Snowden (eds), *A Time to Plant and a Time to Uproot: A History of Agriculture in Papua New Guinea*, Port Moresby: Institute of Papua New Guinea Studies.

–9–

Fluid Forms

Owning Water in Australia
Veronica Strang

Abstract

Drawing on recent ethnographic research in Queensland, this chapter considers notions of ownership in relation to water. It observes that, as a relation between persons and things, concepts of property require some degree of material stasis and it suggests that the material qualities of water elude such conceptual fixity and enable – indeed necessitate – more fluid forms of ownership. Making comparative use of some of the principles of Aboriginal Law, it considers subaltern 'ways of owning' that are processually acquired, subverting the more static concepts of enclosure and separation on which Western notions of property depend.

Water ownership in Australia, as elsewhere, expresses a longstanding ideological tension between the maintenance of collective rights and the desire of individuals and elite groups to enclose and gain control of water 'resources'. There is a parallel divergence in values, between commitments to sustaining social and ecological needs and competitive short-termism. As well as challenging conventional notions of property, alternate forms of water ownership and appropriation draw attention to the separation of economic activities from wider social and ecological processes. This chapter suggests that alternate claims have some potential to support more integrated and thus more sustainable human-environmental relationships.

Introduction

With the aim of contributing to anthropological debates about ownership and appropriation, this chapter proposes several – related – ideas. Building on the precept that human-environmental engagements are mutually constitutive, it suggests that it would be fruitful to pay closer attention to the relationship between notions of ownership and the material qualities of the things that people attempt to own. In doing so it draws on a wider set of theories about the dialectical nature

Figure 9.1 Millaa Millaa waterfall, North Queensland.

of human–environmental interactions (Hegel 1979), and the imaginative use of the material characteristics of the world in formulating metaphors, conceptual schemes and categories (Bachelard 1994; Lakoff and Johnson 1980; Strang 2004). In relation to concepts of property, it extends these ideas to observe that the fluidity of water enables – indeed necessitates – commensurately fluid notions and processes of owning.

A more phenomenological approach to ownership highlights the artificial fixity of legal notions of property, placing 'ways of owning' in spatial and temporal flows of production and consumption, social and economic exchanges, and environmental change. It brings to the fore alternate claims of ownership, not based on legal property rights but processually formed: through the acquisition of knowledge; through creative processes of identity construction; through the accumulation of aesthetic and emotional attachments to place; and through imaginative and physical engagements with material environments. Drawing on the anthropological canon and on recent ethnographic research,[1] this chapter explores such alternate ways of owning. It argues that these constitute a range of counter-claims to exclusive legal constructions of water ownership, and suggests that such claims enable democratic involvement in political processes.

Owning the Country

Property relations are integral to political structures and much has been written about the linkage between property and enfranchisement.[2] The political ecology of resource ownership contains a continuum of possibilities, ranging from egalitarian and relatively collective forms of public ownership, to private and exclusive ownership, with the state playing various potential roles.[3] *How* property ownership is disbursed within a society is vital in defining the degree of equality enjoyed by its members (Widlock and Tadesse 2005). Equality has to be constituted in fact as well as form (Tawney 1952[1931]), particularly in relation to essential resources such as water, the control of which is fundamental to the maintenance of political power (Wittfogel 1957; Worster 1992). This is especially evident when such resources are appropriated, for example in the colonial dispossession and disempowerment of minority or indigenous groups (Attwood and Markus 1999; Dean and Levi 2003; Reynolds 1987; Toussaint 2004).

In a contemporary frame, similar issues are raised by the increasing privatization of water and its appropriation by elite groups in many parts of the world (Verdery 2003). The enclosure of what has been generally regarded as a 'common good' has led to widespread protests, ranging from angry debates, as in the UK under the Thatcher Government (Bakker 2003; Monbiot 2000), to more violent resistance, as in Bolivia in the late 1990s (Albro 2005). There are not only socio-political, but also ecological consequences to these changes. The control of resources by governments or private parties can be considered as alternative regimes of resource management, each of which has implications for social and ecological sustainability (Ophuls 1977; Rose 2004; cf. Godden and Tehan 2010). Hann and others have suggested that a worldwide acceleration in resource privatization denotes a critical shift in property and social relations, from systems that balance short-term self-interest with long-term collective needs, to a newly dominant mode, in which competitive short-termism is unameliorated by collective restraints or moral principles (1998:13, 33; cf. Polanyi 1944; Thompson 1968).

Hardin's influential 'Tragedy of the Commons' (1968) has often been used to suggest that collective management is inefficient in limiting resource use and to promulgate the idea that greater 'efficiency' and investment in sustainability can be gained by privatization. But, as Ostrom has noted (1990), Hardin's examples describe 'open access' rather than 'common ownership' and many limited common property regimes around the world have demonstrated successful long-term sustainability. Aboriginal Australians are often held up as an exemplar in this regard, having sustained a particular economic mode with relatively low environmental impacts for many millennia (Williams and Hunn 1986).[4] Like other place-based groups they provide inspiration for environmentalists and

Figure 9.2 Water rights poster, Mexico City.

other activists hoping to encourage societies to reinstitute more sustainable and collective social forms and resource management practices.

Critics of privatization have also noted that it devolves risks and responsibilities to individual or minority actors poorly situated to meet social or ecological needs, or to transnational corporations more concerned with pleasing shareholders than protecting local lifeways and ecosystems (Lash and Wynne in Beck 2002). This is readily demonstrable in Australia, where small miners and landholders are ill-equipped to manage their activities sustainably and large corporations have often failed to prioritize environmental and social concerns. The result is a loss of environmental flows in many waterways, the pollution of aquatic systems, salination and widespread land degradation. In an arid continent with major variations in freshwater availability, the enclosure and commodification of resources has thus led to increasingly unsustainable practices. The ensuing water crisis provides a salutary tale (Hussey and Dovers 2006).

From Commons to Elites

In Australia transitions in water ownership and use have echoed changes in many Western nations but, rather than taking several millennia, they have 'fast-forwarded' over the last two hundred years. Prior to European colonization of the continent, indigenous groups managed people and resources through a quintessential limited common property regime. In a kin-based network of exchange relations, language groups were sub-divided into clans whose spatially defined identity arose from totemic ancestors located in the landscape. These ancestral beings constituted a sentient environment seen as an 'equal partner' in a highly intimate, localized and deeply affective human-environmental relationship. Population control, a massive lexicon of ecological knowledge and subtle forms of environmental management maintained this socio-economic system for many thousands of years.

Following the massive disruptions of colonization, Aboriginal communities now maintain a hybrid economy (Altman 2006), but customary systems of ownership have persisted, and are regarded as inseparable from other aspects of life. Clans still own the 'country' of their ancestral beings collectively, providing their members with inalienable rights to clan estates through various forms of inheritance. Individual identity is defined by the 'home' place from which a person's spirit emerges (usually in paternal clan land, but sometimes in their 'mother's country'). This is generally a water source of some sort, pointing to an important co-substantiality in personal identity and place, and demonstrating the ways in which 'things' are implicated in social processes (see Morphy this volume).

Rights to land and resources are also acquired processually, for example through the accumulation of knowledge – most specifically sacred (and often restricted) knowledge, but also more general social and ecological knowledge about country. Ownership is gained and affirmed through the use and management of resources, and through the development of affective relations with places and people. Thus indigenous property relations remain fully integrated into a whole range of social and cultural processes, and it has been a lengthy – and only partially successful – challenge to simplify and explicate them sufficiently to enable a land rights or native title process circumscribed by European law (see Attwood 1996; Morphy 2006; Rigsby 2006; Strang 2000; Toussaint 2004; Williams and Hunn 1986; Durie this volume). As noted previously though (Introduction, pp. 4–5), this translation has generated models of alternate – and more fluid – notions of ownership based on social identity, mythological links, knowledge, engagement, usage, long-term historical association and affective attachment.

European colonists in Australia imposed a narrower system of property ownership which was not only more individuated, but also framed land and resources as alienable and thus potentially commodifiable. Until recently, land and water ownership remained congruent, with the land being divided into various forms of tenure – some freehold, but most held under long-term cattle or mining leases – with water rights included in the package. For many decades farmers and miners were able to access artesian water, abstract water from waterways and build dams without any governance or restraint.

Then, as elsewhere, development, intensified production and greater competition for freshwater resources resulted in the imposition of government control, first with a formalized system of water allocations, then in the 1980s a (much resented) requirement for 'Water Allocation Management Plans'. Subsequently (as with fisheries, see Minnegal and Dwyer, this volume) there has been a simultaneous acceleration towards greater restriction and regulation and towards more exclusive forms of water ownership.

Discouraged from direct privatization of the water industry by angry protests against such decisions elsewhere, John Howard's federal government nevertheless moved quite a long way in this direction. Some putative public ownership remains: constitutionally, water is owned by the Australian States and decisions about water allocations were, until recently, made entirely at a state level, in Queensland's case by the Department of Natural Resources, Mines and Water.[5] However, the Howard government made strenuous efforts to wrest the control of water away from the States, initiating a 'National Plan' for water and establishing federally funded 'regional management bodies' to circumvent state control.

Under federal pressure (and sometimes in accord with their own ideological positions) state governments reorganized the departments responsible for water supply into Government Owned Corporations (GOCs) run along commercial lines. These have further devolved many operational responsibilities for water supply to private sub-contractors. As *The Economist* noted when the Thatcher government privatized the water industry in the UK, there are 'more than fifty methods of privatization' (in Alexander 2004:255).[6]

Commodification is fundamental to any transition from common good to individual property and one of the most critical moves towards resource privatization in Australia has been the separation of water from the land and the introduction of water trading. Water allocations previously tied to land and regarded as borrowings from a common pool have been legally separated and reconstituted as private and tradable assets – a form of 'propertization' that, Hann points out, continuously establishes new 'fictitious commodities' (2007:287). Water trading relies on a system of 'virtual' volumetric abstractions theoretically available from particular water sources. Parry observes that such changes in the 'form' of an object

> create new regimes of commodification, new modes of transaction, and a concomitant acceleration of trade and exchange; and with them, a series of challenges for existing property rights regimes... One of the most significant – and I would argue intended – consequences of translating biological materials from a corporeal to an informational state is to make them more mobile and hence more amenable to circulation. (2004:29, 33)

As well as re-forming 'things', this process involves what Minnegal and Dwyer describe as a process of disembedding and imposing ideologies and logic, which 'reshapes the subjective experience of affected persons' (this volume p. 198).

Thus recently imposed changes in water ownership in Australia have used the fluid qualities of water to create a system that both literally and conceptually abstracts it from social and ecological systems, commodifying it and reconstituting it as an asset that can be 'owned'. This narrower form of ownership favours commercial and private interests and largely excludes alternate and indigenous claims[7] (Altman 2004; Wilmore and Upreti, this volume). However, the material characteristics of water, and thus the metaphors that people use for thinking about it, mean that such ownership remains elusive, and there are complex questions about the degree to which such exclusive concepts of property can really 'hold water'.

Holding Water

Contradicting Bentham's notion of property as 'a mere conception of the mind' (in Verdery and Humphrey 2004:1),[8] Godelier suggests that 'property only really exists when it is rendered effective in and through a process of concrete appropriation' (1986:81). Hann also underlines the importance of keeping sight of the materiality of things:

> In focusing on forms of circulation and consumption, there is a danger that anthropologists may overlook the fact that many things (notably land – 'real property' as it is termed by the lawyers), do not circulate so readily. Many patterns of ownership demonstrate important continuities which provide effective stabilizing anchors in even the most rapidly changing, 'post-modern' societies. (1998:31)

As this implies, land is eminently tangible and holdable. The term 'enclosure' communicates this groundedness precisely: encircled with visible boundaries, territory can be 'staked out'. In these terms land is easily appropriated from common ownership. However, such appropriations often require fluidity in the movements of dispossessed people and, conversely, boundaries can be breached and transgressed with 'influxes', 'invasions' and 'floods' of otherness (Strang 2004).

Material culture is equally concrete, but its portability allows for considerable movement: shells and the armbands 'circulate' around Kula rings; grandmother's pearls flow down family lines of inheritance; objects flow over cultural boundaries and across time and space. Material artefacts are in some ways more graspable than land: although they can certainly be appropriated – and their portability simplifies this – they are also easier to control and protect. Thus, material artefacts are sufficiently 'concrete' to be readily perceived as 'real property'.

In effect, as a relation between persons and things, 'ownership' requires some degree of material stasis. The things people own need to be sufficiently concrete to be readily recognized as theirs, and, when things are not portable, people need to be 'in place' sufficiently to claim them exclusively.[9] But, despite the illusions of stasis that are necessary to maintain this perceived fixity, both things and people undergo constant transformation: people and their identities shift and mature; artefacts degrade; environmental change is constant. Thus Strathern has stressed the temporal nature of both identity and ownership, observing that 'ownership gathers things momentarily to a point by locating them in the owner, halting endless dissemination, effecting an identity' (1996:30).

Unlike land and artefacts, water, energy and ideas are not readily 'located': they are intrinsically fluid. They require active containment and storage, and remain difficult to capture and keep. Water readily leaks away, evaporates, flows wherever it can. It may spring up in a particular place, or flow through a particular space, but it won't stay there. And the movements of aquifers and rivers bear little relation to the 'fixed' boundaries staked onto the land around them. Unlike more concrete 'commodities' (such as minerals), or even more viscous fluids (such as oil), water, energy and ideas permeate wider systems in highly dynamic ways, making them difficult to separate out.

Crucially, water is also internal: it flows through people and places. Composing sixty-seven per cent of the human body, it is usefully illustrative of property's internalizing role. As anthropologists of consumption have noted (Lupton 1996), eating and drinking are basic acts of appropriation. In this most fundamental of value transformations, water and food are extracted from the environment to sustain human physical being (Verdery and Humphrey 2004). Material substances are literally embodied into the self and its identity in an intimate relationship between 'people and things' (Hann 1998; Strathern 1999). But while the more solid ingredients of food – minerals, fats and so on – may be integrated into bodily structures, water continues to move, circulating through blood streams and escaping the physical boundaries of the self in urine, sweat, tears and evaporation. Thus even the body, the 'thing' that humans own the most, can only hold water temporarily.

In broader terms water's flow through all organic things, including people, substantiates ideas about common humanity and locates humankind within a global hydrological ecosystem. At a local level it is a vital constitutive element of social identity, connecting bodies and environments and giving 'common substance' to groups and the places that they inhabit. It is thus intrinsic to a process through which identity is dynamically located in a material environment.

In diverse cultural ways, but consistently across cultures, water has been associated not only with social, but also spiritual identity. Hydrological processes provide a common metaphor for the movement of the human spirit through cycles of life and death. As the substance of social and spiritual being, water is also deeply imbued with ideas about wealth and regeneration and the capacity of human groups to be 'wealthy' (i.e. healthy and whole), and to reproduce themselves and the things that they need. Thus water provides a perfect metaphor for the generative creative nature of property relations.

These fluid qualities (and the reality of human needs for water) have ensured that historically, while ways of owning land and material culture have become more exclusive, water has continued to be regarded as a common good. But, as noted previously, its essentiality to all processes of production and reproduction mean that the control of water is directly associated with political empowerment. This linkage has strengthened as 'the economy' has come to be framed increasingly as a separate and primary sphere of activities, encouraging a growing conflict between universal and implicitly egalitarian rights to water (now inscribed in international human rights law),[10] and the competitive desires of individuals or elite groups to gain control of water 'resources'. This tension runs thematically through all debates about the ownership and control of water, and recurs in the interplay between different water users and claimants within major river catchments in Australia. The Brisbane River provides an illustrative case.

Owning the River

Winding for about seventy miles across south-east Queensland, the Brisbane River links resource-based economic production upriver with the sea port that provided the starting point for the city. Just below the cattle stations that predominate in the upper reaches, several large dams supply water to the conurbations along the coast and – until recently – provided fairly unlimited irrigation to an agricultural area in the central valley, which produces fruit and vegetables, wine and some dairy products.

The fertile soils of the Brisbane River floodplains proved attractive to farmers as soon as a British penal colony was established beside the estuary in 1824. Expanding steadily upriver, and at times fighting the indigenous owners of the land for possession of it, 'pioneering' European farmers were central to Queensland's colonial settlement and development. Forming a powerful and highly conservative rural 'squattocracy', they effectively governed the State for much of its history, exerting both physical and political control over the environment.[11]

During this time many farmers built major water storages and these provide some security in the 'holding' of water supplies. There are also thousands of unmetered water bores tapping supplies direct from artesian sources and many

Figure 9.3 Farm dam in the Brisbane River catchment.

more uncounted and unmeasured small impoundments and abstractions from local rivers and creeks. Thus the materiality of land ownership remains the most certain way of holding water, insofar as local ecosystems continue to provide supplies.

However, ecological, social and economic pressures have begun to impinge on this assumed certainty. As noted above, the impoundment and abstraction of water has become more heavily regulated as competition for limited supplies has increased. A commitment to constant growth has driven rapid intensification and the volume of water used in irrigation (and thus dependence on it) has doubled every decade since the 1960s. Along the Brisbane River mining and quarrying require ample water supplies and the lower catchment contains similarly thirsty industries: paper mills, food processing plants, refineries, chemical producers and suchlike. More critically, echoing trends in other industrialized countries, Queensland has seen a major shift from rural to urban life in recent decades, compounded by massive immigration into its coastal conurbations. There has been an economic shift in emphasis from primary to secondary industries. Unlike mining, agriculture no longer makes a significant contribution to the State's economy and it employs a smaller and smaller percentage of its workforce.[12] In a deregulated and increasingly globalized economic context, the agricultural sector has therefore become more marginal and since 2002 lengthy droughts have added further to its woes. Although farmers remain closely involved in political activities, their claim to water has become commensurately tenuous.

While large corporate agriculturalists can afford to buy newly privatized water 'assets', many smaller farmers have found themselves unable to afford to keep their allocations, even when water is available. As illustrated by the controversial giant dams at Cubbie Station (able to impound about a quarter of the water that would otherwise flow down the Culgoa River into the Murray-Darling basin),[13] the commodification of water allocations has made 'holding water' an increasingly speculative activity. Thus in an increasingly volatile and competitive water market, farmers' rights to allocations, though theoretically strengthened by privatization, have been simultaneously weakened.

Running into resource limits has created other pressures. Although all commercial water users theoretically 'own' their water allocations, in times of drought these rights are superseded by the priority given to domestic water users and energy suppliers. With 1,000–1,500 people a week moving to Brisbane, there is an ever-increasing demand for domestic water and electricity. This poses a significant alternate claim for limited water resources. Farmers may 'own' water allocations when supplies are sufficient, but no politician can afford to let the city run dry.

Counter-claims

Along with these immediate pressures, farmers and industrial water users face an array of subtle and not-so-subtle counter-claims to their 'ownership' of water which resonate with 'double movements' discerned elsewhere (see Hann 2007; Filer and Lowe this volume). Local indigenous communities, though long dispossessed of their land and water, still hold a counter-claim to the ownership of the settler population as a whole. There is little hope of many Native Title claims succeeding in the heavily developed south-eastern corner of the State, but the Aboriginal population nevertheless maintains its own concepts of ownership and belonging. This is not without influence: as the Mabo case illustrated, where possession remains in question, there is commensurate pressure for more 'certainty' from those whose control of land and resources is threatened.[14] Perhaps more importantly, in a settler society, the visible presence of a subaltern model of ownership, containing multiple and much more fluid ways of owning, is 'unsettling'.

Alternate claims of water ownership within the non-indigenous population, though more fragmented, contain many of the processual elements that are discernible in Aboriginal Law. They are founded on constructions of identity and belonging; on community membership and involvement; on direct engagement and affective connection with places; on the acquisition of areas of knowledge and expertise; and on the investment of labour and agency. They also share (loosely) some underlying principles, valorizing collective egalitarian ways of holding water and more sustainable human-environmental relationships.

These more fluid forms of owning are readily discernible in the interactions of the 'stakeholders' involved in regional and catchment management groups, and all are influenced by the material qualities of water. Issues of identity and belonging are particularly pertinent in a settler society such as Australia (see Trigger and Griffiths 2003). As noted above, a sense of identity depends, to some extent, on fluid connections: a vision of co-substantiality between people and place, and of common substance within communities. Rural landowners, advantaged by long-standing relations with places and more stable social networks, are particularly assertive in this regard, appropriating Aboriginal discourses, actively valorizing their historic ties and 'cultural heritage', and resisting other claims to land and resources. Conservatively wedded to Western notions of property, however, they present these ties as a valorization of their legal rights, rather than as an alternate basis for ownership.

Assertions of co-substantiality are less achievable for an increasingly mobile urban population, which, as in other industrialized societies, has to seek more fluid ways of connecting with places and people. The ethnographic data suggest that this longing to belong, which Berger *et al.* called 'homelessness' (1973), underlies many counter-claims for ownership and control.

Recreational Claims

A desire to connect is evident in people's increasing engagement with places – and most specifically water places – through recreational activities, such as fishing, sailing, canoeing, swimming or simply gathering for social events. As noted elsewhere, such activities are fundamentally concerned with the 're-creation' of the self through sensory, aesthetic and affective interactions. In communing with 'nature' people seek to relax their normal boundaries and achieve a sense of belonging (Strang 1996, 2009, 2010). Here, too, the qualities of water play a part, providing mesmerizing visual and aural stimuli, pleasurable sensory and aesthetic experiences, and literal opportunities for immersion in places. Recreational water users undertake what Kohn calls 'self-making' (this volume), appropriating and embodying an alternate cultural landscape composed of places and practices that are physically and imaginatively fulfilling.

An important outcome of such interactions is a nascent sense of co-substantiality and connection and a desire to protect recreational environments. The more that people engage and connect with the landscape, gaining knowledge and experience

Figure 9.4 Swimmer, Lake Eacham, North Queensland.

of it, the more they feel a sense of ownership. Recreational water use has therefore fuelled not only a greater demand for direct access to land and water (which in a heavily privatized landscape is proving contentious), but has also generated a fluid and ephemeral sense of belonging in a collective 'back yard', which challenges the exclusivity of the long-standing incumbents.

Conserving Claims

There is a well-documented relationship between recreational engagement with land and waterscapes, and concern for environmental protection (Milton 2002; Saarinen 1998). In Queensland expanding recreational water use and a major demographic shift from rural to urban life have strengthened support for a growing environmental movement. This has encouraged a vocal critique of industrial farming and mining practices and their environmental impacts, to the extent that politicians now have to take these concerns into account. The establishment of regional and catchment-based management organizations is one way in which they have tried to demonstrate a willingness to do so.

With more substantial backing (given greater impetus by anxieties about climate change), conservation groups have become significant 'stakeholders' in these organizations. They have – as they see it – captured the moral high ground with a discourse in which 'nature' (and the 'exemplary' indigenous population seen as aligned with it) must be protected from exploitative short-termism and its destructive effects. Empowered by this narrative, environmental groups now have an influential role in encouraging legislative protection for ecosystems and in the direct management of river catchment areas.

Though still an important subtext, the egalitarian social agenda originally espoused by the environmental movement has been heavily subsumed by a narrower technical approach. Thus the managerial aspirations of contemporary conservation groups are generally framed in terms of having knowledge and expertise about environmental care. Nevertheless, this serves to highlight the importance of knowledge acquisition as a basis for subaltern claims of water ownership. As Aboriginal Law demonstrates, processes of knowing and owning flow together readily and, for environmental groups, specialized knowledge about the environment – and an entire language concerned with 'biodiversity', 'wildlife corridors' and suchlike – provides a keen sense of ownership. They have little hesitation in using possessive pronouns about 'our' river catchment and 'our' environment, which implicitly challenge the practical knowledge of the farming community and transgress established boundaries of ownership.

Expert Claims

There is substantial overlap in the way that 'expertise' validates environmentalist claims and its centrality to the authority of a scientific community equally involved in water management. In a sense they comprise quite similar 'expert communities', differentiated primarily by the extent to which their activities are directed towards scientific investigation or political activism. Both might be said to be part of a larger series of networks or assemblies of people who, though they don't own water or have a political mandate for its governance, influence the ways in which it is managed and controlled.

There are many natural scientists working on water issues in Queensland: ecologists, hydrologists, biologists, botanists, agricultural researchers, soil specialists and so on. They are regular recipients of funding from government bodies including regional management organizations and thus have considerable influence upon their decision-making and on their managerial projects, most of which are therefore focused on practical ecological issues such as weed invasions and pollution.[15]

The importance of scientific authority is particularly well illustrated by the Brisbane River's Healthy Waterways Partnership, which is specifically designed to construct relationships between scientists and other 'stakeholders'. It assesses and reports on water quality in the catchment area, with 'grades' to shame polluters and awards for the 'best' performers. Often the latter are local industries that have cleaned up their operations.

While natural scientists tend to avoid being drawn into overtly political environmentalist critiques of agricultural and industrial water users, their expertise also presents alternative visions of the catchment area, not as 'cattle stations', 'farms' and 'industrial operations', but as landforms, hydrological processes, soil and timber types and flora and fauna distributions. Defined by scientific categories and focused on connective hydrological and ecological flows, this fluid sub-cultural landscape implicitly crosses boundaries and contradicts more static forms of tenure.

Thus in their various ways 'expert knowledges' about the environment, held by scientists and by conservation groups, challenge the authority provided by the local knowledge of farmers and other industrial water users and engender feelings of ownership that appropriate some of the control provided by legal property rights. In this sense 'intellectual property', usually framed as the ownership of knowledge (see Hirsch and Strathern 2004; Coombe 1998 and this volume; Glaskin, this volume), can also be considered as an appropriative process that substantiates alternate claims to resources.

Laboured Claims

Processes of gaining knowledge about places are often coupled with the investment of time and labour which similarly provide a basis for claims of ownership. Historically, the representational focus has been on the way that mining and cattle-raising pioneers 'earned' their place in the landscape through 'hard yakka', reflecting a long-standing Puritanical vision of the rights acquired through labour (as per Locke 1993 [1713]). This foundational national vision has long been central to farmers' resistance to indigenous land claims and today it is also utilized to justify their demands for greater security in access to water resources.

Now, however, other ways of investing labour in water are coming into play. Managerial or scientific professionals may be said to invest their intellectual labour, and such an appropriative rationale is equally discernible among the small catchment groups clustered around the river and its tributaries. There are now approximately thirty-five of these in the river catchment, mostly located in Brisbane's urban areas. In these highly localized groups, as well as engaging imaginatively with the waterways, people quite literally invest labour, working as unpaid volunteers, clearing weeds and debris and planting trees, shrubs and native grasses. Their activities have a dual purpose: to strengthen 'neighbourhood' communities and to 'restore' their local environments.

Figure 9.5 Tree planting on the Brisbane River.

Local catchment groups are part of the grassroots of a broader conservation movement which provides the numbers and votes that have persuaded governments to pay attention to environmental concerns. They are also part of a wider critique of privatization, upholding one of the few remaining forms of direct public management and control of the material environment. They are encouraged not only by their local proximity to the river, but also by the reality that, like recreational water users, they have direct experiential involvement with the river. To some this constitutes an individual claim: people plant riverside trees and want to go back years later to see how 'their' trees are doing. Primarily, though, catchment groups hope to build a sense of community through engagement with and care for a particular locale. As Coombe points out, this reification of notions of community 'does distinctive forms of political and legal work' (this volume, p.118). People draw imaginatively on the connecting qualities of water, defining themselves by the tributaries around which they live, and contextualizing their activities within a larger moral claim for the collective ownership of water and shared long-term responsibility for social and ecological well-being.

Conflicting Claims

Queensland therefore contains a range of groups with alternate claims to water based on fluid and ephemeral notions and processes of ownership and on different narratives about places and things which, as Kaul observes, serve as mechanisms for processes of appropriation (this volume). These are also used to substantiate legal forms of ownership. For example, farmers underline their legal rights by articulating aesthetic and affective interactions with the land and waterscape. They regard their claims as being validated by practical managerial knowledge and large investments of time and labour. They respond to critiques of their activities by expressing the moral value of 'primary production' in sustaining the population and assuring the nation's wealth, and they feel that they make a positive contribution to collective needs.

However, the wider community no longer sees them in this light. Like many areas in Australia, south-east Queensland contains a rapidly widening urban-rural divide. The determination of primary producers to resist 'interference' from government and conservationists, and access for recreational land and water users, has created a gulf that is difficult to bridge. Enclosure doesn't just keep out, it keeps in, separating private owners from collective support in a literally 'anti-social' process opposite to the social appropriation of persons described by Long in this volume. Recently there has been little sympathy for the plight of farmers as they have run into the limitations on growth imposed by an arid continent – and little concern about the pressures created by deregulation and the importation of cheap food from other countries. In this sense material ownership has brought social disownership.

This separation also arises, in part, from major divergences in values. Rural communities and primary industries have continued to hold the productivist views entrenched throughout Queensland's history (and strongly affirmed by Bjelke-Petersen's State government). But the urban population has become more cosmopolitan and open to change. It engages with inland areas largely for recreational purposes, wants an 'unspoiled' environment, and is increasingly willing to blame industrial agriculture and other primary industries for the ecological degradation evident in the river catchment and along the coast. Deeply concerned about the lack of *communitas* in their own experience, city dwellers recognize, at least subliminally, that this depends to some degree on ownership and belonging in place. The urban areas also contain the sectors of the population most likely to harbour grave doubts about the long-term social and ecological consequences of economic rationalism.[16]

Catchment Management

Australia's regional and larger catchment management groups were established partly to reconcile these divergent interests and to balance public and private control over land and water resources through co-management. They are composed of the various 'stakeholders' involved in river catchments: farming, industry, recreational groups, conservation organizations, government agencies, scientific advisors and indigenous groups. Their remit is to achieve 'integration' via a 'triple bottom line' approach encompassing social, economic and environmental concerns.

However, research on these organizations (Lawrence 2005; Strang 2001, 2009) suggests that each group participates to promote its own interests. Thus conservation organizations hope to persuade primary producers to adopt more sustainable practices, and to encourage regulators to enforce environmentally protective measures; indigenous communities want to establish their rights to land and water if not as owners, at least as co-managers; while the farmers and industrial land and water owners are often there (they say) specifically to fend off these pressures and ensure that government representatives – in their mediatory role – hear their 'side' of the story.

In effect catchment and regional management groups contain distinct networks or 'emergent assemblies' through which the social reconstitutes the political (Latour 2005). Each such assembly has ideological alignments with – as one would expect – commercial water users hoping to protect their exclusive ownership and control of land and resources; indigenous communities and their allies asserting native title rights; and non-commercial, urban and conservationist 'assemblies' attempting to uphold alternate, more collective claims. The extent to which each set of interests prevails depends heavily on the political climate.

Two decades after the earliest catchment groups were established in Queensland, the creation of co-management groups has served to give some voice to subaltern concerns, but there is considerable debate about whether this has resulted in real change. Primary producers certainly claim to have espoused principles of 'sustainability' and are anxious to present themselves as good resource managers, but, although some efficiency gains have been made, there is little sign of movement away from an overriding commitment to economic growth and development, or towards broader, more collective forms of ownership.

There are several impediments to change. It is clear that the balance of power is uneven, reflecting the lengthy political dominance of neoliberalism, the legal authority of commercial property rights and the strength of particular social and political networks. Regional catchment groups are heavily dominated by longstanding elites: a 'business community' greatly empowered by its economic centrality, and a farming sector that, although it has lost some social and economic ground, still holds the land, and can still draw on its foundational position in Australian history. Both groups have provided political leadership since the earliest days of European settlement and still maintain close ties with all levels of government.

It has therefore been argued that mechanisms such as catchment management groups are largely performative, giving only a putative democratic 'voice' to alternate claims and interests. Although such groups present an appearance of organizational transparency (but see Strathern 2000), difficult social and polit-ical issues are often avoided in the interests of maintaining superficial harmony. Negotiations and self-interest are concealed and 'collaborative' activities often serve merely to defuse debates, enabling dominant interest groups to conduct business as usual. Thus, while such devolution of decision making to a 'community level' is often represented as enabling democratic control, it is necessary to consider the possibility that it may simply leave the field open to powerful elites, allowing governments to abdicate their responsibilities for resource management and thus for genuinely democratic governance (Lawrence 2005; Strang 2009).

Progress in this regard is further impeded by the fragmentary structural context in which co-management groups are located. In industrialized societies domains of activity – economic practices, religion, the environment, social interaction – have their own laws, languages and operational principles. As long as productive processes are dealt with separately from social and ecological issues, these languages and operational ideas remain oppositional and differentially evalu-ated. This differential also applies to ownership, giving strength to legal forms aligned with economic activities and devaluing alternate, largely non-commercial claims.

Water onto Stone

Despite the apparent intractability of the situation, water issues somehow bring subversion to the surface. In the face of efforts to extend more exclusive forms of ownership, to privatize and enclose water, alternate claims based on fluid notions of ownership have not only persisted over time, they have become more pressing, providing an increasing challenge to the status quo. They raise vital issues about who owns water, and who owns the state, and question the wisdom of giving free rein to economic rationalism and short-term values.

The research on which this chapter is based suggests that this is partly because water itself defies imaginative compartmentalization and containment. Its intrinsic fluidity not only presents practical challenges to people's desire to 'hold' water, but also offers a metaphorical vision of dynamic and holistic – rather than static and divisible – relations between people and things. The meanings encoded in water are processual: it is the symbolic substance of ongoing constructions of identity; of shifting hydrological cycles of social and spiritual being; of a creative ability to generate wealth and health over time. Both internally and externally water connects people and places and reflects fundamental human needs for *communitas*. And, as the most literally essential of substances, it cannot be separated from fundamental issues of enfranchisement and social justice. In the end it is both materially and metaphorically impossible to separate it either from the land, or from the people who inhabit the land.

This reality is readily encompassed in Aboriginal Law, but is less visible in the larger, more fragmentary cosmology that informs non-Aboriginal life in Australia. Dominant discourses don't articulate a holistic view of human-environmental relationships and this lack of integration is painful all round: to those excluded from narrowly conceived notions of ownership and participation and to those who – though they may be winners in a competition for resource control – feel trapped by external pressures to produce, and are ambiguous about being constrained (and in consequence demonized) by a narrow economic role. Interviews with farmers and industrial water users suggest that some would genuinely welcome a return to a more collective, stable and sustainable approach. In effect they feel fenced in by their own enclosures or, as they put it, 'it's hard to be green when you're in the red'.

The counter-claims that promote alternate, more fluid forms of ownership are in many ways a call for reconciliation between the diverse groups who inhabit Australia, and between economic activities and the social and environmental context in which these take place. By challenging putatively 'fixed' notions of ownership, they transgress the intellectual compartmentalization that encourages unsustainable human-environmental engagements. Thus, although most non-indigenous counter-claimants have yet to achieve an integrated and holistic approach, with a literal and political change in climate and a broader societal willingness to adopt more fluid forms of ownership and control, they may get closer to doing so.

Acknowledgements

This research was funded by the Australian Research Council as part of a larger project designed in collaboration with Sandy Toussaint at the University of Western Australia. Both UWA and the University of Queensland provided further support in the form of Honorary Fellowships. The research process benefited greatly from the enthusiastic participation of diverse groups of water users along the Mitchell and Brisbane Rivers, and helpful feedback on the outcomes has been provided, at various stages, by anthropologists in Auckland, Europe and the UK. I would particularly like to thank the Institute of Advanced Studies at Durham University, whose generous 'Water Fellowship' in 2009 provided a supportive and stimulating environment for research and writing.

Notes

1. This research was carried out on two major river catchments in Queensland between 2003 and 2008 as part of a larger collaborative project, 'Under Water', which was funded by the Australian Research Council.
2. This has been well established since Locke pointed to the importance of property ownership as a way of defining membership in the democratic state (1993 [1713]).
3. As Alexander observes, the state can act *as* 'the people' (in which state-owned assets are owned *by* the people); as representatives *of* the people – a more paternalistic idea in which assets are held in trust; and as 'other', with a range of constructions (2004:253).
4. There have been lively debates about the effects of Aboriginal practices on Australian ecologies (e.g. Lewis 1989). Fire management regimes, hunting and domiculture have clearly had some effects, but these are minor in comparison to the massive environmental impacts of 200 years of European settlement.
5. Responsibility for environmental protection lies elsewhere with the (much weaker) Environmental Protection Agency.
6. For those unfamiliar with the song, this is a reference to Paul Simon's 'Fifty Ways to Leave Your Lover'.
7. There has been, to date, only one successful indigenous claim to water rights in Australia, at Blue Mud Bay in Arnhem Land, and this was concerned with the tidal zone rather than freshwater resources (see Morphy and Morphy 2006).
8. See also Gray 1991.
9. As Verdery and Humphrey note (2004:7 citing Collier pers. comm.), there is a relationship between the extent to which identities are seen as individual and boundaried, and the degree to which this is concretized in boundaried land ownership.
10. In global terms, as a signatory to the United Nations Declaration of Human Rights, Australia subscribes to the notion of universal rights to water.
11. Officially, the State was established as such in 1859.
12. In 2006–2007, Queensland's gross farm product, 'a measure of the value added in production contributed by farm businesses', was calculated to be $5.2 billion or 2.8 per cent of the gross state product (Australian Bureau of Statistics 2008). In 2009 primary industries in the state (which include agriculture, fisheries and forestry) employed 3.7 per cent of the workforce (Department of Education and Training 2009).
13. Cubbie Station is situated just north of the NSW border, on one of the major tributaries of the Darling River. Given the extreme ecological degradation

of the Murray-Darling Basin, there was considerable uproar when its owners were permitted to build huge dams along 28 miles of the Culgon River, impounding much of the water that would otherwise have provided substantial flow in the river basin.

14. The acknowledgement of Native Title rights in the 1993 Mabo ruling led directly to a major demand by non-Aboriginal landholders for 'certainty' of ownership.

15. In Queensland it is notable that natural scientists, whose work is directly concerned with material resources, readily find common ground with farmers and primary producers. They are popular advisors with regional management bodies. Focusing on 'the people issues', social scientists are more inclined to be sympathetic to egalitarian perspectives and are thus rarely welcome in stakeholder groups dominated by commercial interests. There is an enticing line of reflexive enquiry to be considered here.

16. In Australia this term generally denotes a neoliberal commitment to the rule of 'market forces' and an assumption that rational decisions are based on primarily economic criteria.

References

Albro, R. (2005), '"The Water is Ours, Carajo!": Deep Citizenship in Bolivia's Water War', in J. Nash (ed.), *Social Movements: An Anthropological Reader,* Malden, MA: Blackwell, pp. 249–68.

Alexander, C. (2004), 'Value, Relations and Changing Bodies: Privatization and Property Rights in Kazakhstan', in K. Verdery and C. Humphrey (eds), *Property In Question: Value Transformation in the Global Economy,* Oxford, New York: Berg, pp. 251–73.

Altman, J. (2004), 'Indigenous Interests and Water Property Rights', in *Dialogue,* 23(3): 29–34.

Altman, J. (2006), 'Nomads Triumphing Today: How Some Hunters in Arnhem Land Engage with the State, the Market and Globalisation', seminar paper, University of Auckland, 3 May 2006.

Attwood, B. (1996), *In the Age of Mabo: History, Aborigines and Australia,* Sydney: Allen and Unwin.

Attwood, B. and Markus, A. (1999), *The Struggle for Aboriginal Rights: A Documentary History,* St Leonards, New South Wales: Allen and Unwin.

Australian Bureau of Statistics (2008), *Agricultural State Profile, Queensland, 2006–2007,* website http://www.abs.gov.au/AUSSTATS, released 19/09/2008.

Bachelard, G. (1994), *The Poetics of Space,* trans. M. Jolas, Boston: Beacon Press.

Bakker, K. (2003), *An Uncooperative Commodity: Privatising Water in England and Wales,* Oxford: Oxford University Press.

Berger, P, Berger, B. and Kellner, H. (1973), *The Homeless Mind,* New York: Vintage.

Coombe, R. (1998), *The Cultural Life of Intellectual Properties*, Durham: Duke University Press.

Dean, B. and Levi, J. (eds) (2003), *At the Risk of Being Heard: Identity, Indigenous Rights and Postcolonial States,* Ann Arbor: University of Michigan Press.

The Economist (1993), 'Privatization: Selling the State', 21 August 328 (7825), pp. 18–20.

Godden, L. and Tehan, M. (eds) (2010), *Comparative Perspectives on Communal Lands and Individual Ownership: Sustainable Futures,* London, New York: Routledge.

Godelier, M. (1986), 'Territory and Property in Some Pre-Capitalist Societies', in M. Godelier, *The Mental and the Material,* London: Verso, pp. 71–121.

Gray, K. (1991), 'Property in Thin Air', *Cambridge Law Journal*, 50(2): 252–307.

Hann, C. (ed) (1998), *Property Relations: Renewing the Anthropological Tradition*, New York: Cambridge University Press.

Hann, C. (2007), 'A New Double Movement? Anthropological Perspectives on Property in the Age of Neoliberalism', *Socio-Economic Review*, 5(2): 287–318.

Hardin, G. (1968), 'The Tragedy of the Commons', *Science*, 162: 1243–8.

Hegel, G.W.F. (1979), *The Phenomenology of Spirit,* translated by A.V. Miller, Oxford: Oxford University Press.

Hirsch, E. and Strathern, M. (eds) (2004), *Transactions and Creations: Property Debates and the Stimulus of Melanesia,* New York: Berghahn Books.

Hussey, K. and Dovers, S. (2006), 'Trajectories in Australian Water Policy', *Journal of Contemporary Water Research and Education*, 135: 36–50.

Lakoff, G. and Johnson M. (1980), *Metaphors We Live By,* Chicago, London: University of Chicago Press.

Latour, B. (2005), *Reassembling the Social: An Introduction to Actor-Network-Theory*, Oxford: Oxford University Press.

Lash, S. and Wynne, B. (1992), 'Introduction', in U. Beck, *Risk Society: Towards a New Modernity,* Newbury Park, CA: Sage.

Lawrence, G. (2005), 'Promoting Sustainable Development: The Question of Governance', in F. Buttel and P. McMichael (eds), *New Directions in the Sociology of Global Development: Research in Rural Sociology and Development,* Vol. II, London: Elsevier, pp. 145–74.

Lewis, H. (1989), 'Ecological and Technological Knowledge of Fire: Aborigines versus Park Rangers in Northern Australia', *American Anthropologist*, 91: 940–61.

Locke, J. (1993) [1713], *Two Treatises of Government,* 4th edn, London: Dent.

Lupton, D. (1996), *Food, the Body and the Self*, London, Thousand Oaks, New Delhi: Sage Publications.

Milton, K. (2002), *Loving Nature: Towards an Ecology of Emotion*, London, New York: Routledge.

Monbiot, G. (2000), *Captive State: The Corporate Takeover of Britain*, London: Macmillan.

Morphy, H. and Morphy, F. (2006), 'Tasting the Waters: Discriminating Identities in the Waters of Blue Mud Bay', *Journal of Material Culture*, 11(1/2): 67–85.

Morphy, H. (2006), 'The Practice of an Expert: Anthropology in Native Title', *Anthropological Forum*, 16(2): 135–51.

Ophuls, W. (1977), *Ecology and the Politics of Scarcity*, San Francisco: W.H. Freeman.

Ostrom, E. (1990), *Governing the Commons*, Cambridge: Cambridge University Press.

Parry, B. (2004), 'Bodily Transactions: Regulating a New Space of Flows in "Bio-information"', in K. Verdery and C. Humphrey (eds), *Property in Question: Value Transformation in the Global Economy*, Oxford, New York: Berg, pp. 29–48.

Polanyi, K. (1944), *The Great Transformation*, New York: Farrar and Reinhart.

Queensland Department of Education and Training (2009), *Primary Industries*, website: http://www.trainandemploy.qld.gov.au/resources/industry/pdf/primary-industries.pdf.

Reynolds, H. (1987), *The Law of the Land*, London, New York: Penguin.

Rigsby, B. (2006), 'Custom and Tradition: Innovation and Tradition', in *Macquarie Law Journal*, 6: 113–38.

Rose, C. (2004), 'Economic Claims and the Challenges of New Property', in K. Verdery and C. Humphrey (eds), *Property in Question: Value Transformation in the Global Economy*, Oxford, New York: Berg, pp. 275–95.

Saarinen, J. (1998), 'Wilderness, Tourism Development and Sustainability: Wilderness Attitudes and Place Ethics', in United States Department of Agriculture, *Personal, Societal, and Ecological Values of Wilderness: Congress and Proceedings on Research, Management, and Allocation*, Vol. 1, General Technical Report, Ogden, UT: USDA Forest Service Rocky Mountain Research Station, pp. 29–33.

Strang, V. (1996), 'Sustaining Tourism in Far North Queensland', in M. Price (ed.), *People and Tourism in Fragile Environments*, London: John Wiley, pp. 51–67.

Strang, V. (2000), 'Not So Black and White: The Effects of Aboriginal Law on Australian Legislation', in A. Abramson and D. Theodossopoulos (eds), *Mythical Lands, Legal Boundaries: Rites and Rights in Historical and Cultural Context*, London: Pluto Press, pp. 93–115.

Strang, V. (2001), 'Negotiating the River: Cultural Tributaries in Far North Queensland', in B. Bender and M. Winer (eds), *Contested Landscapes: Movement, Exile and Place*, Oxford, New York: Berg. pp 69–86.

Strang, V. (2002), *Life Down Under: Water and Identity in an Aboriginal Cultural Landscape*, Goldsmiths College Anthropology Research Papers, No. 7, London: Goldsmiths College.

Strang, V. (2004), *The Meaning of Water*, New York, Oxford: Berg.

Strang, V. (2009), *Gardening the World: Agency, Identity, and the Ownership of Water*, Oxford, New York: Berghahn Publishers.

Strang, V. (2010), 'Water Sports: A Tug-of-War over the River', in J. Carrier and D. Macleod (eds), *Tourism Power and Culture: Anthropological Perspectives*, Bristol: Channel View Press.

Strathern, M. (1996), 'Potential Property: Intellectual Rights and Property in Persons', *Social Anthropology*, 4: 17–32.

Strathern, M. (1998), 'Divisions of Interest and Languages of Ownership', in C. Hann (ed.), *Property Relations: Renewing the Anthropological Tradition*, New York: Cambridge University Press, pp. 214–32.

Strathern, M. (1999), *Property, Substance and Effect: Anthropological Essays on Persons and Things*, London: Athlone Press.

Strathern, M. (2000), 'The Tyranny of Transparency', *British Educational Research Journal*, 26: 309–21.

Tawney, R.H. (1952)[1931], *Equality*, 4th edn, London: Unwin Books.

Thompson, E.P. (1968), *The Making of the English Working Class*, Harmondsworth: Penguin.

Trigger, D. and Griffiths, G. (eds) (2003), *Disputed Territories: Land, Culture and Identity in Settler Societies*, Hong Kong: Hong Kong University Press.

Toussaint, S. (ed) (2004), *Crossing Boundaries: Cultural, Legal, Historical and Practice Issues in Native Title*, Carlton: Melbourne University Press.

Verdery, K. (2003), *The Vanishing Hectare: Property and Value in Postsocialist Transylvania*, Ithaca NY: Cornell University Press.

Verdery, K. and Humphrey, C. (eds) (2004) *Property in Question: Value Transformation in the Global Economy*, Oxford, New York: Berg.

Widlok, T. and Tadesse, W. (eds) (2005), *Property and Equality*, Volume II: *Encapsulation, Commercialisation, Discrimination*, New York, Oxford: Berghahn Books.

Williams, N. and Hunn, E. (eds) (1986), *Resource Managers: North American and Australian Hunter-Gatherers*, Canberra: Australian Institute of Aboriginal Studies.

Wittfogel, K. (1957), *Oriental Despotism*, New Haven: Yale University Press.

Worster, D. (1992), *Rivers of Empire: Water, Aridity and the Growth of the American West*, Oxford, New York: Oxford University Press.

–10–

Appropriating Fish, Appropriating Fishermen
Tradable Permits, Natural Resources and Uncertainty
Monica Minnegal and Peter Dwyer

Abstract

In this paper we ask what happens to fish and to fishermen who are subjected to modern forms of risk management. First, we consider how fish are being or have been reconfigured in the imagination of fishermen, managers and others who have some tie to the fishing industry. Secondly, we ask how the imagination of fishermen is being reconfigured by the imposition of management strategies that, ultimately, translate the uncertainties inherent in macro-level biological and economic systems into lived experience. The two trajectories of meaning are connected. Each influences the other and each entails an appropriation of understandings. We argue that the two trajectories are driven by the same process: a process that may be understood generally as disembedding and, more precisely, as implicit in an imposed ideology and logic that are underwritten by reification, commensurability, categorization and anonymization.

Introduction

Commercial fishing has always been a risky business. Each time a fisherman heads out to sea his life and his livelihood are dependent upon the vagaries of the weather, the movement and population fluctuations of fish and the idiosyncrasies of the market. Within limits, individual fishermen have always been accomplished at managing these essentially local risks. But at broader scales, both social and environmental, there are risks that can only be addressed collectively; for example, preventing the overharvest of fish stocks, or the oversupply of markets, cannot be managed alone. And in the modern global context, where fish – both in the sea and on land – are known to move far beyond the range of fishermen and their communities, responsibility for managing these risks is usually claimed by centralized fisheries agencies rather than being left in the hands of those fishermen and communities.

In this chapter we are concerned with the effect that such centralized management may have on the ways that both fish and fishermen are conceptualized. Much has been written about the emergence of centralized resource management institutions with these often justified in terms of preventing a 'tragedy of the commons' and writers have also considered the impact of these centralized management regimes on the sustainability of resources or communities (e.g. Acheson 2006; Jentoft 2000; Ostrom *et al.* 2002; St Martin *et al.* 2007). Discussion has often focused on the appropriateness of particular regimes, given the character of the resource at stake or the technologies available for its exploitation (Strang, Wilmott, this volume). But such institutional appropriation of the authority to govern access to resources affects more than material sustainability. It effectively reconfigures an inherent capacity to procure a resource as an attributed right and thereby reshapes the subjective experience of affected persons. The resource, too, may be transformed in this process, becoming effectively 'owned' long before it is encountered.

These transformative processes, particularly as they influence the imagination of those with some connection to the fishing industry, are the focus of this chapter. We draw on our research among commercial fishermen in south-eastern Australia, and observations of the impact that the risk management procedures of the Australian Fisheries Management Authority (AFMA) has had on their understandings and ways of life (Dwyer *et al.* 2003; Dwyer and Minnegal 2006; Minnegal and Dwyer 2008a; Minnegal *et al.* 2003). Ultimately, we argue, these procedures have the outcome that generic understandings of both fish and fishermen are appropriated to a neoliberal ideology – underwritten by the disembedding processes of reification, commensurability, categorization and anonymization – that effectively disconnects fish from the reality of the ocean's cycles and fishermen from the relational world that formerly sustained them.

Background

Lakes Entrance, a coastal Victorian town of about 6,000 inhabitants, is home to the largest fishing fleet in south-eastern Australia. Its location at the confluence of inland and ocean fishing grounds, with ready access to both the comparatively shallow waters of Bass Strait and the deeper fishing grounds off the continental shelf, has encouraged the development of a diverse assembly of fishing targets and tactics and a community of fishermen who can switch between these in response to fluctuations in fish stocks.

From 2000 to 2008 there was a decline in fleet sizes, from seventy-five to forty-six ocean-going vessels fishing from Lakes Entrance, and from nineteen to nine vessels fishing in the extensive Gippsland Lakes that stretch westward from the town. The ocean-going fleet includes inshore and off-shore trawlers; boats that target shark, lobster and scallops; a few longliners; squid boats and one purse seiner. The fleet is dominated by owner-operators with about sixty-five per cent of boats in this category. In most of the remaining cases an older owner has given up fishing and hired a skipper – sometimes his own son. The boats are relatively small, ranging in length from ten to twenty-five metres.

The strategic position of Lakes Entrance, roughly equidistant from the major markets of Melbourne and Sydney, has provided flexibility to buffer some of the vagaries of demand for fish. But in the years since 2000, when we first commenced research at this port, we have watched as fishermen struggled to come to terms with a series of structural adjustments in Australian fisheries management. In a process that began long before our arrival, the role of government in managing fisheries has steadily increased as the emphasis of management institutions shifted from development of fisheries to control of fishing. Constitutional agreements between the States (including Victoria) and the Commonwealth have further centralized responsibility for stocks that were found in multiple jurisdictions. While some fisheries, such as lobster-fishing, inshore trawling for prawns and live-fishing on inshore reefs, remain the province of state management, the Commonwealth management agency AFMA is now responsible for managing the major fisheries accessed from Lakes – trawling for scalefish, gill-netting for shark, long-lining for both and scalloping in Commonwealth waters.

The primary management tool employed by AFMA consists of tradable permits in the form of individual transferable quotas (ITQ). The asserted rationale is simple: too many fishermen are chasing too few fish. An annually determined cap is placed on the total allowable catch of each species. That limit is intended to ensure the sustainability of populations of those species. At the outset the total allowable catch is distributed as units of quotas to eligible fishermen, commonly on the basis of their previous catch history. But, thereafter, those units of quotas may be transferred for money from fisherman to fisherman or, in fact, to any interested investor whether or not that person is directly engaged in fishing.

ITQ management thus creates a market in units of quotas that, ultimately, may be realised as fish. In theory efficient operators, or competent investors, accumulate quotas and inefficient operators choose to exit the industry in a version of voluntary redundancy that in this case is not rewarded with financial compensation. The outcomes, according to this idealized model, are sustainable fish populations and a profitable and sustainable fishing industry. The 'invisible hand' of the market does its magic once again.

Few anthropologists will be surprised to hear that it doesn't often work. The introduction of ITQ management does lead to emergence of a quota market. The quota holdings of some fishermen increase; those of others decrease. Entrepreneurs and speculators, who are not fishermen, gradually become important players in the industry. Often these are fish processors who take the opportunity to integrate their businesses vertically. But ITQ management is seldom implicated in substantially reducing the number of fishermen, especially in mixed species fisheries. For these fishermen exit is problematic. Their financial security is tied up in their boats, fishing gear and licences and, as a quota market develops, and quotas become differentially distributed, the market for these commodities collapses. Fishermen who are or become economically marginal are locked in. The only way to remove them – or to 'save' them – is to implement a buyback of licences. From time to time this is what is done, though it is never accompanied by an acknowledgement that ITQ management alone has failed to achieve its intended aims.[1] In fact there is no good evidence that ITQ management or intermittent buybacks ensure the sustainability of fish populations. The models used to assess fish stock are complex and problematic. Their outputs and their confirmation 'on the ground' (or 'in the water') are often questionable (Degnbol 2003; Essington 2001; Finlayson 1994; Wilson 2002; Wilson *et al.* 1994).

But the failures of ITQ management are not the central theme of this chapter. We and others have discussed them elsewhere (Apostle *et al.* 2002; Bradshaw 2004; Dwyer *et al.* 2008; McCay 1995; Pálsson 1998; Pálsson and Helgason 1996; Wiber 2000). Rather we ask what has happened to the fish and the fishermen who have been subjected to these modern forms of risk management. How has the idea of fish and the imagination of fishermen been reconfigured by the imposition of managerial strategies that ultimately translate the uncertainties inherent in macro-level biological and economic systems into lived experience (Minnegal and Dwyer 2008b)?

Appropriating Fish

So what happens to fish? At one level they do what they have always done. As one fisherman said, fish have two roles in life: 'To eat. And not to be eaten' (*New Scientist* 22 March 2008, 'Soundbites' p.10). But many are caught. They tumble out of nets or fall off hooks onto the decks of boats. They may be gutted, decapitated and stored in ice or brine. They are delivered to port, off-loaded, weighed, shipped to markets, auctioned, perhaps exported, delivered to retail outlets and eventually sold and eaten by people or their pets.

Those, of course, are real fish. But the introduction of quota management has created paper fish or virtual fish. These latter are abstractions, commodifications 'of *the idea* of fish' (King 2005:360–5; cf. Pálsson 1990). At one level they are 'signs' of fish; at another, they have taken on a life of their own, indexing 'real' fish, but somehow divorced from them.

Fisherman John, perhaps, is out at sea. He has shot and hauled his net. His catch contains a mix of species. For some of those species he holds a quota; for others, his quota has run out. As he turns for port, he reaches for his mobile phone. While his crew sort and move fish from deck to hold, John's attention shifts from real fish to virtual fish, from driving his boat to pleading and bargaining. His friend cannot help; for the shortfall species he has no spare quota. Another fisherman is willing to lease but the price he sets is too high. John phones his broker. If in the next few hours quotas can be found and leased at an acceptable price, then all John's haul will make it to port. If no quotas are available, or the price is not satisfactory, the surplus fish will be thrown overboard – dead. The penalty for landing fish without a quota is high. For most fishermen it is not worth the risk.

John and other men engaged in practical fishing now experience two kinds of fish. Neither is easy to find and their pursuit calls for different kinds of skills. Past experience and present circumstance are crucial to finding real fish, but an orientation to the future underlies the pursuit of virtual fish. As the following example suggests, the latter are perhaps even more mobile than the former. Quota management was introduced in the Australian Southeast Trawl Fishery in 1992 with quotas for sixteen species allocated to 119 licensed fishermen. In that first year there were 878 quota-leasing events and 133 permanent transfers of quotas between quota-holders (Connor and Alden 2001:390–1). Six years later in 1998 the number of quota-holders had increased to 162, of whom approximately 108 were fishermen, and there were 1,831 leasing events and 230 permanent transfers. In 1998, therefore, the total amount of quotas leased, when translated into weight of fish, exceeded the total catch of fish landed by a factor of 1.2, and the permanent transfers were equivalent to 0.59 of the aggregate total allowable catch for the sixteen quota species. Stated simply, more 'paper' fish were leased than 'real' fish were landed, and more than half the quotas changed owners. Our own analyses for the Australian Southern Shark Fishery are less detailed than those of Connor and Alden, but again reveal the high mobility of quotas (Dwyer *et al.* 2008).

Our illustrative tale of fisherman John has been superseded. In 2006 during a major buyback of Commonwealth fishing licences, John and other fishermen were informed that they would in future have to hold quotas for species that they *might* catch before they put to sea. They would no longer be able to negotiate after the fact. Such a ruling might well mean that more dead fish will be dumped at sea. Certainly as quota holdings come to define not only what fishermen are allowed to catch, but also what they may try to catch, the separation between real fish and virtual fish becomes firmer with the latter, embodied in 'share certificates' and computer entries, now assuming greater salience than the former. 'Virtual' fish, as fishermen had been told, were property, theirs to hold for as long as they chose not to sell. As one fisherman wrote: 'When Quota was sold to us as a management option, it was portrayed to fishers in the Shark Industry and South East Non Trawl as owning blocks of land. Great, we had something for the future!' (AFMA 2003a).

In the course of managing their own quotas, however, it soon becomes apparent to fishermen that the realizable value of quotas has more to do with the intricacies of stock assessment than it has to do with the demands of the market. Quota holdings index a right to take a proportion of an allocated total allow-able catch of fish: they do not represent property as fishermen understand this concept. Indeed, on the latter count, many fishermen assert that fish do not and cannot qualify as 'personal property' until they have been landed; they speak of 'the rule of capture' that confirms a right to the economic benefits that may accrue from landed fish. They consider that uncaught fish are available to all and accept that expressions of co-operation and competition within communities of fishermen provide the ultimate arbiters of individual differences in success. ITQ management introduces a different understanding of 'property', one that ultimately underwrites the shifting understandings of fish and fishermen that are the subject of this paper. Quotas, despite the rhetoric of managers, are held not as 'property' but as 'privilege' (Wiber 2000:277). Virtual fish may last forever, but their translation into real fish is far less certain. The number of units of quota is fixed but the total allowable catch is not. The latter could be reduced to zero, in which case there would be no potential return from a unit of quota.

Fisheries managers writing regulations and enforcing compliance; fisheries scientists modelling stock and recommending total allowable catches; fisheries economists concerned with efficiency and markets; brokers deriving income by facilitating quota-trading; processors reducing costs by vertical integration; entrepreneurs contemplating investment in fisheries, and even environmentalists keeping watch on an extractive industry, increasingly engage with representations of fish that exist within a 'new world' that has parted company with the biophysical world that it was once intended to represent (King 2005).

Fishermen, too, must now navigate that new world in search of those repres-entations. Active fishermen move back and forth between a world in which real fish are, for the most part, hidden beneath the surface of the water and a world in which virtual fish are represented by ever-changing numbers on paper or computer screens. In the world of water, using echo sounders, fishing tackle and crew, the skipper of a boat continues to engage directly with the animals he pursues. In the world of paper and computers, however, direct engagement is no longer possible. Telephones and computers replace nets and lines as tools of the trade. The aquatic environment has given way to industry magazines that advertise quota – *Trade-A-Boat*, *Professional Fisherman* (now *Ausmarine*) – or, with an ironic touch, to Quotaboard, an Australian Fisheries Management Authority website designed by fisheries managers 'to facilitate the trade of Commonwealth quota, Statutory

Fishing Rights and permits and ensure the quota management system functions effectively' (www.quotaboard.afma.gov.au).

Fish have been reduced to units of quota, and interactions that make production possible are mediated by managers, scientists, economists, brokers, processors, entrepreneurs and environmentalists, to most of whom an aquatic world of direct engagement – a world of tangible fish – barely registers.

Appropriating Fishermen

So what happens to fishermen? Before the introduction of ITQ management, fishermen went to sea, caught fish and, after the fact, negotiated their sale. In the initial years of the new management regime, no longer permitted to land fish for which they did not hold quotas, they went to sea, caught fish and negotiated discrepancies between what they had caught and the quotas that they currently held before being able to sell them. More recently with the rules having changed again so that fishermen may not catch fish for which they do not already hold quotas, they must negotiate in advance to ensure they hold sufficient quotas to cover all the fish that they might catch before they even put to sea. Thus they are required to prejudge their likely returns from a risky and ever-fluctuating environment. In this way the logic of fishermen's productive enterprise has been reordered: catch, negotiate and sell has given way to negotiate, catch and sell. Implicit within that reordered logic is a shift in the understanding of the productive process: from one where there was always a sense that returns achieved were a measure of each fisherman's own effort and skill, to one in which potential returns are limited and fixed by an external authority. The result is a sense of loss of control and in parallel a decline in the relevance of practical skill.

For many fishermen much more is at stake. Increasingly a fisherman's professional viability has less to do with his ability to catch fish and more to do with his ability to acquire and hold quotas. As quotas accumulate in the hands of fewer larger-scale operators, or in the investment portfolios of speculators, so smaller-scale operators, who once managed their own businesses, are likely to find themselves beholden to others. Even if they continue to own a boat and a licence to fish, fishermen who had perceived themselves to be self-employed, reconceptualize themselves as employees: employees of one or more quota-holders whom they may neither know nor see. Some whose businesses fail move from owner to skipper or from skipper to crew. In an era in which managers promote forms of co-management – ideally, the sharing of power and responsibility by all stakeholders (e.g. Jentoft *et al.* 1998; Loucks 2007; Sachse and Richardson 2005) – it will be those who hold most quotas and not necessarily those who catch fish whose voices will carry the most weight when decisions are made and implemented. In all of these ways, for those who fish, quota management increases the likelihood of downward mobility and loss of autonomy.

Autonomy is highly valued by fishermen. But, though they assert a 'rugged' individuality, all are entangled in webs of relationship with other fishermen, exchanging information, relying on each other for safety and competing with each other for resources. The 'individuality' of fishermen is embedded in a fluid community of others that, like all human communities, is underlain by relations of trust, reciprocal coercion, cooperation, competition and moral responsibility (Acheson 1975; Blair 2006; King 2006; Knudsen 2008; St Martin 2007). Yet this too is changing. With the introduction of ITQ management, self-identification of fishermen within the frame of an always relational 'rugged' individualism is giving way to self-identification within the frame of a categorical 'utilitarian' individualism (Jentoft and Davis 1993; King 2006). An imposed orientation to the future, the necessity to hold quotas in advance of fishing and the dictates of quota-holders who do not themselves fish, erode trust and conventional expressions of morality and as practical necessity prioritize the needs and wants of individual fishermen in opposition to those of all other fishermen.

As pursuit of those 'virtual' fish – the value of which can be changed at the stroke of a manager's pen – takes up more of fishermen's time and effort, the experience of probabilistic risk always associated with harvesting natural resources is giving way to an experience of existential uncertainty.[2] Once a fishing trip that yielded few fish could be rationalized as 'that's fishing'. Now as a fisherman ventures out to sea, he must wonder whether he can meet the commitments made by acquiring quotas, given that it is impossible to guarantee his boat will perform well, his crew will remain healthy, the weather will be benign and the needed fish will be found.

For fishermen then under recent regimes of management, the significance of practical skill and of engagement with 'real' fish is reduced, autonomy is eroded, downward mobility is an ever-present possibility and utilitarianism and existential uncertainty are emerging as a way of life. Like the fish that they pursue, fishermen are being transformed: quantified and anonymized, reduced to substitutable and transferable productive units, measured by the quotas that they own or lease, judged by the fit between what they are allowed to catch and what they land, rewarded only in as much as they remain in financial good standing. In the bureaucratic world of management they become ciphers, commodifications of the *idea* of fishermen.

Many have responded to these changes with deeply felt frustration; fishermen at Lakes Entrance frequently expressed to us sentiments akin to those articulated in the following extracts from written submissions to a quota reallocation panel in the Southern Shark Fishery (AFMA 2003a,b):

It has been seventeen years of lock down, pending sustainable management. ... Seventeen years of social and economic uncertainty has taken its toll upon fishers and their families.

Removed, down sized, displaced, excised, cut of, dare I suggest it, even mis-appropriated call it whatever you like, even though it was awarded by statute, our fishing permits, are property that has been taken away.

The AFMA Boards token gestures and reluctance to properly listen to industry, the lack of ability to fore-see how hastily conceived decisions can come back to bite them and us. The constantly changing rules and regulations are a humbug and have created uncertainty for a very long time.

[T]he way AFMA manages fishermen across all sectors of the industry means that the malaise, within management, whatever it is, must be deep seated and pervasive. In fact it must underpin the very belief structure within AFMA.

And, sometimes, as irony:

I have often thought that the only way to settle the allocation of shark quota would be to return to the economic policies in vogue during buccaneer times. That is, place all the squabbling factions into a small room..., place $20 million dollars in the middle, throw in a dozen cutlasses, leave and come back in an hour to see if consensus has been reached over how the booty is to be shared. This form of economics has been outlawed, its more subtle nowadays, the factions belts are armed with scientists, lawyers and economists.

Disembedding Fish, Disembedding Fishermen

To commercial fishermen and their customers fish were a commodity long before quota management was introduced, but they were a tangible commodity. As noted above, the difference made by quota management was that the *idea* of fish was commodified. It is this *idea* that from economic necessity has become a focus of engagement for fishermen. In the same sense that fishermen once grew and emerged as fishermen through engagement with 'real' fish and the environments in which these were found – through enskilment at sea (Ingold 2000; Pálsson 1994) – now they grow and emerge through engagement with 'virtual' fish and the environments in which these are found. They are drawn into the wake of the trajectory of the *idea* of fish such that their own trajectory is, inevitably, a mirror of this, to the extent that they too in their own and others' imagination might be understood as commodified.

This story resonates with that encapsulated in Karl Polanyi's seminal work *The Great Transformation* (1944). In an essay published a few years later, Polanyi (1947) wrote that:

Some believe in elites and aristocracies, in managerialism and the corporation. They feel that the whole of society should be more intimately adjusted to the economic system, which they would wish to remain unchanged. This is the idea of the Brave New World, where the individual is conditioned to support an order that has been designed for him by such as are wiser than he.

Polanyi's particular concern was with the impacts of machines – of the industrial revolution – on the political and economic relations of society. He argued that those impacts had the effect that both nature and humans came to be treated as commodities and that this was to the detriment of the 'good society' (Ziegelmayer 2008).

Polanyi's insights have informed many studies in economic anthropology, particularly with regard to change in contexts of 'modernity' and 'globalization'. The mood of many of those contributions is pessimistic. The market engenders fictional realities and, as Taussig wrote, 'it is with these abstractions or symbols that we are forced to operate and comprehend the world' (1990:9). In Africa, Asia, South America and elsewhere, the disadvantaged and oppressed are encompassed by the dictates and indeed the seeming attractions of market economies (e.g. Breckenridge 1995; Comaroff and Comaroff 1993; Coronil 1997; Gudeman 1992; Hart 1990). So too, however, are the well-to-do in developed countries where each resource crisis – of timber, ore and fish extraction, of food production, of carbon emissions, of demand for water, of failing transport systems and power generation and of access to student-clients by institutions of education – is addressed by privatization, tradable permits, commercialized knowledge or some other version of what is presented as a new market (e.g. Bakker 2007; Castro 2007; Cohen 2003; Cooper 2007; Helgason and Pálsson 1997; Smith and Scherr 2003).

But, of course, we are all 'forced' to operate with abstractions and symbols. That is the fate and the fantasy of being human (Fernandez 1991). As Malcolm Lowry wrote, in words that he excised from the third draft of his novel *Under the Volcano*:

Before you knew anything about life, you had the symbols. It was with the symbols you started. From them you progressed to something else. Life was indeed what you made of the symbols and, the less you made of life the more symbols you got. And the more you tried to comprehend them, confusing what life was, with the necessity for this comprehension, the more they multiplied. And the more they multiplied, that is, disintegrated into still more and more symbols which in the first place never had the slightest intention of meaning anything, let alone of being understood, just like human beings in short, the more they liked it, until, in the end, life itself ... fluttered away abruptly, leaving an abstraction behind. (Quoted in Day 1973: 273)

What is really at issue is the form and consequences of the particular abstractions and symbols that characterize the market and, as Malcolm Lowry grasped, the process entailed in the commodification of nature and people. Without knowledge of these matters there can be no way of 'correcting' or 'adjusting' that which we judge to be wrong; each correction or each adjustment is likely to produce 'more of the same'. On the first count the language of management relies on many explicit or implicit symbols that are underwritten by a market-oriented ideology and serve to valorize the neoliberal subject within a context that limits the freedom of that subject. Examples of these naturalized expressions include 'aspirational persons', 'commercial in confidence', 'winners and losers', 'autonomous adjustment' and 'exit with dignity'. All are party to an emerging ideology that elsewhere and with particular reference to Australia we have characterized as one of 'extol and control' (Minnegal and Dwyer 2008c).

Polanyi used the term 'disembedding' to depict the process by which 'capital-ist economic institutions achieved their own, autonomous logic vis-à-vis other dimensions of modern society' (Hornborg 1999:149; see also Humphreys 1969:166; Polanyi 1944). 'Disembedding', as Hornborg wrote, signified 'the alienation of persons, objects or concepts from the *contexts* from which they [had] previously derived their meaning' (ibid.; see also Giddens 1990, 1991; Hornborg 1996). Hornborg's generalization both positions the notion of disembedding within the frame of an ecological semiotics and allows us to see that as a process its relevance to change reaches further and originated earlier than the capitalist underpinnings of modernity and globalization, which are merely catalytic in their effects (Minnegal and Dwyer 1999:76).

This perspective, placing the focus on disembedding as process rather than disembeddedness as product, addresses the concern of Helgason and Pálsson (1997:453; see also Gudeman 2009) that Polanyi's notion of disembedding is flawed in relying on an inappropriately rigid distinction between embedded and disembedded economies and societies. As Gudeman (2009:37) notes, the embedded/disembedded division is 'a continuing dialectic in all economies, where it assumes different historical forms and degrees of tension'. Problems arise, however, where that dialectic is veiled and the underlying logics begin to diverge.

The logic of markets that now governs access to the right to fish at Lakes Entrance is quite distinct from the logic that governs the day-to-day interactions which express the capacity to fish. As these logics have diverged what it means to be a fisherman has been transformed. Capacities and rights are both intangible intersubjective properties of persons. A capacity to fish is acquired and revealed through interactive performance in the tangible landing of 'real' fish. The right to fish – to engage in that embodied performance – has long been seen by fishermen as constituted and demonstrated in that same productive engagement with the sea and those who fish there.[3] The introduction of ITQ management, however, has divorced the capacity to fish from the right to do so; it is now conceivable that a person might have one without the other. And, crucially, the social domain in which the right to fish must now be negotiated (for quota-holdings, like all property, remain inherently relational in form) is divorced from the world of direct engagement with the sea. Rights that were once embedded in a society of fish and fishermen are now, it seems, deployed by individuals who derived them from elsewhere.

It would be easy to assert that the cause of this disembedding – the 'fault' if you will – lay with capitalism and money. This, after all, was an essence of Polanyi's conclusion (Hart 2009). As Bloch (1989:170) expressed it, to Polanyi and to many anthropologists, 'money of itself is seen as an acid attacking the very fabric of kinship-based moral society, an acid operating through the impersonal relationships it introduces'. Drawing on Madagascan ethnography he showed how people may, in fact, incorporate money within their own pre-existing system of relations even as they adjust to it (see also Akin and Robbins 1999). Money is tempting, but its consequences are not inevitable. The temptation resides, not in money itself, but in the logic of money and the ease with which this may be metaphorically extended to non-economic domains of life. Parmentier (2002:51) characterized that logic as dematerialized, depersonalized, decontextualized and conventional while, following others, we have represented it in terms of reification, commensurability, categorization and anonymization (Minnegal and Dwyer 2007; see also Hornborg 1999).

This is what we have been observing with both fish and fishermen at Lakes Entrance and elsewhere: 'ideas' take on a life of their own (reification); fish or fishermen are reduced to substitutable units such that their value may be measured against common standards (commensurability); attributes of things assume greater definitional status than the relational connections between those things (categorization); and fishermen, like fish, are reduced to ciphers amenable to the dictates of managers' models (anonymization). It is these generic processes that are implicated when Hornborg (2007:63) argues that both local meanings and ecosystems are subject to the 'conceptual and physical ravages of global capital'.

However, these related processes and the logic they express may be understood as inherent in the abductive foundations and predilections of the imagination (Dwyer 2005). They are potentials that always exist and according to this argument money may be appreciated as a paradigmatic instance of the imagination made real. It is in those underlying potentials, rather than in money *per se*, that we may understand the processes of appropriation that have enveloped fish, fishermen and so much else in the interconnected worlds of nature and of people.

These processes may be triggered or fore-grounded in situations of perceived crisis such as that entailed in the judgement that 'too many fishermen are chasing too few fish'. In such situations, the easy explanation is to assign fault and blame to an imagined 'other' through the abstracting devices of reification, categorization and so forth. A morality grounded in an understanding that people are beholden to known relational others gives way to a morality grounded in an understanding that they are beholden to anonymous and controlling outsiders. Ultimately, in the imagination, such situations may disconnect – or disembed – fish from the reality of the planet's ocean cycles and the people who depend on fish from the relational world that once succoured them.

Acknowledgements

This paper was first presented in the Panel 'Risky Environments: Ethnographies and the Multilayered Qualities of Appropriation' at the joint conference of the Association of Social Anthropologists of the UK and Commonwealth, the Association of Social Anthropologists of Aotearoa/New Zealand and the Australian Anthropological Society held in Auckland, New Zealand, in December 2008. We thank Sandy Toussaint and Laurent Dousset who with Monica Minnegal convened the Panel and Veronica Strang and Mark Busse who convened the conference, invited us to contribute to the present volume and commented on earlier drafts. We thank the many fishermen – an emic category that includes women who fish – who have contributed so much to our understanding; Simone Blair and Tanya King for many conversations and insights about fishing and fishermen; and both the University of Melbourne and The Australian Research Council for some financial support.

Notes

1. At the time our research commenced, the Southeast Trawl Fishery had been subjected to ITQ management for eight years. In 2001 ITQ management was initiated in the Commonwealth Southern Shark Fishery and in 2002 in the State administered lobster fishery. Commonwealth ITQs have been replaced by quota statutory fishing rights with this change occurring at different times in different fisheries. In 2006 a licence buyback removed approximately one-third of Australian Commonwealth fishing licences. At Lakes Entrance after the buyback in March 2007, 34 per cent of Commonwealth licences had been relinquished, 25 per cent of licence-holders no longer had access to Commonwealth waters, but only 9.3 per cent had abandoned fishing entirely (Minnegal and Dwyer 2008c). However, there has been further reduction in fleet size since that time. These structural rearrangements, combined with

on-going turmoil within the Bass Strait Central Zone scallop fishery, have provided the backdrop to much of our research.

2. We follow Knight (1933:19–20) in treating 'risk' as covering situations in which actors are able to assess the likelihood that a particular event may occur and 'uncertainty' as covering situations in which no such assessment is possible (Dwyer and Minnegal 2006). Further, we extend Svendsen's distinction between situational and existential boredom to a 'typology' of experienced uncertainty: the former is 'of the world', the latter is 'embodied' (2005; see also Musharbash 2007). This distinction is similar to that which Heidegger asserted between 'fear' and 'anguish', where the former refers to a specific fact, is circumscribed and nameable, while the latter lacks clear cause, is provoked by an incapacity to reach decisions and may be ineffable (Virno 2003:32).

3. Glaskin (this volume) writes of the 'strongly relational personhood' that characterizes kin-based societies such as that of Aboriginal Australia, societies in which, as Redmond (2008:76) has noted, 'the processes of self-constitution emerge from an irreducibly social grounding'. Fishermen, too, constitute themselves as subjects within a distinct social field, one in which intersubjective engagements with the sea are perceived as more significant than others (Minnegal *et al.* 2003).

References

Acheson, J. (1975), 'The Lobster Fiefs: Economic and Ecological Effects of Territoriality in the Maine Lobster Industry', *Human Ecology*, 3: 183–207.

Acheson, J. (2006), 'Institutional Failure in Resource Management', *Annual Review of Anthropology*, 35: 117–34.

Akin, D. and Robbins, J. (eds) (1999), *Money and Modernity: State and Local Currencies in Melanesia*, Pittsburgh, PA: University of Pittsburgh Press.

Apostle, R., McCay, B. and Mikalsen, K. (2002), *Enclosing the Commons: Individual Transferable Quotas in the Novia Scotia Fishery*, St Johns, Newfoundland: Institute of Social and Economic Research.

Australian Fisheries Management Authority (2003a), 'Public Submissions Received re Independent Review of Quota Allocation for School and Gummy Shark in the Southern Shark Fishery, 1 August 2003', http://www.afma.gov. au/fisheries/gillnet_hook_trap/notices/submissions/default.php [Accessed 4 August 2003].

Australian Fisheries Management Authority (2003b), 'Second Round of Public Submissions Received re Independent Review of Quota Allocation for School and Gummy Shark in the Southern Shark Fishery, 21 August 2003', http://

www.afma.gov.au/fisheries/gillnet_hook_trap/notices/submissions2/default. php [Accessed 25 August 2003].

Bakker, K. (2007), 'The "Commons" versus the "Commodity": Alter-globalization, Anti-privatization and the Human Right to Water in the Global South', *Antipode*, 39: 430–55.

Blair, S. (2006), 'Shooting a Net at "Gilly's Snag": The Movement of Belonging among Commercial Fishermen at the Gippsland Lakes', unpublished PhD Thesis, University of Melbourne.

Bloch, M. (1989), 'The Symbolism of Money in Imerina', in M. J. Parry and M. Bloch (eds), *Money and the Morality of Exchange*, Cambridge: Cambridge University Press, pp. 165–90.

Bradshaw, M. (2004), 'The Market, Marx and Sustainability in a Fishery', *Antipode*, 36: 66–85.

Breckenridge, C. (ed.) (1995), *Consuming Modernity: Public Culture in a South Asian World*, Minneapolis: University of Minnesota Press.

Castro, J. (2007), 'Poverty and Citizenship: Sociological Perspectives on Water Services and Public-Private Participation', *Geoforum*, 38: 756–71.

Cohen, S. (2003), 'Alienation and Globalization in Morocco: Addressing the Social and Political Impact of Market Integration', *Comparative Studies in Society and History*, 45: 168–89.

Comaroff, J. and Comaroff, J. (eds) (1993), *Modernity and its Malcontents: Ritual and Power in Postcolonial Africa*, Chicago: University of Chicago Press.

Connor, R. and Alden, D. (2001), 'Indicators of the Effectiveness of Quota Markets: The South East Trawl Fishery of Australia', *Marine and Freshwater Research*, 52: 387–97.

Cooper, S. (2007), 'Academic Darwinism: The (Logical) End of the Dawkins Era', *Arena Journal*, 28: 107–17.

Coronil, F. (1997), *The Magical State: Mature, Money, and Modernity in Venezuela*, Chicago: University of Chicago Press.

Day, D. (1973), *Malcolm Lowry: A Biography*, New York: Oxford University Press.

Degnbol, P. (2003), 'Science and the User Perspective – The Gap Co-management must Address', in D. Wilson, J. Nielsen and P. Degnbol (eds), *The Fisheries Co-management Experience: Accomplishments, Challenges and Prospects*, Dordrecht: Kluwer Academic Publisher, pp. 31–50.

Dwyer, P. (2005), 'Ethnoclassification, Ethnoecology and the Imagination', *Journal de la Société des Océanistes*, 120–1: 11–25.

Dwyer, P. and Minnegal, M. (2006), 'The Good, the Bad and the Ugly: Risk, Uncertainty and Decision-making by Victorian Fishers', *Journal of Political Ecology*, 13: 1–23.

Dwyer, P., Just, R. and Minnegal, M. (2003), 'A Sea of Small Names: Fishers and their Boats in Victoria, Australia', *Anthropological Forum*, 13: 5–26.

Dwyer, P., King, T. and Minnegal, M. (2008), 'Managing Shark Fishermen in Southern Australia: A Critique', *Marine Policy*, 32: 263–73.

Essington, T. (2001), 'The Precautionary Approach in Fisheries Management: The Devil is in the Details', *Trends in Ecology and Evolution*, 16: 121–2.

Fernandez, J. (ed.) (1991), *Beyond Metaphor: The Theory of Tropes in Anthropology*, Stanford, California: Stanford University Press.

Finlayson, A. (1994), *Fishing for Truth: A Sociological Analysis of Northern Cod Stock Assessments from 1977 to 1990*, Newfoundland: ISER Publications.

Giddens, A. (1990), *The Consequences of Modernity*, Cambridge, UK: Polity Press.

Giddens, A. (1991), *Modernity and Self Identity: Self and Society in the Late Modern Age*, Stanford, California: Stanford University Press.

Gudeman, S. (1992), 'Remodelling the House of Economics: Culture and Innovation', *American Ethnologist*, 19: 141–54.

Gudeman, S. (2009), 'Necessity or Contingency: Mutuality and Market', in C. Hann and K. Hart (eds), *Market and Society:* The Great Transformation *Today*, Cambridge, UK: Cambridge University Press, pp. 17–37.

Hart, K. (1990), 'The Idea of Economy: Six Modern Dissenters', in R. Friedland and A.F. Robertson (eds), *Beyond the Marketplace: Rethinking Economy and Society*, New York: Aldine de Gruyter, pp. 137–60.

Hart, K. (2009), 'Money in the Making of World Society', in C. Hann and K. Hart (eds), *Market and Society:* The Great Transformation *Today*, Cambridge, UK: Cambridge University Press, pp. 91–105.

Helgason, A. and Pálsson, G. (1997), 'Contested Commodities: The Moral Landscape of Modernist Regimes', *Journal of the Royal Anthropological Institute*, 3: 451–71.

Hornborg, A. (1996), 'Ecology as Semiotics: Outlines of a Contextualist Paradigm for Human Ecology', in P. Descola and G. Pálsson (eds), *Nature and Society: Anthropological Perspectives*, London: Routledge, pp. 45–62.

Hornborg, A. (1999), 'Money and the Semiotics of Ecosystem Dissolution', *Journal of Material Culture*, 4: 143–62.

Hornborg, A. (2007), 'Learning from the Tiv: Why a Sustainable Economy Would Have to Be "Multicentric"', *Culture and Agriculture*, 29(2): 63–9.

Humphreys, S. (1969), 'History, Economics and Anthropology: The Work of Karl Polanyi', *History and Theory*, 8: 165–212.

Ingold, T. (2000), *The Perception of the Environment: Essays in Livelihood, Dwelling and Skill*, London: Routledge.

Jentoft, S. (2000), 'The Community: A Missing Link of Fisheries Management', *Marine Policy*, 24: 53–9.

Jentoft, S. and Davis, A. (1993), 'Self and Sacrifice: An Investigation of Small Boat Fisher Individualism and its Implication for Producer Cooperatives', *Human Organization*, 52: 356–67.

Jentoft, S., McCay, B. and Wilson, D. (1998), 'Social Theory and Fisheries Co-management', *Marine Policy*, 22: 423–36.

King, T. (2005), 'Crisis of Meanings: Divergent Experiences and Perceptions of the Marine Environment in Victoria, Australia', *The Australian Journal of Anthropology*, 16: 350–65.

King, T. (2006), 'Between the Devil and the Deep Blue Sea: Negotiating Ambiguous Physical and Social Boundaries within the Shark Fishing Industry of Bass Strait, Australia', unpublished PhD thesis, University of Melbourne.

Knight, F. (1933)[1921], *Risk, Uncertainty and Profit*, Boston: Houghton Mifflin Company.

Knudsen, S. (2008), 'Ethical Know-how and Traditional Ecological Knowledge in Small Scale Fisheries on the Eastern Black Sea Coast of Turkey', *Human Ecology*, 36: 29–41.

Loucks, L. (2007), 'Patterns of Fisheries Institutional Failure and Success: Experience from the Southern Gulf of St. Lawrence Snow Crab Fishery, in Nova Scotia, Canada', *Marine Policy*, 31: 320–6.

McCay, B. (1995), 'Social and Ecological Implications of ITQs: An Overview', *Ocean and Coastal Management*, 28: 3–22.

Minnegal, M. and Dwyer, P. (1999), 'Re-reading Relationships: Changing Constructions of Identity among Kubo of Papua New Guinea', *Ethnology*, 38: 59–80.

Minnegal, M. and Dwyer, P. (2007), 'Money, Meaning and Materialism: A Papua New Guinean Case History', *SSEE Working Papers in Development*, 2/2007, School of Social and Environmental Enquiry, University of Melbourne, pp. 1–27.

Minnegal, M. and Dwyer, P. (2008a), 'Managing Risk, Resisting Management: Stability and Diversity in a Southern Australian Fishing Fleet', *Human Organization*, 67: 97–108.

Minnegal, M. and Dwyer, P. (2008b), 'Fire, Flood, Fish and the Uncertainty Paradox', *The Australian Journal of Anthropology*, 19: 77–81.

Minnegal, M. and Dwyer, P. (2008c), 'Mixed Messages: Buying Back Australia's Fishing Industry', *Marine Policy*, 32: 263–73.

Minnegal, M., King, T., Just, R. and Dwyer P. (2003), 'Deep Identity, Shallow Time: Sustaining a Future in Victorian Fishing Communities', *The Australian Journal of Anthropology*, 14: 3–71.

Musharbash,Y. (2007), 'Boredom, Time, and Modernity: An Example from Aboriginal Australia', *American Anthropologist*, 109: 307–17.

Ostrom, E., Dietz, T., Dol ak, N., Stern, P., Stonich, S. and Weber. E. (eds) (2002), *The Drama of the Commons*, Washington, DC: National Academy Press.

Pálsson, G. (1990), 'The Idea of Fish: Land and Sea in the Icelandic World-view', in R.G. Willis (ed.), *Signifying Animals: Human Meaning in the Natural World*, London: Unwin Hyman, pp. 119–33.

Pálsson, G. (1994), 'Enskilment at Sea', *Man* (N.S.) 29: 901–27.

Pálsson, G. (1998), 'The Virtual Aquarium: Commodity Fiction and Cod Fishing', *Ecological Economics*, 24 (1998): 275–88.

Pálsson, G. and Helgason A. (1996), 'Property Rights and Practical Knowledge: The Icelandic Quota System', in K. Crean and D. Symes (eds), *Fisheries Management in Crisis*, Oxford: Fishing New Books, pp. 45–60.

Parmentier, R. (2002), 'Money Walks, People Talk: Systemic and Transactional Dimensions of Palauan Exchange', *L'Homme*, 162: 49–80.

Polanyi, K. (1944), *The Great Transformation: The Economic and Social Origins of Our Time*, New York: Farrar and Rinehart.

Polanyi, K. (1947), 'Our Obsolete Market Mentality. Civilization Must Find a New Thought Pattern', *Commentary*, 3: 109–17.

Redmond, A. (2008), 'Time Wounds: Death, Grieving and Grievance in the Northern Kimberley', in K. Glaskin, M. Tonkinson, Y. Musharbash and V. Burbank (eds), *Mortality, Mourning and Mortuary Practices in Indigenous Australia*, Farnham: Ashgate, pp. 69–86

Sachse, M. and Richardson, G. (2005), 'Moving from Input Controls to Output Controls Using the Partnership Approach in Australia's Southern Shark Fishery', *e-Journal of Northwest Atlantic Fishery Science*, 35, Art. 40.

Smith, J. and Scherr, S. (2003), 'Capturing the Value of Forest Carbon for Local Livelihoods', *World Development*, 31: 2143–60.

St Martin, K. (2007), 'The Difference that Class Makes: Neoliberalization and Non-capitalism in the Fishing Industry of New England', *Antipode*, 39: 527–49.

St Martin, K., McCay, B., Murray, G., Johnson, T. and Oles, B. (2007), 'Communities, Knowledge and Fisheries of the Future', *International Journal of Global Environmental Issues*, 7: 221–39.

Svendsen, L. (2005), *A Philosophy of Boredom*, London: Reaktion Books.

Taussig, M. (1990), *The Devil and Commodity Fetishism in South America*, Chapel Hill: University of North Carolina Press.

Virno, P. (2003), *A Grammar of the Multitude: For an Analysis of Contemporary Forms of Life*, translated from the Italian by I. Bertoletti, J. Cascaito and A. Casson, Cambridge, Massachusetts: Semiotext(e).

Wiber, M. (2000), 'Fishing Rights as an Example of the Economic Rhetoric of Privatization: Calling for an Implicated Economics', *Canadian Review of Sociology and Anthropology*, 37(3): 267–88.

Wilson, J. (2002), 'Scientific Uncertainty, Complex Systems, and the Design of Common-pool Institutions', in E. Ostrom, T. Dietz, N. Dolŝak, P.C. Stern, S. Stonich, and E.U. Weber (eds), *The Drama of the Commons*, Washington, DC: National Academy Press, pp. 327–59.

Wilson, J., Acheson, J., Metcalfe M. and Kleban, P. (1994), 'Chaos, Complexity and Community Management of Fisheries', *Marine Policy*, 18: 291–305.

Ziegelmayer, E. (2008), 'The Great Transformation at Sea: Fictitious Commodities and the Crisis of Marine Fisheries', paper presented at the annual meeting of the American Political Science Association, Boston, Massachusetts, 28 August 2002 [available at http://www.allacademic.com/meta/p66292_index.html].

Can't Find Nothing on the Radio

Radio Spectrum Policy and Governance in Nepal

Michael Wilmore and Pawan Prakash Upreti

Abstract

This chapter examines the relationship between state and civil society institutions in South Asia through an examination of radio broadcasting regulations in Nepal. The development of new forms of media and wider media access are often regarded as instrumental to the transformation of social and political identities, especially through the roles media play in the construction of civic institutions, of new relationships with the nation-state and in the emergence of information as the basis for many common goods and services. This chapter argues that, if we are to evaluate people's ability to take advantage of the potential that media may offer in bringing about political empowerment, the theorization of these transformations must encompass an understanding of the state's role in regulating media activities, especially the licensing of broadcasting and publication. It examines these issues in the context of the dramatic increase in independent radio activity in Nepal, where Equal Access, a non-governmental organization producing programmes on social change, has produced the first survey of broadcast signal reach for independent radio organizations.

Introduction

Recent proliferation of FM radio activity in Nepal has created broadcasting with vibrancy unparalleled in the South Asian region and with considerable political importance given the country's recent civil conflict. However, this medium is also suffering the effects of overuse through signal interference, leading to problems for both radio listeners and broadcasters. It is also clear that radio stations' and government regulators' attempts to deal with this problem through purely technical solutions do nothing to solve the persistence of inadequate institutional arrangements for the governance of radio broadcast licensing and the operation of stations. Having been utilized during the past decade in effect as a common resource to which anyone potentially had access rights, there is a risk that a strict regime of use and property rights will be imposed in the name of avoiding signal interference, thus restricting access to the state broadcaster, Radio Nepal, and a minority of wealthy commercial organizations. The dozens of community radio stations that give Nepal's radio environment unprecedented diversity may disappear into the static of history.

Chris Hann (2005:122) notes that 'new technologies are continuously creating new forms of property objects and straining the capacity of the standard liberal model [of property relations]'. Radio spectrum provides a rich example of how new technologically mediated resources have been appropriated and used by different agents. Such analysis is important given that 'the predominant pattern in broadcasting was the persistence of early constitutive choices' (Starr 2004:384) and the paths laid down by those choices are 'not easily diverted' once laid. The choices now being made about what form rights over radio spectrum use will take in Nepal are likely to structure relationships between media producers, their audiences and the state for decades to come. If 'technological innovation is always and inevitably the site of contestation and struggle' (Wurtzler 2007:289), to what extent is there any recognition in Nepal that diverse choices in spectrum use are even possible?

This chapter addresses this question by considering theoretical analyses of commons, particularly work on so-called common-pool resources, of which the radio spectrum is a prime example. We examine why radio has *not* been developed as a common-pool resource in most situations through a brief review of radio policy, governance and property rights that have subsequently become international norms. This is followed by a brief description of the development of radio broadcasting in Nepal, highlighting the growth of independent FM stations (commercial and community-based), and evidence that some of these utilize broadcasting practices that both help and hinder attempts to avoid signal interference. We conclude that Nepalese radio originated within a commons-like context, which in part enabled radio broadcasting to play its vital political role in the past decade, but that this potential will be undermined if concerns regarding signal interference lead to the imposition of the type of property regimes that are widely seen internationally, either wholesale state appropriation, privatization or a hybrid of these. We argue that commons-based solutions provide the best means to ensure that radio continues to play this important role, but renewed emphasis on understanding the sociological dimensions of what has hitherto been seen as a purely technical issue is required. However, this also opens up a new and daunting range of challenges to researchers and to those tasked with the design and implementation of spectrum policy, especially in a political context that already provides innumerable obstacles to success.

Understanding the Radio Spectrum as a Common-pool Resource

The portions of the electromagnetic spectrum used for transmitting radio signals have become in the past century 'one of the most valuable pieces of "real estate"—and one of the keenest objects of speculation' (Campbell 2003:64). This value derives from continuing innovation in uses of this resource, especially for telecommunications and media vital to the functioning of complex societies and their economic activities. Whilst undoubtedly a part of nature, the technologically mediated exploitation of the spectrum, implemented via institutional arrangements based on private or public ownership, is entirely a human construct. There is nothing inevitable about how the spectrum is used, either technologically or sociologically. Other arrangements for the use of this resource are both possible and supported by many users and policy analysts, particularly use of the spectrum as a commons, but these alternatives are invariably rejected on a number of grounds.

Primary amongst these is the risk of signal interference due to excessive competition over frequency use. Increasing reliance on wireless communication in modern industrialized societies makes this a potentially devastating tragedy of the sort described by Garrett Hardin (1968). Governments and commercial organizations have been quick to advocate solutions to the 'tragedy of the commons' implied by signal interference through one or other of the options described in Hardin's highly influential article, either public or private forms of ownership. In practice systems of spectrum governance have tended to involve a mixture of these solutions. The approach adopted in the USA of state ownership with licensing of limited spectrum use rights to private agents has become the global norm and one of the best examples of a diffusion of policy instruments internationally (Best and Thakur 2009). The counter challenge to this hybrid approach to spectrum governance comes from two directions.

Firstly, there are those who accept Hardin's reasoning regarding the inevitability of the destruction of commons, but criticize the pragmatic ways in which spectrum governance policies have developed to avert this risk, usually advocating more radical forms of private ownership as more efficient in maximizing both the economic and social value of the spectrum (Hazlett 1990; Snider 2003). Second, the basic premises of Hardin's argument have been questioned through theoretical and empirical work that re-examines commons and their use. Given that much of the radio spectrum lies 'idle at any given instant and location ... there is growing debate over whether the "shortage" arises from outdated spectrum policies that allow little sharing' (Forge and Blackman 2006:8), which makes signal interference inevitable given that frequencies are unnecessarily licensed to users who are given sole rights over their use.

Elinor Ostrom's work on common-pool resources is particularly significant in this respect because she revokes the accepted conceptualization of goods as only either privately or publically owned and utilized. She demonstrates that four rather than just two ideal-typical goods exist through consideration of the characteristics of 'exclusivity' and 'subtractability' used to define goods (that is the relative difficulty in restricting usage and likelihood of subsequent erosion of the resource due to its use) (Hess and Ostrom 2003). Public and private goods remain in opposition due to difficulties in excluding access to and low subtractability of the former (for example, anyone can enjoy a sunset, but such enjoyment in no way diminishes that of anyone else) and the corresponding ease of exclusivity and high subtractability of the latter. Two other types of goods remain: common-pool resources (CPRs) which potentially anyone can use, but which have high levels of subtractability, and those goods (such as club facilities) that have highly exclusive access, but experience little or no erosion through use. Resource use may become particularly rivalrous in situations of high subtractability but low exclusivity, which appears to be the case with the radio spectrum and the justification for policy measures that shift it into the realms of either private or public ownership.

Ostrom emphasizes that these descriptions of goods are idealizations based on theoretical consideration of logical possibilities arising from these fundamental characteristics of exclusivity and subtractability. Her core criticism of Hardin's thesis, laid out in her path-breaking work *Governing the Commons* (1990), is that his prediction of tragic resource destruction is based on an unrealistic evaluation of idealized commons in which these characteristics are pushed to their limits. Hardin assumes that commons exist as goods to which there is entirely open access (a total lack of exclusivity) and in which all users exert the same capacity for the exploitation of the resource (anyone can subtract as much as anyone else). The empirical work upon which Ostrom's critique is based demonstrates that such ideal situations seldom if ever exist and as such the ownership arrangements suggested by Hardin may be solutions to a tragedy that is far from inevitable; it is instead a possibility arising only in the most extreme situations. Actual arrangements for the use of common-pool resources tend to prevent destructive over-exploitation through self-organized collective action that both formulates and then enforces regulations proscribing access to and use of commons (Ostrom 1990, 2000). These regulations may incorporate forms of private and public ownership by excluding third party access, but retaining less exclusivity amongst those regarded as the collective owners of a resource (Wellenius and Neto 2006).

The theoretical work involved in identifying and distinguishing common-pool resources from other types of goods does not itself help predict what solutions will be reached to avert potential resource destruction in any given context. At the same time, as Ostrom (2000) notes, simply referring to this as a contextual problem does not assist us in moving towards a wider theoretical understanding of how and why particular systems of resource governance and property regimes develop as they do. It is one thing to demonstrate that self-organized collective action carried out by the users of a resource may provide a maximally efficient solution to the problem of averting a commons tragedy. It is entirely something else to explain what leads one resource to survive through such actions as a commons *sui generis*, whilst another resource might be destroyed due to the failure of effective user self-organization or changed into a good of entirely another type by alteration of the institutional arrangements and norms that prescribe rights over its use. 'The question is shifted from the existence of one or another form of property rights to why some communities succeed in preventing or ameliorating problems in the use and management of common resources and others do not' (MacCay and Jentoft 1998:25). MacCay and Jentoft conclude that the real tragedy might be that the solutions implemented to prevent resource destruction – state or private, market regulated ownership – destroy the capacity of communities of resource users to maintain systems of self-governance that not only protect but also maximize the potential value of CPRs to users:

> A more ethnographic and hence complex perspective on human/environment relations … calls for careful specification of property rights and systems of resource use and their embeddedness within discrete and changing historical moments, social and political relations, and environmental conditions.
>
> A 'thicker' perspective calls into question the value of relying heavily on any theoretical model when trying to account for and understand particular situations. (ibid.: 24)

The need for such 'thicker' perspectives provides an incentive for anthropologists to contribute to an important area of interdisciplinary research, whilst also presenting challenges in the application of existing theories and methodologies to new questions. So-called 'new commons' research (Hess 2000) draws our attention to cultural innovations that have CPR characteristics, such as wireless communication, and challenges us to incorporate insights from recent CPR research to develop an understanding of the moral economies applied to their use. Increasingly it is recognized that such understandings require theoretical perspectives and methodologies derived from anthropology, even as these must be applied through negotiation with practitioners and perspectives developed in other fields, especially the approaches of economists that have hitherto dominated the analysis of property allocation and associated policy development (Bardhan and Ray 2008). Edelman and Haugerud (2005), for example, identify several questions as 'under-explored' (pp. 20–1), each of which is highly pertinent to the problems of understanding common-pool resources identified in this chapter.

These include 'the invention and trading of new – and intangible – commodities' and 'the persistence in the late 20th and early 21st centuries of "moral economies," ... which in country after country – and transnationally – have constituted a political obstacle to the imposition and implementation of pro-corporate free-market policies' (ibid.: 21), the latter often seen most evidently in connection to community activities relating to CPRs.

The radio spectrum is a good example of a common-pool resource in that access is hard to control once the initial entry barriers of cost of purchasing transmission equipment are overcome, but subsequent overcrowding of the spectrum by users appears to degrade the resource as a whole. 'The intelligibility or the quality of a signal is a function of its strength (power) at the point of reception relative to the strength of *other* signals received simultaneously at that point – the level of noise or interference' (Minasian 1969:391; emphasis in original). This leads Minasian to conclude that, 'consequently, a system must exist which, by restricting the uses of frequencies, holds down the interference to a tolerable level' (ibid.:391). The existence of signal interference as a result of rivalrous use by broadcasters is not in doubt. It is a real threat. But the questions of what system should be used to deal with this problem and what counts as tolerable levels of interference remain open to debate.[1]

Systems for regulating access to spectrum may operate through markets, governments or communities (Aitken 1994:687). In most instances governments have stepped in to appropriate sole access and use rights, and then either provided media as state broadcasters in their own right (as is the case in Nepal with Radio Nepal), created publicly owned and accountable broadcasting institutions (as with the BBC in the UK), or licensed private broadcasting funded through commercial activities, primarily on-air advertising (as has been predominantly the case in the USA). Most states currently operate hybrid systems of broadcasting that include state, public and commercial broadcasting, although the latter dominate in terms of total contribution to broadcasting globally. Community-controlled and run radio stations are found in almost all places where media are not entirely state-controlled, but have tended to exist on the margins of broadcasting systems, utilizing a restricted range of frequencies (Hungbo 2008). They operate despite the existence of dominant public and private commercial broadcasters, rather than defining the paradigm for spectrum access and use.

'A generally well-designed regulatory framework' (Salmon 2004:168) is essential to the provision of effective wireless broadcasting services, even when an effective system for allocating licences is in place. Without the former it is likely that 'undesired consequences' (Hann 2005:122) will ultimately result. In the case of radio these are the eradication of diversity in broadcasting, particularly where such diversity is vested in alternative forms of economic organization and governance (Atton 2002:10; Wurtzler 2007:174; see also Strang this volume).

Technical issues have tended to remain centre-stage, however, when systems of regulation and licence allocation have been determined on the grounds of public service by governments. For Wurtzler (2007) the reasons for this are simple: such arguments serve those who are able to mobilize their capital to develop the most technically 'perfect' systems of media production and transmission and then lobby governments to have this accepted as the benchmark for public service.

Lawrence Lessig (2002) argues that a radio spectrum commons has never subsequently been able to flourish in any developed industrialized country, despite the benefits that might accrue to users under such arrangements, because from its inception as a medium even the possibility of efficient organization of broadcasting through commons-like institutional arrangements has been summarily dismissed by commercial broadcasters and their supporters in government. Technical arguments regarding spectrum scarcity have repeatedly been mobilized to justify this rejection of a spectrum commons. This has occurred despite the fact that economic modelling demonstrates that, 'while the theoretical optimum achievable by government in an ownership regime exceeds predicted welfare for a commons regime, for most model specifications the difference is not large and an ownership-regime can easily under-perform a commons regime if imperfectly-informed policy makers set policy variable incorrectly' (Wildman *et al.* 2006:83). We now turn to examine how these possibilities are being realized in practice in Nepalese radio broadcasting.

Radio in Nepal

In 1997 when the Nepalese government issued the first FM broadcasting licence to Radio Sagarmatha (a not-for-profit radio station run by a coalition of non-governmental organizations led by the Nepal Forum for Environmental Journalists), there was almost no expectation that the radio sector would grow to the extent that it subsequently did. It took a couple of years of political lobbying for Radio Sagarmatha's radio licence to be issued, but during the next ten years the number of FM radio licences issued reached almost three hundred; more than 172 independent FM radio stations were operational by the end of 2008. Out of these about eighty-five of the operational radio stations are community-based and run by either non-governmental organizations or cooperatives. As the Nepali media academic and journalist Pratyoush Onta states, 'while there are inadequacies in the independent radio sector...., its achievements constitute a slap in the face to those who make it their business to repeat the cliché that "nothing happened during the era of multiparty democracy"' (2006:119).

The growing importance of radio broadcasting in Nepal was underlined in 2006 when King Gyanendra was forced to relinquish power and restore parliamentary democracy. Raghu Mainali, a founder of Nepal's Association of Community Radio Broadcasters (ACORAB), goes so far as to say that 'communication is the fuel for everything—for democracy, for development and for many other things. Without fuel, the light was very dim. We poured the fuel, and the light became very bright' (quoted in Deane 2008:39).

Communication is indeed increasingly recognized as fundamental to wider socio-economic development, although in practice it may be overlooked in the face of seemingly more pressing aspects of poverty (Benkler 2006; Deane 2006; Sen 2000). It is especially important to examine the media and communication sector in Nepal because it is clear that independent FM radio broadcasting is potentially undermined by their extremely rapid proliferation (Bhattarai 2007; Pringle and Subba 2007). The sustainability of radio stations is closely connected to the possible degradation of radio broadcasting due to signal interference. However, for the reasons detailed above it is clear that the solutions to this problem are as much social as they are technical.

No distinction is currently made between community and commercial ownership in the licensing of radio stations in Nepal. Community stations receive no government subsidies or protection from competition, which means that all stations must seek whatever resources they can to sustain themselves. Advertising has become the main source of revenue for almost all radio stations, although stations are also sometimes paid to broadcast programmes made by INGOs and NGOs (including Equal Access, who conducted the nationwide study of radio signal propagation with funding from USAID under the direction of one of the present authors, Upreti). This is obviously a massive disincentive to the creation of radio stations in areas where there is simply no population of sufficient wealth or with access to markets in which to purchase the goods or services advertised on these stations. Income from government advertising alone is insufficient to sustain even very small-scale stations given the costs associated with licensed radio broadcasting.

A member of the board of governors of a community radio station run by a cooperative/NGO organization noted during a recent interview conducted by Wilmore that the station's motto was 'hour, power and tower'. They had increased the number of hours broadcast daily from fourteen to nineteen to ensure that listeners were less likely to retune their radios, despite the recent problems with electricity shortages that caused many stations to drastically cut back on broadcast time; they had increased their transmission power from an original 100 watts to 1,000 watts; and they next planned to move their transmission tower from its existing lowland location in the Terai (the low-lying southern border area) to a point in the hills. Although the station wished to maintain a service that met the needs of its own district's people, they were simultaneously pursuing an expansion plan that might see their broadcasts covering up to fifty of Nepal's districts in order to compete for advertising revenue with commercial broadcasters (see below regarding the further implications of this).

This latter point about the location of transmission is important because FM radio transmission is greatly affected by geography. Nepal faces particular problems in relation to variations in signal reach because it is one of the most extreme and varied landscapes in the world. Not only is the propagation of signals blocked, but reception often goes far beyond that expected because of abnormal propagation and the non-applicability of normal assumptions regarding line-of-sight propagation. Abnormal signal propagation allows the radio signals to travel further than the normal propagation where sometimes the signals undergo different physical factor such as signal scattering, diffraction, reflection, enhancement or ducting (Sinclair 1997). Government licensing of stations on the same frequency has not taken this pattern of propagation into account and signal interference then becomes inevitable, especially given the poor tuning capabilities of most listeners' cheap radios. Until recently the practical effects of this have been little understood by independent broadcasters in Nepal and not taken into account during either the government licensing process or by station owners. Equal Access's signal mapping project enabled the growing problems of signal interference and spectrum erosion to be identified for the first time. In particular there is a severe danger that the decisions radio broadcasters are making to further their own need to increase signal reach and ensure sustainability, such as boosting transmission strength and shifting transmitter tower location, will have potentially dire consequences for everyone who increasingly relies on the radio spectrum for communication in Nepal.

This is the potential commons tragedy hidden in the radio signal map shown in Figure 11.1 because the seemingly impressive range of coverage in some areas is either creating reception problems for others or actually reflects the propagation of signals from distant areas that then interfere with local broadcasting. Again it is those most vulnerable and reliant on the niche service that very local community-based radio stations provide who are most likely to find their voices drowned out amidst the growing cacophony of radio signals. Whereas a system of regulation firmly based on the principles of common ownership might allow for the development of mutually beneficial arrangements for the sustainable management of this resource, the present system of licensing actively discourages cooperation in favour of destructive competition over sources of revenue.

Solution to Signal Interference in Nepal

The challenge is now to put in place institutional arrangements through which some of the worst impacts of signal interference problems can be ameliorated. It will be clear that this invariably requires the application of detailed contextually

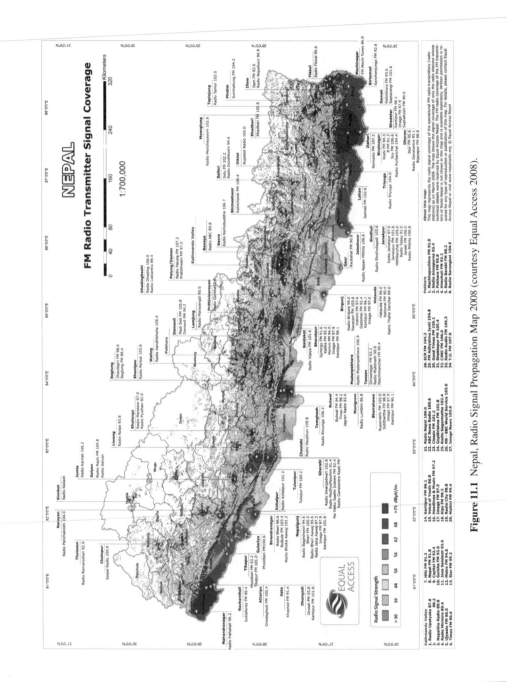

Figure 11.1 Nepal, Radio Signal Propagation Map 2008 (courtesy Equal Access 2008).

aware understandings of the local circumstances in which such interventions are proposed, especially given the cultural and linguistic diversity of Nepal. In particular this situation demands that we develop a clearer picture of how transactions occur between actors situated at different levels of institutional activity, from the village communities that aspire to run ultra-small-scale radio stations, to large-scale commercial producers and to complex governmental bureaucracies undergoing massive political transformation. We must avoid seeing national governments and other state-level agents as simply external to the 'local' situations or communities seen as our primary concern (Ostrom 1990:215). As such radio provides a perfect example of the challenges posed by the formation of 'global commons' (Ostrom *et al.* 1999), in particular the processes through which collective action requires a grasp of how 'vertical' as well as 'horizontal' reciprocity contributes to the varieties of self-organization involved in common-pool resource governance (Tang and Tang 2001).

It is most appropriate to begin at the level of the broadcasters themselves, especially the self-identified community broadcasters, because as with other common-pool resources it is self-governance and local solutions that are most effective in either dealing with or preventing a commons tragedy (Ostrom 1990). One of the most important innovations occurring in radio broadcasting at the present moment is the increasing provision of content that is in the minority national languages of Nepal (Martin *et al.* 2007; Martin and Wilmore 2010). Radio stations seldom provide a service in any language other than Nepali, but many community stations recognize that provision of substantial 'minority' language programming in areas where speakers of these languages are a majority of the population creates a significant point of differentiation between themselves and commercial broadcasters who have no interest in meeting the needs of these audiences. The most significant factor inhibiting these innovations in multi-lingual broadcasting is the comparative lack of minority-language speakers with broadcasting experience. Formal and informal training in radio broadcasting almost always requires fluency and literacy in Nepali, as this is the medium of all higher education and business.

Language is the most important factor in ensuring the sustainability of community radio stations, because it is crucial in their development of a distinctive voice – literally in the case of radio – that distinguishes them from commercial and national broadcasters (Rodriguez and El Gazi 2007). Providing alternative content, especially in languages that your audience members can understand (including simple, non-technical scripting), has time and again been shown to be the best means through which an audience can be built and retained by small-scale broadcasters (Martin *et al.* 2007; Tacchi and Kiran 2008). Unfortunately the capacity issues referred to above and the reliance of stations on paid advertising and programming shared by many other stations militates against the development of such distinctiveness. Stations must by law broadcast in the national languages of Nepal (i.e. those included in the constitutional list), although this only applies to presentation and talk shows, so songs in other languages are permitted. At present, only one organization, Voice of Youth, is allowed to broadcast in other 'international' languages, but stations openly flout this rule: many transmit Hindi broadcasts to capture advertising aimed at the Indian market, which is unintelligible to most of their potential Nepalese listeners.

Community stations are exploring new sources of revenue, often based upon the ideal of local representation that provides them with their main legitimacy as a broadcaster. An interesting example is Rupakot Radio in Khotang District, Diktel VDC. This is run as a type of cooperative with each shareholder being a household in the broadcast area. Households gave NR100 minimum as a levy at the time the station was set up, although some gave as much as NR10,000 (the motivations for such variations are not presently known). In return the households receive a minimum of NR100 per year. Approximately a thousand homes are divided into five areas that vote to elect an area representative for the station board. Rupakot Radio has been in operation for less than three years and currently faces no competition in the immediate locality. There is little signal interference suffered by the station at present, but this is bound to change as new stations transmit in the area. Other significant questions remain to be answered about this model of community media ownership and organization: can new households subsequently join the cooperative? How will the station deal with inevitable pressure to increase transmission power?

More typical of community radio resourcing is Vijaya FM (VFM), which was started in 2004 under the auspices of the Vijaya Development Resource Centre (VDRC). The VDRC takes a two-legged approach to its work: working as an NGO for the governance structures that this provides and as a cooperative for better sustainability. Working as a cooperative provides income and purpose to their activities. The radio station matched the cooperative's aims and ambitions by making their work known to as many people as possible. The VDRC also runs a micro-finance organization that occupies the ground floor of the VFM building and is a shareholder in the radio station. VFM has many other shareholders due to the cooperative ideal under which it was founded. Some are individuals, but many are institutions such as the microfinance organization, VDCs, schools (both public and private), NGOs and community forest user groups. The maximum level of shareholding is set by the regulations of the cooperative in order to maximize participation and prevent any one shareholder wielding undue power over VFM. Radio Madan Pokhara (RMP), possibly the most celebrated example of community broadcasting in Nepal, is run by the Village Development Committee in a similar way and illustrates another approach to the reciprocity required to construct the type of collective agreements to organize common-pool resource rights. Financial contributions from the local population are collected on a purely voluntary basis, but the station is still reliant on advertising. However, the station has put in place strict self-imposed guidelines about the types of products and services advertised in its programming; for example it has banned junk food and soft drink advertising. As such it does not compete with local commercial stations for these particular sources of advertising revenue and preserves the community-welfare orientation of the station's programming.

At present there is no separate licence structure for community broadcasters. The Nepal Association of Community Radio Broadcasters (ACORAB) defines radio stations that are eligible for membership in their organization according to the wholly negative criterion that they are not owned by commercial organizations (private limited companies). At the same time the content and service provided by broadcasters also tends to be more uniform than might be expected and there are no licensing requirements to ensure that self-proclaimed community broadcasters restrict their content in any way. Many do, of course, attempt to fulfill a clear community service remit, especially in relation to self-imposed guidelines to regulate their advertising content. Radio broadcasting is also becoming increasingly politicized with a number of instances of political parties operating radio stations being widely known, if not explicitly proclaimed (Luitel 2007).

The irregular separation of frequencies due to poor allocation at the licensing stage creates problems that are particularly intractable because, once established, stations are extremely reluctant to change their broadcast frequency. One of the best solutions to the problem of radio signal interference would be the construction of low-powered transmitters within a network, which would also have the added advantage of allowing small-scale broadcasters to operate through the sharing of transmission facilities. Unfortunately, the current government licensing regime rules this out for all but the wealthiest commercial broadcasters because each transmission facility requires a separate licence: the licence is issued for the individual transmitter, rather than for the broadcaster as an individual media organization. Transmission facilities that broadcast one station's output even on the same frequency are regarded as entirely separate for the purposes of licensing. Considering this, one of the best solutions for community broadcasters would be the reservation of a defined portion of the radio frequency for their exclusive use and this is a key element of ACORAB policy (ACORAB 2008). ACORAB is currently lobbying for this change to be adopted, but as noted above any enforced change to frequencies allocated to licence holders ordered as a result of the adoption of such a policy would probably be fiercely resisted by many broadcasters, including even some of the more established community broadcasters. Amicably dealing with this issue could provide the most vivid exemplar of the self-organization of common-pool spectrum resources suggested by Ostrom.

Some of the terms under which licenses are held have been recently changed, but these are not enforced on existing stations retrospectively and the technical problems associated with frequency allocation are not being properly addressed by the Ministry of Information and Communication (MOIC). Whether such new regulations help improve the situation will of course be largely dependent on the willingness and ability of the government to enforce them. Understanding how and why this might not occur presents a challenge to researchers and radio broadcasters alike who invariably find it hard to access, let alone influence, processes of elite decision making. According to Whalley (2006:68), 'The ability of the regulator [created by the Nepalese MOIC] to act impartially has been curtailed to a limited degree. This should not be interpreted as suggesting that the regulator has been sidelined, but rather as an indication of the increasing polit-icization of the industry as well as the protracted decision-making process of the regulator.'

Whether centralized bureaucratic governments, especially in a state like Nepal traumatized by recent conflict, can fine tune policy quickly and carefully enough to keep up with the pace of media innovation is a moot point. Deitz, Ostrom and Stern are 'guardedly optimistic' (2003:1910) in general about the possibilities for 'adaptive governance' in relation to common-pool resources, but Edmunds and Wollenberg (2001) strike a note of caution by pointing out that the power differentials in multi-stakeholder negations over commons governance invariably lead to the kinds of developments noted earlier in relation to the radio broadcasting in industrialized states. Goulden (2005) also points to the need for skilled contextually aware policy makers in developing media environments in order to avoid such difficulties, although the persistence of an emphasis on 'hard' technologically focused training or content creation in media education restricts their availability. The development of media policy in many developing countries remains in the hands of inexperienced legislators and bureaucrats or is the burden of a few chronically over-stretched experts due to the high cost of providing such services (Grätz 1999; Whalley 2006).

It should be noted that the vibrancy, not to say creative chaos, of the Nepali radio scene is often contrasted with the much more cautious approach adopted in India, where the government has not faced the same difficulties as in Nepal and retained much greater control over broadcasting (Page and Crawley 2001). As noted above, it is in part this relative lack of control over the regulation and governance of broadcasters that encouraged the formation of a radio spectrum commons – or at least a 'commons-like' situation – in Nepal. However, as in the USA in the 1920s when a similar situation of creative chaos ensued (Hitchens 2006), it is increasingly likely that government will impose ever stricter licensing measures that benefit existing commercial interests under the pretext of protecting a public resource. In addition the post-conflict political environment under which the media operate in Nepal encourages national governments to seek legitimation for their policy developments in the eyes of the donor nations that they rely on for international development aid, further reinforcing the conservatism of spectrum policy (Best and Thakur 2009).

Conclusion

The intangibility of the radio spectrum might explain initial ambiguities regarding its value as a resource, but it is apparent that once this period of uncertainty passed it was rapidly appropriated by states and commercial interests (Wurtzler 2007:175). Debates about signal interference and the presentation of such debates as solely concerned with technological causes and solutions to the potentially tragic erosion of a natural resource served to make this a more tangible problem that could be presented as a cause for universal concern (cf. Strang this volume). We have explained that such ambiguities in contemporary Nepal, as elsewhere, have occurred primarily through uncertainties surrounding the institutional arrangements for use rights in relation to the spectrum. Such ambiguities allowed for 'claims that permit a flexible exploitation of those having less power by those with more' (Verdery 1998:171), claims then naturalized as the accepted common sense of spectrum management (see, for example, Withers 1999).

We do not dispute that the radio spectrum tends in practice to be used as a rivalrous and at least partially exhaustible resource. Rather we have questioned the near universal rejection of the viability of commons-based solutions to problems of resolving access and use rights over the radio spectrum predicated on problems of signal interference. These potential solutions have seldom been realized in *practice* because control of the spectrum has been usurped by states and use rights have then been allocated only through systems of licensing and privatization. However, following Ostrom's (1990) examination of the governance of commons, it is important that we recognize that actual examples of common-pool resource use indicate that it is very difficult to generalize about practical outcomes, even if the various theories of use provide some clear expectations.

Radio broadcasting in Nepal illustrates this insight well: failures of governance appear to inexorably lead towards the spectrum becoming a rivalrous and exhausted resource, but regulatory failures also earlier resulted in the development of radio spectrum use with many commons-like characteristics. While many countries with more fully developed and enforced systems of broadcasting regulation have not yet been able to realize the potential of broadcasting for development, especially community broadcasting (India is a case in point), the relative lack of governance in Nepal allowed for widespread radio activity. Although systems of regulation do exist in Nepal, what also now exists amongst the population at large is a keenly felt sense that despite – or maybe even because of – attempts to limit freedoms to broadcast, access to the radio spectrum is a fundamental right of Nepal's people (see Wilmore 2008a and 2008b).

If this is the case, then it is vital that we understand the ways in which this common resource is threatened by misuse and acknowledge that users themselves may have already created ways to maintain it as a non-rivalrous resource. The risk, however, is that instead those 'customs' encouraging signal interference – the drive towards increases in so-called 'hour, power, and tower' – will thrive and become a convenient excuse for the destruction of radio as a commons in Nepal through wholesale state appropriation and privatization, which obviously serves the interests of larger commercial networks. McCay and Jentoft (1998) go so far as to warn that 'external' interference in established or emerging processes of self-organized collective action may actually provide the circumstances under which commons tragedies occur by disrupting the delicate balance of reciprocity involved in such relations. Alternative customs that have arisen out of relations between radio stations are emerging, but remain fragile. How these can be best supported and encouraged so that the radio spectrum remains available to all as a common-pool resource is a question that at present can only be answered negatively, because we can be sure that established forms of state appropriation will surely only bring this experiment in community broadcasting to an abrupt end. If this happens we can also predict that those who stand to lose most are listeners who only recently experienced the novelty of hearing people from their own communities talk on the radio (Brinson 2008). The spectrum itself may survive, but the spectrum of ideas and opinions will be tragically diminished.

Notes

1. Forge and Blackman (2006:12) note that some commentators on this issue have gone so far as to assert 'that spectrum is an intellectual construct, whose utility is rapidly decreasing as technology develops'. Although they emphasize the technological reasons for this, others, notably Lawrence Lessig (2002), argue along lines with clearer antecedence in Karl Polanyi's (1968) famous assertion that the appropriation of certain natural resources within a system of capitalist market relations is a 'commodity fiction'. McCay and Jentoft (1998) provide a more extensive discussion of the connections between Polanyi's ideas and common-pool resource theory.

Acknowledgements

First, apologies to REM for the appropriation of lyrics from 'Radio Song' off their album 'Out of Time' in the title of this chapter! We would like to acknowledge the support of all our colleagues, too numerous to list here, working under the auspices of the *Assessing Communication for Social Change* project (http:// ac4sc.org/en/wiki/about). This project involves collaboration between Equal Access Nepal (http://www.equalaccess.org/country-nepal.php), the University of Adelaide, and Queensland University of Technology. This project is funded through an Australian Research Council Linkage grant (LP0775252) and we are grateful for the financial support of the ARC and Equal Access Nepal. The original radio signal mapping research to which we refer was originally carried out under the auspices of Equal Access's *Digital Broadcast Initiative* project funded by USAID. We would like to thanks Martin Fuchs and Assa Doron for convening the panel at the ASA 2008 conference in Auckland in which this paper was originally presented and the helpful comments of all present on that day. Finally, the valuable comments of our editors, Mark Busse and Veronica Strang, and the input of Chris Hann, have helped to greatly improve our chapter. The authors, of course, have sole responsibility for all chapter content.

References

ACORAB (2008), *Community Radio for Information, Expressions and Development*, Kathmandu: Association of Community Radio Broadcasters (ACORAB) Secretariat.

Aitken, H. (1994), 'Allocating the Spectrum: The Origin of Radio Regulation', *Technology and Culture*, 35(4): 686–716.

Atton, C. (2002), *Alternative Media*, London, SAGE Publications.

Bardhan, P. and Ray, I. (2008), 'Economists, Anthropologists, and the Contested Commons', in P. Bardhan and I. Ray (eds), *The Contested Commons: Conversations Between Economists and Anthropologists*, Oxford: Blackwell Publishing, pp. 1–24.

Benkler, Y. (2006), *The Wealth of Networks: How Social Production Transforms Markets and Freedom*, New Haven: Yale University Press.

Best, M. and Thakur, D. (2009), 'The Telecommunications Policy Process in Post-conflict Developing Countries: The Case of Liberia', *Info*, 11(2): 42–57.

Bhattarai, B. (2007), 'Nepal: Picking up Steam, but Political Bottlenecks Ahead', in K. Seneviratne (ed.), *Media Pluralism in Asia: The Role and Impact of Alternative Media*, Singapore: Asian Media Information and Communication Centre, pp. 132–75.

Brinson, S. (2008), 'Radio's Covenant: The Regulatory Failure of Minority Ownership of Broadcast Radio Facilities', in M.C. Keith (ed.), *Radio Cultures: The Sound Medium in American Life*, New York: Peter Lang, pp. 9–21.

Campbell, B. (2003), 'Compromising Technologies: Government, the Radio Hobby, and the Discourse of Catastrophe in the Twentieth Century', in S.M. Squier (ed.), *Communities of the Air: Radio Century, Radio Culture*, Durham and London: Duke University Press, pp. 63–75.

Deane, J. (2006), 'Why the Media Matters: The Relevance of the Media to Tackling Global Poverty', in M. Harvey (ed.), *Media Matters: Perspectives on Advancing Governance and Development from the Global Forum for Media Development*, Paris: Internews Europe, pp. 35–44.

Deane, J. (2008), 'The Role of Community Radio in the Nepali Crisis: An Interview with Raghu Mainali', in *Fighting Poverty: Utilizing Community Media in a Digital Age*, Montreal: AMARC, World Association of Community Radio Broadcasters; Berne: SDC, Swiss Agency for Development and Cooperation; Paris: UNESCO, pp. 34–41.

Deitz, T., Ostrom, E. and Stern, P. (2003), 'The Struggle to Govern Commons', *Science*, 302: 1907–12.

Edelman, M. and Haugerud, A. (2005), 'Introduction: The Anthropology of Development and Globalization', in M. Edelman and A. Haugerud (eds), *The Anthropology of Development and Globalization: From Classical Political Economy to Contemporary Neoliberalism*, Oxford: Blackwell Publishing, pp. 1–74.

Edmunds, D. and Wollenberg, E. (2001), 'A Strategic Approach to Multistakeholder Negotiations', *Development and Change*, 32(2): 231–53.

Forge, S. and Blackman, C. (2006), 'Spectrum for the Next Radio Revolution: The Economic and Technical Case for Collective Use', *Info*, 8(2): 6–17.

Goulden, B. (2005), 'Building ICT Regulatory Capacity in Developing Economies: A Learning Framework for Regulators', *Info*, 7(4): 3–7.

Grätz, T. (1999), 'Local Radio Stations, Political Transformation and the Demonopolisation of Public Communication: The Case of *Radio Rurale Tanguieta* (Northern Benin)', *Sociology of Development Research Centre, Working Paper* No. 321, Bielefeld: Sociology of Development Research Centre, University of Bielefeld.

Hann, C. (2005), 'Property', in J.G. Carrier (ed.), *A Handbook of Economic Anthropology*, Cheltenham: Edward Elgar, pp. 110–24.

Hardin, G. (1968), 'The Tragedy of the Commons', *Science*, 162: 1243–8.

Hazlett, T. (1990), 'The Rationality of US Regulation of the Broadcast Spectrum', *Journal of Law and Economics*, 33(1): 133–75.

Hess, C. 2000. 'Is There Anything New Under the Sun? A Discussion and Survey of Studies on New Commons and the Internet', paper presented at 'Constituting the Commons', the eighth biennial conference of the International Association for the Study of Common Property, 31 May to 4 June 2000, Bloomington, Indiana.

Hess, C. and Ostrom, E. (2003), 'Ideas, Artifacts and Facilities: Information as a Common-pool Resource', *Law and Contemporary Problems*, 66(1/2): 111–45.

Hitchens, L. (2006), *Broadcasting Pluralism and Diversity: A Comparative Study of Policy and Regulation*, Oxford: Hart Publishing.

Hungbo, J. (2008), 'The Wilderness of the Public Sphere: Clandestine Radio in Africa', paper presented at 'Governing the African Public Sphere,' 12th General Assembly of the Council for the Development of Social Science Research in Africa (CODESRIA), 7–11 November 2008, Yaoundé, Cameroon.

Lessig, L. (2002), *The Future of Ideas: The Fate of the Commons in a Connected World*, New York: Vintage Books.

Luitel, G. (2007), 'Voice of the Party', *Nepali Times eSpecial*, http://www.nepalitimes.com/issue/350/Nation/13572 [Accessed 24 February 2009].

McCay, B. and Jentoft, S. (1998), 'Market or Community Failure? Critical Perspectives on Common Property Research', *Human Organization*, 57(1): 21–9.

Martin, K., Koirala, D., Pandey, R., Adhikari, S., Acharya, D. and Kiran, M. (2007), 'Finding the Local Community in Community Media: Some Stories from Nepal', *Asia Rights*, 8, http://rspas.anu.edu.au/asiarightsjournal/Issue%20Eight_Martin%20et%20al.htm [Accessed 24 February 2009].

Martin, K. and Wilmore, M. (2010), 'Local Voices on Community Radio: Introducing 'Our Lumbini' in Nepal', *Development in Practice*, 20(7): 866–78.

Minasian, J. (1969), 'The Political Economy of Broadcasting in the 1920s', *Journal of Law and Economics*, 12(2): 391–403.

Onta, P. (2006), *Mass Media in Post-1990 Nepal*, Kathmandu: Martin Chautari.

Ostrom, E. (1990), *Governing the Commons: The Evolution of Institutions for Collective Action*, Cambridge: Cambridge University Press.

Ostrom, E. (2000), 'Collective Action and the Evolution of Social Norms', *Journal of Economic Perspectives*, 14(3): 137–58.

Ostrom, E., Burger, J., Field, C.B., Norgaard, R.B. and Policansky, D. (1999), 'Revisiting the Commons: Local Lessons, Global Challenges', *Science*, 284: 278–82.

Page, D. and Crawley, W. (2001), *Satellites over South Asia: Broadcasting, Culture and the Public Interest*, New Delhi: Sage Publications.

Polanyi, K. (1968), *The Great Transformatiom: The Political and Economic Origins of Our Time*, Boston: Beacon Press.

Pringle, I. and Subba, B. (2007), *Ten Years On: The State of Community Radio in Nepal*, Paris: UNESCO.

Rodriguez, C. and El Gazi, J. (2007), 'The Poetics of Indigenous Radio in Colombia', *Media Culture Society*, 29(3): 449–68.

Salmon, T. (2004), 'Spectrum Auctions by the United States Federal Communications Commission', in M.C.W. Janssen (ed.), *Auctioning Public Assets: Analysis and Alternatives*, Cambridge: Cambridge University Press, pp. 147–76.

Sen, A. (2000), *Development as Freedom*, New Delhi: Oxford University Press.

Sinclair, J. (1997), *How Radio Signals Work*, Sydney: McGraw-Hill Book Company.

Snider, J. (2003), *An Explanation of the Citizen's Guide to the Airwaves*, Washington, DC: New America Foundation, Spectrum Policy Program.

Starr, P. (2004), *The Creation of the Media: Political Origins of Modern Communication*, New York: Basic Books.

Tacchi, J. and Kiran, M. (2008), ' "Finding a Voice" in Context', in J. Tacchi and M.S. Kiran (eds), *Finding a Voice: Themes and Discussions*, New Delhi: UNESCO, pp. 25–46.

Tang, C. and Tang, S. (2001), 'Negotiated Autonomy: Transforming Self-governing Institutions for Local Common-pool Resources in Two Tribal Villages in Taiwan', *Human Ecology*, 29(1): 49–67.

Verdery, K. (1998), 'Property and Power in Transylvania's Decollectivization', in C.M. Hann (ed.), *Property Relations: Renewing Anthropological Traditions*, Cambridge: Cambridge University Press, pp. 160–80.

Wellenius, B. and Neto, I. (2006), 'The Radio Spectrum: Opportunities and Challenges for the Developing World', *Info*, 8(2): 18–33.

Whalley, J. (2006), 'Recent Developments in the Telecommunications Industry of Nepal', *Info*, 8(1): 57–71.

Wildman, S., Bauer, J. and Ting, C. (2006), 'Spectrum Governance Regimes: Efficiency Properties and Policy Choices', *Info*, 8(2): 83–96.

Wilmore, M. (2008a), 'Urban Space and the Mediation of Political Action in Nepal: Local Television, Ritual Processions and Political Violence as Technologies of Enchantment', *The Australian Journal of Anthropology*, 19(1): 41–56.

Wilmore, M. (2008b), *Developing Alternative Media Traditions in Nepal*, Lanham, MD: Lexington Books.

Withers, D. (1999), *Radio Spectrum Management: Management of the Radio Spectrum and Regulation of Radio Services*, 2nd edn, London: Institute of Electrical Engineers.

Wurtzler, S. (2007), *Electric Sounds: Technological Change and the Rise of Corporate Mass Media*, New York: Columbia University Press.

Part Three
Ownership as Social Communication

–12–

The Village That Wasn't There

Appropriation, Domination and Resistance

Adam Kaul

Abstract

Corporate and Government appropriations of tourist destinations are often characterized as exploitative of local people who are displaced, commodified and/or essentialized. But what happens when it is the local people themselves who appropriate their own spaces by transforming a collection of grassroots tourism-related commercial interests into a fully fledged corporate-led tourist industry in a matter of only a few years? What impact does the appropriation of the physical spaces of a destination have on the narrative of what the place is about? Conversely, how do changing discourses about a place change physical spaces?

In 2003 locals in the village of Doolin in County Clare, Ireland, created a development plan. Since then more development has occurred than ever before in the history of the village. Using ethnographic accounts of the planning process and its subsequent implementation, this chapter tracks the transformation, essentialization and the auto-appropriation of a tourist destination. It analyses not only the corporate appropriation of the physical spaces of the village, but also the narrative appropriation of the definitions of the place. It considers how contestations over these created a village that wasn't there before – a process of discursive emplacement that began long before it culminated in the concrete reality of development.

Introduction

When asked where I conduct my ethnographic research, I often describe my 'fieldsite' as the small coastal village of Doolin (pop. 600) in County Clare, which has been a major tourist destination in western Ireland since the late 1960s. Yet this characterization is a little simplistic: in reality definitions of this locale are complicated, fluid and contested. While Doolin is a real place inhabited by real people, it is also the physical manifestation of an ever-becoming constantly retold narrative, a community whose story seems to have changed recently as a result of tourism. In this chapter I look at how stories about this community relate to the ways in which its built environment comes into being and conversely how that built environment changes the narratives about the place.

At the core of this analysis is the claim that the stories people tell about places are everyday acts of knowing and owning them. In that sense, a 'telling of place' can simultaneously be an act of appropriation, a claim to ownership and belonging, or an act of resistance to others' claims to own and belong. There is nothing passive about this process: as Barbara Bender wrote, '[t]he landscape is never inert, people engage with it, re-work it, appropriate it, and contest it. It is part of the way in which identities are created and disputed, whether as an individual, group, or nation-state' (1993:3). This argument stems from a broader foundation laid by Foucault who in *The Archaeology of Knowledge* analyses the relationship between discourse and the formation of objects or, as he himself put it, the relationship between 'words and things' (1972:54). He argues that discourses are in fact 'practices that systematically form the objects of which they speak' (ibid.). While people make landscapes – both literally and also by the way in which a landscape is 'framed' visually, socially and metaphorically (Bender 1993:1) – it is equally true that social interactions and power relations are heavily influenced by the places in which they are carried out (Foucault 1984:239). In other words there is a 'recursive relationship between ideational and material spaces, between ways of knowing the world and ways of being in the world' (Farrar 2008:8).

This resonates with Howard Morphy's contention in this volume that we must understand 'objects in the context of action'. For Morphy the *product* of Yolngu art that he writes about must be seen 'as a way of acting in the world', a representation of the *process* of creating group identities and asserting ownership. In Doolin my focus is not on art but on the recent development of buildings in the landscape, though the principle is the same. Places are *dynamic fields of action* – acted upon and active – rather than inert and empty vacuums, and the activity and dynamism of physical places has a great deal to do with the stories that people tell about them.

In this case I am interested in how conflicting and evolving discourses about buildings and landscape form group identities and re/create power structures. Because of its dramatic history and setting and its lucrative tourism industry, narratives about Doolin are important for tourists, the tourist industry and Clare County Council developers. The village is sandwiched between three of Ireland's most famous natural landscapes: the Cliffs of Moher, the Burren and the Aran Islands just off the coast. The recent social history of the village is equally dramatic, especially in terms of its 'musical landscape'. Since the late 1960s Doolin has been one of several locales at the centre of a revival of traditional

Irish music. All of this has resulted in a very strong and diverse tourist 'product'. It is beyond the scope of this chapter to delve too much into that history and its impacts,[1] but all of this attention makes Doolin a densely storied place.

Owning Places by Knowing and Naming Them

Ireland's obsession with landownership came up recently in a conversation I had with an informant, Charles,[2] as we sat in the basement of the bright new offices of the Clare County Council in the town of Ennis. As he described planning procedures to me, he raised his eyebrows and said with a gasp, 'landownership here is regarded as sacred!' Charles is not Irish: he was transplanted there to fulfill a temporary appointment as a 'forward planner' working on regional development issues for the County Council. The value that the Irish place on land, as well as the intricacies of defining places – how they are delineated and named – came as something of a surprise as he began his work with local communities. But this veneration of landownership is nothing new. Brody (1973:59–64) describes in detail how land became an increasingly valuable commodity following the Famine of the mid-1800s, sometimes even to the economic and social detriment of a landowner's own offspring who were forced to emigrate because holdings were increasingly consolidated into the hands of a single heir rather than subdivided. For well over a century this economic reality catalysed the fetish of landownership. More recently the Celtic Tiger economy provided many new opportunities such as tourism, so patterns of emigration caused by landlessness have slowed and even reversed. Still, the intense value placed on land remains and it is vividly expressed by the detailed way in which every minute field and feature in the landscape is named. Names have great power as spaces are appropriated into places (Frake 1996:235). In the Irish context, '[n]aming has long been recognised as an important part of the act of claiming and confirming possession over space' (Jarman 1993:126). In precolonial times there was even a whole toponymic poetic tradition called *dindshenchas* that solely recounted the stories of particular place-names.

Traditionally the Isle of Ireland is composed of four regions: Leinster, Munster, Connaught and Ulster, which are sub-divided into thirty-two counties. The land is further divided into baronies and then into civil parishes. Finally parishes are parcelled into townlands, which range in size from less than an acre up to several hundred acres. There are approximately 60,000 individually named townlands across Ireland, and well over 2,300 in County Clare alone. Many examples in and around the village of Doolin are simply descriptive, like *moymore* ('the big field') or *tir gan ean* ('place of rabbits'), while others have more intriguing names like *ballysalach* ('the dirty village') or *poulnagun* ('the dog's cavern') that obviously describe something more than just the physical features of the place. This naming tradition illustrates how stories about places coalesce into a kind of collective memory or knowledge that helps to formulate community identities.

During the past few centuries many Gaelic place-names were lost as the English dominated the Irish landscape both by physical force and also through renaming. As Nash (1999:460) points out, the 'colonial impulse to name and simultaneously claim newly "discovered" or explored land' through renaming was as common in Ireland as it was in many other colonized regions of the world. Resistance to this practice has also been common and the process of re-appropriating the land through the reclamation of Gaelic place-names became an important aspect to Irish cultural nationalism and Republicanism in the twentieth century (ibid.:461). In some areas of Ireland the result has been a continued dispute to the present day about what places are called. The most famous example is the city of Derry in Northern Ireland, called Londonderry on British maps, where the name itself has long been a symbolic flashpoint in the conflict between Catholic and Protestant communities. Indeed one of the most famous murals in Northern Ireland stands in the Catholic neighborhood of Derry called the Bogside. It simply but authoritatively names the place: 'You Are Now Entering Free Derry'. Likewise it is significant that, although bilingual signs have been common in Southern Ireland since the 1930s, the posting of Gaelic place-names in the North was still officially illegal up until 1995 (O'Reilly in Nash 1999:462). Place-names are therefore much more than simply the names of places, they are a means of affirming community, dominating peoples and engaging in what Scott might call 'symbolic resistance' (1985:282–3).

As ethnographers have noted in other European contexts (Cohen 1987; Kohn 2002; Pine 2001) and elsewhere (Anderson 1998), being inculcated into the everyday intricacies of local systems of knowledge is a fundamental part of belonging in and to a community. In this way, naming can be considered an act of possession. In Doolin local people have a longstanding and detailed understanding of the locale which includes the traditional names of places and also of the families who have occupied these over the years. Doolin is not unique in the sense that people are associated with particular tracts of 'ground' in the collective memorate. In years past, according to Arensberg and Kimball, the perceived relationship between the landscape around Doolin and the generations of people who occupy it – both past and present – was also extended to the way that buildings and houses in particular were constructed (1968[1940]:129–30).[3]

Arensberg describes the close relationship between people and the land: 'A particular ancestral line is inseparable from a particular plot of earth. All others are "strangers to the land"' (1959:83). Kinship and landownership become intertwined and to a large extent this is still true today. For example, like many local people in the village, Martin Mackie's family presence in Doolin goes back beyond memory. Martin is a gentle quiet man who lives in a traditional cottage passed down to him through the family. His ancestors were fishermen and today he is one of the last fishermen in the village. On long walks across the parish he translated Gaelic place-names for me, pointing out sites associated with particular people who once lived there or where some dramatic episode occurred. He told me,

> To become a local, your blood has to be here for a few years. It's just like if you're germinating some plant or something, and you want to get the proper one, you have to have it in the ground for so many years, for so many generations, so many times, before it will actually become the right seed from the ground. Well, the exact same thing works with people.

Martin's sense of rootedness, his idea that people, like plants, are naturally adapted to and spring from specific environments, is not unusual. Mary, a traditional Irish musician, once described the localized west Clare style of fiddle playing, not by describing various musical techniques, but rather by describing the landscape. She said that the local style of fiddle playing derives from the gentle rolling pastureland to the east, the roiling sea along the west coast and the high lofty Cliffs of Moher to the south. She also claimed that the rabbit-warren of caves that undercut the parish give her playing a deep energy. Many traditional Irish musicians speak in similar terms – as if they have not mastered traditional music so much as they have entered into a mutually appropriative relationship with the genre. One musician therefore suggested that traditional musicians are not using their instruments to play traditional music; instead, the musician becomes the instrument for the continuation of the tradition.

To the north the bare-rock limestone 'mountains' of the Burren extend across the northern stretches of County Clare and into County Galway. In a sense the Burren exemplifies the claim that landscapes are human-made (Bender 1993:1), not just in the way that they are metaphorically framed by narratives, but also quite literally in the way in which they are physically created and delineated. Some stretches of the Burren support vegetation in the cracks between the great slabs of limestone 'pavements', but much of it is almost completely bare rock. Farmers in the Burren and on the (geologically similar) Aran Islands used to harvest kelp from the sea which they then burnt or composted into soil. Centuries of this slow methodical activity created arable gardens.

Similarly it took many generations to create the elaborate network of dry-stone walls, held together by nothing more than gravity and friction, which separate the diminutive fields. The walls protect gardens from herds of sheep and cattle, they mark the edges of townlands, or the sections of townlands owned by particular families, and they also provide a place to put loose limestone rocks. For the latter reason some of the walls rise impressively high, well above eye level. From a distance the overall impression is of a complex web of stone draped over the rocky hills – stone on stone encircling an occasional patch of bright green.

One day when I helped Martin repair a stone wall that lined one of his family's fields, he explained that today's locals are simply the stewards of the land in the present, but that its relationship with the people of Doolin is much deeper than any simplistic notion that people own or possess the land. The land, Martin explained, lays claim to him as much as he lays claim to it. In many cultural contexts this type of close tie to the land is characterized as a kind of reciprocal gift-giving, but Anderson, in a very different ethnographic context, describes this more accurately as a mutual appropriation (1998:73). It is knowledge of the land, according to Anderson, that creates this mutual possession. In Doolin mutual possession stems not only from practices of land stewardship, but also comes through the knowledge of place-names, local family histories and local musical aesthetics.

Because local parish nomenclature is complicated and extensive and because it includes both official and colloquial names, the act of simply naming the village is far from simple. Doolin is the name of a single townland in Killilagh Parish, a parish that easily spans several hundred acres, but the name for this one townland eventually extended across the whole area. Even identifying what makes up the village is not straightforward. What is called Doolin today is a scattering of buildings spread out across several miles of road. When I lived there in 2002 and 2003 there were two main sections. The stretch of buildings called Fisherstreet that runs along the parish's Aillee River bears most resemblance to the Anglo-American stereotype of a village with a tightly packed assemblage of buildings. Another section called Roadford, about two miles further inland, is much more dispersed with large tracts of green pasture between buildings.

A basic confusion about what to call this place is evident on older maps, which occasionally label the whole area 'Doolin', but just as often use more localized names. In recent decades, though, the tourist narrative, which demands sound-byte-simplicity about destinations, has just used the name 'Doolin' and more recent official maps of the area have followed suit in using the overarching name 'Doolin' instead of more specific names for the various parts of the village. This is not a small point if, as Nash suggests, place-names reflect local histories of power (1999:457). In this way tourism has played a major role in essentializing one place-name over others and therefore consolidated the very *idea* of Doolin as well.

The dialogic 'telling of place' through knowing and naming by locals, by tourists and as we will see below, by corporations and government agencies, is in fact a process of narrative place-making, something Peace has called 'emplacement' (2001). Naming, knowing and narrating places are all acts of owning and appropriating them. Recently this process has placed a fluid cultural interaction with a landscape quite literally 'on the map' and by formalizing it, has reduced complexity to commensurable simplicity.

This parallels a distinction that Minnegal and Dwyer make in this volume between *fish* and the *idea of fish*. In their case study on Australian commercial fishers, they argue that the creation of *virtual* fish as a technocratic quota issued by the state – a quantifiable number on paper– has appropriated the ways that fishermen relate to the actual fish that they catch. In the case of fish quotas in Australia and development in Doolin, it is the state that increasingly defines the terms by which narratives about fish and land are constructed.

The Village That Wasn't There

The idea that the built environment itself is created by discursive practices is not just an abstraction in Doolin: it has very real consequences. The built environment of the village expanded by approximately one third between 2005–2008. Thus the amount of construction over these three years was the same as in the previous quarter of a century. Almost all of it is geared towards tourism, an industry that is on the decline in the region.

Nearly all of this expansion occurred in the space colloquially known as 'Fitz's Cross', a crossroads almost exactly halfway between Fisherstreet and Roadford (Figures 12.1 and 12.2). Prior to 2005 there were a few old cottages in this locale, but nothing that could be called a subsection of the village like Fisherstreet or Roadford. In fact its most prominent feature was the way in which the space

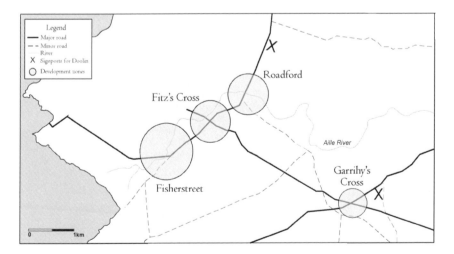

Figure 12.1 Zones of development in Doolin.

Figure 12.2 New developments in Doolin.

directed tourist traffic *away* from Fitz's Cross towards Fisherstreet or Roadford (Figure 12.3). Now, however, this has become the 'centre of the village' by all accounts. What is more, not only is this a 'village that wasn't there before', but since the new construction consists almost solely of holiday homes, shops and hotels, it is also a place in which barely anyone actually lives.

The rapid development that has occurred over the last three years is a direct result of two factors. One was the implementation of a regional development

Figure 12.3 Signposting at Fitz's Cross.

plan for the northern part of County Clare which officially zoned certain areas of Doolin for tourism-related commercial development. The other factor was the expiration at the end of 2004 of a tax-relief programme by which individuals or corporations could receive generous tax-write-offs by investing in tourism schemes. These two factors created a flurry of activity in which Ireland's new Celtic-Tiger-bourgeoisie flooded planning offices with building applications. In the weeks prior to the expiration of the tax-incentive scheme, plans for approximately 170 non-residential holiday homes were submitted to the County Clare planning office. This is despite the fact that one of the primary purposes of the development plan was to create '*sustainable* development of the area' (North Clare Local Area Plan: 2, my italics). In an unusually unanimous voice (not typical in a community known for independent individualism and privacy when it comes to economic matters) locals energetically resisted most of these plans with a media blitz and by swiftly submitting formal objections to the county council. This was a classic moment of the kind of collective resistance described by James C. Scott, characterized by a principled concern for the welfare of the group over individual self interest (1985:292), and in this instance it was moderately successful. About 120 of the proposals were halted. But the building projects that were approved have had a dramatic impact on the built environment. In addition to several dozen holiday houses, two hotels were built along with a large 'strip-mall' style commercial center.

As a result of all of this development at Fitz's Cross, there has been a rerouting of capital flows and consequently political capital as well. Previously coach tours stopped at Fisherstreet and to a lesser extent at Roadford to offload hundreds of tourists per day. They would eat lunch at the pub and browse in the gift shops. In 2002–2003 Fisherstreet was the centre of this very lucrative tourist trade. But now, given its easy access from the main road and it modern amenities, this traffic has been redirected to the new hotel at Fitz's Cross and business along Fisherstreet has slowed significantly. Prior to 2005 Doolin's tourist industry was almost solely owned and operated by local families running guest houses, restaurants and shops. But several of the major new developments were built either by investors from other parts of the country or by corporate interests with local ties, so the profits from these new ventures do not necessarily stay in the village. Tourists bring in a great deal of monetary activity, but in these cases it immediately flows out again into the non-local corporate coffers. Thus the financial channels that used to terminate in Doolin, benefiting the local community, have in part been rerouted to terminate elsewhere, reframing Doolin as simply a host-site for others' profits.

These changes have been exacerbated by the fact that the development process has become more and more removed from local control. The rapid instantiation of the narrative about 'place' into an actual built environment reflects altered social relations at the local level, and a shifting power dynamic between the local community and influences extraneous to it at the county, national and transnational scales. But exactly how has all of this come about? It is instructive to consider the history of tourist-oriented development in order to understand the factors that led up to collective resistance in early 2005 and the events that followed. To return to the central thesis of this chapter, the meta-narratives about a place are powerful forces for their re/creation, so careful attention must be paid to those who control them. There have been three primary groups whose rhetorical voices and devices have impacted development in the past half of a century: the local, the touristic and the State. Each of these voices has narrated and appropriated the place of Doolin differently.[4] Over time the *dominant* narratives have become simplified, essentialized and centralized.

Narrative Re/creation of Place

Several sets of ideas are useful in thinking through these issues in the context of Doolin. Henri Lefebvre's central ideas from *The Production of Space* (1991) are particularly relevant. Spaces for Lefebvre are not empty, nor are they separate from sociality and imagination: the process of the social production of space and the spatial product itself are inseparable aspects of one another. Lefebvre usefully distinguishes between the *appropriation of place* by local people for their own purposes and use-value from the *domination of place*, typically by governments, in order to facilitate State power and reproduce capital (see also Molotch 1993:889). In this sense Lefebvre's use of the term 'appropriation' does not have the negative connotations that it sometimes carries in other contexts. Other writers have suggested that 'the space in which tourism happens is an *inert field of action* predicated by its representation' (Crouch 2002:208, my italics), but if Lefebvre is correct there is nothing inert about it.[5] It is not only the act of place-making that exerts ownership over spaces; places themselves actively reflect and reinforce the power structures of the representations that predicated them. The processes, in other words, are reciprocal.

Also useful in this context is the way in which Bruner and Gorfain (2005) apply Bakhtin's concepts about the dynamism and discourse inherent in language to the narrative construction of tourist places. They argue that stories about tourist places are told in a polyphonic cacophony of voices, a *dialogic narrative* that resists attempts towards its opposite – a singular authoritative voice: in other words, a *monologic certitude*. Narratives about places 'not only define and empower storytellers but also help constitute and reshape society' (ibid.:169). Others have made similar claims that tourist sites are polysemic (Bender 1993:3) and that people 'see' very different landscapes when looking at the same site

(Orlove 1991, 1993:29, 40–41). This is readily evident in the case of Doolin. The development of built environments and the power structures that they represent and embody are preceded by and follow on from the narratives about them.

In Doolin tourist-oriented developments can be divided into two distinct phases. The first was in the late 1960s when tourism began, and extends into the early years of the new century. This was followed by the period after the expiration of the tax incentive scheme at the end of 2004. In the first phase tourism slowly but almost completely subsumed the farming and fishing base of the local economy, to the point that today these industries are peripheral. As this occurred, many of the older 'traditional' cottages in the village (small thick-walled stone structures sometimes with thatched roofing, but more often roofed with flagstones or slate tiles) were renovated and turned into tourist-oriented businesses like restaurants, hostels and music shops. Fisherstreet was wholly appropriated by tourist ventures, and the pier, instead of being the locus of the fishing economy, was appropriated by ferry companies transporting tourists to the Aran Islands. Fishing has not been a strong economic activity in Doolin for many decades, and in 2002–2003 only three fishing boats remained. By 2008 two of these had ceased fishing as well.

Pastureland and fields were also appropriated for the construction of new buildings. Individuals built new homes and businesses on their property, mostly along the major roads. Especially during the 1980s and 1990s, buildings sprung up across the parish in a confetti-like pattern that the county bureaucrats call 'ribbon development'. This follows a long-standing tradition of building practices in rural Ireland, in which small clusters of homes are built by extended family members on their own property rather than concentrated in urban centres. As a result what may seem like random development is actually purposeful. To some extent the way that houses relate to one another across the rural landscape reflects the relationship between members of extended family units. Pine (2001:446) describes a similar set of practices among the Górale people in Highland Poland, where 'kinship is articulated in such a way that the house and the land take on some characteristics of the lineage ... [i]n a way, it is not the people who accumulate their land, but the house and the land which can be seen as recruiting their people'. As a palimpsest, a stratigraphy of past and present human occupation (Winer 2001:266), the landscape provides an important bonding agent in the formation of local identities, and also reveals and represents complex social and kinship relations.

Despite the relatively large amount of autonomous local control in this earlier phase of development, the voice of tourism was influential in the dialogue because the changes in the built environment in Doolin are appropriations that occurred *for tourism*. The tourist narrative is extremely diverse, coming as it does from such a diverse population; but it is also an essentializing voice, one that simplifies the complex history of a place into a handful of sound-bytes. As Martin's cousin

Ciarán pointed out, one of the deep ironies of the tourist discourse is that it is the tourists, not the locals, who want places like Doolin to remain unchanged, frozen in some preconceived form of authenticity, and they express a desire to 'get away from all the tourism'. Newer tourism-oriented developments are perceived by many tourists to be somehow polluting or inauthentic, but locals like Martin and Ciarán have seen many changes and know their home to be a dynamic place.

Tourist sites are particularly pregnant with romantic narratives, prompted by the way in which they are marketed to a consuming travelling public. The seamier realities of history may be papered over while the local 'character' is buffed to a high gloss. Many tourists seek out information about destinations before travelling to them, and therefore their perception of the place, the way in which it is re/created, begins in the imagination. Travlou (2002:108) has argued that tourist guidebooks in particular mediate 'the interaction of the tourists with the destination place. The tourist, the site and the guidebook – as part of the group of markers – are bound in an empirical relationship, constructing the tourism experience.' One aim of this chapter is to extend this argument and posit that over time such narratives have the power to assist in the literal and figurative construction of the place itself, and influence the identities of the people who live there.

In some cases the touristic narrative is wildly misrepresentative, playing into romantic tropes about authenticity. For example in the 2007 edition of *Fodor's Ireland* guide, one passage states that 'On Doolin Pier ... fisherfolk sell their fresh catches right off the boat' (2007:422). As noted above, fishing has all but died out in Doolin, and even when it was a major part of the local economy, the so-called 'fisherfolk' did not sell their fish at the pier. But the narrative that Doolin is a small fishing village is particularly common, as exemplified in this description of Fisherstreet from the third edition of *Ireland for Dummies*: it is a 'row of thatched fisherman's cottages' (Albertson 2005:339). These buildings were once cottages, but this is no longer true. Some were thatched forty years ago, but only two still have thatched roofs today (although one of these is painted bright pink – hardly a 'traditional' colour).

There are other representational activities that help create the tourist narrative. Several dozen coach tours pass through Doolin everyday in the busy summer season, stopping in one of the pubs for lunch after visiting the Cliffs of Moher. On their way down into the village the coach tour operators provide their own detailed romantic stories. In a few short sentences the passengers are given an anticipatory 'frame' for the experience they are about to have (Kaul 2009:76–7). Likewise other voices from the local tourist industry – the staff and owners of hotels, gift shops, restaurants, B&Bs and so on – tell similar stories about Doolin's history and its musical fame. More often than not, they are as brightly polished and reductive as the narratives in travel guides.

Along with the consolidation of the name of Doolin, these stories have concretized what once was a multifaceted knowledge of the locale into a singular,
much narrower idea of what Doolin is all about. This was mutually important
to community stake-holders and to the consuming tourist public. The authors of
guidebooks require a name and a concise description in order to present pragmatic information for readers. Locals also understand the necessity of marketing
a consistent 'Doolin brand'. We might go further and claim that this narrative
essentialization is a powerful mechanism for reinforcing or rewriting what
Cohen has called the 'symbolic boundaries' around the community's 'character'(1987:15–16).[6] However misrepresentative or superficial these narratives
may be, they are part of a local auto-appropriation of place and space that has a
symbiotic relationship with tourist narratives about places.

It is important to distinguish between the *content* of the changes that have
occurred (e.g. the reuse or construction of older buildings for a new tourist economy)
and the *processes* by which they have come about (e.g. the auto-appropriation
by local individuals and families versus the more recent changes resulting from
new zoning laws). In the earlier phase of development people did occasionally
critique touristic appropriations of the traditional built environment, the ribbon
development in the previously empty spaces, and the narrative essentialization of
the 'Doolin story', seeing it as commodification and as an erosion of some sort of
authenticity. However, the key point for local people is that physical or narrative
appropriations have a far greater potential to be perceived as detrimental when
they are wrested from local control. In previous decades local people themselves
rarely found anything wrong with their own appropriations. By contrast they are
confused and frustrated today when, for example, they are denied permission by
the County Council to build homes or establish new tourist ventures on their own
land for their own families because the land is not properly zoned while at the
same time they must live with developments built by investors from outside the
community.

The earlier period of development was not, of course, entirely community-
oriented and harmonious. The touristic supplanting of traditional economic
activities in Doolin also created new tensions. It created new class distinctions,
exacerbated older ones, and spurred conflicts (occasionally legal and sometimes
even physical) in the competition for tourists. Still, Lefebvre might describe this
phase of appropriation – and I would agree – as *empowering* the local community.

Doolin's more recent phase of development represents a major shift in power
and a third narrative – that of the State. There is a movement afoot in Ireland to
regulate development more purposefully. Although based on older practices of
land use, 'ribbon development' has been deemed undesirable by the Government
at the county and national levels. Government agencies now go to great lengths
to slow down and reverse such development by encouraging more concentrated

development in particular areas while restricting it in others. As a Doolin inhabitant put it: 'The national goal is to put people into the towns'. To do this the Government is garnering increasing control by regularly updating and extending regional development plans, which run on a six-year cycle before being renewed.

Some have argued that this is a larger project of national 'modernization' and transnational integration into Europe (Wilson and Donnan 2006:160), a process that is leading to the implementation of development policies inspired by those of the EU. Collinson (2005:291) notes that the Europeanization of development policy has created a seismic political shift in Ireland, 'altering the relationship between local communities and the Irish government in profound ways'. In theory the *intention* is to encourage grass-roots development planning while also demanding transparency, but the *result* has undermined local representation (Wilson and Donnan 2006:160–1) and favoured top-down approaches to development policy. As has been pointed out by Herzfeld (1992) and Strathern (2000a, 2000b:4–5), transparency and accountability are quite often weakened by new regimes of neoliberal politics in Europe. This is ironic given that the emergent 'audit culture' style of governance is characterized by demands for accountability (Strathern 2000b) and individual 'freedom' (Lawrence 2005:41). These contradictions are exacerbated as they are refracted through the prism of the older 'machine style' politics in County Clare (Peace 2005:505; Wilson and Donnan 2006:160). Political parties worked for decades to foster very strong loyalty and personalized patronage between regional politicians and individual members of the public (ibid.). Now, the voice of local politicians is undermined by the increasingly influential voice of regional technocrats who largely control the development process. This mirrors the top-down governance style of the European Commission, which at its founding was 'heralded as a "technocratic elite"' (McDonald 2000:108).

Charles, the forward planner for County Clare, confirmed that in regard to planning policies the result has been a rapid centralization of authority at the county level and a correlative decrease in power and public input at the local level. He also suggested that, while the Irish system of development planning used to allow more local autonomy than other European contexts, the localized planning process occasionally became 'a tool to settle old scores against neighbours'. Bureaucracies like the Clare County Council often have their own momentum. Individual unelected technocrats like Charles who work within a bureaucratic structure come and go, but the project itself keeps moving forward. Thus in the County Clare Development Plan a revolving door of planning experts created an environment ripe for shifts in power dynamics. Again the parallel with Minnegal and Dwyer's contribution to this volume is striking. In both cases government attempts to regulate economic activities created major unintended consequences for those people whose livelihoods depended on them.

Local peoples' voices are included at three key moments in the process of creating and renewing development plans in County Clare. First, there is an initial public consultation period with local communities. Then, following the public posting of a draft of the Plan, individuals can privately submit their own changes. Finally, individuals can privately file official objections to specific developments that find their way into the Plan in the previous stages. During the initial consultation period, county officers organize focus groups and public meetings to ascertain local concerns and desires regarding zoning issues. This exemplifies what James Scott calls the 'public transcript' of political discourse (1990:4–5). A number of public meetings took place in Doolin during the spring months of 2003 when the North Clare Development Plan was first being composed (Kaul 2009:97–98). Elected officials attended these meetings, and there were carefully worded debates. The process of arriving at a single community statement took a great deal of effort because this community has no formal political structure, such as a mayor or a town council. Much of the 'real' decision-making took place in the form of quiet conversations in the corners of pubs before and after the public meetings. Eventually, after various factions had met more privately, a plan was publicly voted on and submitted to the county planner's office.

What happened next was far more influential. With respect to their own properties, individuals were allowed to submit changes or additions to the plan directly to the county bureaucrats, and according to Charles these submissions were all 'rubber stamped'. The submissions were extensive – so extensive in fact that they filled a booklet almost an inch thick, while the original community development plan that had necessitated so much public and private debate was by contrast only a few pages long. From the State's point of view this part of the process gave additional voice to local people; however, in practice it meant that regional representatives were once again bypassed in the process while the bureaucracy of technocratic State power was centralized and solidified further. It also meant that some local actors undermined the collective voice in favour of their own personal interests. From the point of view of the county technocrats, this was a 'democratic' and 'transparent' move in the sense that decision-making was dispersed amongst a broader public, but in reality some individuals in the community (e.g. landowners) were empowered while others were disempowered (e.g. non-landowners). Furthermore those who own land within newly zoned areas were empowered more than those whose land falls outside development zones. For non-landowners in particular collective community action would seem to be one of the only avenues for resistance to development.

The third avenue for local people to exert control in decisions about the built environment comes in the form of objections to particular planning applications brought to the county in the first two phases in the planning process. This brings us back to the moment in late 2004 when around 170 planning applications were submitted to the County Clare planning office and the community rallied against them. While members of the local community have these three avenues for making their voices heard, only the latter two – making individual submissions and objecting to someone else's plans – seem to have much impact. Furthermore, despite the fact that the whole process is meant to be 'public' and 'transparent', clearly individual claims, rights and objections outweigh the collective voice during the initial planning period. The County Council, through its continually revised regional planning documents, now defines the terms by which the community can control future growth and development. Intentionally or not they have divided local communities into camps objecting to one another's individual plans, thereby undermining the narratives about community that have been developing at the local level for decades in favour of their own top-down understanding of what Doolin ought to be. And, given the government's desire to concentrate development into villages and towns, large corporate developers – a new phenomenon in Doolin – have begun to move in. Since land is instantly more valuable as soon as it becomes zoned for development, individual sellers may garner huge profits from the sale of land, but typically only large corporate investors can afford to purchase it. Simultaneously individuals who want to build properties, even for their own purposes on their own land, are thwarted if it is not zoned for development. In one sense if ownership is in part about control, then the Council now 'owns' Doolin a little more than before.

Power accrues to those who control the dominant narrative about a place whether they seek that domination or not. Cosgrove might claim that the '[l]andscape of the dominant culture' (1989:128) of State and corporate powers overrode the 'alternative landscapes' (ibid.:131) of the local population who attempted to maintain control over the places in which they lived and worked. Doolin has its own 'geograph[y] of resistance', a circumscribable space in which power and resistance to power occurs (Pile 1997:2). That resistance has been initiated both individually and collectively. Scott suggests that group resistance is inherently more effective because it is selfless and 'negate[s] the basis of domination itself' (1985:292). This is opposed to what he calls 'token' resistance, which is unsystematic and characterized by self-interest. This is ineffective precisely because it feeds into the dominant system (ibid.). Scott's analysis mirrors the events in Doolin in the sense that effective forms of resistance to imposed developments occurred when people acted together rather than individually.

Conclusion

The interplay between narrative and physical constructions of places is not merely a theoretical metaphor. Over the past forty years Doolin has been appropriated and re/created by tourism and, more recently, dominated by State-driven 'modernizing' narratives about place-making in Ireland. Constructing places is, as various writers have pointed out,[7] a deeply political process: one that embeds and inscribes power structures and conflicts into the material production of places. In other words political conflicts do not simply exist during the act of place-making; they also exist in the physical developments that result from that process. Foucault (1980:69) points us towards this nexus between power and place: 'Once knowledge can be analysed in terms of region, domain, implantation, displacement, transposition', he writes, 'one is able to capture the process by which knowledge functions as a form of power.' This leads us 'to consider forms of domination designated by such notions as field, region, and territory' (ibid.:69). Narrative-making is therefore an act of appropriation, an act of claiming or reasserting ownership, and re/created places lead to new narratives.

Places can therefore be seen as sites in which the built environment reveals and also creates the social environment. Knowledge, narratives and power articulate and interact with buildings, land and boundaries. In his discussion of Yolngu art in this volume, Morphy goes to great lengths to show that the physical product is only a touchstone for the creation and expression of knowledge that underlies its production. This encapsulates the relationship between processes of knowledge acquisition and expression on the one hand, and the material things that these generate on the other. In this sense the difference between earlier appropriations of the built and unbuilt spaces in and around Doolin, and its more recent domination by corporate and government interests, is a difference in scale and a difference in who controls the process. The faultlines between county technocrats and local communities form along the demarcation between their perspectives about who truly controls and therefore owns the land – or, more precisely, to what *degree* different parties 'own' it. If property ownership is really a relationship between people rather than one between people and things (Hann 1998:4; Strang 2009:44), then it is clear that local people now own their land a little less than they did before. Unfortunately, given that local resistance often remains decentralized and manifests itself largely in the form of objecting to the sale or development of land by neighbours, the weight of the local voice in the dialogue has been diminished over time. That said, the fact that the community came together in 2004 and 2005 to stem the flow of development shows that 'real resistance' can be effective. Positive forms of resistance like this are a testament to the abilities of even small communities to collectively push back against the centralization of external power, and to make a claim that they ought to have a voice in determining their own future.

Notes

1. See Kaul 2009 for a detailed historical analysis of how tourism has impacted traditional Irish musical performances in Doolin.
2. All names used here are pseudonyms.
3. The place Arensberg and Kimball call Lough in *Family and Community in Ireland* is in fact a townland in the same parish that includes Doolin.
4. See Waldren 2007 for a similar discussion.
5. See also Foucault 1980:70.
6. In fact the word 'character' came up quite a lot in the early public meetings about a development plan for Doolin.
7. For example, Lefebvre (1991), Bender (1993), Farrar (2008), Foucault (1972, 1984).

Acknowledgements

Many thanks to Veronica Strang, Mark Busse, Chris Hann, Tamara Kohn, Hazel Tucker and Rebecca Rice for their very helpful comments on earlier drafts. Thanks to Augustana College which funded a large part of the research for this paper. Thanks to Sean Murphy and Jen Burnam for the cartography. As always, many sincere thanks to the people of Doolin.

References

Albertson, L. (2005), *Ireland For Dummies*, 3rd edn, Indianapolis, Indiana: Wiley Publishing.

Anderson, D. (1998), 'Property as a Way of Knowing on Evenki Lands in Arctic Siberia', in C. Hann (ed), *Property Relations: Renewing the Anthropological Tradition,* Cambridge University Press: Cambridge, pp. 64–84.

Arensberg, C. (1959), *The Irish Countryman: An Anthropological Study,* Gloucester, MA: Peter Smith.

Arensberg, C. and Kimball, S. (1968 [1940]), *Family and Community in Ireland,* Cambridge, MA: Harvard University Press.

Bender, B. (1993), 'Introduction: Landscape, Meaning and Action', in B. Bender (ed.), *Landscape: Politics and Perspectives,* Oxford: Berg, pp. 1–18.

Brody, H. (1973), *Inishkillane: Change and Decline in the West of Ireland,* New York: Schocken Books.

Bruner, E. and Gorfain, P. (2005), 'Dialogic Narration and the Paradoxes of Masada', in E. Bruner (ed), *Culture on Tour: Ethnographies of Travel,* Chicago: University of Chicago Press, pp. 169–90.

Clare County Council (2005), *North Clare Local Area Plan*. Ennis, County Clare, Ireland: Clare County Council.

Cohen, A. (1985), *The Symbolic Construction of Community*, London and New York: Tavistock.

Cohen, A. (1987), *Whalsay: Symbol, Segment and Boundary in a Shetland Island Community*, Manchester: Manchester University Press.

Collinson, P. (2005), 'Development, Democracy and the New Europe in the Irish Borderlands', in T. Wilson and H. Donnan (eds), *Culture and Power at the Edges of the State: National Support and Subversion in European Border Regions*, New Brunswick and London: Transaction Publishers, pp. 289–320.

Cosgrove, D. (1989), 'Geography is Everywhere: Culture and Symbolism in Human Landscapes', in D. Gregory and R. Walford (eds), *Horizons in Human Geography*, Totowa, New Jersey: Barnes and Noble Books, pp.118–35.

Crouch, D. (2002), 'Surrounded by Place: Embodied Encounters', in S. Coleman and M. Crang (eds), *Tourism: Between Place and Performance*, Oxford, New York: Berghahn, pp. 207–18.

Farrar, M. (2008), *Building the Body Politic: Power and Urban Space in Washington, D.C.*, Champaign, Illinois: University of Illinois Press.

Fodor's Ireland (2007), Fodor's Travel, New York: Random House.

Foucault, M. (1972), *The Archaeology of Knowledge*, London: Tavistock Publications.

Foucault, M. (1984), 'Space, Knowledge, and Power', in P. Rabinow (ed), *The Foucault Reader*, New York: Pantheon Books, pp. 239–56.

Foucault, M. (1980), *Power/Knowledge: Selected Interviews and Other Writings, 1972–1977*, New York: Pantheon Books.

Frake, C. (1996), 'Pleasant Places, Past Times, and Sheltered Identity in Rural East Anglia', in S. Feld and K. Basso (eds), *Senses of Place*, Santa Fe, New Mexico: School of American Research Press, pp. 229–57.

Hann, C. (1998), *Property Relations: Renewing the Anthropological Tradition*, Cambridge: Cambridge University Press.

Herzfeld, M. (1992), *The Social Production of Indifference: Exploring the Symbolic Roots of Western Democracy*, New York: Berg.

Jarman, N. (1993), 'Intersecting Belfast', in B. Bender (ed.), *Landscape: Politics and Perspectives*, Providence and Oxford: Berg, pp. 107–39.

Kaul, A. (2009), *Turning the Tune: Tourism, Traditional Music, and Social Change in an Irish Village*, New York and Oxford: Berghahn Books.

Kohn, T. (2002), 'Becoming an Islander through Action in the Scottish Hebrides', *Journal of the Royal Anthropological Institute*, 8(1): 143–58.

Lawrence, R. (2005), 'Governing Warlpiri Subjects: Indigenous Employment and Training Programs in the Central Australian Mining Industry', *Geographical Research*, 43(1): 40–8.

Lefebvre, H. (1991), *The Production of Space*, Oxford: Blackwell.

McDonald, M. (2000), 'Accountability, Anthropology, and the European Commission', in M. Strathern (ed.), *Audit Cultures: Anthropological Studies in Accountability, Ethics, and the Academy*, New York: Routledge, pp. 106–32.

Molotch, H. (1993), 'The Space of Lefebvre', *Theory and Society* 22(6): 887–95.

Nash, C. (1999), 'Irish Placenames: Post-Colonial Locations', *Transactions of the Institute of British Geographers*, 24(4): 457–80.

Orlove, B. (1991), 'Mapping Reeds and Reading Maps: The Politics of Representation in Lake Titicaca', *American Ethnologist*, 18(1):3–38.

Orlove, B. (1993), 'The Ethnography of Maps: Cultural and Social Contexts of Cartographic Representation in Peru' *Cartographica*, 30(1): 29–46.

Peace, A. (2001), *A World of Fine Difference: The Social Architecture of a Modern Irish Village*, Dublin: University College Dublin Press.

Peace, A. (2005), 'A Sense of Place, a Place of Senses: Land and a Landscape in the West of Ireland', *Journal of Anthropological Research*, 61(4): 495–512.

Pile, S. (1997), 'Introduction: Opposition, Political Identities and Spaces of Resistance', in S. Pile and M. Keith (eds), *Geographies of Resistance*, New York and London: Routledge, pp. 1–32.

Pine, F. (2001), 'Naming the House and Naming the Land: Kinship and Social Groups in Highland Poland, *Journal of the Royal Anthropological Institute*, N.S. (2): 443–59.

Scott, J. (1985), *Weapons of the Weak: Everyday Forms of Peasant Resistance*, New Haven and London: Yale University Press.

Scott, J. (1990), *Domination and the Arts of Resistance: Hidden Transcripts*, New Haven and London: Yale University Press.

Strang, V. (2009), *Gardening the World: Agency, Identity, and the Ownership of Water*, New York: Berghahn.

Strathern, M. (2000a), 'The Tyranny of Transparency', *British Educational Research Journal*, 26(3): 310–22.

Strathern, M. (2000b), 'Introduction: New Accountabilities', in M. Strathern (ed.), *Audit Cultures: Anthropological Studies in Accountability, Ethics, and the Academy*, New York: Routledge, pp. 1–18.

Travlou, P. (2002), 'Go Athens: A Journey to the Centre of the City', in S. Coleman and M. Crang (eds), *Tourism: Between Place and Performance*, Oxford: Berghahn Books, pp. 108–42.

Waldren, J. (2007), 'Reframing Place, Time and Experience: Leisure and Illusion in Mallorca', in S. Coleman and T. Kohn (eds), *The Discipline of Leisure: Embodying Cultures of 'Recreation'*, Oxford, New York: Berghahn, pp. 73–90.

Wilson, T. and Donnan, H. (2006), *The Anthropology of Ireland*, Oxford, New York: Berg.

Winer, M. (2001), 'Landscapes of Fear and Land Loss on the Nineteenth-Century South African Colonial Frontier', in B. Bender and M. Winer (eds), *Contested Landscapes: Movement, Exile and Place*, Oxford, New York: Berg, pp. 257–71.

–13–

'Not Just Pretty Pictures'

Relative Autonomy and the Articulations of Yolngu Art in its Contexts

Howard Morphy

Abstract

This paper explores the utility of the concept of relative autonomy in understanding the ways in which the Yolngu people of Eastern Arnhem Land in northern Australia have used art as a mode of action. Yolngu are aware of the different properties of their visual and performing arts and the ways in which art can be used in different contexts. The context of use, including engagement with the colonial 'other', contributes to maintaining its diversity and its potential as a form of acting in the world. In the contemporary context Yolngu do not have any sense that they have lost control of their art or reduced their capacity to produce it. Relative autonomy needs to be seen as a principle of action as well as an analytic concept. As a principle of action it concerns the capacity of human beings to both separate phenomena in space and time and be aware of their interconnections.

Introduction

Property is one of those areas where an anthropologically grounded cross-cultural category is of broad theoretical and practical relevance. The nature of property rights and the very conception of property vary cross-culturally and temporally. Making different systems of rights and different conceptions of property compatible is as relevant to global trade as it is to national discourse. In Australia the politics of Aboriginal property rights have involved two related processes. The first was a process of recognition in which Aboriginal rights in land or other property were finally acknowledged and established in law. The second is a process of implementation through the establishment of a legal framework that enables the particular nature of Aboriginal property rights to be incorporated in statute and legal practice.

In Australia discourse over Aboriginal property rights has occurred in two main areas – rights in land and rights in art and cultural property. In the case of land rights the focus has been on the spiritual nature of the relationship between people and land and in the vesting of rights in groups rather than individuals. In the case of art the issues have centred on intellectual property, copyright and moral rights (Coleman 2005).

The process has involved changes in the Australian legal system. The Land Rights (Northern Territory) Act 1976 and the recognition of native title, for example, addressed the question of property rights in land. In the case of art the change was more one of legal practice – copyright legislation was extended to cover Aboriginal as well as non-Aboriginal art. Attitudinal changes were also required in the dominant society – an understanding that Aboriginal people had property-like relationships to land and art. The recognition of Aboriginal property rights and their codification under Australian law also required significant adjustments in those rights and a loss of autonomy in exercising those rights. However, these changes also resulted in the extension of previous rights into new domains and the creation of new rights in a transforming global context.

This chapter is focused on Yolngu art. Because part of the difference of Yolngu art is that it is integral to land ownership and the system of rights that also apply to land, from a Yolngu perspective rights in land and rights in art are not easily separable. The objective of the chapter is not so much to demonstrate the relationship between rights in art and rights in land which I have discussed in detail elsewhere. Rather it is to develop a theoretical framework which shows how Yolngu have been able to use their art in postcolonial contexts and at the same time maintain its relative autonomy as a mode of action in both internal and external contexts.

Complexity and Relative Autonomy

Any anthropologist who has undertaken long-term fieldwork accumulates a body of knowledge about that society that can both overwhelm with the density of connections and possible interpretative frameworks, yet at the same time has a sense of coherence and trajectory. As one becomes more part of a society one is more able to predict how people are going to respond to events, what possible forms of action exist and which impositions or influences from the outside are going to meet strong resistance or go horribly wrong (Morphy and Morphy 2007). Over time anthropologists are likely to apply concepts in context to explain what they see in the present and what was recorded in the past. And if they have been fortunate, as we have been, to work with a society that has an immense history of anthropological research, the body of knowledge extends back into the archives, notebooks and publications of earlier researchers.

This chapter is a palimpsest of moments in time covering a period of forty years. There are two main theoretical ideas or interpretative themes: one is that of relative autonomy allied to the concept of articulation, and the other is of art as a mode of action. I will be exploring these concepts with reference to the last eighty years of Yolngu history. My major aim is to present a perspective on how I have analysed data and why I find the ideas of relative autonomy and art as action useful.

Relative autonomy occurs in the context of the articulation between Yolngu and the colonizing Australian society. Clearly Yolngu society has never been isolated from neighbours, precisely bounded or contained. But European colonization has juxtaposed it with very different systems of social organization, institutional structures, value trajectories, modes of production and so on. And over eighty years the picture has been an ever-changing one.

I first encountered the idea of relative autonomy in the writings of Althusser (1969) and Godelier (1977) and then much later applied the concept to the properties of material form. I apply the term relative autonomy at two levels. The first is between different domains within the same regional socio-cultural system, for example between the kinship system, the system of technology and production, the ideational system and so on. In this context I argue that technological systems have certain properties and potentials that are relatively independent of kinship systems and their associated values. The concept still has much in common with Althusser's, though freed from the Marxist discourse, which required that economic structures remain 'determinant in the last instance' (Althusser 1969:113).[1]

The second level of application is in the context of socio-cultural systems that were previously on very different historical trajectories. I will argue that the socio-cultural trajectory of the Yolngu people of Eastern Arnhem Land is very different from that of the encapsulating 'dominant' society. Relative here refers to the fact that adjacent societies that interact over periods of time inevitably influence each other and create mechanisms and modes of adjustment that ramify internally. In the case of settler colonial societies and indigenous societies, the adjustments required by the state are often unequal.[2]

The two uses of relative autonomy are related. The structures and processes of articulation within regional socio-cultural systems, which ensure that the autonomy of any one domain is only relative, give the overall society characteristics that differentiate it from others that have fundamentally different histories. These structural relations are extremely durable since individuals are socialized into them (Morphy, F. 2007; Morphy, H. 2007). Communication and articulation between relatively autonomous worlds is clearly integral to human history and some individuals move easily between different worlds – anthropologists are trained to do so. In postcolonial contexts such processes become vital components in trajectories of change. But I would argue that models that move the future of societies to the space in between, before that space is largely occupied – hybridity theories, theories of the intercultural – can deflect attention away from where the core variables and value-creating processes are located.

Art as Mode of Action in Yolngu Society

The focus of this chapter is on Yolngu art in the context of relations between Yolngu and European Australians. Yolngu art can be approached most product- ively as a way of acting in the world (Morphy, H. 2009). Yolngu art is a form of representational and expressive practice that can be used to achieve or at least attempt to achieve certain objectives; these can vary from transporting a person's soul, to affirming group identity, to demonstrating rights in land or the ownership of a motor vehicle. The question of what something is used for or what something means is only part of the process of analysis. How something can be used and how something means are essential to understanding objects in the context of action. That Yolngu art can be used in action depends in part on its properties and these properties are relatively autonomous of its use. Any body of practice, any technology, has potentials that have yet to be utilized. *How* always has more potential than *what* – hence any system of action always contains the possibility of acting in new contexts (Morphy 1991, chapter 9). However, the possibilities for action may be constrained by contextual factors that have nothing to do with the properties of the system. For example, Yolngu art is one of the ways in which knowledge is controlled in Yolngu society. The fact that certain forms can only be used in restricted contexts can act as a constraint. Works that were once restricted can be opened up to more public contexts, but opening them up requires decisions to be taken that create a precedent. And this chapter is partly about the ways in which Yolngu have used their art by extending it to new contexts, changing the trajectory of their society, and in the process creating innovative new works.

Looking at the use of art in two contexts separated by forty years shows how Yolngu artists created works of art for new situations and effected change both within their own society and in the world outside. These changes in Yolngu art and performance are best seen as part of the trajectory of Yolngu society and art rather than hybrid artefacts occupying an intercultural space.[3] The first event is the painting of the Yirrkala church panels in 1962, and the second is Djambawa Marrawili's participation as a selected artist in the 2006 Sydney Biennale.

Before looking at these events I need to introduce two relatively autonomous properties of Yolngu art that affect its use and perception in context: the fact that Yolngu art is semantically dense, and the fact that it has expressive properties or is aesthetically powerful – it encodes meanings and it has impact on the senses. Yolngu art often combines these elements: there is no absolute separation between the aesthetic and the semantic.

Figure 13.1 Painting of the Wawilak sisters by Wuyulwuy Wanambi, 1974, private collection. Copyright the artist, reproduced by permission of Buku Larrnggay Art Centre, Yirrkala.

Wuyulwuy Wanambi's painting represents an episode of one of the most renowned Yolngu myths, that of the Wawilak sisters (Figure 13.1). At their journey's end the two sisters are swallowed by the ancestral snake Yulunggurr at the waterhole of Mirrarmina. But this painting relates to an earlier phase of the journey: it represents one of the sisters, Gandjalala, hunting a kangaroo through the open forests. She is using fire and the kangaroo's skin is singed by the flames, but she never quite catches up with it. Instead the sisters feast on honey which they get by cutting down stringy bark trees and prising them open. So the painting appears to encode in figurative form the ancestral woman moving through the forest on her travels.

Shortly after he completed this painting in 1974, Wuyulwuy told me that he was making another one exactly the same. He may have detected an expression of disappointment passing across my face, quickly repressed. As a poor graduate student I did not have the budget to acquire too many paintings that were exactly the same. However, I should have known from his eagerness to show me the 'same' painting that it might be a little different (Figure 13.2). Thirty-five years on I can still recall the excitement I felt when seeing it for the first time. 'This is the same painting?' I asked. 'Just the same' was the reply.

It is not my aim here to fully decode the painting, but I do need to discuss the sense in which it is the same painting (see Morphy H. 1991). My interpretation will inevitably set the two works in dialogue with one another. Wuyulwuy's

Figure 13.2 'The same' painting of the Wawilak sisters by Wuyulwuy Wanambi, 1974, private collection. Copyright the artist, reproduced by permission of Buku Larrnggay Art Centre, Yirrkala.

second painting is 'the same' because the two paintings belong to the same set and, in Yolngu ontology, the first painting is derived from the second. All the meanings encoded in the first painting are present in the second, and the paintings share a key element. The divided oblong motif that occurs in each is a clue to the relationship: it is a clan-owned design element that signals the ancestral set. Gandjalala was hunting the kangaroo with fire and, though she never caught the kangaroo, its coat was singed. The oblong represents the kangaroo, the dividing line its backbone, and the red hatching the burnt hair. Hence the oblongs can be interpreted as the kangaroo being chased through the forest. The kangaroo ran into the stone country: its feet hit the hot rocks and small flakes flew off hitting the chasing women and making them bleed. The flakes were stone spearheads. The oblong in the first painting represents the making of stone spears by humans or ancestral kangaroos. The small square is a hammer stone, the fissure in the middle of the oblong representing the flake being struck off.

Having failed to catch the kangaroo, the ancestral women had to live off honey. Where they cut down the stringy bark trees to obtain this, different features of the landscape were created: in one place a watercourse, in another a giant ceremonial ground around which the women danced. In another place the honey was transformed into lumps of rock that were the source material for the stone spearheads traded across Arnhem Land. For the purposes of trade the stone spearheads were wrapped in paperbark and stuffed inside special woven bags. In the first painting the oblong can be interpreted as the woven bag and the crosshatched bands represent the stone spears and the paperbark wrappings.

The elongated triangular forms in the second painting (Figure 13.2) represent different places where the ancestral women cut down the trees. In one place the shape represents a watercourse, in another the ceremonial ground, and in another the stone quarry of Ngilipidji. In this painting the stone quarry is the one that has the three oblongs in the centre representing the kangaroo and blocks of stone and the women hunters. But it could equally have represented the ceremonial ground since that ground in turn refers to the stone quarry.

However, my aim in discussing Wuyulwuy's paintings is not to go into the iconography of the paintings in detail, but to illustrate that Yolngu art has both semantic and expressive qualities and that the two are relatively autonomous. An aesthetic property that Yolngu emphasize is the creation of *bir'yun*, which I have translated as 'shimmering brilliance' or 'shine' (Morphy 1991:193ff.). The effect is interpreted as a sign of the ancestral power inherent in the designs. *Bir'yun* is present to in all Yolngu art because of the use of cross hatching and glistening pigments, but it is most intensely present in the more geometric paintings that are seen to be closest to their ancestral origin. All Yolngu sacred paintings have this dimension, and it is relatively autonomous of the semantics of the work: it is the expression of ancestral power wherever it is manifested. But the ancestral world itself is differentiated, and the closer we come to the event the more differentiated it becomes. In the case of Wuyulwuy's paintings and the associated songs and ceremonial performances, iconography locates that power in the particularity of the events: the shine is that of the glistening honey, of the fresh hard clean brilliance of the surface of the struck stone, or the light in the flower of the eucalyptus tree where the bees seek out the nectar and pollen.[4] As we have seen, all three of those are closely connected. The honey comes from the eucalyptus and is transformed into the rock – a process that the Yolngu refer to as 'cooking'.

Meaning in Yolngu art is not generally communicated by this kind of formal exposition – rather it is gained through participation in ceremonies and experienced in place and then applied to images. Wuyulwuy's paintings are connected to the Djungguwan, a major regional ceremony (Dunlop 1990).

The ceremonial ground (Figure 13.3) is the elongated triangular shape first created where the stringy bark tree fell. The shape was replicated a number of

Figure 13.3 The djuwany posts at dawn on the Djungguwan ceremonial ground, Gurka'wuy, Trial Bay, 1976.

Figure 13.4 Re-enactment of Gandala's journey, Gurk'awuy, Trial Bay 1976.

times in the more geometric painting (Figure 13.2). The three djuwany posts set along the centre refer to the ancestral women, to the trees filled with honey, and to each stage of the ancestral beings' journey from the quarry inland to the shore where one of the felled trees ended up. The feather string suspended above the posts represents the flight of the bees and the journeys of the women. In a ceremony like this groups of people gather to re-enact the ancestral law of a particular set of ancestral beings, each group acting out its own geographic section of the journey.

As part of the ceremonial performance women re-enact Gandjalala's journey (Figure 13.4). The male initiates are painted with the same designs the ancestral women had on their faces (Figure 13.5). The face painting is directly connected to the ancestral journey and its meanings can vary. In this ceremony the primary focus was on the stringy bark trees the women cut down. The ceremony was held at Gurka'wuy on Trial Bay where an ancestral tree cascaded down from the hilly country inland and gouged out the course of the river. The face painting is a

Figure 13.5 Male initiate with face painting design worn by ancestral women, Gurka'wuy, Trial Bay, 1976.

semantically dense image, which can refer to the structure of the hive, and to the bees, flowers and pollen. The songs sung during the ceremony contain these and other referents. The shimmering brilliance of the design can be seen to reflect the light of the stringy bark tree and the glistening of honey. In other contexts it can refer to the froth of the waves or bubbles rising to the surface of fresh water. *The expressive potential of dancing light and movement is relatively autonomous of the semantic.*

Before I leave Wuyulwuy's paintings I need to say something about their differences. The largely geometric painting is referred to by Yolngu as a *likanpuy miny'tji* or a *madayinpuy miny'tji* – a painting from the sacred domain. A painting just like this could have been photographed by Donald Thomson in 1937 on a boy at circumcision, or on the chest of a dead person.[5] Today precisely the same painting could be seen in analogous contexts. The more figurative painting is an example of a type of painting that has developed since European colonization. Figurative representations are not entirely absent from the set of *likanpuy miny'tji*, but they were reduced in number and frequently absent altogether.[6]

Art for Sale

From the beginning of missionization Yolngu produced paintings both to earn money and communicate with outsiders. Three factors influenced the increasing use of figurative representations. One is that purchasers were attracted by recognizable figures: even as late as the 1970s wholly geometric paintings were very difficult to sell. Second, the figurative representations modified the form of the sacred paintings making them more suitable for public viewing. The figures acted as an internal mask deflecting the viewer and making it less like the underlying *likan'puy min'tji* (Morphy and Layton 1981). Third, the figurative representations acted as a pedagogic device which indigenous communities used to teach Europeans about their law. The artist would select meanings associated with an element of predominantly geometric painting and represent them figuratively so that interpretation of the painting could be guided in a particular direction. Thus Wuyulwuy's painting shows Gandjalala hunting the kangaroo through the forest and the trees cut down for honey. The paintings would often be sold with an accompanying story. Paintings were also important components of the discourse between Yolngu and missionaries and anthropologists (see Morphy 2008). Many of the founding missionaries in Yolngu country were interested in Yolngu art and religion, and three of the first anthropologists to work at Yirrkala, Donald Thomson, Ronald Berndt and Charles Mountford, used paintings as part of their fieldwork methodology. However, Yolngu art cannot be easily divided into art for inside the society and art for outside the society. The modified designs began to be used in a number of internal contexts, for example as paintings on coffin lids, on schoolroom walls and in the classroom. They can also be seen in the Yirrkala church panels.

The Yirrkala Church Panels

The Yirrkala church panels (Figure 13.6) were produced in 1962, and when Frances Morphy and I first undertook fieldwork there between 1973 and 1976 they were still in the church on either side of the altar. The following year they were thrown out of the church by a fundamentalist minister who saw them as heathen idols. Today they are in a special chapel of their own in Buku Larrnggay Mulka art centre. The origin of the church panels has both a complex and a simple story associated with them, or rather several of both kinds. The simple story begins with a new missionary superintendent Edgar Wells arriving at Yirrkala in 1961 (Wells, A. 1971; Wells, E. 1982). He had previously been superintendent at Milingimbi for nearly a decade. He was a church builder and, on arrival, decided that the community needed a new church. He was also passionate about Aboriginal art and saw it as an expression of religious values. He held a meeting with community leaders to discuss his plans, and after the meeting Narritjin Maymuru suggested to him that two panels should be made to be placed either side of the altar to show that Yolngu also had a deep religious law. The Reverend Wells thought that it was an excellent idea and his wife documented the whole process of producing the paintings (Wells 1971).

Figure 13.6 Yirrkala church panels. Photograph Ron Croxford, 1962.

The main reason for creating the paintings given by Yolngu at the time was to show Europeans that they too had a sacred law and a religious life. The inclusion of their paintings in the church made a statement about the equivalence of the two systems. Yolngu accepted Christianity, but did not see its beliefs as being incompatible with Yolngu religion. There had been a history of religious discourse with the missionaries since the founding of the mission in 1935 (Morphy 2005). Wells also sought compatibilities between the two bodies of practice and theologies, and helped create an environment in which syncretism was possible (Wells, E. 1982).

The panels on either side of the altar were divided on the basis of moiety and the sections within them on the basis of kinship and clan. The church panels represented the core components of Yolngu society and its cosmological under-standings. From that perspective the panels made the architecture of the church commensurate with Yolngu society, thus constituting the church as a ceremonial ground. The story is beginning to look complex.

The second reason given for the church panels was to assert in a European context Yolngu rights in land. At that time Yolngu had begun to use the analogy between their paintings and title deeds to land. The need for this arose because Yolngu had recently discovered a threat to their tenure, with prospectors from a French aluminium company setting up camps and drilling the ground. Yolngu paintings encode the relationship between people and land, and it is perfectly logical that they should be used as a means of demonstrating Yolngu rights in land to outsiders. Placed in the church the panels would be a statement of authority. Arguably, as a form of action, it worked. Soon after the church was consecrated a Labor parliamentary delegation visited the community and, after they had seen and been instructed about the panels, one of them, Kim Beazley Senior, suggested that a petition on painted bark might be the best way to engage the attention of Parliament. The Yirrkala bark petition became one of the icons of Aboriginal land rights movement (see Morphy 2008:63–7). The church panels and the bark petition proved effective in communicating cross-culturally. Their aesthetic qualities certainly made a difference in attracting attention, but it was because they were seen as objects of meaning that they came to be used in this way.

How did it become possible to utilize the paintings cross-culturally? The church panels comprise a palimpsest of paintings previously produced on surfaces no larger than the human chest. Yolngu did produce larger works in the form of hollow log coffins, but not painted with *likanpuy* designs. The paintings had previously been used in restricted contexts and were generally masked, the surface smudged before people moved out into the open. Yolngu ceremonies were usually focused on a specific ancestral track, or were organized in relation to a particular person's genealogical connections.

The church panels in fact comprise a regional inventory of ancestral designs, beautifully organized, with an internal structure. The panels map the distribution of sacred designs on a regional basis, focusing on Yirrkala mission station as a central point and extending to Blue Mud Bay in the south and Buckingham Bay in the west. They are not comprehensive and are biased towards the ancestral law associated with the major regional ceremonies – the Dhuwa and Yirritja moiety Ngarra ceremonies. In the case of the Dhuwa moiety, they are associated with the journey of the Djan'kawu sisters and in the case of the Yirritja moiety with fire and honey.

How did it become possible conceptually to make paintings of this scale, and what decisions within Yolngu society had to be made for the panels to be placed on either side of the altar in a public place of worship? The use of art in this way required adjustments in Yolngu society, and in this respect, although I have presented the church panels as if they were a moment in time, in reality they were the result of long-term (and continuing) processes.

The scale of the paintings is remarkable and was clearly facilitated by the availability of new materials, in this instance the masonite used in building the church. Yolngu had always created works of art that reflected the geographic range of their ancestral stories, but the church panels were more comprehensive. They comprise a series of paintings that belong to different places. Each of these has a set of sacred law associated with it – paintings, sacred objects, songs, dances, power names – all of which can be substituted for one another, or complement each other, in the context of ceremonial performance.[7] Every Yolngu ceremony involves the selection and organization of sacred law from different places in a particular sequence. Thus in Wuyulwuy's painting a journey of several hundred kilometres is compressed into a painting that could fit on a person's chest. And in the ceremony the whole length of the journey is performed through different representations of the *madayin* (sacred law). If three boys are being circumcised, each may have a painting belonging to a different place connected with the Wawilag sisters. Other places may be represented by the same basic ceremonial ground, contextualized by related songs or dances. Each djuwany post in turn represents a different place.

Major regional ceremonies are usually restricted to a particular ancestral journey that traverses the estates of a number of clans (Keen 1994; Dunlop 1983), but in circumcision ceremonies and mortuary rituals the performance cross cuts those ancestral divisions. For example, in a burial ceremony one objective is to guide the soul from the place of death to a spirit place in his or her own clan country (Morphy 1984). Thus in constructing the ceremony people compose a journey across country in which responsibility is handed on from one set of ancestral beings to another, creating an individual pathway across the network of ancestral tracks that underlie the surface form of the world.

The church panels were created by selecting the paintings out of the body of *maḏayin* or sacred law from each place and compiling a map of the region surrounding Yirrkala. Although the panels are not comprehensive, and there are many other paintings that could have been included, they were deliberately chosen to be representative of the clans of the region.

However, the map is bisected on the basis of moiety. From a European perspective it might have seemed logical to organize the painting alternating clan countries on a moiety basis along the coast, but Yolngu ontology requires that the relative autonomy of the moieties be retained. One major constraint operates in structuring ritual performance – in operationalizing the ancestral network – and that is that the performance comprises the *maḏayin* of one moiety only. Ceremonies can be held in parallel and synchronized, but the sequence of *maḏayin* is always moiety specific. Indeed the division of the world on the basis of moiety is partly what the church panels are intended to demonstrate and reproduce.

The movement towards larger composite paintings had a number of precursors, apart from the latent possibilities provided by the virtual archive that underlies every ceremonial performance. Yolngu began making art for sale in the first year of missionization. Ronald Berndt's commissioned set of crayon drawings contained many, which took the form of regional maps in which clan designs were represented geographically (Hutcherson 1995). In the late 1950s, with the visits of Tony Tuckson of the Art Gallery of New South Wales and its sponsor Stuart Scougall, paintings began to be produced on extremely large sheets of bark (see Morphy 2008). This enabled composite paintings to be produced containing a palimpsest of smaller paintings ordered in culturally significant sequences.

Opening Up and Widening Out

The church panels were part of a process of opening up Yolngu society and at the same time widening its influence in the public sphere. In producing the panels the artists were representing in concrete form something that already existed as a virtual archive in people's heads. However, that archive was also a contested and dynamic domain. I have shown elsewhere that there was a great deal of agreement concerning the overall body of knowledge, as indeed there had to be, since it was the basis of every Yolngu ceremony, every marriage and every journey. But such knowledge was often implicit, and the connection between individual people and groups to the *maḏayin*, which included the paintings, lay at the heart of the politics of Yolngu society. A single representation was not going to end contestation, but in producing this virtual archive in concrete form the artists sought to get maximal agreement from clan leaders across the region

The church panels also made public paintings that, although not secret in any absolute sense, usually occurred only in specific contexts where their viewing was controlled and their manifestation temporary. Works produced for outside consumption were subject to similar constraints. The Scougall bark paintings, for example, were produced in a men's camp out of sight of the main community. Placing such paintings in the church, where they were open to all members of society, was a significant change of Yolngu cultural practice.

This was part of a complex process gradually opening out Yolngu paintings to a wider audience. An even more dramatic precedent occurred in the neighbouring Yolngu settlement of Galiwinku, where a memorial was created through the public installation of a set of sacred objects outside the Galiwinku church (Berndt 1962). Berndt's phrase 'adjustment movement in Arnhem Land' captures the spirit of the process – *adjustments that maintained the relatively autonomous trajectory of Yolngu society in its articulations with the encompassing colonial world*. The church panels certainly were directed towards non-Yolngu in expressing Yolngu rights in land, with the intention of gaining the recognition of those rights by the colonizers. And they were part of a continuing process of persuasion that used the semantics of art to communicate an understanding of Yolngu society and its values to outsiders – for example, emphasizing the significance of moiety and clan.

The church panels were also part of the process of change that was occurring within Yolngu society: a very conscious process that included widening the effective Yolngu polity and changing some of the ways in which gender roles were demarcated.[8] The church panels represented a public statement of agreement over the distribution of rights in *madayin* of the kind usually restricted to the ceremonial ground, and presented it in such a form that it remained on record. This supported a wider regional polity in which the sacred law became as central to political relationships with non-Yolngu society as it was within Yolngu society. The panels did not freeze Yolngu political relations at a particular point in time, but they did create something that showed that Yolngu law was built on solid foundations.

The church panels can be seen as a step towards a more general opening out of ceremonial performance and giving women public access to knowledge of sacred paintings. The paintings were produced (rather as djuwany posts were) in an enclosed male space and then revealed in the public sacred space of the church. The clan elders who played a leading role in painting the panels subsequently encouraged their daughters to paint sacred paintings for sale. And on rare occasions their daughters substituted for their brothers in previously male ceremonial contexts.

The church panels were also directed towards a different enterprise that can perhaps be seen as a form of intercultural production – the creation of a Yolngu Church asserting the equivalence and compatibility of Yolngu and Christian religious practice. The challenge to boundaries that this represented is not only reflected in their eviction from the church little more than a decade later, but also in a reality that Yolngu remain divided about their inclusion.

The trajectory of change in which the church panels were components is reflected in their form in a number of ways. I have noted several of these already – the composite nature of the design for example. However, the form and compositional structure of the individual paintings also reflects interaction with the colonizers, echoing the pedagogic theme in Yolngu art introduced earlier. They contained the clan designs that are the basis of all Yolngu sacred art, but also included a large number of figurative representations directing interpretation in a particular way. They differ in two main ways from paintings seen, for example, on the chest of a boy at a circumcision ceremony. One is that animals associated with the ancestral law of the place concerned are represented figuratively. Thus, in the Yirritja panel, an ancestral crocodile that is readily seen by Yolngu as immanent in the Madarrpa and Gumatj clan designs is represented explicitly. A painting by Gumbaniya Marawili of the Madarrpa crocodile at Yathikpa illustrates this well (Figure 13.7).

Figure 13.7 The ancestral crocodile, Bäru. Section of a painting by Marira Marawili, Madarrpa clan, Australia National Maritime Museum. Copyright the artist, reproduced by permission of Buku Larrnggay Art Centre Yirrkala.

The crocodile Bäru is closely associated with fire. In ancestral times (*wangarr*) the hut in which he slept was set on fire by his angry wife. He rushed to the sea, his back blazing with strips of burning bark, and dived into the water. The background pattern of a Maḏarrpa clan design therefore represents, among other things, the fire, the turbulent sea, and the pattern burnt into the back of the crocodile. The pattern itself is sufficient to represent the crocodile at Yathikpa.

The other figurative addition is of ancestral beings in their human transformation. This is illustrated in a painting by Mawalan Marika, commissioned by Stuart Scougall in 1959 for the Art Gallery of New South Wales (Figure 13.8).

The painting covers the journey of the Djan'kawu from Buralku to Yalangbara in the Riratjingu country represented in the lower section of the Dhuwa moiety church panel. The Djan'kawu mythology centres on two female ancestral beings accompanied in the Riratjingu version of the story by their brother.[9] The painting

Figure 13.8 The journey of the Djan'kawu. Section of a painting by Marira Marawili, Madarrpa clan, Australia National Maritime Museum. Copyright the artist, reproduced by permission of Buku Larrnggay Art Centre Yirrkala.

is divided into sections depicting different stages of the journey of the Djan'kawu from the island of Buralku in the east to Yalangbara on the Eastern Arnhem Land coast. They travelled just before dawn, following the light of the Morning Star. From Yalangabara they travelled from east to west following the passage of the sun. They created waterholes with their digging sticks, and where they left these sticks in the ground they were transformed into the trees that surround the waterholes. In different places they gave birth to the various clans of the Dhuwa moiety. The paintings show the Djan'kawu women paddling their canoe with their brother resting in the bottom. Opposite, disturbed by the passage of the canoe, a group of whistling ducks take off from the water. In the upper and lower panels the Djan'kawu are shown plunging their digging sticks into the ground. The panels do not follow a simple geographical logic. The Morning Star and the sun are represented in the lower left, referring to the diurnal and seasonal patterns that underlie the symbolism of the journey. The figurative images fill a gap in the interpretation of the images that in Yolngu ceremonial contexts is performed in dance and song. If the figures were removed, in most cases the painting left behind would be precisely as it would be produced in a ritual context. To quote Narritjin Maymuru, when I asked him if the painting would be the same if painted in a ritual context: 'it would be just the same but wherever you see the animal we would just put a mark'. The church panels are not an intercultural or hybrid production: they are works produced by Yolngu for a cross-cultural context, but which are also a part of processes of internal adjustment and transformation.

Expression across Cultures

For the final part of the story we move forward in time forty-five years to the Sydney Biennale of 2006 and to an exhibition of big bark paintings by Djambawa Marawili (Figure 13.9), who became the first Yolngu artist to be featured in the programme. In comparison with the paintings on the church panels the barks had relatively few figurative representations.

At the time of the paintings in the Yirrkala church Aboriginal art was relatively unknown, though beginning to have an impact. The main market was comprised of people who had a strong interest in Aboriginal culture as well as an appreciation of art. The art market tended to frame Aboriginal art as ethnographic, and the main exhibition contexts were museums as opposed to art galleries. The collections made by Scougall and Tuckson showed that some influential individuals were trying to move Aboriginal art into the art gallery, but there was little evidence that they were going to succeed.

In the last thirty years the situation has changed dramatically. Within Australia indigenous art produced in continuing traditions has gained recognition as

Figure 13.9 Painting by Djambawa Marawili, 2006, private collection. Copyright the artist, reproduced by permission of Buku Larrnggay Art Centre Yirrkala.

contemporary art, and increasingly the paintings that have been given the greatest recognition are those that appear to be most abstract. Indeed in many contemporary indigenous Australian art traditions, the figurative component has become largely absent in paintings produced for sale.

One consequence of the acceptance of Aboriginal paintings into the fine art category has been a shift to appreciating the works on the basis of pure form – on their aesthetic properties alone. Thus the relatively autonomous formal properties of Yolngu art – the vibrant surface forms, the scintillating light that emanates from the paintings – have been the ones seized by the market. Ironically a coincidence of value has been created between what Yolngu see as 'dear' art (art of high spiritual and cultural value) and the market value of such objects in the Australian art world. The contemporary art market plays down the pedagogic dimensions of

Aboriginal art: the paintings are certainly marketed because they are believed to express the spiritual beliefs of the 'oldest living culture', but it almost adds to their value that their meaning is ultimately unknowable. Indeed, information about their cultural context makes them into ethnographic objects, threatening their value as objects of aesthetic appreciation.

While it is possible to see the artworld's appreciation of Yolngu art as an appropriation of value, this does not reflect the Yolngu view of what has occurred. Artists are aware that they produce aesthetically powerful objects and they have been engaged in a long-term struggle to create equivalences of value between their cultural production and way of life and those of other cultures. They resist attempts to present their art as an individual expression of universal values, though pushed in this direction by elements of the Australian art world and the market. From their perspective these are performative works. Djambawa was aware of the tendency of Europeans to separate the aesthetic from the semantic components of art, and in his artist's statement he declared, 'I don't want to go to exhibitions and galleries and see people only looking at pretty pictures any more. I want people to look at our paintings and recognise our law' (Marawili 2006:21).

The paintings that Djambawa produced for the Sydney Biennale can be see as part of the trajectory of engagement with European Australians that resulted in the church panels. The church panels and the bark petition had contributed in a significant way to the passage of the Northern Territory Land Rights Act, which granted Yolngu ownership of the land down to the low water mark. This left an area of ambiguity as to who owned the sea that covered the land at high water mark. Government and private enterprise in the form of the fishing industry assumed that, when the tide came in, they had the right of access. In consequence Yolngu began to lose control of their shoreline as governments granted fishing licences and nets were set across estuaries at high tide. Yolngu became deeply concerned over the intrusion into their land, and a crisis point was reached when fishermen left the severed head of a crocodile in the mangroves close to the place important to Bäru, the ancestral crocodile sacred to the Madarrpa clan. This led to a long campaign, which began with Yolngu producing an exhibition of paintings demonstrating their rights in coastal waters with explicit reference to the church panels and the bark petition (Buku Larrngay 1999). Producing these paintings again required a period of negotiation within the community: rather than focusing on a single clan estate, they covered precisely the same set of clans that had been represented in the church panels. They then took the Government to court by initiating the Blue Mud Bay native title claim. The 2006 Biennale and its preparations overlapped with the hearing of the court case and the various appeals against the decisions that were made.

Djambawa was very conscious of the context, as it was he who had led the legal case from the beginning. The paintings appreciated by the European

Figure 13.10 Dancers from Blue Mud Bay, performing at the opening of exhibition of paintings and hollow log coffins by Djambawa Marawili, as part of the 2006 Sydney Biennale.

artworld for their aesthetic power all centred on the *madayin* of the ancestral crocodile at Yathikpa (Figure 13.8) and the neighbouring Madarrpa estate of Baraltja. The opening of the exhibition was one of the main events of the 2006 biennale. Djambawa led a group of dancers from the north of Blue Mud Bay. They performed one of the key dances associated with Bäru creating his nest in the dense mangrove forests of the river estuary.

Rather than making an opening speech Djambawa sang about Mungurru, the powerful Yirritja moiety current that flows into the bay and moves with the tide into the shores of the bay (Morphy and Morphy 2006). The audience was deeply moved without most having any idea about the meanings of the songs or paintings. They were, however, a powerful expression of a culture that was different to their own. It was plain that these paintings were not just 'pretty pictures'. And in quite a different context, that of the federal court, paintings by Djambawa and other clan elders were accepted as primary evidence, in a court case that, after the final appeal to the High Court had been heard, recognized Aboriginal ownership over eighty per cent of the coastline of the Northern Territory (Morphy, F. 2009).

Conclusion: Ownership Appropriation and Relative Autonomy

The theme of ownership underlies the argument in this chapter. In Yolngu society art cannot be separated for long from a discourse over rights. Most acts of painting are a claim to rights in ancestral law and to associated rights, including rights in land. Historically art has been used by Yolngu as the main medium for demonstrating these rights to outsiders and trying to gain recognition for them. At the same time Yolngu have used performance as a way of engaging outsiders with the richness of their way of life and the affective power of their *maḏayin*, and they have traded art objects as objects of exchange in the market. These two objectives – the recognition of rights and cultural production for trade and exchange – have never been entirely separated (Morphy, H. 2006).

It could be argued that in both contexts Yolngu art has been in danger of appropriation by the encapsulating society. When Yolngu use paintings as evidence to gain recognition of their rights under European law, they can be seen as subordinating their cultural production to a European legal process (Morphy, F. 2009). Their art is positioned in a particular way, subjected to alien rules of evidence and legal categorization and opened up to cross-examination – *likanpuy* paintings get referred to as 'title deeds' to land. When paintings are made to be appreciated on the basis of form alone, surely they have been appropriated from their cultural context. And when Yolngu perform at the opening of such an exhibition in order to contextualize the paintings and signal their ownership of them, the fact that most of the audience are unaware of the significance of the dance and treat it as mere theatre again opens up possibilities of appropriation. After all, those same images are used to attract visitors from all over the world to come to Australia and appreciate *its* Aboriginal culture (see Lattas 1991).

Yet in other contexts precisely the same dance performance is part of the body of evidence used to convince a court that Yolngu do have their own system of law, and that under this system of law they own the land they have occupied for thousands of years. While that recognition has been granted by an encompassing colonial legal system, it has also been granted under laws that only apply to indigenous Australians as a consequence of their determined and persuasive political actions. The aesthetics of art and performance have been integral to that process of persuasion (Morphy 2006).

While Yolngu are aware that both the politico-legal context and the national arena of cultural performance pose risks of appropriation, or perhaps because they are aware of these dangers, they never talk as if either of these uses of their art were appropriations. They are, however, extremely concerned about issues of copyright and any unauthorized use of their art. Yolngu are conscious of the different properties of their art and its capacity for use in innumerable different contexts. The contexts of use contribute to maintaining its diversity and its potential as a form of action in the world. They do not feel that they have lost control of their art or their capacity to produce it.

Relative autonomy needs to be seen as a principle of action as well as an analytic concept. As a principle of action it concerns the capacity of human beings to both separate phenomena in space and time and also to be aware of their interconnections. Yolngu use the same paintings in different contexts where the presuppositions and objectives of the participants are very different. The same design may be produced in a circumcision ceremony or a funeral, be used as a design at a graduation ceremony, in a court case to establish native title or copyright, or purely to elicit aesthetic pleasure. In each of these contexts the design is associated with different value creation processes that have the potential to affect its use in other contexts. The demands of the western art market or juridical system may affect conditions of access to works of art and the formal trajectory of cultural production.

Yet much can be carried over from one context to another and much can be shared. Given time and willingness, the Australian legal system can participate in processes of cultural translation where they begin to understand why Yolngu draw an analogy between paintings and title deeds. At an individual level Yolngu dancers can experience a similar sense of heightened awareness and aesthetic pleasure as their western audiences, even if they interpret and understand the performance in different ways. Over time the meaning of things and the potential for action change, and acting in widening contexts, is part of the process of socio-cultural transformation. Too often indigenous peoples have had changes forced upon them, losing their relative autonomy to choose, either because no one takes account of their actions or because the encapsulating society has constrained the choices they can make. Yolngu continue to act with an awareness of the relative autonomy of their artistic system; they continue to stress the need for it to be learnt and practised in context, and for each engagement in a new context to be considered both for its effectiveness and for the consequences it might have on other occasions and at other times.

Notes

1. Indeed as Althusser put it (1969:113): 'the economic dialectic is never active in the pure state; in history, these instances, the superstructures, etc. — are never seen to step respectfully aside when their work is done ... From the first moment to the last, the lonely hour of the "last instance" never comes.' Cavadino and Dignan argue that given the ideological and political dimensions of social formations are equally determining according to Althusser's own formulation, then economic determination in the last instance is maintained as 'an essentially metaphysical, almost religious assertion' (Cavadino and Dignan 2007:73).

2. Dianne Austin-Broos in her study of the Arrernte of Central Australia over time refers to 'a gnawing tension between two regimes of value and their unequal power' (2008:5).

3. In this context I would argue strongly against the position adopted by Eric Michaels (1988) in which he attributes hybridity to western desert acrylics on the basis of the use of new materials to produce works for new contexts of consumption and exchange.

4. Ian Dunlop's film monograph *Djungguwan at Gurka'wuy* is a detailed account of the ceremony associated with Wuyulwuy's paintings. The film provides detailed exegesis from Yolngu participants on the expressive dimension of the ritual.

5. Donald Thomson's collections and photographs provide a rich window in Yolngu art and ceremonial performance at the beginning of intensive European colonization in Eastern Arnhem Land (see e.g. Peterson 1976).

6. For a detailed discussion of Yolngu art and changes that have occurred over time see Morphy 1991 and 2008.

7. The organization of Yolngu ritual performances is discussed in Morphy 1984 which centres on a burial ceremony filmed by Ian Dunlop (1979). Ian Keen (1994) provides an overview of Yolngu ceremonial organization and discusses the Dhuwa moiety Ngärra ceremony centred on the Djan'kawu sisters in some detail. Ian Dunlop's *In Memory of Mawalan* is a film of such a ceremony at Yirrkala and relates closely to the iconography of the Dhuwa moiety Church panel.

8. There are many excellent analyses that have built on Berndt's original and insightful ethnography. Maddock's (1972) understanding of the adjustment movement as an exercise in remodelling society is particularly salient to my own analysis.

9. The Riratjingu clan following an initiative of the artist and clan member Banduk Marika worked with anthropologist and curator Margie West to produce a book on paintings from Yalangabara which documents them in detail and places them in the context of the landscape and Djan'kawu mythology (see West 2008).

References

Althusser, L. (1969), *For Marx*, London: Allen Lane.

Austin-Broos, D. (2008), *Arrernte Present, Arrernte Past: Invasion, Violence and Imagination in Indigenous Central Australia*, Chicago: University of Chicago Press.

Berndt, R.M. (1962), *An Adjustment Movement in Arnhem Land, Northern Territory of Australia*, Paris: Mouton.

Buku Larrngay M. (1999), *Saltwater: Yirrkala Bark Paintings of the Sea Country*, Yirrkala: Buku Larrnggay Mulka Centre in association with Jeniffer Isaac publishing.

Cavadino, M. and Dignan J. (2007), *The Penal System: An Introduction*, London: Sage.

Coleman, E.B. (2005), *Aboriginal Art, Identity and Appropriation*, Aldershot: Ashgate.

Dunlop, I. (director) (1979), *Madarrpa Funeral at Gurka'wuy*, Sydney: Film Australia.

Dunlop, I. (director) (1983), *In Memory of Mawalan*, Sydney: Film Australia.

Dunlop, I. (director) (1990), *Djungguwan at Gurka'wuy*, Sydney: Film Australia.

Godelier, M. (1977), *Perspectives in Marxist Anthropology*, Cambridge: Cambridge University Press.

Hutcherson, G.M. (1995), *Djalkiri Wänga: The Land is My Foundation. Fifty Years of Aboriginal Art from Yirrkala, Northeast Arnhem Land*, University of Western Australia Berndt Museum of Anthropology, Occasional Paper No.4, Perth: University of Western Australia.

Keen, I. (1994), *Knowledge and Secrecy in an Aboriginal religion*, Oxford: Clarendon Press.

Lattas, A. (1991), 'Nationalism, Aesthetic Redemption, and Aboriginality', *The Australian Journal of Anthropology*, 2(3): 307–24.

Maddock, K. (1972), *The Australian Aborigines: A Portrait of their Society*, London: Penguin.

Marawili, D. (2006), 'Artists Statement', *Zones of Contact Handbook,* Sydney: Biennale of Sydney.

Michaels, E. (1988), 'Bad Aboriginal Art', *Art and Text*, 28: 59–73.

Morphy, F. (2007), 'Uncontained Subjects: "Population" and "Household" in Remote Aboriginal Australia', *Journal of Population Research*, 24(2): 163–84.

Morphy, F. (2009), 'Enacting Sovereignty in a Colonized Space: the Yolngu of Blue Mud Bay Meet the Native Title Process', in D. Fay and D. James (eds), *The Rights and Wrongs of Land Restitution: 'Restoring What Was Ours'*, Abingdon: Routledge-Cavendish.

Morphy, F. and Morphy, H. (2007), '"Soon We Will Be Spending All Our Time at Funerals": Yolngu Mortuary Rituals in a Time of Constant Change', paper presented at the 106th meeting of the American Anthropological Association, Difference (In)equality and Justice, 28 November-2 December 2007, Washington, DC.

Morphy, H. (1984), *Journey to the Crocodile's Nest*, Canberra: Australian Institute of Aboriginal Studies.

Morphy, H. (1991), *Ancestral Connections: Art and an Aboriginal System of Knowledge*, Chicago: University of Chicago Press.

Morphy, H. (2005), 'Mutual Conversion: The Methodist Church and the Yolngu, with Particular Reference to Yirrkala', *Humanities Research*, XII(1): 41–53.

Morphy, H. (2006), 'Sites of Persuasion: Yingapungapu at the National Museum of Australia', in I. Karp, C. A. Kratz, L. Szwaja and T. Ybarra-Frausto (eds), *Museum Frictions: Public Cultures/Global Transformations*, Durham: Duke University Press.

Morphy, H. (2007), 'Anthropological Theory and the Multiple Determinacy of the Present', in D. Parkin and S. Ulijaszek (eds), *Holistic Anthropology: Emergence and Convergence*, Oxford: Berghahn.

Morphy, H. (2008), *Becoming Art: Exploring Cross-Cultural Categories*, Sydney: University of New South Wales Press.

Morphy, H. (2009), 'Art as a Mode of Action: Some Problems with Gell's *Art and Agency*', *Journal of Material Culture*, 14(1): 5–27.

Morphy, H. and Layton, R. (1981), 'Choosing among Alternatives: Cultural Transformations and Social Change in Aboriginal Australia and the French Jura', *Mankind*, 13(1): 56–73.

Morphy, H. and Morphy F. (2006), 'Tasting the Waters: Discriminating Identities in the Waters of Blue Mud Bay', *Journal of Material Culture*, 11: 67–85.

Peterson, N. (1976), 'Mortuary Customs of Northeast Arnhem Land: An Account Compiled from Donald Thomson's Fieldnotes', *Memoires of the National Museum of Victoria*, 37: 97–108.

Wells, A. (1971), *This is their Dreaming*, St Lucia: University of Queensland Press.

Wells E. (1982), *Reward and Punishment in Arnhem Land*, Canberra: Australian Institute of Aboriginal Studies Press.

West, M. (ed.) (2008), *Yalangbara: Art of the Djang'kawu*, Darwin: Charles Darwin University Press.

Index

Acheson, J., 198, 204
activism, 106–7, 110–11, 117, 187
    and fisheries, 202–3
    and water, 173–4, 183–4
    see also counter-movements;
        environmentalism; participation
aesthetics, 244, 282
    see also art; senses
agency, 4, 240
    art, 9, 29, 261–70 passim, 282
        as title deeds, 282–3
    fluid, xvi
    induced, 114
    object, 29
    performance, 50
    personhood, 4, 9, 29
    political, 6, 113
    property and, 6, 105
    see also discourses; narratives
aggression, 27, 30
    see also conflict
Agrawal, A., 112, 117
Albro, R., 173
Alexander, C., 12, 176
alienability, 175
    see also inalienability
alienation, 171
    of concepts, 207
    of land, 10, 134, 138–9, 141, 149–61
        passim, 167
    of persons, 207
    of resources, 175
    of water, 173, 175
    see also customization; disembedding;
        privatization; reification; rights
Althusser, L., 263
Altman, J., 175, 177
Amit, A.,117
Anderson, D., 242, 244
Andolina, R., 108, 110, 114, 115

anthropology, 1, 2, 4, 31, 57, 221
    and cultural diversity, 4, 6, 13, 230
    and cultural translation, 13, 263
    and law reform, 148
    in property claims, 2
appropriation, xv, 1, 3
    and agency, 4, 9
    and *bricolage*, 80
    and communication, 4, 8, 9
    and creativity, 4, 82
    and dispossession, 3, 13, 119, 151, 167,
        173
    and embodiment, 69, 73, 83, 182
    and identity, 60
    and negotiation, 4
    and personhood, 5, 9
    and violence, 4
    auto-appropriation, 239, 251
    bodily, 69, 71, 74, 75, 79–81, 83
    by the state, xv, 13, 51, 218, 232, 239
    definitions of, xv–xvi, xvii, 4, 44, 248
    enclosure, 10, 11, 145, 171–4, 177, 187
        see also privatization
    mutual, 8, 46, 244
        see also mutual possession
    of built structures, 44, 251, 255
    of cultural practice, 282
    of culture, 113, 145
    of knowledge, 206
    of land, xv, 10, 13, 135, 151, 159–67
        passim
    of narrative, 187
    of objects, 4, 45
    of persons, 4,8, 43–9 passim, 59, 167,
        187
        see also borrowing, of persons;
            figureheads; mutual possession;
            persons
    of physical spaces, 239, 251, 255
    of place, 9, 239, 248, 251

of resources, 208, 218
of text, 43–4
of value, 280
of water, 173, 178
process, xvi, 4, 8, 46, 59
through narrative, 187, 239–40, 249–50,
    251, 255
through renaming, 241–2
    see also naming
see also consumption; displacement;
    ownership; possession; privatization
art, 93–96, 98–100, 261–83 passim
and appropriation, 9
and knowledge, 264
as a form of action, 9, 240, 261, 264–70
as statements about ownership, 9
body art form, 66, 78–9
market, 94–5, 98–100, 278–9, 283
semantics, 267, 275
see also aesthetics
Attas, D., 43
Atton, C., 222
Attwood, B., 173, 175
Auge, M., 74
authenticity, 8, 71–2, 78–83, 91–100
    passim, 109, 113
authenticity, and tourism, 250–1
    see also identity; tradition
authorship, 88, 90
autonomy, 99, 107–9, 140, 204, 252, 262
indigenous, 112, 114
political, 112, 114, 120–1
relative, 261–4, 274, 281–283
see also agency; self-determination

bad faith, 8, 43, 45, 56–7, 58, 59–60
Bakker, K., 173, 206
Bales, K., 4
Bardhan, P., 221
Battaglia, D., 35
Bauman, Z., 65
belonging, 5, 25–6, 82, 182–3, 242
and ownership, 181, 187
and subjectivity, 46
claim to, 240
identity and, 181–2
knowledge and, 242
land, 7–8, 143

non-belonging, 73
spiritual, 7–8, 173, 175, 143, 262
    see also citizenship; identity; ownership,
        ancestral; possession; property
Bender, B., 240, 243, 248
Benkler, Y., 224
Bennett, T., 115
Berlin, B., 118
Berlin, E., 118
biodiversity, 119
    see also Convention on Biodiversity
biopiracy, 116, 118
    see also property
bioprospecting, 113, 118
    see also property
Bollier, D., 10
Bondi, L., 106, 114
borrowing, 5, 9, 23–4, 26–31, 74–7, 83
of persons, 34, 36–7
    see also appropriation, of persons
    see also possession; sharing; theft
Bourdieu, P., 70
Bratich, J., 115
Brosius, J. P., 117, 118
Brown, M., 2, 12, 105

Candea, M., 46
capitalism, 10, 13, 88, 144, 149, 208
anti-capitalism, 108, 11
    see also counter-movements
economic rationalism, 187, 189
Carpenter, K., 5, 7, 8
Carrithers, M., 6
Castro, J., 206
citizenship, 48, 106–7, 121
and subjectivity, 46, 121
collective, 115
differentiated, 114
market, 121
new forms, 108, 112, 120
    see also belonging
claims, 3–10 passim, 92, 105–14 passim,
    117, 137, 181–7
against the state, 131, 140, 148, 280
and belonging, 240
collective, 116, 118
counter-claims, 172, 181–2, 190
    see also counter-movements

cultural, 119, 120
egalitarian, 33
identity, 119
individual, 254
to ethnic sovereignty, 47
to genre, 99–100
to knowledge, 82
to water, 142, 171–2
see also naming; ownership; ownership,
    alternate forms, naming; rights
Clarke, J., 106, 115
Clifford, J., 65
Cohen, A., 242, 251
Cohen, S., 206
Coleman, E.B., 262
collective interests, 26
see also ownership, collective
Collier, J., 115
Collinson, P., 252
colonial legislation, xvii, 282
colonization, 13, 47, 137, 174–5, 263, 270
decolonization, 110
    see also counter-movements
dispossession, 3, 13, 151, 167, 173
history, 135–42 passim
see also empowerment,
    disempowerment
Comaroff J., 105, 113, 206
Comaroff, J. L., 105, 113, 206
commercialization, *see* commoditization
commodification, *see* commoditization
commodities, 11, 178, 200
commodities, humans as, 206
commoditization, 77–8, 176, 251
new regimes of, 176
of art, 98–100
of difference, 106
of expertise, 77, 113
of fish 11, 200, 205
of history, 77, 79
of knowledge, 83
of land, 136
of persons, 204, 286–7, 241
of resources, 174–5
of ritual, 88–9, 94–6, 100
of water, 10, 11, 174, 177, 181
see also markets; privatization;
    propertization

commodity chain, 118
common good, 144, 176, 179, 217
see also commons
common pool resources, 176, 218–22,
    228–32
see also commons
common resources, 10, 221, 232
see also commons
commons, 1, 10–12, 174, 218–23
enclosure, 10
non-rivalrous resources, 11–12, 232
radio as, 1, 218–23, 225, 227, 232
rivalrous resources, 12
'tragedy of the commons', 12, 173,
    220–3 passim, 225, 227–32 passim
water as, 1, 174
see also common good; communalism;
    government, state ownership;
    land tenure; ownership, forms of,
    collective; resource management
    regimes
communal, 26, 35, 91, 97
communalism, 144
see also common good; commons
communication, xvi, 3–4, 6, 9, 93, 263,
    272
and development, 224, 231
see also development
community, 107, 114–16
concepts of, 13, 25–7, 114, 117–18, 251
construction of, 105–6, 117–19, 121, 253
place-based, 242
see also government, decentralization;
    identity, co-substantiality
compensation, 116, 140, 155
competition, 48–50, 52–5, 147, 202, 224–8
    passim, 251
for resources, 11, 180, 190
see also markets
concepts, xvi, 5, 23–7, 29–34, 138, 171
categories, 172
displacement of, 31, 33, 35–6
metaphors, 172
schema, 172
conflict, 1, 13, 131, 133, 217, 230, 242,
    251
civil, 217
historical, 135–141 passim

massacre, 156
protests, 134, 138, 141–2, 173, 176
urban-rural, 187
see also aggression; property, competing
perceptions; violence
conflicting narratives, 186–7, 239–45
passim, 248–50, 254
see also discourses
conservation, 111, 112, 117, 120
see also environmentalism
consumption, xv, 12, 34, 172, 177, 178
as appropriation, xvi, 69–70,74
see also appropriation
Convention on Biodiversity, 110, 112, 116
see also biodiversity
Coombe, R., 5, 7–10, 186
Cooper, D., 25–7, 28, 32
Corsin Jimenez, A., 31, 32, 33, 35
counter-movements, 10
conservation, 183–5
grassroots, 11, 106–10 passim, 186
see also activism; capitalism, anti-
capitalism; claims, counter-claims;
social movements
creativity, 2, 4, 36, 82, 90–1
Creed, G., 117, 118
Crouch, D., 248
Csordas, T., 70
cultural diversity, 4, 13, 30, 111–12,
120–1, 131–2
cultural heritage, 105, 110–16 passim, 182
see also identity; property, intellectual;
reification; traditional knowledge
cultural survival, 7, 108
see also counter-movements
customization, of alienated land, 10, 150,
167
see also alienation
customs, *see* tradition

Damasio, A., 75
dance, 87, 91, 93–9, 273, 278, 281–3
competition, 55
Dean, B., 173
debt, 33
Deitz, T., 230
development, 106–11, 114–16, 149–51,
166, 176, 188

alternative, 106, 116
and aid, 108, 120, 150, 224, 231
and communication, 224, 231
see also communication
and NGOs, 108–12, 115–20, 224, 228
economic, 10, 159, 188, 224
growth, 180, 188, 254
intensification, 176, 180
see also environmental issues
organizations, 117, 119
planning, 108, 239, 245–6, 252–3
regional, 241, 246–7, 249
rural, 149, 249
see also sustainability
discourses, 69, 75–6, 111–12, 117, 182–4,
248
academic, 107
and achievement, 50, 58
and identity, 47, 114
and ownership, 9
and place, 9, 239–40, 250
and property, 2, 28, 262
and rights, 5, 105–7, 113, 120–1, 281
and subjectivity, 57
appropriation of, 182
art as, 270, 281
dominant, 190, 253
emancipatory, 120
see also social justice
legal, 105
multicultural, 108
national, 261
see also agency; narratives
discrimination, 47, 52
see also paternalism; racism
disembedding, 177, 197–8, 205–8
see also alienation; immateriality;
reification
disempowerment, *see* power
displacement, 92–3, 98, 255
see also appropriation; dispossession;
emplacement
dispossession, 3, 13, 119, 151, 167, 173
see also appropriation; displacement
disputes, *see* conflict
Doane, M., 113
Dweck, C.S., 50
Dwyer, P., 176, 177, 245, 252

Edelman, M., 221
Eidson, J., 2
elites, 12, 35, 174, 188–9, 206
embodiment, 50, 69, 73, 75, 79–83
    as methodological paradigm, 70
    habitus, 46, 70
    of water, 178
    of landscape, 178
    see also appropriation; enskilment;
        identity; self-making
emplacement, 9, 239, 244
    see also displacement
empowerment, *see* power
enclosure, *see* appropriation
enskilment, 59, 67–9, 83, 205
    see also embodiment
entitlement, *see* rights
environmental issues, 155, 160
    climate change, 183
    ecological degradation, 174,
        187
    fish stocks, 11, 197–8, 200, 206
    industrial agriculture, 187
    intensification, 176, 180, 198, 220
        see also development
    logging, 155, 160–1, 166, 206
    pollution, 174, 184
    salination, 174
    short-termism, 171, 173, 184
    water, abstraction, 176, 180
    see also resource management;
        sustainability
environmentalism, 107
    and fisheries, 202–3
    and water, 173–4, 183–4
    as part of political strategy, 111
    environmentalist politics, 117
    environmentality, 112
    see also activism; conservation;
        governance
equality, 33, 173, 179, 182, 184
    and property, 173
    inequality, 47, 120
    see also social justice
Escobar, A., 119
ethnocentricity, 2, 13
Eudaily, S., 113
evolutionist theories, xv, 1

exchange, 3, 4, 9, 109, 172, 282
    gifts, 25, 28, 108, 136–7, 167, 244

Farrar, M., 240
Ferguson, J., 65
fictitious commodities, *see* immateriality
figureheads, 43, 45
    see also appropriation, of persons
Fingleton, J., 150, 151
Firth, R., 1, 136
fish quotas, *see* regulation
Florez, M., 113
Fortes, M., 6
Foucault, M., 8, 66, 115, 240, 255

Geismar, H., 2
Gell, A., 29, 99
gender, 90, 275
geneaology, 7
genetic resources, 113
    bioprospecting, 113, 118
    see also property
Giddens, A., 207
gifts, *see* exchange
globalization, 113–14, 206–7
Gluckman, M., xvi, 1
Godden, L., 173
Goodale, M., 113
governance, 12, 26, 107–15 passim,
        227–8, 252
    democratization, 112, 120
    of resources, 175, 184, 189, 217–21,
        227, 230–1
        see also resource management
        regimes
    participation, 108–9, 117, 119, 172
    state control, 176, 217
    surveillance, 112, 120
    see also environmentalism; government,
        regimes of; participation; regulation;
        resource management regimes; self-
        governance
government, 115, 120
    decentralization, 47, 108–9
        see also community
    depoliticization, 107, 120
        see also neoliberalism
    national, 227, 231

policy, 137
　instruments, 106, 219
　international, 105–6, 219
　land, 133, 151
　regimes of, 152
　see also governance
state and civil society, 217
state authority, 11
state institutions, 117
state ownership, 11, 152, 219
　see also commons
state, 12–14, 45, 109–11
　role of, 13
　see also ownership, of the state
transnational, 12, 119
governmentality, 105, 115, 117, 120
　community-based, 118
　concept of, 8, 107, 115
　environmentality, 112
　mentality of, 57
　neoliberal, 106, 115, 121
　see also neoliberalism
Gow, D., 110, 112
grassroots, *see* counter-movements
Gray, K., 24–5, 27, 28
Green, T., 7
Greene, S., 118
Griffiths, G., 182
growth, *see* environmental issues,
　intensification
Gudeman, S., 206, 207
Gupta, A., 65
Gustafson, B., 112

habitus, *see* embodiment
Hale, C.R., 113
Hamilton, A., 13
Hann, C., 1–2, 4, 173–81 passim, 218,
　222, 255
Hardin, G., 173, 219–20
Hart, K., 206, 208
Haugerud, A., 221
Hayden, C., 113, 118
Hegel, G., 6, 172
Helgason, A., 200, 206, 207
heritage, *see* cultural heritage
Herzfeld, M., 73, 74, 252
Hess, C., 220, 221

hierarchy, 28, 58
　rankings, 50, 52, 55, 58
　see also power
Hirsch, E., 2, 3, 4, 98, 185
Hirsch, S., 115
Hitchens, L., 230
Hornborg, A., 207, 208
human resources, *see* appropriation, of
　persons
human rights, *see* rights, human
Humphrey, C., 1, 2, 5, 6, 88, 89, 106, 177,
　178
Hunn, E., 173, 175
hybridity
　economy, 175
　identity, 167
　intercultural production, 275, 278
　property regimes, 167, 218–19, 222
　space, 151, 264
　theories of, 264
　see also intercultural

identity, 8
　and cultural survival, 7
　anonymization, 197–8, 204, 208
　census, 5
　collective, 5, 7, 10, 109, 264
　construction, 115, 172, 181, 189
　　see also self-making, self-realization
　cosmopolitan, 187
　co-substantiality, 136, 175, 182, 186
　　see also community
　cultural renaissance, 138
　essentialized, 113, 118
　ethnic, 47
　indigeneity, 114
　language, 8, 108, 175, 227
　place-based, 106, 175
　spiritual, 175, 178–9
　temporal, 178
　through enskilment, 59, 67, 69, 205
　see also authenticity; belonging; cultural
　　heritage; embodiment; tradition
immateriality, xv, 2, 14, 69, 105–7, 116,
　120
　fictitious commodities, 176
　virtual commodities, 11, 200–2, 245
　　see also disembedding; materiality

inalienability, 7, 111, 175
Inda, J., 115, 120
indigeneity, 109, 113–14
individualism, 204, 247
  possessive, 7, 88, 98, 101
  see also persons
inequality, *see* equality
Ingold, T., 43, 205
inheritance, 3, 4, 28, 92, 175, 177
  rules of, 92, 161
intangible, *see* immaterial
Intangible Heritage Convention, 116
intellectual property, *see* property,
  intellectual
intercultural, 8, 67, 100, 275, 278
  identity, 65
  personhood, 98
  spaces, 83, 264
  see also hybridity
interculturalism, 112
interdisciplinarity, xvi, 221
international law, *see* law, international
intersubjectivity, 7–9, 87–92 passim,
  95–96, 100, 207
  see also property, as sociality

Jackson, M., 6, 66
Jameson, F., 10
Jentoft, S., 198, 203, 204, 221, 232

Kalinoe, L., 2, 4
Kingfisher, C., 106
kinship, 36, 73, 133, 175, 263, 272
  and land, 242, 249
  kin-based economy, 89
  moral society, 208
  obligations, 9, 27, 33, 89
  see also sharing
Kopytoff, I., 91, 100

labour, 25, 51, 157–63 passim, 182, 185,
  187
  collaborative, 109
  collective, 110
  theory of ownership, 3
land, rights, *see* rights
land tenure, xv, xvi, 138, 149, 161
  see also commons

land, xv, xvi, 3, 51, 112–13
  and identity, 7, 8
  and spiritual connection, 7
  customary, 10, 133–5, 149–50, 153,
    159–61, 165–6
  occupation, 3, 13, 136, 138–9, 141, 145
    see also ownership, occupation
  ownership, xvi, 1, 7, 10, 133, 143, 180,
    241–2, 262
    individual ownership, 131
    public ownership, 173, 176
  tenure, xv, xvi, 138, 149, 161
    freehold, 150–1, 160, 175
    leasehold, 150, 152
Lash, S., 174
Latour, B., 188
Laurie, N., 106, 108, 109, 114
law
  ancestral, 269, 272–5, 276, 281
  common law, 3, 13, 25
  constitutional agreements, 199
  customary,106, 111, 113, 116, 120,
    136–7, 145
    see also ownership, forms of,
      customary; tradition, customary
      management
  inheritance, 92, 161
    matrifiliation, 91
    patrifiliation, 91–2
  international, 118
    conventions and treaties, 106, 109,
      110, 116
    courts, 120
    UN Declaration on the Rights of
      Indigenous Peoples, 140, 145
  legal title, 3, 109, 139–41, 144–7,
    150–2, 159–61
  native title, 175, 181, 188, 262, 280, 283
  see also legal frameworks; legislation;
    ownership; rights
Lazarus-Black, M., 115
Leach, J., 2, 4, 51
legal anthropology, xvi
legal entities, 8, 9
legal frameworks, 118–19
  see also law
legal order, 25, 133
  see also queuing

legal recognition, 120
legislation, xvii, 134, 138, 262
    see also law
Levi, J., 173
Li, T. M., 117, 119, 120
Lie, J., 8
Lindholm, C., 88
Locke, J., 3, 185
Lupton, D., 178

Macpherson, C.B., 2, 7, 88
Malinowski, B., xvi, 1
marginalization, 117
markets, 197, 199–202 passim, 206–7,
    222, 279–283
  and subjectivities, 114
  commercial art, 94–5, 98–100, 278–9,
    283
  environmental, 112
  free-market, 2, 14
  in knowledge, 113
  market-based economy, 89
  transferable fish quotas, 11, 141, 199,
    245
  water market, 181
    see also water, trading
  see also commoditization; competition;
    neoliberalism
Markus, A., 173
Marxism, xv, 115, 263
Maskovsky, J., 106
materiality, xvi, 2, 5–6, 10–12, 177, 180
  and portability, 177
  fluidity, 10, 172, 189
  invisibility, 11
  material qualities, 171, 182
    see also immateriality; property,
      intangible; tangible
matrifiliation, 91
  see also law, inheritance
Maurer, B., 7, 115
Mauss, M., 1
McDonald, M., 252
memory, 73, 91, 96, 153, 155, 242–3
Milton, K., 183
Minnegal, M., 2, 10, 11, 12, 176, 177, 245,
    252
mobility, 51, 65–6, 69, 77, 201, 204

Monbiot, G., 173
moral economies, 221–2
    see also social justice
moral responsibility, 204
Morphy, H., 9, 13, 87, 93, 99, 175, 240,
    255
Morphy. F., 271
Moutu, A., 2
music, 12, 240–1, 243–4, 250
    see also songs
mutual possession, 8, 46, 60, 244
    see also appropriation, mutual

naming, 5, 241–2, 244
    see also appropriation, through
      renaming; claims; ownership,
      alternate forms, naming
narratives, 50, 254
  and landscape, 243
  and tourism, 240, 244, 249–51
  appropriation, 239
  emplacement, 9
  environmentalist, 111
  historical, 9
  of achievement, 50
  of place, 186, 239–40, 244, 247–51,
    255
  of self-making, 59
    see also agency; appropriation, through
      narrative; discourses
neoliberalism, xv, 2, 14, 106–7, 110–14
    passim, 188, 198
  neoliberal conditions, 115–16
  neoliberal governmentality, 105–6, 108,
    120–1
  neoliberal politics, 252
  neoliberal subject, 107, 207
    see also government, depoliticization;
      markets
non-rivalrous resources, *see* commons

objectification, *see* reification
Ong, A., 115
Ophuls, W., 173
oral history, 92, 155
Orlove, B., 249
Ostrom, E., 12, 173, 198, 220, 227–31
Overing, J., 6

ownership
  alternate forms, 4, 12, 171–2, 175–90
    passim
    affective relations, 172, 175, 187
    community membership, 181
    historical association, 175
    identification, 172
    knowledge, 172, 175, 182–5, 241–5
    labour investment
    mythological links, 175
    naming, 241–5, *see also* claims;
      naming
    occupation, 3, 13, 136–9, 144, 155,
      242
    physical engagement, 10, 172
    use of land and resources, 175
  as processual, xvi, 4–14 passim, 43, 59,
    175
  as social action, 3–4, 8–9
  as symbolic communication, xvi, 4
  clear-act principle, 3
  forms of
    ancestral, 111, 136
    collective, 108, 173, 177, 186,
      225, *see also* commons; rights,
      collective
    customary, 10, 149–66 passim, *see
      also* law, customary
    indigenous, 150
    individual, 131, 141
    private, 142, 219, *see also*
      privatization
    public, 152, 173, 176, 219, *see also*
      commons
  of airwaves, 1
  of cultural property, 7, 9, 105, 109, 262
  of development, 247–52
  of fishing quotas, 141, 199–204, 208
  of heirlooms, 7
  of heritage, 1
  of human organs, 7
  of identity, 58, 69
  of intellectual property, 12, 88, 99, 185,
    262
  of knowledge, xv, 9, 71, 81–3, 185, 264
  of land, xvi, 3, 131–48 passim, 149–67
    passim, 179–80, 241–2
    see also land, occupation
  of material culture, 10, 179
  of minerals, 3
  of persons, 4,8, 43–9 passim, 59, 167,
    187
  of physical space, 239
  of resources, 173
  of the state, 12, 189
    see also government
  of water, 3, 173, 178
  through labour, 3
  through occupation, 3, 13, 136, 144
  see also appropriation
  see also claims; law; rights

Palsson, G., 67
Parry, B., 176
participation, 6, 108–9, 117–19, 190, 228,
  267
  see also activism; governance
Passes, A., 6
paternalism, 132
  see also discrimination; racism
patrifiliation 91–2
  see also law, inheritance
peoplehood, *see* persons
performance, 51, 91–4, 282
  and appropriation, 75, 282–3
  and art, 264, 28and ownership, 91
  as evidence, 282
  ceremonial, 267, 269, 273–5
  contests, 50, 54–8 passim
  non-rivalrous, 12
  ritual, 87–8, 100
persons
  peoplehood, 7, 8
  personhood, 4–7, 9, 11–13, 51, 87–90,
    95–8, 100–1
    individual, 6–7, 35, 65, 87–9, 95, 98,
      204, *see also* individualism
    relational, 8, 87, 89, 95, 98–101, 204
  see also appropriation, of persons
phenomenology, 10–11, 66, 172
Pile, S., 254
Polanyi, K., 173, 205–8
political ecology, 173
political economy, xvi, 114
  transnational, 9, 12, 174, 222, 252
Posey, D., 2

possession
  first possession, 25
    see also queuing
  legal claims, 105–6
    see also appropriation; belonging;
      borrowing; rights; sharing; theft
power, 4, 120, 188, 240, 251–3, 255
  ancestral, 267
  and narrative, 255
  and objects, 280, 282
  and the state, 12, 218, 231–2
  bodily transmission, 75
  disempowerment, 173
  empowerment, 110, 179, 217
  indigenous empowerment, 112
  regimes of, 120
  state, 12–13, 114, 119–20, 248, 253–4
    see also hierarchy
privatization, xv, 10, 173
  and the state, 12, 218, 231–2
  elites, 12, 232
  of water, 176, 181, 186
  risks and responsibilities, 174
  transnational, 12, 174, 221–2
    see also alienation; appropriation,
      enclosure; commoditization;
      ownership, forms of, private;
      propertization
productivism, *see* environmental issues,
  intensification
propertization, 176
    see also commoditization; privatization
property
  and enfranchisement, 173, 189
  as privilege, 202
  as sociality, 28–9, 35, 121
  communal, 1, 13, 26, 91, 109
  competing perceptions, 135
    see also conflict
  concepts of, 3–4, 142, 261
  dance as, 91, 143
  genetic resources, 112
  history, 120
  intangible, 10–11, 116, 143, 176, 200–2,
    204–5
    see also materiality
  intellectual, 2, 7, 12, 88–100 passim,
    120, 185, 262

copyright, 116, 262, 282–3
  patents, 112–13, 116
    see also cultural heritage; traditional
      knowledge
  land as, xv–xvi, 1
  material culture, 10, 177–9
  music as, 12
  regimes, 12–14, 43, 120, 142–8 passim,
    173, 218, 221
  relations, 1–6 passim, 12, 88–9, 96, 173,
    175, 179
  songs as, 91, 96, 143–4
  stories as, 143
  water as, 3, 171–96 passim
    see also belonging; biopiracy;
      bioprospecting; rights
Proudhon, P.-J., 3
Prudhon, W.S., 112
public symbols, *see* appropriation, of
  persons

queuing, 23, 25–7
    see also legal order; possession, first
      possession
quotas, 11, 141, 199–204, 245
    see also regulation; resource
      management regimes

racism, 132
    see also discrimination; paternalism
Radcliffe, S., 106, 108–10
Rao, P., 2
Rapport, N., 117
Ray, I., 221
Reardon, J., 116
Recht, J., 3
regulation, 115, 220
  multilateral, 112
  of fishing quotas, 141, 202, 205, 245
  of radio, 217, 222–3, 225, 228, 230–1
  of water, allocation, 176
    see also governance; resource
      management regimes; subjectivity
reification, 197–8, 208
  of communities, 107, 118
  of cultural heritage, 3, 9
  of culture, 3
  of peoples, 3, 186

of persons, 6, 208–9
of relations, 6, 208–9
see also alienation; disembedding;
    traditional knowledge
Reisman, P., 6
resistance, *see* activism
resource management regimes, 117, 173–4
    centralization, 198
    co-management, 187–9, 203
    indigenous, 111–12, 173–4
    local, 117, 173
    national 138, 173, 199
    water, 173–4, 176, 182–8
    see also commons; governance;
        regulation; sustainability
resource management, 117, 138, 173–4,
    189, 198
    see also environmental issues
Reynolds, H., 173
Ricoeur, P., 43–5
rights
    collective, 109, 171
        see also ownership, collective
    customary, 155
    human, 107–108, 111–13, 179
    indigenous, 105–111, 116
    individual, 140
    recognition of, 282
    to clan estates, 175
    to cultural property, 109, 262
    to foreshore and seabed, 134–5, 142, 148
    to land, 109, 135–41 passim, 159,
        165–7, 175, 262
        land rights movement, 272
    to sea, 13, 280
    to use, 13, 91, 142–8 passim, 219, 222,
        231
    to water, 142, 171–9 passim, 188
    see also alienation; claims; law;
        ownership; possession; property
Rigsby, B., 175
Rio Declaration on Environment and
    Development, 110
risk, 11, 54, 161, 201–4 passim, 218–19
    risk management, 197–8, 200
ritual, 88–90, 92–3, 99–100, 267, 270–8
    knowledge, 9
    objects, 70, 87

rivalrous resources, *see* commons
Robbins, J., 98, 208
Rodriguez-Garavito, C., 107
Root, D., 43
Rorty, A., 95
Rose, C., 3–4, 173
Rosenthal, J., 119
Ryan, A., 3, 6

Santos, B., 107, 113
Sartre, J.-P., 8, 56–7
Schwab, G., 7
self-determination, 108, 119
    see also autonomy
self-governance, 111, 115, 221, 227
    see also governance
self-government, 110, 140
    see also sovereignty
self-making, 59, 66, 69, 74, 182
    self-expression, 26, 32
    self-fashioning, 45, 57, 59
    self-realization, 5, 7, 26, 68
    see also embodiment; identity,
        construction; self-governance
senses, 73, 75, 264
    see also aesthetics
shadow concepts, xvi, 5, 24, 32–7
    shadow images, 33, 35
sharing, 5, 25–35 passim
    power and responsibility, 203
    see also borrowing; kinship; possession;
        theft
signal interference, 217–19, 222, 224,
    225–33 passim
social capital, 108–10, 114, 120
social justice, xvi, 120, 184, 189
    see also equality; moral economies;
        sustainability
social movements, 106, 108, 110, 112, 114
    see also counter-movements
social networks, 89, 182
    see also transnational networks
Solms, M., 91
songs, 87–91 passim, 96, 99, 267, 278, 281
    and ceremony, 270
    and dreams, 91, 95
    and property, 143–4
    and sacred law, 273

songs as sovereignty, 47, 116, 131, 137–8
see also music; property, songs as
squatters, 163
St Martin, K., 198, 204
Starr, P., 218
stealing, *see* theft
Stern, P., 230
Stewart-Harawira, M., 113
Strang, V., xv, xvi, 45, 89, 198, 222, 231, 255
Strathern, M., 2, 3, 4, 5, 6, 7, 9, 13, 51, 75, 96, 178, 185, 189, 252
Suarez-Navaz, L., 115
subjectivity, 7–8, 57–60, 95
  and agency, 45
  and appropriation of people, 46
  and appropriative relationship, 50
  and practice, 66
  collective, 114
  embodied, 8
  market-based, 114
  political, 114
  see also regulation
sustainability, 107, 188, 224
  of communities, 198
  of ecosystems, 12–13, 173
  of fish populations, 199–200
  of radio stations, 224–8
  sustainable development, 110–11, 247
  see also development; environmental issues; resource management regimes; social justice
Sykes, K., 30, 98
symbolic communication, 4

Tadesse, W., 173
tangible, 177, 203, 205, 207
  see also materiality
Tarde, G., 46, 60
Taussig, M., 206
Taylor, C., 6
Tehan, M., 173
territory, 108, 111–17 passim, 135, 151–6 passim, 161, 255
  ancestral, 111

theft, 29
  see also borrowing; possession; sharing
totems, 94–5, 97, 175
Toussaint, S., 173, 175
tradition, 35–6, 83, 94–5, 99, 106, 108–20 passim, 136, 148, 243, 249, 278–9
  ancestral values, 138, 140
  customary management, 135
    see also law, customary
  invented, 106, 113
  traditional cultural expression, 116, 120
  see also authenticity; identity
traditional knowledge, 105, 110
  and genetic resources, 112–13, 116
  as property, 112, 114
  ecological knowledge, 175
  use of, 109
    informed consent, 116
  see also cultural heritage; property, intellectual; reification
traditional economic regime, 32, 136
transnational networks, 12, 109
  see also social networks
Trigger, D., 182
Tsing, A., 117, 120
Turnbull, O., 91

Ulloa, A., 110, 111–13

value, 280
Van Meijl, T., 3
Verdery, K., 1, 2, 5–6, 88, 89, 173, 177, 178, 231
violence, 4, 13, 30, 173
  see also conflict
virtual commodities, *see* immateriality
voice, *see* agency
Von Benda-Beckmann, F., 11
Von Benda-Beckmann, K., 11

water
  abstraction, 180
    see also environmental issues
  allocations, 10, 176, 181
    see also regulation
  rights, *see* rights, to water

trading, 176
   see also commoditization; markets;
     privatization; resource management
     regimes
   see also common good; ownership of
Wiber, M., 200, 202
Widlok, T., 173
Wildman, S., 223

Willerslev, R., 31, 32, 33, 35
Williams, N., 173, 175
Wilmore, M., 2, 10, 11, 12, 14, 177
Wittfogel, K., 173
Worster, D., 173
Wynne, B., 174

Ziff, B., 2